SAILOR'S MULTIHULL GUIDE
Second Edition

By Kevin Jeffrey & Charles E. Kanter

from Avalon House Publishing
in cooperation with

MULTIHULLS Magazine

Cover Photographs of Industry-Leading Multihulls:

FRONT COVER
upper left: Victory Catamarans, *Victory 35*
upper right: Island Packet Yachts, *Packet Cat 35*
lower left: PDQ Yachts, *PDQ 36 Mk III*
lower right: Contour Yachts, *Contour 34 SC*

BACK COVER
upper left: Voyage Yachts, *Mayotte 500*
upper right: KKG, *Macro Spaceshuttle*
lower left: Prout Catamarans, *Prout 45*
lower right: Lagoon/Jeanneau, *Lagoon 57*

INSIDE FRONT
upper left: Prout Catamarans, *Prout 37*
upper right: Performance Cruising, *Gemini 105M*
lower left: Fountaine Pajot, *Bahia 46*
lower right: Catana, *Catana 411*

INSIDE BACK
upper left: Manta Enterprises, *Manta 40*
upper right: Maine Cat, *Maine Cat 30*
lower left: Corsair Marine, *F-28*
lower right: Dufour Yachts, *Nautitech 395*

AVALON HOUSE
PUBLISHING
sustainable living • marine

ISBN 0-9627562

D1285873

Avalon House Publishing

Editor   Kevin Jeffrey
Book Design   Avalon House Publishing

Printed in the United States Of America

Cataloguing in Publication Data

        Jeffrey, Kevin, 1954–
            Sailor's multihull guide to the world of cruising
        catamarans and trimarans

        2nd ed.
        Includes index.
        ISBN 0-9627562-5-3

        1. Catamarans. 2. Trimarans. I. Kanter, Charles E., 1930–
        II. Title.

        VM311.C3J44 1997   623.8"223   C97-900919-7

        797.124—dc 20

Marine Trade Orders

Multihulls Magazine
421 Hancock St.
Quincy, MA 02171 USA
Toll Free: (800) 333-6858
Tel: (617) 328-8181
Fax: (617) 471-0118
email: MultiMag@aol.com

Outdoor & Standard Book Trade Orders

Menasha Ridge Press
700 South 28th Street
Birmingham, AL 35233 USA
Toll Free: (800) 247-9437 ext. 100
Tel: (205) 322-0439 ext. 100
Fax: (205) 326-1012
email: ppalmer@menasharidge.com

ACKNOWLEDGMENTS

We would like to thank everyone who helped make this book possible. Our special thanks go out to all of the contributing authors, and to all of the industry professionals, including builders, designers and sales agents, who contributed information and drawings of their boats for use in this book.

ABOUT THE AUTHORS

—Kevin Jeffrey and his wife, Nan, live in Prince Edward Island, Canada, and are writers and owners of Avalon House Publishing, a small press specializing in sustainable living and marine books. Their current titles include *Sailor's Multihull Guide, Adventuring With Children—An Inspirational Guide to World Travel and the Outdoors, Bahamas—Out Island Odyssey*, and *The Independent Energy Guide—Electrical Power for Home, Boat & RV*. The Jeffrey family has cruised extensively on multihulls, and their articles on family adventuring, multihulls, and renewable energy have appeared in numerous sailing magazines. Kevin also designs and consults on electrical power systems and writes a regular electrical power column for *Multihulls, SAIL* and *DIY Boatowner*.

—Charles E. Kanter and his wife, Corinne, are free-lance marine writers and owners of SAILco Press, a small publisher specializing in marine books. Their current titles include *The Galley K.I.S.S. Cookbook* and *The Cruising K.I.S.S. Cookbook*, nautical best-sellers written by Corinne. Corinne writes a regular cooking column called "Corinne's Culinary Corner" for *Multihulls* magazine. Charles Kanter's articles have appeared in numerous sailing publications. He is an experienced yacht surveyor and delivery captain, a long-time member of the Society of Naval Architects and Marine Engineers, a commodore in the Seven Seas Cruising Association, and a member of the American Boat and Yacht Council, the Chesapeake Cruising Multihull Association and the Multihull Association of Southern Florida. Charles and Corinne purchased their first multihull in 1971 and have cruised extensively since 1980.

—Robin Rule contributed to the article *Multihull Term Chartering*, Tom Kintz, Randy Hogen, John Sykes, and Patrick Boyd contributed to the article *Buying Through A Broker*, Kurt Hughes contributed to the article *Owner Building A Stock Design* and *Basic Sailing Techniques I*, David Williams contributed to the article *Multihull Insurance*, and Victor Shane contributed to the *Drag Devices* section of the article *Basic Sailing Techniques II*.

Contents

Financing A Cruising Multihull

Owning A Cruising Multihull

Multihull Seamanship

Color Photo & Advertising Section

Production & Semi-Custom Catamarans

(Production & Semi-Custom Catamarans Continued)

Production & Semi-Custom Trimarans

Stock Catamaran Designs

(Stock Catamaran Designs Continued)

Stock Trimaran Designs

Reference Section

Introduction

Publisher's Note

A few words about this edition

Avalon House Publishing is pleased to present the second edition of the SAILOR'S MULTIHULL GUIDE. We would like to thank the thousands of readers who made the first edition such a success. This book remains the only up-to-date, single-source guide to the world of cruising catamaran and trimaran sailboats. It reflects the effort and dedication of countless multihull professionals, as well as our personal love of these superior sailing craft and the cruising experiences they offer.

Multihulls continue to create the real excitement in the sailing scene around the world. The SAILOR'S MULTIHULL GUIDE is for anyone who finds himself caught up in that excitement, for those eager to discover how currently available catamarans and trimarans fit into their cruising aspirations.

As you browse through this book, we ask that you keep several thoughts in mind about the content and format. Our intent in publishing this guide is to provide a single comprehensive resource for both prospective buyers and multihull professionals. As such, we have combined a collection of how-to articles with detailed specifications on over one hundred and fifty cruising multihulls. We feature production and semi-custom boats in all sizes and price ranges, as well as popular stock designs for

owner or professional building from the best multihull designers around the world. The articles help you figure out what to look for and what is involved in chartering, buying, building, sailing and handling a cruising multihull, while the featured boats are a good representation of the best cruising multihulls currently available on the market.

Each boat is presented in an objective two-page format, allowing readers to judge for themselves which boat best meets their needs. While this guide is invaluable for comparing the various boats and narrowing down your options, a buyer's final selection should come only after gaining as much knowledge and first-hand experience as possible with a particular boat, its designer and its builder.

The two-page boat layouts are arranged alphabetically by builder (for production and semi-custom boats) or designer (stock designs), and catamarans are listed separately from trimarans. Each layout includes the following:

General information

The name of the boat designer is followed by the approximate cost of the boat or stock plans. If a price was not available or it varies depending on the configuration you choose, we simply suggest you call for the current cost. A general boat classification is given to help the buyer understand what each boat is primarily intended for. The contact information for the builder or sales agent (production and semi-custom boats) or stockist (stock designs) is followed by the year the boat or design was introduced and the number sold or built as of September 1997, and a list of other cruising multihulls by the builder or designer. Many builders and designers were unable or unwilling to supply us with the year a boat or design was introduced and an accurate estimate of how many boats were built or plans sold. We feel this is important information since it distinguishes new designs from older ones, and gives the buyer some history about a particular boat and its builder or designer.

Main features

This section describes the distinguishing features of each type of boat, including its hull and sail plan, the deck and cockpit layout, the accommodations, the steering system, and the auxiliary engine(s).

Description

A brief description of each boat gives the reader a condensed version of what that particular cruising multihull is all about, its strong points, and an indication of what type of cruising it is best suited for.

Specifications

We have attempted to give a complete set of specifications for each boat so that buyers could accurately compare different makes and models. It continues to be a difficult task, since the level of information provided by builders and designers varies widely. In some cases the exact nature of certain specifications provided, such as displacement, payload, and wing deck

clearance (catamarans) was ambiguous. In many cases the information was simply unavailable. Builders and designers should be aware that not providing complete information only leads to confusion for the prospective buyer. Our hope is that our format will encourage standardization in the industry for specifications on all sales and descriptive literature.

Displacement. Displacement can refer to the boat's gross empty weight as it comes fitted out from the builder (also known as displacement lightship or unloaded; we use this definition in the specifications), the displacement at design waterline (gross empty weight plus recommended normal payload), or the maximum displacement (gross empty weight plus the maximum payload). The most useful measure to cruisers is the recommended payload that makes the boat ride nicely at its design waterline. Adding more payload can adversely affect safety and performance. When talking with builders and designers, be sure to ask exactly what displacement they are referring to.

Standard auxiliary. This describes the standard auxiliary engine recommended by the designer or builder. Other power options, if any, are described in the Features section under Engine(s).

Overall length. Also referred to as the LOA, this measurement is given in feet and inches as well as in meters.

Waterline length. This measurement, known as the LWL, describes the boat's length at the design waterline. Note that on boats with near vertical bows and reverse transoms, the LOA and the LWL are close to the same.

Bridgedeck length. This measurement, describing the length of the rigid bridgedeck section of a catamaran, is not a specification normally talked about. We have included it, however, since it helps illustrate the variance in the usable rigid bridgedeck section between boats of different design. Some boats have rigid bridgedecks almost the full length of the boat, while others have modest to large areas of trampoline netting incorporated into the fore or aft section between the hulls. The *Privilege* boats from Jeantot and a few other designs such as the new *Prout 45* are unique in that the center of the bridgedeck section extends forward similar to the main hull of a trimaran, with small areas of netting on each side. There is no right or wrong type of bridgedeck configuration to look for, since on each boat it has been designed to relate well to the other specifications.

Beam. This measurement is given in terms of maximum beam, or beam overall (BOA), for both catamarans and trimarans, and minimum or folded beam describing the width of a folding trimaran. For some trimarans, the folded beam is also the beam when trailered.

Draft. The draft of the boat is given in terms of the maximum draft, a fixed number for boats with low-aspect-ratio keels, and the minimum draft, or the draft of the hull(s) on boats with daggerboards, center-boards, and retracting or pivoting rudders.

Mast height. This measurement is most commonly given in terms of the height from the waterline to the top of the mast. It is also occasionally given as the mast height off the deck. Mast height off the deck indicates the actual height on boats where the mast rests in a tabernacle on deck.

Sail area. Some manufacturers and designers give only total sail area, while others list the sails individually. Some use the quantity of sail area at 100% of jib and main triangles, while others list the total

area of a standard sail plan, including the mast if it's a rotating wing shape, the roach of a fully battened mainsail, and the roller-furling genoa. We've chosen to list the actual area of each sail, with the total area representing the standard sail plan. This includes wing mast area, the area of the genoa, and the area of the staysail on cutter rigs. Smaller jibs are listed where applicable. Optional sails such as spinnakers are listed below the total sail area.

Capacity. In this section we list information of great interest to cruisers. The capacity of the boat is described in terms of the number of berths available (listed as either singles or doubles, even though many doubles are actually queen-size or larger), the number of separate staterooms (a sleeping cabin with some standing room and a door), the number of head compartments, the fuel and fresh water capacity, and the recommended payload. Keep in mind that some designers use onboard water-making capability to reduce the water storage capacity required. Watermakers now allow boats with relatively small water storage capacity to have a long-distance cruising range.

We hope you enjoy reading the SAILOR'S MULTIHULL GUIDE as much as we have enjoyed producing it, and that it will help steer you toward the perfect cruising catamaran or trimaran for your needs. We welcome your comments and suggestions for the next edition.

Best wishes for level sailing,

Kevin Jeffrey
Avalon House Publishing

Cruising Multihull Update

Industry trends, a review of the choices

From the vantage point of being the fastest growing segment of the cruising sailboat industry, multihull professionals are coming to the conclusion that they must be doing something right. In the four years since the original publication of the SAILOR'S MULTIHULL GUIDE sales of cruising catamarans and sport trimarans have increased to 35% of the market. Consumer problems with multihull insurance or boat yards are just a faded memory, as are the most virulent of prejudices. Who could have predicted four years ago that the yacht charter industry would so unhesitatingly embrace cruising catamarans, that the SORC, long a bastion of traditional racing, would be mostly trimaran speedsters, and that there would be almost as many multihulls as monohulls at the Miami International Boat Show?

The news on the catamaran front is positively exciting. In North America the new *Gemini 105M* from Performance Cruising leads the pack in number of boats sold, while other forerunners include the *Manta 40* from Manta Catamarans, the *PDQ 32 MkII* and *36 MkIII* from PDQ Yachts in Canada, the *Endeavourcats* from Endeavour Catamarans, the *Packet Cat 35* from Island Packet Yachts, and the *Victory 35* from Victory Catamarans. Relatively new to the market, but making their presence felt are

the *Maine Cat 30* from Maine Cat, and Chris White's *Atlantic 42* from Lombardi Yachts. Leading trimaran builder Corsair Marine is introducing their new *Corsair 3600* cruising catamaran based on the former *Parallax 11m* design.

On a semi-custom basis in North America you'll find the *Luau 350* from Luau Boats, the *Conser 47* from Conser Catamaran, the *Horizon 48* from Horizon Boats, the John Shuttleworth designed *ShuttleCat 31 & 40* from Dale Schneider and the luxurious *ShuttleCat 52* from Pedigree Cats, the *Featherlight 43* from Mastermold Composites, and the *Even Keel 37* from Greene Marine. TomCat Boats have just introduced a combination sailboat/runabout in their *TomCat 6.2*, while Symons Choice is offering a new version of their *C-Cat* design.

Commercial cruising cats on the market include the *Elan Extreme 36* from Multi-Winds, the *ProCat 43* from ProCat Marine, the John Marples/Jim Brown designed *Newport 5400* from Newport Multihulls, and the Kurt Hughes designed *Sunchaser 58* from Lightspeed Marine.

Down in the Islands Roger Hatfield and Gold Coast Yachts of St. Croix continue to produce high quality, high performance multihulls. The cats from Voyage Yachts in South Africa are marketed and chartered by Voyage Charters in the Virgin Islands. And a dynamic new catamaran company has surfaced in the Caribbean, Aikane Trinidad building the *Aikane 56 & 72* luxury cats.

Builders and designers in the UK are busy satisfying their customers. Prout is undergoing a complete redesign of their entire line with the introduction of the *Prout 45* and the new *Prout 38*. Heavenly Cruising Yachts introduced the *Heavenly Twins 36*, a long-awaited sistership to the popular *Heavenly Twins 27*. For those on a budget with an appreciation of the past, Blue Water Catalacs is reviving some of the older classic designs by offering new versions of the *Catalac 900* and *Sunstar 32*. And James Wharram has released two new *Tiki* designs, the *38* and *46*, that should ensure the future of this line of stable, affordable, aesthetically pleasing open-bridgedeck catamarans.

The French have lost some of their dominance in the multihull market but none of their class, as evidenced by the lovely cats from Catana, Dufour (the *Nautitech* line), Fountaine Pajot, Lagoon, Jeantot (the *Privilege* line), Naval de Cordouan (the *Kennex* line), and Naval Force 3 (the *Piana* line). For those who want high performance at a modest price, Edel has reorganized and released their new *Edel 11m* cat.

M&M Boat Builders in the Netherlands now offer three semi-custom catamaran cruisers, the *Nimble 39.3, 39.9, & 49.4*.

The new cats from Down Under include the Grainger-designed *Oasis 380* from Catamaran Developments, the *Chincogan 520* from Chincogan Cats, and Overell & Stanton's *Lightwave 10.5*. Coming recently to the forefront is the *Tasman Elite 4000* from Tasman Yachts and the classic cruiser and motorsailer designs from Peter Brady & Associates. Jeff Schionning continues to expand his portfolio of sleek stock design cats with his new *Cosmos* line.

And the open bridgedeck *Seawind 1000* from Seawind Catamarans, now available with a hardtop and enclosed cockpit, holds the interest of multihull buyers.

The South African catamaran builders remain active, with the majority of their boats entering the charter trade. South African built cats include the *Norseman 430* and *Mayotte 500* from Voyage Yachts, the new *Moorings 4500* built by Robertson and Caine for The Moorings, the *St. Francis 44* from St. Francis Marine, and the *Wildcat 350* and *Royal Cape Cat 45* from Charter Cats S.A..

KKG of Austria remains the multihull builder furthest from open water, yet their state-of-the-art designs such as the *Novara 50RC & 52C*, along with their new *Spaceshuttle* cats, are captivating prospective clients around the world.

South American custom builders are producing some truly amazing multihulls. Alwoplast can hardly keep up with demand for their combination cruiser/sport fishing catamarans such as their *Crowther 45*.

Affordable trailerable catamarans are meeting with good success; boats of interest are the *Aquilon 800* from Stanek Marine, the Kelsall designed *X-Cats*, and the Woods designed *Savanah 26* from Advanced Cruising Designs. Other popular modest-sized catamarans include the *Hirondelle 23* and the *Maine Cat 22 & 30*. The *Seawind 850* and *Prout 26* are technically still available; all you have to do is convince the builders to produce one for you.

Some of the best catamaran stock designs are available from Rober Harris of British Columbia; Ed Horstman, Kurt Hughes, John Marples & Jim Brown, and Chris White of the United States; James Wharram and Woods Design of the UK, Crowther Associates, Tony Grainger, Jeff

Schionning and Roger Simpson of Australia; and Angelo Lavranos and Malcolm Tennant of New Zealand.

In the past four years there has been a renaissance of the trimaran, with companies such as Corsair (*F-series*), Contour Yachts (*Contour 30 & 34*), and Quorning Boats (*Dragonfly 800, 920 & 1000*) leading the way and others quickly catching up. For trailer-sailing no other boat even comes close to satisfying the consumer's demands as these remarkable folding sport trimarans. Other companies in the race are Colorado Composites (*F-25*), Essential Boats of Australia (*Essential 8*), Moore Sailboats (*Antrim 30+ & PC 34*), Multi-Winds (*Elan 26 & 7.7m*), Naval Force 3 of France (*Challenge 30 & 37*), and the Tremolino Boat Co. (*T-Gull 25 & Argonauta 27*).

Trimaran stock designs are also popular, including those from John Marples and Jim Brown, Ian Farrier, Allan Hartley, Ed Horstman, Kurt Hughes, Dick Newick, and Chris White. And Gold Coast Yachts offers their *GC 56C* tri on a semi-custom basis.

For a truly unique trimaran, investigate the stunning *Zefyr 43* from Walker Wingsail Systems. This tri has no soft sails at all; the rig is a sophisticated computer controlled raked monoplane wing.

Do you feel two or three hulls just aren't enough? Try the new *Quadcat 28* from Encore International Multihulls, with two main hulls plus two retractable amas.

Amid the enthusiasm and progress in the multihull industry a few caution flags are being raised. In an effort to jump on the multihull bandwagon a few monohull builders have leapt into multihull construction and sales without fully understanding the technology or the rationale behind it. Without a good

grounding in the fundamentals of multihull design, safety features may be compromised, including lack of sufficient bridge-deck clearance. In addition, shallow draft (one of the major multihull advantages) and centerboard technology appear an endangered species as the demand for the convenience of fixed keels and higher payloads increases. And it still has not become an industry norm for a builder or designer to publish a complete set of specifications for each boat, including a recommended payload or weight-carrying capacity estimate. This publication works hard to lobby the industry for standardized specifications so buyers can compare boats of different make and model accurately.

Another issue to contend with is cost. The scarcity of cruising multihulls with a modest price tag continues to frustrate those in the lower income brackets. While prospective owners have to come to grips with the economic reality of what it costs to build seaworthy multihulls today, it's fair to say that the market is still ripe for more cruising multihulls with a modest price tag. The growth of the new boat multihull market over the past decade should ensure an increasing supply of pre-owned multihulls, which in turn should help stabilize prices. If you find that new boats are simply out of your league, keep your sights on the used boat market and you may just find the perfect boat in your price range.

The multihull industry is still young and will experience some growing pains as it strives to give customers what they want. As we head into the next century there are many unknowns for customers and professionals alike, but one thing is clear—cruising multihulls are definitely here to stay.

The Cruising Dream
The romance of multihull sailing

Leaving behind the tight, companionable anchorage at Samana on the east coat of the Dominican Republic, we sailed out towards Los Haitises National Park. A handful of adventurous cruisers had raved about it, urging us to spend a few days in this veritable coastal paradise. When asked what made it so special, so worth the five hour sail, they remained curiously inarticulate. It had to be seen, they insisted, to be believed.

So we sailed, making the crossing of Samana Bay in a brisk afternoon breeze. Approaching the opposite shore, our first impression was of complete solitude. No human sounds disturbed the quiet, no habitations intruded. For as far as we could see, we were the only people anywhere, something frequently experienced at sea, but rarely by land. Great mounds of coral rock, like miniature hills, rose from the water, their steep sides covered in dense, tropical growth, their appearance reminiscent of some exotic destination in the Far East. As the exquisite beauty of this seaside park unfolded before us, our sense of isolation was electrifying. Anchoring off a tiny white sand beach, we soon discovered many of the park's secrets: the dark, mysterious, mangrove-choked creeks waiting to be explored by dinghy; the deep caves hidden in the thickly wooded hills;

the abandoned, overgrown banana grove with its ripening fruit; the flocks of tropical birds that returned nightly in great wheeling masses. Sitting in our cockpit within a stone's throw of shore, surrounded by a peace that only nature can impart, it occurred to us that this was the epitome of a cruiser's dream. We had experienced it numerous times before during our years as sailors, but never so intensely, so completely.

Pursuing some personal dream is, of course, what lures all of us aboard sailboats initially. Yearning for an independence, an excitement, a challenge that supersedes our lives on land, we turn to the water to find it. There is something about severing ties with the mainland that appeals to many people, as though they had also left behind the responsibilities and pressures of modern life. This is why islands are so popular. Boats take the whole issue one step further, especially sailboats large enough to live and cruise on. Once on the water one's whole perspective of land and life on it alters. Noises recede and crowds vanish. The pace slackens and the world shrinks. Life regains equilibrium as you find yourself dealing with the intimate environment of a sailboat. Simple pleasures become paramount and simple acts rewarding. A destination reached, an anchor well set, a sail properly trimmed, a hot meal prepared; these are the accomplishments that add up to the soul-satisfying business of cruising.

Taking stock of our idyllic surroundings in the heart of Los Haitises, I knew that the realization of our dreams of cruising were strongly linked to our choice of a catamaran for a boat. After a youthful indoctrination into the world of cruising on a classic wooden monohull, I realized that such a craft, while charming and unquestionably lovely, was completely inappropriate for a family with two young children.

So what is it about a multihull that renders it so compatible with the cruiser's dream? Why is it that the popularity of cruising catamarans and trimarans has escalated tremendously in recent years? For anyone who has sailed or cruised aboard a multihull, the answer is obvious, the reasons multiple. Multihulls have so much to offer so many different types of sailors. Despite their unquestionable turn of speed and attendant excitement, they are easy to sail. Gone are any preconceived convictions that beating to windward means clinging to your seat, fighting a weather helm, and crawling around at an alarming angle while spray washes over you with irritating regularity.

If your dream is to sail the waters of the world in some recognizable degree of comfort, a multihull is the perfect solution, for it offers a veritable home on the water. With its permanently made-up double bunks, spacious galley, cavernous lockers, roomy cockpit, panoramic saloon, and light, airy interior, it is unquestionably the most livable boat ever built. Families with young children as well as older retired couples welcome this gentler approach to sailing, as do numerous women who would otherwise leave the business of bluewater cruising to men. Gone are the steep companionways, gimballed stoves, narrow berths and habitual post-sail shambles belowdecks that once typified cruising. Home life, I quickly discovered, can continue to function no matter what the conditions, with children cavorting on the foredeck, bread baking below, and a good novel enjoyed, all while sailing downwind in a 40 knot wind and steep seas. When it comes to anchoring, a multihull continues to show its superiority with its delightful shoal-draft. Beaches can be literally landed on, cozy, well-protected corners sought out, and

crowded anchorages handled with equanimity as you maneuver past the masses to drop anchor a few yards off shore.

When enjoying such comfortable conditions, the speed of a multihull comes as a continual surprise. Even our "floating cottage" first catamaran had a gratifying way of out-sailing most other boats around. With a permanently mounted spinnaker pole, twin headsail arrangement and good sail inventory, we quickly found ourselves enjoying far better averages than predicted. For those who relish the excitement of racing, a cruiser/racer offers the opportunity to compete while still maintaining a comfortable cruising craft, an often impossible compromise in the world of sailboats.

The desirability of multihulls was brought home to me the other day while in the company of friends. A large family of five adults and two young children, they began outlining their dream of owning and living on a sailboat. Tired of the cost and maintenance of a home, the continual company of neighbors, the lack of travel, the predictable quality of their lives, they wanted to go sailing. Becoming positively starry-eyed, they insisted a multihull was

what they not only wanted, but needed. Why? Because it offered the necessary room, the degree of comfort, the required privacy, and the interior elegance they sought. More than that, they knew after a two-day charter aboard one that multihulls are forgiving boats. Amateurs under sail, they sought a craft that would allow them to learn and travel at the same time. We understood perfectly, having once shared that sentiment as we took possession of our first catamaran, only to find ourselves raising sails upside down, anchoring backwards, running aground, breaking battens, and accidentally jibbing, all in that first extraordinary season of learning to sail.

Surrounded by books and brochures, charts and travelogs, the family outlined their hopes and dreams, their plans and ambitions. Looking down at the glossy photograph of a multihull, they knew instinctively that only a boat like this would fulfill their aspirations yet supply them with a home, would satisfy the adventurous members of the family yet still serve the needs of the children. Choosing a multihull would make their dream become a reality.

Characteristics of a Cruising Multihull

Boat Classification
Sorting out the various makes & models

Before plunging into the specific characteristics of what sets cruising multihulls apart from their single-hulled cousins, we should first attempt to answer the questions many of you may be asking, namely, "What exactly is a cruising sailboat? What defines it? What differentiates it from other types of sailboats?"

We all use the word cruising, yet it is a highly subjective term and probably means different things to different people. *Webster's Dictionary* defines it as "sailing or driving about from place to place, for pleasure or in search of something."

This aptly describes what most of us have in mind when we think of buying a cruising sailboat, to travel about in a pleasurable fashion, searching for new places to see and people to meet. What differs is how each of us envisions the boat itself, the style of travel and the destinations we wish to explore.

While it can be said that it's possible to cruise successfully in almost any type of sailboat, for the purposes of this guide we have limited our focus to multihull sailboats that offer some type of interior sleeping and cooking accommodations. Additionally, to help the reader sort out which type of craft best suits their needs, we have classified cruising multihull sailboats into five separate categories: Racer, Cruiser/Racer,

Trailerable Sport Cruiser, Cruiser, Luxury Cruiser, and Charter Cruiser.

As you might guess, when it comes to sailboats there is a substantial amount of overlap between these categories. When does a racer become a cruiser/racer? When is a trailerable sport cruiser also a cruiser/racer, and when is it no longer just for coastal cruising? When does a cruiser become a luxury cruiser? Our intent is not to create rigid boundaries that cannot or should not be crossed, but to provide a loosely-defined guide that suggests the type of sailing a particular type of boat, given its design and how it is outfitted, is best suited for.

Perhaps it would be helpful to draw the analogy to buying a motorized vehicle for the purpose of cruising on land. As with boats, your choices are varied according to the compromises you are willing to make. At one end of the spectrum is a van, which will carry you along in conservative luxury. Based on its size and load-carrying capacity, you have the option of filling it up with all sorts of diversions and accessories.

At the other extreme is a highly tuned sports car, in which you can experience the ecstasy of brilliant performance, high acceleration, superb cornering and the like. For these pleasures you greatly sacrifice interior room, load-carrying capacity and the comforts of a larger vehicle.

Between these two opposite poles lies a series of vehicles with their own inherent compromises. Somewhere in the middle is the sedan which has better performance than the van, yet more carrying capacity than the sports car. The analogy could go on, but the point is taken since most of us have made this type of decision and lived with the consequences.

Thus it is with sailboats, no matter how many hulls they have. The issue is not that you can't use one particular type for another purpose, it's simply that for the purpose of comparing and purchasing a cruising sailboat you should be aware of the intent of the designer and the nature of the compromises relating to the activity of cruising.

Years ago at a multihull symposium it was suggested that the definition of a cruising multihull be "any boat that did not win the race." While we can all appreciate the humor, we must also come to grips with the irony. The diagram below might help explain the dilemma we face in creating categories.

In the diagram, each circle represents a specific primary design intent and usage for vessels. They are racing, cruising, and general recreation, general recreation being defined as all other casual uses. Note where the circles intersect. These areas of intersection are the grey areas of classification. Classification is especially difficult in the central area where all three categories overlap. There is always a certain amount of controversy between those who make classifications and those who design and build boats.

The following five classifications are of our own devising and intended solely for the use of our readers.

Racers

Pure racing machines are well beyond the scope of this book. There are, however, many boats in this guide that have competed successfully in racing events. While we consider a racing boat to be fit for cruising when the designer and builder have placed an appropriate degree of

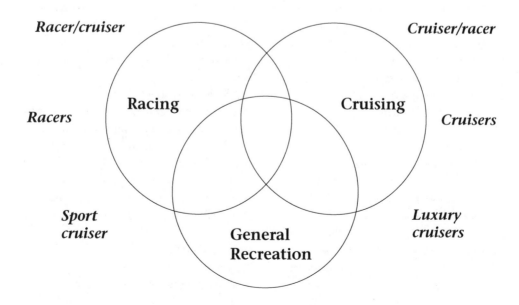

emphasis on comfort, it is a subjective decision as to where the line is drawn between racer and cruiser/racer. For instance, all ocean-racing boats must have some bunk and galley accommodations for the racing crew, but that alone doesn't make them acceptable for cruising. To us, an indication of comfort should also include things such as how easy the boat is to sail and handle, to maneuver under power, and to live aboard in a variety of conditions.

Cruiser/racers

As mentioned above, for the purposes of this guide a sailboat becomes a cruiser/racer when it has permanent bunks, some sort of cooking facilities, and an appropriate degree of comfort for the crew and their guests. Notice that we have placed the word cruiser ahead of racer for the purposes of this guide. Boats listed in this category could also be termed performance cruisers, as they have been designed and outfitted primarily for fast cruising and secondarily for the purpose of being competitive on the racing circuit if the owner so desires.

On a cruiser/racer, compromises have often been made in order to make the boat suitable for both recreational and competitive sailing. The addition of heavy cruising equipment such as refrigerators, freezers, generators, and dinghies in davits can seriously affect the boat's rated performance. High windage items such as Bimini tops are eschewed and entire systems are often eliminated to save weight and complexity. Many racing enthusiasts, for instance, prefer tiller steering to wheel steering to save weight, reduce the need to carry spare parts, and to enable them to use simpler, lighter, less-costly auto pilots.

If a cruiser/racer is to be raced competitively, you might find on board a more

sophisticated and extensive sail inventory, larger winches and other sail-control apparatus such as backstay adjusters. Special slick bottom coatings may be used and special emphasis given to bottom fairings and shapes. Smaller auxiliary powerplants, lightweight anchors without all-chain anchor rodes, and similar lighter weight equipment choices would be made.

Trailerable sport cruisers

This category is represented by many folding and demountable trimarans: the *Contour 30 MkII* and *Contour 34*, the *F-Series* of folding trimarans designed by Ian Farrier, including those built by Corsair Marine, the *Essential 8m*, the *Antrim 30+* and *PC 34*, the *Elan 26*, the *Dragonfly Series* from Quorning Boats, and the *T-Gull 25* & *Argonauta 27*. There are also a few trailerable catamarans such as the *Aquilon 800* and *Savannah 26* in this group. These boat are labeled as sport cruisers since they are so much fun to sail, and are mostly used for a combination of coastal cruising and sport racing.

The intent in classifying these boats as we did is to emphasize that, in general, a trailerable boat has made such compromises in order to be demountable and small enough for trailering that it is best suited for inshore sport cruising, although even some of the smaller models have made successful bluewater voyages. Keep in mind that most of these designs can be highly competitive on the racing circuit with the proper rigs, while some boast sufficient comfort and stability to make them appropriate for fast off-shore cruising—the *Contour 34*, the *Dragonfly 1000*, and *F-31* come to mind.

Cruisers

In some ways this is the most difficult classification to define, yet most cruising multihulls on the market fall into this middle ground since a balance is sought in their design and construction. A boat that is simply classified as a cruiser should be designed for safety and stability, be able to perform reasonably well on all points of sail, and provide adequate living accommodations and load-carrying capacity for short term or extended cruising.

It should be noted that many boats designated as cruisers can easily become cruiser/racers or even luxury cruisers depending on the way they are rigged and outfitted.

Luxury cruisers

A luxury cruiser can be more easily defined by the intent of the design and the amenities installed. In general, a luxury cruiser has more emphasis on comfort than on performance, since the weight and windage of the equipment and appointments that cause it to be labeled a luxury craft almost always detract from its performance. Once a vessel has permanently installed air-conditioning, for instance, it is easily considered a luxury cruiser. Most luxury cruisers are known for their ambiance. Freezers, ice-makers, heat and air-conditioning, generators, sophisticated

audio systems and electronic navigation systems are typical appointments. Lavish interior design fabrics and accessories and sumptuous cabin layouts are the norm. These boats are made to be lived on.

Charter cruisers

Boats that have been specifically designed and equipped for the charter industry should be considered in a class of their own, even though many of them can be outfitted as successful family or private-owner cruisers. In fact the opposite is also true, that almost any boat could be used for some type of charter enterprise, whether for day chartering, sight-seeing, or some form of term chartering. We have chosen, however, to label sailing multihulls built primarily for commercial use as charter cruisers.

Conclusion

Try not to place too much importance on the general categories or the specific way in which we have classified a particular boat. Keep in mind that it was done to give you a reference point. How you classify your sailboat, and where or how you choose to sail her, is entirely up to you.

Cruising Considerations
What to look for in a good cruising multihull

 ### Costs

How much does it cost to own a multihull cruising sailboat? In relative terms it costs no more to own a multihull than any other type of vessel; expenses are related to the size and complexity of the boat. To get a clear understanding of cost you must break it down into the four categories of: initial cost, depreciation, interest and maintenance.

Initial cost. This varies widely depending on the nature of the cruising multihull you choose. In general, cats and tris are a good bit more expensive per foot to build, and therefore to purchase, than monohulls, but then you can also get similar accommodations in a much smaller boat with a cruising multihull. Many cruisers on smaller budgets have a hard time finding a good production multihull in their price range. Demand has kept the price for both new and used boats high, although the level of production over the past few years has created an abundance of used boats on the market and competition will force prices down a bit.

Depreciation. Depreciation will be the difference between what you pay for the vessel and what you receive when you sell it. Some production catamarans actually appreciate in value, while cats in general and most production tris do exceedingly well on the resale market, much better than

their monohull counterparts. It is not prudent, however, to count on that when you buy. Expect a reasonable amount of depreciation since times and fashions change and there are more multihulls being built every day.

Just like monohulls, good multihulls will remain popular and retain their value, poor ones will not. Multihulls, unlike automobiles, do not eventually lose all their value, though it is probably good accounting to figure about 20% the first year and about 5% a year thereafter. Inflation counteracts some of the depreciation, as we have seen in past decades.

Interest. Most people figure both the interest they pay on a note and the interest they lose by not having that block of capital invested in interest-bearing securities. This cost is strictly personal, but should be taken into account.

Maintenance. Maintenance must be broken down into its component parts: docking/mooring/storage, repairs/replenishment and insurance/registration/taxes. Docking/mooring/storage fees are most often set by length. Overall length has been the arbiter of charges for years. During the last five years, however, there has been a surge of charges by the square foot: length x beam. This change was triggered by design changes in powerboats. Many yards and marinas, realizing that they could no longer fit as many boats in the same space as they previously did, changed their way of charging. With regard to beam, folding designs that can reduce their width for docking purposes have a distinct edge over their competition.

Marina fees on the U.S. East Coast vary from fifty-cents per foot of length per day to well over one dollar per day, depending upon location. Other areas vary accordingly. In certain areas there are plenty of slips, yet in the hot-spots they continue to be in short supply. The future is uncertain concerning both availability and cost. If England is a precursor, harbor dues will soon be universal.

Mooring costs vary depending upon location—they can be delightfully inexpensive or unbelievably pricey. Moorings in Whittaker Creek, North Carolina, can be had for $75 to $100 per month, while in Newport, Rhode Island, a similar mooring is $25 to $30 per day!

Regarding storage, the vessels with the greatest advantage are those you can take home with you—the trailerable cruisers. These boats have other advantages: they can be towed with a smaller, lighter, less expensive auto than comparable monohulls, and they may be launched from virtually any launch ramp, and often from the beach. Monohulls need a ramp with a steeper incline and deeper water.

Winter storage costs again depend upon your location. Out-of-water storage is less expensive than in-water storage, even considering haulout charges. Figure the costs of winterizing as well.

Haulout costs are of great concern to multihull owners. It's no surprise that boats with moderate beam have the fewest difficulties finding haul-out facilities. In areas of the world where no haul-out facilities exist, everyone is in the same situation—you use the local beach set aside for that purpose. The shallower your draft, the greater your advantage because you will have the longest periods of dry between tides. Monohulls either have to find a dock or wall to lie against, or careen the boat on the beach. Careening means at least two tide changes to get both sides painted. Consideration must be given to haul-out facilities, their capabilities and their prices in the areas you intend to cruise.

As for maintenance items, some cost more for a multihull and some less. Bottom coating usually costs more. Boats used in salt-water need their bottoms coated with anti-fouling yearly. A moderate-size catamaran will use about two gallons of coating. With wholesale prices over one-hundred dollars per gallon, this is a significant expense. Bimini tops and dodgers typically cost more on a multihull because of their wider beam.

Costs for other maintenance items such as sails, rigging, engines, zincs, cutless bearings, filters, through-hull fittings, and electronics depend on the type of boat and how it is outfitted. Many cruising multihulls have smaller sailplans than monohulls of similar length, and many have outboard auxiliary engines that are less expensive to maintain. Most other maintenance costs will be the same as for a monohull.

Hull configuration

Every boat design, without exception, is a series of compromises, and this applies to the hull configuration as well. Sometimes the compromises are made in favor of low cost or ease of construction, other times for ultimate stability or comfort, and still other times for high performance or shallow draft.

Only you can decide which boat is right for your needs, but the most successful cruising designs tend to provide the most overall balance without compromising too heavily in any one area.

The three main hull considerations are the materials used in construction; the general hull shape, including cross section, bow and stern design and the amount of freeboard; and the method used to achieve windward ability.

Hull material. Almost all hulls on production cruising multihulls are made of FRP (fiberglass-reinforced plastic, commonly just referred to as fiberglass) using master female molds. The vast majority of boats have solid FRP hulls with a composite construction of foam or balsa panels and fiberglass for the decks, although many production boats are built using composite construction throughout. Some builders replace a portion of the glass fibers with more exotic reinforcing materials such as Kevlar and carbon-fiber that are stronger and lighter in weight. Custom-built or owner-built hulls are predominantly made using composite construction, wood/epoxy, or the strip plank method of cedar strips and epoxy.

Hull shape. Hull shapes on cruising multihulls vary considerably, the major differences being the shape of the cross section, including beam and freeboard, and the shape of the bows and transoms.

—Hull Cross Section. Most modern cruising hulls have rounded or U-shaped underwater cross sections that continue the same smooth shape above waterline. Some designers use flared (knuckled) hull sections that have a smaller waterline imprint for better performance, then flare out above waterline to increase the interior space and provide reserve buoyancy when reaching.

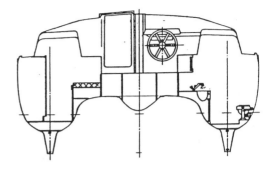

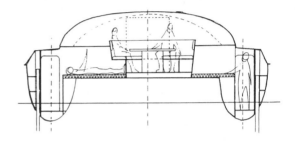

Above: catamaran with standard beam, U-shaped hulls, central nacelle and fixed keels. Below: catamaran with wide beam, U-shaped hulls, no nacelle and daggerboards.

—Hull Length/Beam Ratio. For the individual hulls, the length-to-beam ratio is a clue to how well the boat performs and what its carrying capacity is. For a start, thinner is faster. A high-performance boat will often have hull L/B ratios of around 12:1 or even greater. That means a 32 foot racing catamaran with a 12:1 hull L/B ratio will have a maximum hull beam of 32 inches. The higher the performance expectations, the higher the hull L/B ratio.

The trade-off in hull L/B ratio is carrying capacity. As boats are designed closer to cruising specifications they will have much lower hull L/B ratios. Many cruising catamarans and trimarans are in or around the 8:1 hull L/B category. While this hull L/B ratio still projects above-average speed, it lowers top speeds.

—Freeboard. Cruising catamaran design, since its inception, has had to face the conundrum of standing headroom versus excessive freeboard. To have a properly proportioned vessel, with both sufficient bridgedeck clearance above the water and standing headroom inside, a minimum of forty feet in length was required. In earlier years, this conundrum was faced by either not even attempting standing headroom (except in the hulls) or building a "nacelle" in the center of the bridgedeck section. Most recently, aesthetic prerequisites have been relaxed to include vessels of less than forty feet with considerable freeboard.

Above: catamaran with flared bows, fixed keels, plumb transoms and inboard rudders. Below: catamaran with near-plumb bows and reverse transoms.

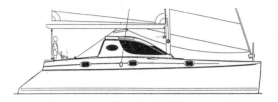

Excessive freeboard in a small vessel creates a host of problems. First is handling the vessel around docks and piers. Low docks and floating docks present a serious access problem. Getting on and off the vessel while docking, especially while clearing the dock, is difficult. Next is excessive windage and high center of gravity. Multihulls with high windage share the same wind-related maneuvering problems as houseboats and top-heavy, single-screw motor yachts. Care must be taken to offset the high center of gravity, which creates excessive pitching and poses a safety hazard.

—Bow & Transom Design. Cruising multihull bows are either narrow (fine-entry) or moderate in cross section, and either flared (with an overhang) or plumb (straight up and down). Transoms are either flared or raked aft (reversed). Flared bows have more reserve buoyancy, while plumb or near-plumb bows increase the waterline length and potential speed significantly. Boats with fine-entry bows have greater performance, but they also have less reserve buoyancy and therefore, in general, require a higher degree of skill to operate. Almost all modern cruising

multihulls have reverse transoms that incorporate some type of boarding steps or swim platforms.

Keels, centerboards & daggerboards. Cruising multihulls use one of three methods to give them windward ability: low-aspect-ratio keels (mostly catamarans), pivoting centerboards (mostly trimarans), and daggerboards. A few boats use a combination of these methods.

Catamarans with fixed low-aspect-ratio keels and spade rudders have the following attributes:

—Protection from grounding damage.
—Simplicity; no moving parts.
—Easier to sail, with no board to trim.
—No trunk to clog or to leak.
—Simpler, more interior room.
—Less expensive to build.

Multihulls with centerboards, daggerboards and transom-hung or kick-up rudders have the following attributes:

—Very shallow draft with board(s) up.
—Better windward performance.
—Better overall sailing performance.

—Better tacking ability

—Ease of rudder maintenance/repair.

Length & beam

This section discusses the various considerations of length (either LOA or LWL) and overall beam (BOA).

Length. It's easy to talk about the implications of length on a cruising boat. Adding length to a boat increases its speed and its ability to provide comfort and carrying capacity in almost every conceivable way. It also, unfortunately, increases the cost in almost every conceivable way, including initial purchase or construction cost, the cost of outfitting, and the ongoing cost of docking, maintenance and storage. Although most modern designs are set up for easy handling, longer boats generally require more crew to sail them.

Wide vs. standard beam. It must be noted that the standard boat length overall-to-beam overall ratio (LOA/BOA) for cruising catamarans over the preceding four or five decades has been BOA=approx. 1/2 LWL. This standard is still adhered to by many present catamaran manufacturers, including Performance Cruising with their immensely popular *Gemini* series. This beam ratio will be considered the "standard" beam for the sake of the following descriptions. It has been proven to provide sufficient initial, athwartships, fore & aft and transverse stability.

Having a standard beam on a cruising multihull allows greater access to canal, marina and repair facilities. Most standard beam catamarans have full rigid bridgedecks instead of trampoline netting foredecks and afterdecks.

Fully decked catamarans have a drier ride, less maintenance, a simpler headstay attachment and better utility for anchoring and mooring. Standard beam craft often have a better ride and can be designed with less freeboard, thus less windage and more traditional appearance.

Cruising catamarans with wide beams have enormous amounts of interior volume, huge deck areas and luxurious interior and exterior layouts. Having a wider beam in high-performance craft also allows the carrying of significantly taller masts. The controlling principle is the lever-arm, with leverage being figured at one-half beam over mast height. Leverage works in all directions, however, and while athwartships stability increases with beam, fore-and-aft stability does not—that would require an increase in length. Most cats with a wide beam compensate by reducing their bridgedeck length and mounting trampoline netting forward and even aft in some cases.

As stated elsewhere, overhanging flared bows and flared hulls are designed to increase buoyancy when immersed by pressure. Fine-entry, plumb bows have less reserve buoyancy, and when combined with taller rigs they create the need for more operator skill to prevent the tendency of the leeward bow to submerge. That is the price you often pay for high performance. In most modern production catamarans, this tendency is diminished by adding weight in the aft end and incorporating more conservative rigs. Trimarans typically counter this tendency by the shape/position of the amas.

Wider beam also reduces or eliminates the possibility of hull-wave interference. All hulls generate some sort of wave, although thinner hulls with finer entries create the least. Boats that are heavily loaded with the hulls more deeply immersed tend to create much larger wave patterns. If those waves meet under the bridgedeck they can cause wave slamming and the drag can be considerable, especially if there is a center nacelle introduced into this turbulence. That is why adequate bridgedeck clearance above waterline and strict adherence to the designer's recommended payload should also be factored into the equation along with beam, length and hull shape.

Displacement

As mentioned in the *Publishers' Note*, the term displacement can be used in several ways. Displacement is a common term that usually refers to the estimated gross weight of the vessel before payload.

The Displacement At Design Waterline is the gross weight plus the payload, or recommended carrying capacity. While designers and builders vary on how they arrive at the recommended payload, that is a number you need to know on any boat, power or sail, monohull or multihull. Payload dictates how much "stuff" you can put on board.

Maximum Displacement is a figure that, according to the recommendation of the designer and builder, you should not exceed. You do not expect a compact car to haul a palette of bricks and likewise you should not expect your boat to exceed its recommended Maximum Displacement without becoming a poor performer and possibly even dangerous.

Multihull displacements are continually decreasing because of new construction materials and techniques. The implications of this trend are higher average boat speeds as well as greater carrying capacity, due in part to the fact that cruising gear also continues to get smaller and lighter.

Sail plan and rigging

The sail plan and rig of a cruising multihull should be simple and basic,

designed to maximize speed while ensuring the ease of sailing and sail handling. A good cruising boat can be designed to be fast enough in all conditions by simply providing enough sail area. Most of the expensive and complicated speed enhancing gear should be reserved for racers who want to use them.

There are two conditions to consider when cruising. One is moderate-to-heavy air when a boat can easily be sailed at or near its maximum speed. The other is lighter air when there may not be enough wind power to reach maximum speed. Since moderate-to-heavy wind provides enough energy to sail at maximum speed, the sail plan for these conditions should be as convenient to handle as possible. The ideal would be a simple working sail plan such as an easily-reefed mainsail with a small, easily-tacked or self-tacking headsail. A square-top main can reduce mast height and lower the center of drive, and it provides sort of an automatic first reef, since the square top tends to distort in a gust.

In lighter winds the boat will not sail at maximum speed with just the working sails, so it is necessary to add sail area. While the working jib could be lowered and replaced by a large overlapping genoa, it is more convenient to leave the working jib as it is and set a larger headsail on a second forestay attached farther up the mast and extended farther out on the bow or onto a bowsprit. Thus we increase both sail area and the area of wind we are using. If sailing to weather, the larger headsail could be a light genoa fit with roller furling gear. If sailing off the wind, the headsail could be an asymmetric spinnaker.

Having established the characteristics of the ideal cruising rig, let's examine the popular sail plans and rigs found on the cruising multihulls featured in this book. The three most popular rigs are the fractional sloop rig, the masthead sloop rig, and the mast-aft cutter rig. In addition, there are some unconventional rigs that bear consideration: the cat rig, the schooner rig, Forespar's AeroRig™, and the Walker Wingsail.

Fractional sloop rig. This is by far the most popular cruising rig in current use. It is a high-performance rig where the headstay attaches to a point that is some fraction of the full mast height instead of at the masthead. Its use for cruising is an outgrowth of its tremendous success on the racing circuit. Having only three wires to support the mast, the headstay and two shrouds, it is the most efficient rig and has the least parasitic drag. With no backstay, generous roach of the mainsail is possible, as are rotating wing masts. Many have a self-tacking jib as part of the standard sail plan, with a roller-furling genoa and an asymmetrical spinnaker available as options. On fractional rigs, the main drives the boat and the smaller jib tends to act as a guide or lead for the main.

An example of a fractional sloop rig

Fractional rigs do have a few disadvantages: on larger vessels, the fully battened main becomes heavy and one needs to be rather athletic to raise one with aplomb; on mainsails with extreme roach, the upper battens tend to press inward on the mast track, requiring costly mechanisms to keep them raising and lowering easily; and with no backstays it's hard to get proper headstay tension, although it's less important on rigs with smaller headsails.

Masthead sloop rig. Running a close second in popularity is the standard masthead sloop rig. This rig usually has twin backstays, a single headstay, double lower shrouds and single or double upper shrouds. This rig spreads the most sail for the least cost, uses a shorter and lighter mast section and has the option of a variety of headsails. Mainsails are typically not fully battened and roller-furling jibs are prevalent. On some cruising multihulls, the rigging base is wide enough to eliminate the need for spreaders, a considerable advantage. Some designs use a double headsail set-up; in light airs these boats carry main and genoa, in stronger winds the genoa is replaced by a small high-cut jib and the forestaysail is set. The masthead sloop is a utilitarian rig and a good compromise between performance, cost and flexibility.

Mast-aft cutter rig. The mast-aft cutter rig, like that used extensively in the Prout Catamarans line of cruisers, has some distinct advantages. The main is small and easy to handle on these boats. It is mainly a headsail-driven rig, with the low aspect ratio headsails creating a certain amount of lift at the bows. There is always an inner forestay for conveniently mounting staysails and storm jibs. For those who like large roller-furling headsails or multiple headsails, this is a good rig. Another nice feature is that the mast is mounted aft on the main bulkhead; the mast is easy to reach with all lines dropping into the cockpit, and the mast support doesn't pass through the saloon cabin.

There are, however, some compromises associated with mast-aft cutter rigs; the rigging geometry is such that the backstays are at a more acute angle to the mast than the headstays. In practice, this means it can be difficult to get a really tight headstay, a must for great performance, even when the backstays are fully tightened.

Cat rig. The cat rig has a single sail set on a mast stepped well forward, as on the *C-Cat 3214.* This rig has always had admirers for its simplicity and ease of sailing, and because of the substantially wider beam, a cat rig on a multihull doesn't create the same weather helm for which monohull catboats are noted. The ease of sailing, however, only applies to light-to-moderate conditions. As soon as the wind increases and you need to reef, you must handle a single sail of considerable size. With all of the sail area contained in one sail, a taller mast is needed to fly the same sail area as a sloop rig. As long as the boat size is moderate this isn't a problem, but if the mast height goes much beyond 45 feet cruising utility begins to be lost. The Endeavourcats are essentially cat rigged but with a small self-tacking headsail to spread the sail area.

Schooner rig. The Wharram designs are noted for their balanced, easy to handle two-masted schooner rigs. Most of these designs use two gaff-headed, boomless soft wingsails with a small headsail; the sails are easier to set and easier to handle than those on standard rigs. And the schooner rig enhances the traditional appearance of the Wharram designs.

An example of Forespar's Aero-Rig™

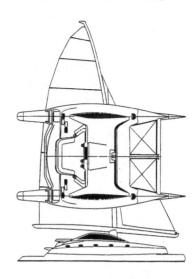

Forespar's Aero-Rig™. This efficient rig is gaining popularity in the multihull sailing community. It is essentially an unstayed, rotating mast and rig that allows both the boomless main and headsail to be simply rotated as a unit into position for proper sail trim. In most cases the sails can be reefed from the cockpit. This system is efficient, yet rather expensive and not for traditionalists who want to handle sails in the conventional way.

Walker wingsail. This patented rig takes the concept of a rotating mast foil to the extreme. According to designer John Walker, this rig unites the precision world of aircraft science with the exhilarating world of sailing. The rig consists of a rigid, raked carbon-fiber monoplane wingsail. Mounted on a free bearing like a weathervane and computer controlled, it responds to every wind shift or course change to keep the wing section perfectly trimmed. It also provides automatic tacking and jibing, reverse thrust for air braking and going astern, and electronic governing to prevent overpowering and capsize.

Sail handling aids. Many cruising multihulls with large mainsails now feature aids to sail handling such as "lazy jacks", Dutchman™ systems or other methods of gathering a lowered mainsail on the boom. Lazy jacks are a centuries-old method of containing a lowered mainsail, consisting of a series of fixed light lines. They are inexpensive and effective, although they tend to catch the leach of the sail while it is being raised. The Dutchman™ system requires mainsail and cover modifications, but it avoids the tendency of catching the leach of the sail. It features a series of parallel lines, suspended from the topping lift and woven through the mainsail, to gather the sail as it lowers.

There are also options available that roll the mainsail up on the boom or in the mast, but they tend to be complex and more expensive. In-the-mast furling requires a considerable amount of hardware, including a special mast section. Once in place it is as convenient as a roller-furling jib, although its expense, added weight aloft, inability to handle full battens and the typical whistling sound over the opening are considerations.

In-the-boom furling has the advantage of convenient stowage, simple operation and no need for special lines. Its disadvantage lies in the initial cost and the fact that the boom must be absolutely square to the mast for proper operation.

Self-tacking jibs can be truly trouble-free when fitted with a Camber Spar™, a curved rod sewn into a pocket in the sail that acts like a wishbone boom. The sail maintains an efficient shape, and is kept from flapping when headed into the wind.

Deck layout

Deck layout, including foredeck design, cabin design, side-deck accessibility, and cockpit arrangement are important items to consider on a cruising multihull.

Foredecks. There are two types of foredeck construction on cruising catamarans, solid bridgedeck and trampoline nets of various shapes and sizes. The ability to manufacture a proper cruising boat with a solid foredeck is limited by the beam of the boat. When the overall beam (BOA) exceeds one-half the waterline length, trampoline netting begins to become a necessity rather than an option. Standard beam vessels with solid foredecks have the advantage of solid footing for anchoring, sail changes and dinghy handling. Headstay attachment is simplified, as is anchor handling equipment, and a drier ride is experienced in rough going.

There are various types of trampolines and foredeck construction and management systems. The simplest and most straightforward is to have a net fill the entire area. The advantages are light weight and minimum windage. The disadvantages are that you must walk in the nets every time you go to the bow to handle anchors, docklines and headsails.

On many catamarans the foredeck is split into two by a promenade down the center. This solid area gives good footing for anchor handling, a solid base for anchor tackle and divides the trampoline area in half, thus allowing lightweight net materials and a lower maintenance quotient. This promenade often has grooves molded into it to retain anchor chain and keep chain, shackles and rode from damaging the netting. This central promenade also doubles as a boarding ladder on some models.

On some catamarans the forward trampoline area is rather small, and a rigid deck section is placed just aft of the netting to house self-draining storage lockers. This is a nice compromise between fully netted and fully rigid foredecks.

On boats with trampoline foredecks there is a forward cross-beam. This unit has several functions: it distributes the headstay load, handles the compression load between the hulls and provides trampoline attachment. There are two basic methods of distributing the headstay load, a bridle and a gull-striker.

The bridle is the simplest, lightest and most effective. Its disadvantage is that it raises the tack of the headsail off the deck, thus reducing somewhat the performance of the sail. On the other hand, raising the sail up increases visibility from the helm. On modern fractional-rig cruising boats, minor differences in performance are of lesser importance than visibility and simplicity. A bridle transfers the headstay tension to the bows using a tube as its compression member. It is also possible to keep a tighter headstay with this arrangement because the headstay itself is shorter, there are fewer connections and the loads are distributed in straight lines.

The gull-striker is essentially a truss arrangement that allows the tack of the jib to be placed on the forward cross-beam itself, thus allowing the maximum possible length of headstay. Most often, the gull-striker has an A-frame arrangement serving as the compression portion of the truss, and a wire across the top of the frame serving as the tension member. The tension load created by the headstay is distributed through the compression frame to the tension wire to the bows of the boat.

There is considerable torque and tendency toward wracking, including from anchor rode-handling equipment, in any forward cross-beam arrangement. This

makes proper design critical. The best forward crossbar designs are bolted rather than welded. It is not good engineering practice to pull directly on a weld, especially an aluminum weld.

Occasionally you will see some excellent fiberglass composite forward cross-beams. An interesting and effective approach is the curved arch, as used in the *Manta 40* and others.

Many forward cross-beams, especially those that are free-standing and have neither gull-striker nor promenade, are not strong enough to anchor from the center in severe conditions. Rather than placing enormous force in the center of the tube with nothing to counteract it, it's best to use a bridle from the hull deck cleats. This is especially true with all-chain rodes, which are capable of generating enormous shock loads in heavy weather.

Most modern trimarans have trampoline netting between the main hull and the amas, although some new designs and quite a few older designs do feature rigid side decks.

Whether on a catamaran or a trimaran, trampolines offer some of the finest aspects of multihull sailing. Lying in the trampolines, watching the water and the dolphins, basking in the sun or sleeping under the stars are experiences that cannot be equalled or even approached on any other type of vessel. They are, however, a high-maintenance item. If not maintained, they represent a serious safety threat. Any trampoline should be capable of supporting the weight of the entire crew. Proper materials, design and attachment are necessary to achieve that goal. Trampoline attachment is often the weak link. Check this area carefully when comparing boats.

Cabins & side decks. On boats with

bridgedeck cabins, the slope and height of the cabin sides, the width of the side-decks, and the hand-holds available are especially important considerations for cruisers. It is necessary to climb on cabin tops to get to the mast, handle sails and sail-covers, and to make adjustments or repairs to sail lifting and handling apparatus, so easy, safe and secure access is also an important item. Cabins with extreme slopes and height can be difficult to maneuver around or climb on.

The most user-friendly cruisers have good access and secure footing at the mast base. Many cabins with extreme slopes also let in excessive sunlight, thus requiring special curtains to contain it and negating one of a cruising catamarans best attributes: its panoramic view from the interior. Some cats such as the *Moorings 4500* have molded steps up the forward slope of the cabin. High cabin tops sometimes interfere with visibility from the cockpit and can adversely affect the boat's aesthetics.

The Fontaine-Pajot catamarans have an interesting design to the cabin, allowing for good visibility and a shading overhang that reduces solar gain into the main cabin.

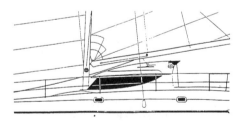

Cockpits & afterdecks. On most cruising multihulls the cockpit is located aft, although a few have center cockpits with aft sleeping cabins. Center cockpits, or aft cockpits with wide protective side decks or afterdecks, give a great feeling of security when at sea. Wide side decks next to the cockpit and afterdecks also provide good places for storage, lounging and sunbathing. Afterdecks, as with foredecks, can be fully rigid or made of trampoline netting. Cockpit seating is either aft, port & starboard or complete wrap-around. Most cruising multihulls have storage lockers under some portion of the cockpit seating.

The Chris White designed *Atlantic 42* has a unique arrangement: the cockpit is located forward of an aft wheelhouse, allowing for complete visibility from the cockpit helm in good weather, and a protected steering station in the main saloon cabin in bad weather. Most of the Wharram designs have a similar central helm station on the open bridgedeck.

Steering systems

Tiller vs wheel. Each system has its adherents. A tiller is by far the simplest system. It weighs less, costs less and allows for the use of less expensive autopilots. It is more sensitive to the touch and has the most steering feedback of any system. Most of the current production trimarans are tiller-steered, while many of the stock designs feature wheel steering.

Wheel steering is the preferred system on larger boats. It is familiar to people and lends itself to preferred cockpit locations and remote steering stations. There are three basic types—hydraulic, mechanical and cable—as well as several sub-types or combinations of types seen in modern boats.

Hydraulic systems. These are most often used in the more complex vessels, especially those with multiple steering stations. The hydraulic system gets its initial thrust from a permanently contained pressure reservoir. It is without doubt the most complex of all systems, requiring many spare parts, appropriate tools and above average mechanical savvy. Hydraulic systems are noted for their lack of feedback and feel of the helm.

Cable systems. Cables are the most common. They are further divided into pull-pull systems and push-pull systems. The TELEFLEX® cable within a cable is an example of push-pull. Most outboard-powered boats use this system as do some of the small-to-medium sized catamarans.

Pull-pull cable systems such as the EDSON® are used on a majority of boats. The system is a closed loop of cable, guided over sheaves (pulleys). The system pulls equally in each direction depending upon which way the wheel is turned. The system is easy to repair and adjust, requires the fewest spares and has great longevity.

Mechanical systems. Straight mechanical systems hook wheels to tiller cross-bars of various types and then to modified quadrants or tiller heads. These systems are simple, easy to maintain, rugged and foolproof.

In any boat capable of passage making, there should be an emergency tiller or other emergency steering system available.

Helm locations. Steering station location is most often based upon the primary design orientation of the vessel. While tiller steering aft is the preferred system for multihull sport boats, many of the larger charter boats have twin-helm wheel steering in the aft-quarters of the boat; that location keeps the crew and working lines as far away as possible from paying passengers.

An aft helm is often used on racing boats in order for the helmsman to best see the sails. That location is not, however, so good for general visibility and ease of

maneuvering, and on some designs the helmsman is practically perched above the waves on small seats at the stern, not the best arrangement for comfortable cruising. The majority of cruising boats have the helm forward against the cabin bulkhead, allowing for maximum protection from the elements and giving good all-around visibility.

Inside steering stations are very useful, especially for those who sail in cold weather and wish to extend their sailing season. They are much less relevant to those boats in tropical waters. They complicate the steering system and most use hydraulic systems.

Auxiliary engine(s)

For auxiliary power, trimarans typically have either a single outboard engine mounted aft or a single diesel engine installed inboard. Those with outboards use clever techniques for mounting and handling them.

Cruising catamarans, however, have five standard options for auxiliary power:
• Single or twin outboard, mounted on the transom or in a cockpit well.
• Twin inboards with twin screws.
• Single inboard with catamaran drive leg.
• Single inboard with twin hydraulic drives.
• Inboard engines with saildrives.

Outboard. There are a number of advantages to having an outboard as your auxiliary engine.

—The engine is outside the boat.

—No latent heat inside the boat.

—The danger of gasoline aboard is minimized because tanks and engines are outside, vented from below.

—The engine is easily removed for service with no haulout.

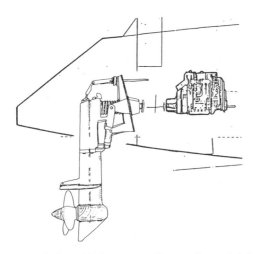

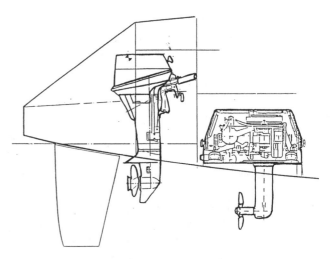

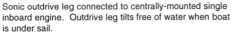

Sonic outdrive leg connected to centrally-mounted single inboard engine. Outdrive leg tilts free of water when boat is under sail.

Transom-mounted outboard engine (left) and inboard engine with saildrive mounted in the hull (right).

—Service organizations worldwide.

—Inexpensive (usually less than one-third the cost of a comparable diesel installation).

—Lightweight (usually less than one-half that of a comparable diesel.

—Reasonably reliable and dependable.

—Can be completely retracted from the water, thus lessening drag and electrolysis.

—Can often be adjusted for depth.

—Maneuverability (most outboards are connected to the rudders, dramatically improving close-quarters handling).

There are also some disadvantages:

—Fuel consumption: The rule of thumb for fuel consumption: two-cycle engines burn one gallon per ten horsepower per hour, four-cycle engines burn one-half gallon per ten horsepower per hour, diesel engines burn one-quarter gallon per ten horsepower per hour.

—Traditionally low electric output.

—Cavitation problems (certain vessels are more affected than others).

—Ease of operation. There are very few outboard installations that are as user friendly as a well-installed inboard, where you just touch a button and are under way.

—User acceptance. There exist cruisers who will not accept outboard power simply because it is outboard power! To them, an outboard has negative connotations of jury rig or of not being truly seaworthy. No amount of persuasion will alter their prejudice. This has implications for resale.

Inboard, twin screw. This is one of the most popular arrangements, with the engines mounted one in each hull just aft of midships. The advantages of this type of auxiliary power are:

—Nothing is as user friendly and easy to handle around docks and piers as a well designed twin screw catamaran. The wide beam makes it far more maneuverable than even a twin screw powerboat.

—There is safety in numbers. If one fails, the second engine will get you back.

There are also a number of disadvantages to inboard, twin screw installations:

—You have the cost of two engines.

—You have the weight and complexity of two installed engines.

—You have the same underwater protuberances and chronic problems of struts, shafts, through hulls, zincs, galvanic action etc. as your monohull counterpart, only you have it double.

Inboard, catamaran drive leg. Most of these installations are in a "nacelle" between the hulls of the catamaran. They are comparable to the inboard/outboard of motorboat circles. That is, the drive leg raises, lowers and turns, though it is seldom hooked directly to the rudders or steering system in the manner of outboards. This is a most practical setup, and perhaps has the most advantages and fewest disadvantages. The advantages are:

—Retractable leg, nothing in the water to drag, corrode or conduct electricity, when under sail or at the dock.

—Engine is outside the living quarters, therefore, less heat, noise, smell, mess.

—Low fuel consumption.

—Able to power belt-driven accessories such as refrigeration, alternators, and hydraulics.

—Easy access for maintenance/repair.

The only disadvantages are its weight and cost over an outboard and the possible difficulty of finding parts and service for the Sonic Drive leg.

Inboard, twin hydraulic drives.

This once popular system has almost faded into oblivion. In the days when marine diesels were outrageously expensive and inordinately heavy, it made good sense to use a single engine and hook it to two propellers via hydraulic motors. With the coming of the lightweight, high-speed diesel, it has become an unnecessary, complicated arrangement. This system has the additional disadvantage of introducing

yet another expensive, complicated component, hydraulic drives, into the boat. The engine is coupled to a large hydraulic pump instead of being hooked to a drive shaft. This pump in turn feeds through a manifold and director valves into hydraulic motors, which turn the propellers.

Those in existence have most of the advantages of twin screws. You cannot run the propellers at different speeds, however, thus limiting your maneuverability. There is also considerable power loss through the hydraulic system and most are rather noisy.

With hydraulic drives you still have the disadvantage of any drive system that has fixed propellers on shafts: catching trash, galvanic corrosion, vulnerability to damage, and the need to haul out for maintenance.

Saildrives. Inboard engines with saildrives are a clever marriage between a fixed leg and an engine/transmission mounted directly on top of it as a one-piece unit. These units are typically found mounted well aft in each hull, sometimes even accessible from above on the aft deck of the hull. The original saildrives, built by OMC, were derived from their standard outboard motors. In addition to the advantages and disadvantages listed above for all diesel installations, saildrives have these additional advantages:

—In some installations it is possible to remove the entire unit without haulout.

—Lighter, simpler, fewer parts.

—Eliminates the drive shaft, shaft log and stuffing box.

—Drive is perpendicular to waterline, thus not having the propeller thrust loss associated with an angled drive shaft.

—More compact, uses less space.

—Eliminates alignment problems.

—Quieter because of rubber bellows.

—Some units have the water intake

incorporated in leg, thus eliminating a through-hull fitting

The additional disadvantages over any inboard installation are:

—In some cases it is not possible to locate the engine far enough forward to properly distribute the weight.

—May be more drag than a conventional shaft and folding prop if the leg is not raised under sail.

—The vertical leg may catch trash which is difficult to remove.

Single inboard engine. Occasionally you will come across a catamaran with a single diesel engine installed in one hull with a conventional or a sail drive. This can be a satisfactory arrangement. Boats powered in this way are handled like any other single-screw vessel. You'll find that quite often it is not apparent in which hull the engine is installed.

Electric drives. There is a growing interest in quiet, reliable electric auxiliary drives for multihulls. In an electric drive system single or twin electric motors are matched with appropriate drives, either standard prop shafts or retractable legs. The motor(s) draw electrical power from a large battery bank, typically not the bank that supplies house loads. The horsepower requirements for electric drives are modest compared to typical combustion engines; 6-8 horsepower of electric drive (either single 6-8 hp or twin 3-4 hp) will provide ample power for moderate-sized cruising multihulls. In addition to the motor and drive, these systems include controls, throttles, and instrumentation to monitor motor and battery performance.

Motor voltage usually varies with the motor size. The electric drives of a leading manufacturer are rated at 3hp@36V, 4hp@48V, and 8hp@72V. Batteries must be

connected in series to achieve the desired voltage, and DC-to-DC converters used to step the voltage down to 12 volts if house loads are to be supplied. Renewable power sources can help replenish the power supply.

Electrical power system

Having a reliable source of electrical power on board is crucial to being able to enjoy your time cruising. The further afield you travel, the more you'll find this to be true. Ask anyone who has finally made it to the Islands, only to have his stay in paradise ruled by the constant need to run the engine for battery charging. The threat of dead batteries looms large on every cruiser's mind, yet maintaining an adequate supply of power can be easy, especially for those cruising on multihulls.

In many ways, the ease of finding an energy solution relates to how you approach the problem. For a start, most cruisers don't take their energy situation seriously enough until it's too late. They are used to having power whenever they need it at home, dockside, or in an automobile, so they make do with inadequate energy equipment while they upgrade all the other systems onboard. What they tend to forget is that many of those other systems are dependent on a reliable supply of electrical power.

On a boat, as soon as you leave the dock you are essentially managing your own little electric utility company on board. You have to accept the responsibility this position entails or suffer the potential consequences. Your job as utility manager is to select power-generating equipment and adequate storage capacity, then establish a comfortable charging routine that avoids brownouts and blackouts. You also want to choose efficient appliances that reduce your load without sacrificing performance. They may cost a bit more initially, but efficient appliances mean less generating power needed to run them, and that can yield big savings for a modest investment. Now you're starting to think like a utility manager!

You should also have proper monitoring equipment so you'll know exactly how your system is performing at all times. Energy meters and monitors make electricity visible, thus helping to eliminate the mystery. The rest is simple. Balance the energy produced with the energy consumed and you're well on your way to energy independence. It takes a little effort and a reasonable budget for initial set-up, but managing your own energy supply can be intensely satisfying.

How do you go about setting up a proper energy system? Many cruisers can piece together a reasonable system on their own using a comprehensive resource such as the *Independent Energy Guide.* To avoid unnecessary effort and expense, however, most cruisers use books as a primer for working with a qualified energy professional who can accurately assess their needs, is capable of supplying a complete energy package and, most importantly, is willing to stand behind his product if a problem develops in some far-off cruising ground.

Before embarking on an energy system design, it's advisable to become familiar with the various types of marine energy equipment currently available. A good place to start is with the equipment that generates power, including gear that uses renewable sources of energy such as solar panels and wind or water-powered generators, as well as engine-driven gear such as high-output alternators, portable generators, and gen-sets. Unlike any other piece of marine equipment you buy, renewable

energy gear actually pays for itself over time. Cruising multihulls, with their wide decks and transoms and their superior speed, are perfectly suited to gear using renewable sources of energy. The extra weight of the gear is more than offset by the reduction in engine fuel for charging batteries.

Solar panels. Most cruising multihulls have abundant space for locating a sizeable array of PV (photovoltaic) solar panels that transform sunlight directly into electricity. Don't let anyone delay your purchase of solar panels by saying how they're the thing of the future. Like multihulls themselves, this technology is perfected and ready for tough cruising conditions right now. In fact, today's solar cells are more efficient at converting light to electricity (12-16%) than incandescent bulbs are at converting electricity to light (only 10%). Over the years, forward-thinking multihull enthusiasts have helped bring PV solar use into the mainstream. Today sailors are finding creative ways to mount entire arrays of solar panels, either the flexible UniSolar panels mounted on Biminis and dodgers or rigid panels mounted on rails, davits, hardtops, stern arches or on frameworks over the cockpit. It's not unusual to see boats with over 200 watts of solar power capable of handling their entire electrical load.

Wind-powered generators. Cats and tris also offer a wider selection of mounting locations for wind-powered generators. Wind units come in two basic types. High power, large prop units made in the U.S. use 60-72 inch diameter wind blades to produce up to 20 amps of current in 20-25 knots of wind. They can be mounted on a pole at the stern, hung in the fore-triangle for use in port, or mounted on the front of a mizzen mast. Look for units that have overspeed

Air Marine wind generator

protection in high winds (over 25 knots) and can be converted to a water generator for longer passages.

Small prop, multi-bladed units produce much less power, but are typically self-limiting by design and pose less of a hazard when mounted on a boat. With their 36-40 inch diameter blades, they work best in windy locations or as part of a diverse energy package. The *Air Marine* three-bladed wind generator is small, lightweight, and attractively styled, with a surprising output in higher windspeeds, although you may be disappointed with the output in light winds. There were problems with blade noise and low output in some of the earlier units, but these seem to be corrected and the factory is excellent at handling warranty claims.

Water-powered generators. These are by far the most underrated and least understood source of marine electrical power. They use the motion of a sailboat, or the power of the wind on the sails, to produce electrical power. Most units currently available are Trailing-Log types. A small prop mounted on a stainless steel shaft is trailed through the water on 60-100

feet of tightly wound line. As the line spins, it turns an electrical generator mounted on the stern of the boat.

Water-powered generators can also be Strut-Mounted units that trail in the water just behind the boat from a submerged strut, Outboard-Leg type units that mount on the transom like an outboard motor, or Prop-Shaft units that utilize the power of a rotating prop shaft while the boat is under sail. The drag of a water-powered generator is negligible on a multihull. Don't let the small size of these machines fool you; the high average cruising speeds of a multihull produce a truly phenomenal amount of power, with daily averages approaching two to three hundred amp-hours!

High-output alternators. For those with an inboard engine, a high-output alternator gives you the most power for the smallest financial investment. These units are not just standard alternators with a higher output. They are quite different in how they are constructed and controlled. They run cooler, produce more power at lower rpm (revolutions per minute), and charge batteries more quickly and more fully. These units are moderately priced and the small- and large-case models are made to be direct replacements for the standard alternators found on most engines.

Portable generators & gen-sets. Some cruisers find it advantageous to have an engine-driven source of power that is separate from their auxiliary. A small portable generator can provide AC power for tools and other appliances, but typically the DC output is minimal (8-10 amps). You can get around this by plugging in a battery charger to the AC side of the portable generator (or run the generator output into your shorepower connection) and use its full AC capacity to charge batteries efficiently. Remember that while they are an efficient source of power, they are best-suited for occasional use or as part of a diverse energy package. As a favor to yourself and those anchored near you, look for the quietest unit you can find and don't attempt to use it as your sole power source.

The same applies to permanently mounted gen-sets. Some cruisers need the kind of power that only a gen-set can provide. Any time they are operating you can direct a large portion of their power output into battery charging. But many AC loads are either small-to-moderate or are intermittent, and these can easily be handled by the noiseless, maintenance-free operation of an efficient DC-to-A C inverter. Small 200 Watt inverters can run some power tools, blenders, computers, TVs and VCRs, while larger units can provide 2500 Watts or more of continuous AC power. Keep in mind that inverters are taking stored energy from your batteries, so you must also have an adequate means of DC charging to replace that power.

Accommodations

As with many other cruising consider-ations, trimarans by nature have accommo-dation plans similar to those found on monohulls. No modern trimarans have accommodations on the wingdeck between main hull and amas, and the forepeak of the main hull is typically used for a double V-berth. For that reason our discussion of accommodation considerations will focus on cruising catamarans.

Cabins & cabin access. Most cruising catamarans have three main areas of accommodation, one in each hull and one on the bridgedeck. In almost all cases the hull accommodations are accessed from inside the bridgedeck saloon cabin, al-

though on some models such as the *Edel 11m* the three cabin areas are all accessed separately. The advantage of separate access is that it gives the bridgedeck cabin more usable space without the need for steps and walkways to the hulls. The disadvantage is that in bad weather you must go outside to the hulls.

On most cats the hull access steps from the main saloon cabin are located aft and directly opposite from each other. Occa-sionally you'll see variations on this theme. The *Nimble 39.3* and the *Hughes 45* have access steps to one hull located aft and the other forward, allowing for an L-shaped galley aft and an L-shaped settee forward. Some of the larger cats, such as the *Oasis 380*, the *Tasman Elite 4000* and the *Norseman 430* have two sets of steps to one or both hulls, allowing access to fore and aft staterooms without passing through heads located midships. The *Catseye Bay 10.8* has dual access steps to each hull; the steps pass either side of a nav area midships in the port hull and a refrigeration compartment midships in the starboard hull.

You'll notice that on some of the cruising catamarans featured in this book, such as the *Aquilon 800*, the *Maine Cat 30*, the *Seawind 1000* and the Wharram *Tiki* designs, the bridgedeck cabin has been eliminated in favor of an open deck plan. This type of layout offers some advantages, including a great deal of deck space, low windage, ease of construction and lower cost. On a boat with an open bridgedeck, the hulls are accessed separately through hatches on either side of the cockpit, and one portion of a hull, usually adjacent to the galley, often serves as a lounge or dining area. Some open bridgedeck designs have a soft or rigid enclosure over the central bridgedeck area that offers weather protection for a table and seating area and the access hatches to the hulls.

A variation of the open bridgedeck is the partial bridgedeck design, where a low headroom superstructure is integrated into the cockpit and deck plan. On boats with this layout such as the *ShuttleCat 31 & 40*, the partial bridgedeck offers a place for low-headroom berths (accessed from the hulls), storage lockers (inside and out) and some degree of protection for the cockpit.

Chris White's *Atlantic 42* has a unique layout where the cockpit is actually forward of the main cabin that also serves as an enclosed wheelhouse. Access to this cabin, and thus the hulls, is from a door at the aft end of the cockpit. The area forward of the wheelhouse is a partial bridgedeck design, with bridgedeck berths that are accessed from the hulls.

The galley. Cruising multihull galleys, especially those found on catamarans, have certain advantages over those found on monohulls. Because of the reduced motion of the boat, there is little need for galley harnesses or gimballed stoves. Few cruising catamarans have fiddle rails on tables or counters. Most have simple edging, the same type you would find in a shoreside home environment. Catamaran galleys are noted for exceptional amounts of counter space, cabinet space and user-friendly layout. Most are airy with good natural ventilation, are spacious and have a view out the windows.

Many cruising catamaran galleys have double sinks, a delight for the cook and clean-up crew. For those of you who are new to cruising, a few of the advantages are: you can use the second sink as a dish drainer (cruisers simply leave them there, safely protected for the next use); the second sink makes a convenient rough-weather,

temporary storage for items most often left on the counter top; it is a handy place to stow your thermos, your coffee cup or other beverage when the going gets rough; a second sink allows a second person to clear and safely stack while the first person washes; for those who like to keep sinks filled with soapy wash water, one can be filled while the other is used for rinsing; and you have plenty of room for salt-water taps, soap dispensers, spray heads and other accessories.

There are two basic configurations used in catamaran galleys. One is to have the galley on the same level as the bridgedeck as an integral part of the main cabin. While most galley-up layouts are on the larger cats, the *Renaissance 320* and *Tobago 35* are examples of this arrangement on modest-size boats. The second method is to have the galley down in one of the hulls. Each galley design has particular advantages.

There are several popular layouts in the galley-up style. There is the galley at the back of the main cabin, as in the *Victory 35*, the *Catana 381*, *Nautitech 395* and the *Manta 40*. Then there is the side of the cabin arrangement as seen in the boats from Voyage, Fountaine Pajot, Lagoon, and others. There is even a central layout as seen in the *Packet Cat 35* and *Nautitech 475*. All these arrangements tend to support the theme that the galley should be an attraction in and of itself and be a central part in the entertainment/living center.

Galley-up gives the chef a panoramic view of the main cabin, and lends itself more readily to lots of people. That is a particular life-style choice, and there are those who will always congregate in the kitchen. The spacious feeling of the galley-up relates to the proximity of the rest of the main cabin. The galley work or serving area is often expanded by using the navigation station or chart table if it is located on the bridgedeck.

Having the galley and navigation areas up on the bridgedeck means that the hulls serve strictly as sleeping accommodations, with head compartments and storage areas as desired. Some might say that the galley-up arrangement is informal, whereas the galley-down is more formal. I suppose that depends on whether you consider anything formal on a small sailboat.

The basic galley-down arrangement means that the galley is configured in one of the hulls, by far the most popular layout. The cats from Corsair, Performance Cruising, Prout and PDQ are examples of this technique. They have the galley layout in a straight line, or two lines back-to-back with an aisle through the middle. The advantage to this arrangement is that the muss and fuss of cooking and dish-washing is farther from sight. There is considerably less traffic through the galley area. The galley, being

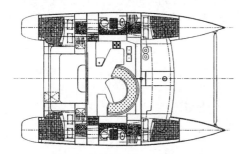

Galley up style shown above and galley down below

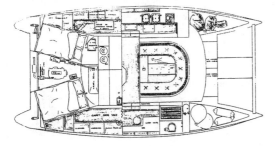

separate, allows more open space in the main cabin. Galley-down arrangements are proportionately larger. In most galley-down catamarans, the head is on the opposite side from the galley, eliminating that cross-traffic.

Navigation area. The navigation area, a vital space to serious cruisers, is often neglected on boats primarily used for coastal cruising or charter work. A proper navigation area provides a good space for chart work and serves a growing need for a temporary office on board. Over the years a popular arrangement has been to have the nav station located midships in one of the hulls facing the main cabin. This allows the chart table to slide under a counter or settee when not in use. On smaller boats the nav seat is usually a fold-down affair, stored on the opposite wall of the hull. On larger boats there is often a comfortable pull-out seat. In either situation a crew member seated at the chart table takes up the entire width of the hull. If the space forward of the nav area is a stateroom or work/storage area this layout works well, but if the only head is forward of the nav area, the person working at the chart table must pack up his work and move to allow passage to the head.

Having the nav area in the saloon cabin avoids this problem. Many of the newer boats place the galley up to one side of the forward saloon area and the nav area on the other side, with a curved settee in the middle. Often an extension of the settee serves as the nav seat. This layout gives the navigator less privacy, but provides greater access to the cockpit, a much better vision of the surroundings, and a permanent work area out of the normal traffic patterns.

Sleeping accommodations. Modern cruising catamarans and trimarans offer permanently made-up double berths, with many cats having one in each corner of the boat. Keep in mind that what we refer to as doubles in the two-page boat layouts are most often in fact queen-sized berths.

You might ask, "When does a berth become a cabin, or a cabin become a stateroom?" A berth becomes a cabin when it is closed off from through traffic, even if it is only by a curtain. A cabin becomes a stateroom when it contains more amenities than simply a berth and a place to hang your clothing. Staterooms contain items such as dressing tables, mirrored vanities, hanging lockers, sitting areas and even washbasins. Staterooms are denoted by having their own solid door as a closure and a walkway in addition to the berth. Most cruising catamaran accommodations fit into the stateroom category, while most trimarans and many cats have a combination of staterooms, cabins and convertible settee/berths.

Cruising catamaran berth layouts fall into two general classifications, berths on the bridgedeck and berths in the hulls. In addition, these berths can be placed forward, aft, or in both locations. Examples of a single stateroom forward with a double berth on the bridgedeck are the *Gemini 105* and the *Privilege 37*. An example of a boat with two double staterooms forward with double berths on the bridgedeck is the *St. Francis 44* and the *PDQ 36*.

Most of the larger luxury cruising catamarans have the berths athwartships on the bridgedeck as opposed to fore and aft in the hulls. Bridgedeck berths are easier to access, though many cruisers find the motion more comfortable in berths positioned fore and aft. The *Heavenly Twins 27 & 36* and the *Ocean Twins 38* illustrate twin aft staterooms in a center cockpit design,

with the double berths running fore-and-aft on the bridgedeck. Some models have a large forward stateroom with a double berth on the bridgedeck that is open from both sides of the vessel in a large master suite arrangement.

Head compartments. One of the most striking aspects of a cruising catamaran is its ability to have an abundance of heads. All head compartments on cruising cats are located in the hulls, either forward, aft or midships. Some are enclosed within a private stateroom, while others are accessible to all crew members. Some are located in the corners of the craft, others midships. Some head compartments placed midships span the entire width of the hull and must be "walk-through" in order to access the cabin beyond, unless there are dual access steps from the bridgedeck. On larger boats a midships head compartment can be placed outboard with a separate walkway connecting fore-and-aft accommodations.

While the majority of boats have just one head, or possibly one head in each hull, many of the boats intended for the charter trade have up to four or five separate head compartments.

Privacy. One striking advantage of the accommodations on a cruising catamaran is the feeling of privacy. Berths are typically diagonally across from each other, maximizing the distance between them. Due to the shape of the boat, sound does not travel easily. Catamarans easily lend themselves to having widely separated cabins in the four corners of the boat. Those with solid doors for closure do not share that door with other compartments. With the main cabin up on the bridgedeck, cruisers can have full use of the lounging and eating facilities without disturbing those in the sleeping cabins.

Chartering a Cruising Multihull

The Charter of Choice
Why multihulls are so popular for chartering

Once the exclusive domain of monohull sailboats, well over one hundred charter fleets worldwide now offer cruising multihulls in their flotillas. Demand has spurred this remarkable change, a demand reflected by the explosive popularity of multihulls in general. Increasingly the boat of choice by today's customer, cruising multihulls provide maximum value in the charter industry, which explains why they are now the most popular of all charter vessels. The same characteristics that make them so appealing to private owners apply even more to charter customers, for whom a limited time investment, varied levels of expertise, a vacation mentality, and often a desire for privacy all play an important role. Coupled with a substantial money investment, these considerations put specific demands on chartering that cruising multihulls can easily meet.

With limited time at their disposal, charterers want to sail to a variety of places, enjoy their stay in each one, and experience that rare combination of exhilarating yet comfortable, relaxing sailing. Characterized by their fine turn of speed, cruising multihulls can generally cover considerably more territory than a monohull of comparable size, allowing for a more flexible cruising itinerary. In addition, while the speed of a multihull provides plenty of excitement, the noticeable ease of handling their simple rigs, manageable sail plans, and level sailing make the whole experience much less tiring than on a monohull. Cruising multihulls are also forgiving boats, a serious consideration for novice sailors who want to experience the world of sailing without trepidation, mishap, or necessarily the need to employ a captain and crew. Numerous first time charterers find themselves permanently sold on multihulls after enjoying this gentle introduction to sailing.

The sheer comfort of a cruising multihull, both topsides and below, lends itself well to the nature of chartering where customers want the fun of sailing without the discomforts that often attend it. With only their short vacation time at their disposal, charterers are looking for comfort and convenience while cruising. Often escaping a fast-paced, urban life-style, they seek the peaceful aspects of life out on the water as well as the adventurous ones. Multihulls offer all the enjoyment of cruising with a host of additional attributes. Even small multihulls boast cockpits that are large enough to host a party, yet they remain dry under sail. Deck space is expansive, with plenty of room for maneuvering, sail-handling, sunbathing, and carrying assorted paraphernalia like dinghies and sailboards. Level sailing means that even a stiff beat to windward can be an enjoyable experience for those who want to lounge on the foredeck, sunbathe aft, or just bury themselves in a good book. And boarding has become immeasurably easier on these high free-board craft, with most charter designs now incorporating steps into the twin transoms.

When it comes to comfort, nothing can beat the interior layout of a cruising multihull. Light and airy cabins, panoramic windows, cockpit-level saloon seating, spacious galleys, cavernous locker space, and private sleeping cabins are all the norm, even on the smaller charter boats. Catamaran staterooms often feature queen-size berths, a seat, hanging locker, storage, and even vanities, washbasins or private heads with a shower. Privacy is a prime feature, an important consideration when chartering with one, two, or even three other couples. A number of yachts incorporate the galley-up concept, an especially workable design on crewed charter boats as it lends easy access to the dining area for the cook. Luxury multihulls can also easily include a bar with stools, dual dining areas, and an entertainment center, all on the bridgedeck and away from the sleeping quarters. No other charter vessel of comparable size can match this degree of privacy and acoustical seclusion.

Cooking is always a pleasure on a boat that stays level under sail and has an easy motion when anchored in swells. The galley area is usually spacious and very workable, separated from the main flow of traffic either on the bridgedeck or located in one hull. And eating, drinking and relaxing inside are especially enjoyable on a boat with eye level windows and a panoramic view.

Multihulls exhibit another decided advantage when it comes to their shoal draft. As most charter operations are located in popular cruising grounds, finding a secure anchorage can be a challenge in crowded harbors. For novices the situation is doubly challenging as they strive to cope with not only the logistics of anchoring, but locating a viable spot to drop anchor. Here again, multihulls offer the significant advantage of shoal draft, allowing them to anchor in cozy, isolated corners inaccessible to deeper draft craft. Not only do anchoring possibilities increase dramatically on a multihull, but day outings guests can often step right from boat to shore.

Beyond the practical reasons why charter customers like multihulls, there's the pure magic of sailing on these craft. Nothing can match the thrill of flying through the water in exotic, adventurous surroundings while enjoying the comforts of home. As many sailing enthusiasts have already discovered, a charter cruise on a multihull offers one of life's greatest pleasures.

Multihull Day Chartering
Just for fun or as a first step toward ownership

Day charter multihulls have sprung up on the world's waterfronts, bringing a new range of possibilities to chartering: boats that appeal to the imagination; a greater range of day destinations due to the faster speed of a multihull; a wider appeal because of their pronounced stability and comfort; the fascination of their cutting-edge looks, concepts and technology.

You can choose to day charter on just about any kind of multihull that's been built. There is, however, a tendency in many tourist destinations for big new catamarans designed specifically for day chartering to dominate the business. Offering a smooth, level ride that's fast and dry, these impressive boats can accommodate numerous passengers while still providing roomy comfort for all.

In most places there is still a choice of smaller cruising cats and tris for day charter as well, each with its own appeal and advantages. While a little less smooth and dry, they usually offer a more personal situation for anywhere from two to a dozen or so people.

Each kind of boat and trip offers a unique type of experience. Perhaps after a day charter on one of the smaller multihulls, you might find yourself considering buying or building one of these vessels as your own personal boat.

The developing taste for what is being called eco-tourism finds one of its finest expressions in multihull day charters. Efficient, fast and comfortable, multihulls can seek out lovely natural havens that are often the most perfect and unspoiled areas in their region. Another itinerary might offer a 15 mile beat into a fresh tradewind to some delightful destination, where you disembark for some relaxed shopping, sight-seeing, or beach time before re-embarking and surfing back in the afternoon under spinnaker.

Day chartering can also offer other rewards. Anyone reading this book is interested in sailing and knows that books can be great fonts of knowledge. But there is no teacher like experience, in this case an experience that is readily available by day charter. These charters offer the opportunity to gain insight into just about any kind of multihull you might be interested in, all for about the price of a visit to a good restaurant.

If you already own a cat or a tri, you might want to compare your boat with other types of multihulls. Or maybe you're a salty soul with years of experience sailing monohulls who's curious about these multihulled boats and how they feel under sail. Perhaps you've considered term chartering a multihull to get a taste of the experience. Before committing yourself to a week or more on one type of boat, try day charter as an alternative. If you want to get first-hand knowledge of the boat you're considering building or buying, the day charter offers a pleasant, relaxed research opportunity.

Day charter boats are out cruising almost every day, as are the people who sail them. Charter operators can give you valuable information about the boat they sail and, frequently, about others as well. Among day charter skippers you will find transatlantic racers, cruisers who have sailed around the world, and people who have built and sailed these boats for years.

You'll find that day chartering is a combination of the sea, beaches, the boats and their crew, and the insight you'll gain from the experience—that's what makes multihull day chartering so memorable.

Day charter boats

In the past three decades we've witnessed the sailing multihull become the vessel of choice for the majority of commercial sailing passenger operations worldwide. The commercial sailing industry can be divided into two areas. The most visible segment, perhaps due to heavy advertising, is the term charter market. The other side of the commercial sailing industry is the phenomenon of the growing day charter market, which has given millions of people a healthy sailing experience.

Day charter multihull layouts are passenger friendly and safe. The boats are designed so that passengers have ample areas for lounging and sunbathing, and so that the boat can be handled by a minimum crew. Amenities such as comfortable seating with sun and rain protection are considered standard. Comforts may extend to include full service bars, dining arrange-

ments, men's and women's spacious toilets with push button flushing, and full 'stairways' for swimming and snorkeling access. These day charter multihulls (and catamarans in particular) have optimized hull shapes for both minimizing wetted surface and enhancing slow-speed maneuverability. The majority of vessels carry 49 passengers or less, since craft carrying between 50 to 65 seats must comply with more stringent USCG regulations. Above 65 passengers (and up to 149), charter boat owners can begin to amortize the added regulatory expense.

Though there are large numbers of "walk-on" customers climbing aboard, most commercial operators depend on advance bookings marketed through an affiliated hotel or resort for which the vessel has a signed concession agreement. A large portion of the pre-booked market is the cruise ship industry. And growing group of travel agents book individuals and groups as part of a complete travel package. Sailing tours are frequently marketed as 'eco-tours', though the vessels are usually seen plying the same old routes out to the favorite old anchorages, beaches and snorkeling grounds. To rise above the competition many operators are advertising higher performance craft or offering specials such as on-board diving instructions.

It's interesting to note the construction of the larger day charter vessels. Most are built as 'one-offs'. Simple hull moulds are typical, with the majority of the parts and pieces being hand-crafted. Most of the vessels are composite in nature, with epoxy resins being used to glue cedar planks (strips) which are then glassed both inside and out with epoxy resins and unidirectional glass cloths. There are some balsa-cored vessels and a few foam-cored vessels.

Solid glass and aluminum construction are simply too heavy to be considered competitive in today's market.

Propulsion. Auxiliary propulsion in the commercial market seems divided between inboard and outboard systems. These decisions partially depend on vessel size and route, with the trend towards greater inboard power. Unlike the cruiser, the commercial craft owner gets to pick his route and weather. In the tropics where the weather is consistent, outboards have proven ample and demonstrate the lowest initial investment. More variable or rougher routes dictate inboard diesel installations. The saildrive option is the favorite, with its simple installation and low sailing drag.

Rigs. Most commercial vessels geared for high performance are using fractional sloop rigs, often with rotating masts. If the primary sail is to be a large main, then a rotating, self-supporting spar begins to make sense. The wing mast, with its fewer parts, greater efficiency, lower corrosion and lighter weight, is beginning to gain popularity.

Multihull Term Chartering
The best way to try before you buy

Most sailors in the market for a multihull spend a great deal of time sorting out the various cruising cats and tris, trying to balance their cruising needs and budget with boat size and style. They send away for brochures and spend endless time talking with builders, brokers, friends, acquaintences, in fact anyone who can give them insight into their chosen vessel. If possible they visit boat shows or local dealers to view the choices first-hand. It's great to actually walk around the deck, sit in the saloon cabin and cockpit, try out the berths, and peek into the lockers. All of this effort helps narrow down the choices, but how do you make that final decision with confidence, knowing that it's the right boat for you?

The very best way, especially if you are new to cruising multihulls, is to try before you buy. An afternoon test sail is a good start, and all builders and brokers are happy to accommodate those seriously interested in purchasing. For a more relaxing experience where you are guaranteed to get straight answers to tough questions about a boat's performance, a day charter on your boat of choice is another good option. The problem with a day sail, either with a builder, broker or day charter operator, is that it provides only a short time on board and the experience of only one set of conditions. If winds are light you'll wonder how she handles in more wind; if the wind is up you'll wonder if she performs in light winds. You'll also have lingering concerns about what it's like to anchor, to cook, perform chart work under sail, motor in various sea conditions, and so on. Just days after the test sail you'll be trying hard to remember what certain aspects of the boat were like.

What you really need is to spend some time on board your prospective boat, say a week or so in pleasant surroundings, to sail her in varying conditions and get familiar with her more subtle characteristics. Term chartering is the perfect solution. Either bareboat or crewed chartering allows you to combine a pleasant vacation with the perfect opportunity to put your boat of choice through its paces in some of the world's best cruising grounds. The cost of the experience is modest when compared to the expense of buying the wrong boat. If more than one boat is in the running as your next cruising vessel, take your time and try chartering each one in order of preference. With a week or more to sort out the pros and cons of a particular multihull, you'll quickly know when you've found the right cruising boat.

Of course, you don't have to be in the market to buy a multihull to charter one. In fact sailing without the responsibility of ownership, or the prospect of ownership, is part of the fun. Just relax and have a good time. Some sailors charter year after year without ever actually owning a boat.

Where to charter

The charter locations for cruising multihulls is almost unlimited today. For wintertime charters the Caribbean is an obvious choice, though other warm destinations include Florida and the Keys, the West Coast or Gulf Coast of the U.S., the Bahamas, Guatemala, Belize, Greece, Turkey, Corsica, Australia, New Zealand, Polynesia, and many other good cruising grounds. Most of these popular cruising areas have good charter potential all during the year. You can reduce the cost of your charter vacation by avoiding peak season.

Before you make the decision of where to charter, consider several factors. If you are only mildly interested in buying a boat, choose a charter spot by which travel destination you are most interested in exploring. If you are serious about buying a boat, it makes more sense to choose a charter location that has the model you are considering buying in an area similar to the one you plan to cruise in most often. This helps you find out if your boat of choice performs as needed in the conditions you expect to encounter.

Another helpful hint is to plan your charter around the things you expect to do as an owner. If you like to dock at marinas and explore new restaurants, choose a charter destination with areas like this nearby to give yourself docking experience and a taste of how you plan to cruise. If you prefer secluded anchorages or diving and snorkeling, pick a boat and a charter area well suited to these activities. Even if you plan to sail offshore, term chartering allows

you to see if your choice of multihull performs adequately in the varied wind and wave patterns you experience while cruising.

Bareboat or crewed charter?

Bareboat chartering allows you and your crew to have complete control over the sailing and handling of a cruising multihull. It affords you the most privacy and is certainly more affordable, but bareboat chartering is not for everyone, especially if you are still gaining experience with multihulls or sailing in general.

The term "bareboat" is a little misleading to those unfamiliar with chartering. You may be envisioning an empty hull, but don't worry; charter boats are typically well appointed and equipped. It's simply that what you are renting is the boat itself—you and your guests make up the crew. Multihulls have such great accommodations for their size that it's easy to bring along some friends to help defray the cost of chartering. Having friends on board gives you some idea of what it will be like to have guests on your own boat, something that inevitably happens when you have a multihull in a desirable location.

Crewed chartering is best for those who would like to ease into sailing a multihull, or for those who want experience with a larger boat. Boats over 50 feet are typically only available for crewed charter arrangements because of the complexity of the sail handling and the systems on board. The "crew" in these situations can consist of a captain, cook, and deck hands, or simply a captain who directs your involvement as the crew. A crewed charter situation allows you to completely relax and take as much of an active part in the sailing of the boat as you wish. It is a great way to learn the art of sailing, sort of like a personalized sailing school. And the captain also serves as a knowledgeable guide to the area you are cruising in, ensuring that you take best advantage of your vacation.

Choosing a charter company

Having chosen a potential boat and cruising ground, you still need to select the right charter company. Several avenues are open to help you find companies with the type of multihull you have chosen in the area you want to cruise:

— Many reputable charter operations that specialize in cruising multihulls are listed at the end of this chapter.

—Search through ads in the popular yachting magazines. Most of the larger publications have annual charter issues that feature qualified charter companies.

—Spend time talking with factory reps and yacht brokers. They'll direct you to the companies that specialize in the type of boats you are considering buying.

—Contact owners of the same kind of boat you've selected to charter. Some of the more popular multihulls have owner associations.

Once you have your potential list together, call each charter company and ask the following questions:

"What sailing conditions and climate can I expect when I plan to charter?"

"Are captained or bareboat charters available?" Bareboat chartering gives you responsibility for the boat and more closely approximates ownership.

"Do I meet the necessary qualifications to bareboat?" Some companies require bareboat certification in order to charter, but many don't. In most cases, sailing experience as a skipper is sufficient. If you are hesitant about bareboating in a new cruising ground, or would like assistance with the boat, a captain is usually available. Most companies are flexible; you can get a captain for as little as half a day, or for the duration of the charter.

"What is the age of the boat?" If buying a used boat, try to choose a charter vessel of approximately the same vintage.

"Are there limits to the cruising grounds?" The company's insurance limitations often dictate whether you can go where you had planned.

"What are the security deposit requirements and when will the deposit be returned?"

"What equipment is on the boat and what do I need to bring?"

"Are there travel restrictions, visa requirements, or health precautions to be taken?"

Read the charter contract thoroughly before sending in a deposit. Make sure you are able to meet all the terms and conditions, and understand what you are signing. Ask for an explanation if something is unclear.

Ask the potential charter company about their check on procedures. Make sure all boat systems will be explained to you and that you know where all the safety equipment is stored and how to use it. Additionally, make sure a company representative will go over the local charts with you to recommend good anchorages or places to avoid, and to suggest possible itineraries.

If you are chartering a boat with the thought of purchasing one, ask when the charter operators might have some time to discuss the boat with you. Remember—the management company has probably spent more time with the boat than most owners. Ask them about the boat's strong points, shortcomings and the annual repair and maintenance costs.

The cost of renting the boat itself will vary greatly depending upon its size, age and location. The more remote or exotic a location is, the more it will cost, partly because this increases the company's costs for getting parts, supplies and reliable, knowledgeable employees.

Ask the company what other expenses you can expect to incur. In most cases you receive the boat with full fuel and water tanks and it is your responsibility to return it the same way. Some charter companies provide food packages as well, saving you the time and effort required to stock up for the week. Ask what these costs are likely to average. If you choose to stay in marinas

each night, find out how much this is going to cost. Ask what additional charges are possible, such as boarding the boat early, renting a dinghy, the daily cost of a captain if needed, or entering different territorial waters such as visiting the BVIs from the U.S. Virgins or vice versa.

Ask the right questions before you charter and you'll avoid unpleasant surprises. Once you settle on the boat, the location, the type of charter and the charter company, make the most of this pre-purchase test cruise. If you find your first choice of cruising multihull doesn't live up to your expectations, don't be discouraged—you'll get to spend another week in paradise trying out the next boat.

company	charter area	multihulls in their fleet	telephone
Allied Yacht Charters	Chesapeake Bay	Lagoons, F. Pajots	(410) 280-1522
AYS Charters	Chesapeake Bay	PDQ, Gemini, Seawind	(800) 382-8181
BareCat Charters	Virgin Islands	PDQ, Privilege	(800) 296-5287
Blue Water Yacht Charters	Bahamas, FL Keys	Solaris, Edel, Lagoon	(800) 522-2992
BOAT/U.S. Yacht Charters	Worldwide	Assorted boats	(800) 477-4427
California Multihull Charters	Tortola, Tahiti	Voyage, Crowther	(619) 222-9694
Charter Cats of the Bahamas	Bahamas	PDQ, Prout, Americat	(800) 446-9441
Crusader Yachting	Turkey	full range of Prouts	(44) 07-00-015-1500
Cumberland Charter Yachts	Australia	Elite, Parallax, Seawind	(61) 7-946-7500
Florida Sailing Charter Club	Florida E, W & Keys	Gemini, Americat, PDQ	(800) 468-4440
Florida Yacht Charters	Florida, Bahamas	F. Pajots, Lagoon, Manta	(800) 537-0050
Island Yacht Charters	Virgin Islands	Packet Cat, Lagoon	(800) 524-2019
Multihull Marine Center	California, Caribbean	F-27, F-31, Tobago 35	(310) 821-6762
Paradise Yacht Charters	Caribbean Islands	Privilege cats	(800) 258-8753
Sail Abaco	Bahamas	PDQ 32, 36	(800) 678-6096
Sea Safari Sailing	Florida Gulf Coast	C-Cat, Gemini, Americat	(800) 497-2508
Southernmost Sailing	Florida Keys	Tobago 35, PDQ 32, 36	(888) 352-7245
Sun Yacht Charters	Carib, S. Pacific, Med	F. Pajot, Voyage	(800) 772-3500
The Moorings	Carib, Med, Austral	Lagoon, F. Pajot, Moorings	(800) 535-7289
TMM Bareboat Vacations	Caribbean, Belize	F. Pajot, Lagoon, Privilege	(800) 633-0155
Tropic Island Yacht Management	Virgin Islands	F. Pajot, Voyage	(800) 356-8938
Vacation Yachts	SW Florida	F. Pajot, Gemini, Seawind	(800) 971-0101
Voyage Yacht Charters	Virgin Islands	Voyage catamarans	(809) 494-0740
Wind Works Sailing Center	Pacific NW	Corsair F-31, Gemini	(206) 784-9386

Choosing Your Own Cruising Multihull

Buying A New Boat

The choices and the process of purchasing new

The appeal of buying a brand new boat looms large in the minds of most prospective buyers, especially those who make the pilgrimage to the boat shows where a host of beautiful multihulls are on display. As with buying a new home or car, there is nothing quite like being the very first owner. Economic reality often tempers this enthusiasm, but for those who can afford to make the plunge the experience can be superb. The customer in the market for a new boat has several choices, either a production boat or one that is built on a semi-custom basis using a stock design.

Buying a production boat

Buying a new production boat has advantages to those who like a particular boat as it is displayed at boat shows or offered as standard from the factory, and don't want to be burdened with a host of decisions through every step of construction. Some owner wishes can almost always be accommodated, but production boats are typically produced by larger companies focused on offering a particular design with little flexibility for changes. True production yards keep costs to a minimum by setting up an assembly line and schedule for each model offered, and by standarizing materials, methods of construction, and design choices relating to deck and interior layouts, rig and sailplan, and individual boat systems as much as possible. Major deviations from the standard design are either not offered or offered with a steep price tag.

Each builder handles minor variations differently. Some yards offer their customers more options than others. It really depends on what their market focus is. If the focus is churning out large numbers of boats for the best possible price, few customer choices are offered; in fact choices are usually only in the form of interior finishes or optional add-ons. Production builders who really want to concentrate on building boats don't even like to install the options such as solar charging systems, davits, dodgers, watermakers and such; they'd rather have a subcontractor do this time-consuming work so they can make room for another boat in the assembly line. If the market focus of the builder is to offer flexibility to customers willing to pay a bit more, then more choices are available and more of the installation of options is done in house.

Production boats are offered directly through the builder or through regional agents or brokers. The cost is usually the same whether you go through an agent/broker or not, so you might as well take advantage of having someone local to help you through the process.

Buying a semi-custom boat

Boats built on a semi-custom basis can usually be finished off to suit an individual client's requirements. This service is dictated either by the builder's philosophy or by the nature of having a limited client base, where personal service is the result of building only a few boats per year.

Semi-custom boats aren't necessarily more or less expensive than true production models, nor are they necessarily superior or inferior in quality. It all depends on the amount of labor involved in transforming the customer's wishes into reality, the builders construction methods and quality control, the materials selected, and so on. Boats built on a semi-custom basis often don't have the economics of scale of those built by larger production yards, but then the semi-custom builder usually operates with much less overhead and can pass the savings on to his customer.

Customers buying a semi-custom boat can typically choose their own interior layout and finish (as long as no structural conflicts arise), type of rig, auxiliary engine and other on board systems, as long as standard design conditions are met. To be able to offer comprehensive changes and still keep the boat performing as it should a custom builder needs to work closely with the designer. The customer should be aware of this necessity and make sure that the builder is offering realistic choices.

Semi-custom boats are usually available direct from the factory, although some are also marketed through regional agents and brokers. These boats are almost always available in any stage of completion.

Making the choice

With so many multihulls available in all shapes, sizes and prices, making a choice is hard and takes much soul searching. Making a satisfactory decision on which production or semi-custom multihull to buy first requires some analysis of your own particular requirements. Are you looking for a weekend cruiser, a sport boat, a bluewater cruiser, or a charter boat? Are you going to use the boat alone, as a couple, or with the family? Do you plan to cruise short-term or live aboard? Once you have thought through how you are actually going to use your boat, select a number of models you feel are well suited to your needs. Naturally, aesthetics will affect your choice to some extent. After developing a short-list of final contenders, it's time to carefully compare their design.

Design

Boat design is heavily dependent on intended function, and each builder selects the design they feel best meets their requirements. Since each type of boat is designed to suit its intended purpose, different parameters may be applied for coastal cruising or sport sailing rather than safe ocean cruising. With charter boats, the parameters are again different—here you look for interior layouts featuring privacy for multiple guests, large cockpits for outside entertaining, and lots of sunbathing areas. Once you have made your decision on the type of boat you are interested in and short-listed three or four models, visit the builders and have a look around the yard. Does it look professionally run and well organized? Would you trust this company to build your dream boat?

Construction

You can tell a great deal about how your boat is going to be treated during construction from the attitude of the employees to their work and the care and attention they show to detail. Peek under boat floors and lockers, in those forgotten corners; notice how much care has been taken in places you wouldn't normally look.

If you're in the market for a production boat, find out what construction standards the yard builds to. Does the yard have a credited quality control system? This makes a tremendous difference to the standard of construction and the uniform quality guaranteed with each boat produced. Semi-custom builders should also adhere to strict quality control standards. Ask if the yard building the design you've chosen has an extensive in-build checking system for both constructional details and final fitting out.

Look at the construction of the boat on the factory floor. Pay particular attention to the following critical areas:

Hull-to-deck joint. Are the joints bonded the entire way around the periphery of the hull-to-deck to make a one-piece moulding, thus avoiding leaks and structural problems?

Bonding. Are all the bulkheads bonded to the hull and deck, and are any of them stuck with rovings or mechanically fastened to the hulls and decks to avoid bonding failures of the structure? Are items such as floors, tanks and furniture bonded in for additional strength and security?

Reinforcement. If the boat has fixed keels are they reinforced for grounding, either in the original lay-up or as an addition in the form of some kind of keel shoe? This is important if you are going to an area where there is coral or you plan on grounding or beaching periodically.

Lamination. What is the laminating schedule for the mouldings? Is this to an approved standard and with approved materials?

Warranty. What sort of hull warranty is given? It is common now for a production builder to give a 5-10 year hull warranty against osmosis. More importantly, do you feel the builder will be able to make good on warranty claims after the sale?

It is important that the factory exercises care when building a quality yacht, protecting finishes, gelcoat and equipment to prevent unnecessary damage during construction. A good yard will cover all decks with some type of peelable coating and protect all finished bulkheads during the building process.

You should satisfy yourself that the materials used in construction, including the deck gear, are of a quality commensurate with the standard and value of the vessel you are considering buying.

Engineering

Take a good look at the engine bay and the wiring. Is it neat and tidy? Does it look professional? Ask about the test procedures for all the mechanical and electrical equipment, including the gas and water systems.

Is a formal and traceable process attached to their quality control system? This can save endless problems when you take delivery of the vessel. Ensure that the yard fully trial-tests each boat before it is handed over to the customers. Most of today's cruising multihulls are highly complex, often fitted with a range of sophisticated equipment: electronics, generators, watermakers, even air conditioning. These all should be tested and their use and operation explained to the prospective owner.

Make sure the yard is prepared to give enough time to help you settle into your boat, and as the inevitable "teething" problems occur, will work with you to sort them out and help you get everything ready to sail away. Once you have had a look around the factory and satisfied yourself on these points, it's time to go for a sail.

Demonstration sail

Try to pick a day when there is a good breeze and a bit of a sea running. Make sure you sail the boat on all points—beat to windward, see how the boat tacks, reaches, runs, motors and maneuvers under engine in tight quarters. Go down below and see how comfortable she is under sail. Handle the boat yourself, steer her and handle the sails, see how easy her rig is to handle. Most people want boats that can be controlled from the cockpit without having to climb all over the decks. This creates a much safer boat at sea, especially at night.

Once you have satisfied yourself with all aspects of sailing the boat, look at the track record of the company building the boat. Is it a well known, reputable company that has been in business for a number of years and is likely to be there in a few years' time? If it is a relatively new company, check the credentials of the boat designer and builder.

For established production boats, ask the builder if there is an owners' association. If not, find one or two owners of the type and model you are interested in and contact them. Most manufacturers are happy to offer a reference. Ask owners their unbiased opinion of the factory and product; this will give you insight into the boats and the company with whom you are considering spending your money.

After sales service

It is prudent to find out the attitude of the yard to after-sales service. Ask what their standard policy is. Do they have a formal warranty claim procedure? Is there a dealer network that can offer support? Do they back up the product fully and offer spares and replacement parts?

Re-sale value

Cruising multihulls of sound design, and built by a reputable yard under strict quality control, will retain their value well. With these boats, you'll almost certainly get your money back and find a ready re-sale market when it comes time to sell. Beware of boats built strictly for the charter market, as they may be unsuitable for private ownership and liveaboard use. You'll also find that these boats are often sold on the used boat market at lower prices, showing fairly high depreciation after only a few years in charter management, and this may lower the value of privately-owned versions of these particular models. This is a specific problem that will continue to develop over the next few years as large numbers of used charter multihulls hit the market.

Conclusion

The cruising multihull market is expanding rapidly, with more and more choices available to confuse the potential buyer. Most are well-built, value-for-money boats, but prospective purchasers must look carefully at how each model is going to suit their intended use. Budget and taste will play an important part in the selection of any boat, but the wise customer is the one who looks in detail at the product and the company producing it. Thorough research and careful selection help to ensure that buying your boat is a pleasure and not a chore, and that your final selection is as near to what you wanted as possible.

Buying Through A Broker
Words of wisdom from experienced professionals

Choosing the right boat
—by Tom Kintz,
Adventure Yacht Sales

The phrase "horses for courses" can be aptly applied to yachts, and multihulls are no exception. The best multihull design for bluewater cruising will probably not be the best design for trailer-sailing. Ask yourself if you will really be sailing around the world. The reality is that although many people dream of sailing over the horizon a very small percentage actually do it. Don't pay for more boat than you need. Those who end up enjoying boating the most are those who have best matched their choice of yacht with their boating life-style. Yachts that have not been chosen with this in mind often sit idle at the dock while the owners pursue another hobby—or work overtime to pay for the floating millstone they have purchased.

If after careful consideration you feel the cruising life is for you, make sure that the multihull you choose is well suited for offshore service. Your yacht is your only protection from a sometimes hostile environment.

Recently I was contacted by a client who asked me to find a multihull that he could use for local cruising now and world cruising in about ten years. He indicated that he wanted his yacht to fulfill both functions. I advised him to buy his local cruising yacht now and not worry about the world cruiser until later. My reasoning was that in ten years his cruising plans may have changed radically, and multihull design and construction methods are constantly evolving and will have advanced by the time he is ready to go world cruising. Another consideration is that a multihull for local cruising is less expensive than a world cruiser. It would be wiser for him to invest that savings until the cruise nears. My message to prospective buyers is to purchase a yacht that will meet your present needs. Don't plan too far down the road.

Most people looking for multihulls have champagne tastes and beer budgets. It is still possible to purchase a multihull capable of open ocean cruising for US$20,000, but you must expect a very Spartan vessel, typically built of glass over plywood by the owner.

Production multihulls cost more than monohulls of the same length, and for good reason. A typical catamaran has much more surface area than a monohull, is often built of more expensive materials, has two engines, two rudders, heavier rigging and a much larger interior. I encourage my clients to consider the amount of accommodation instead of overall length when comparing monohull and multihull prices. Comparing apples and apples, a multihull may actually be less expensive than a monohull.

If your purchase target date is several years away, you will not be making the best use of your and your broker's time by collecting listings on used yachts. The yacht you like will probably not be on the market when you are ready to purchase. It would be more efficient to spend the time reading all you can about the subject, researching the various designs, visiting multihulls at the boat shows and perhaps chartering yachts that interest you. When you are ready to make your purchase, you will have a much better idea of what to look for.

Every design strikes a compromise between accommodations and performance. Generally speaking, increasing accommodations in a given length multihull will decrease performance. If carried too far, maximizing accommodation can decrease the yacht's sea-keeping abilities. Weight and windage increases and bridgedeck clearance (the distance between the surface of the water and the underside of the bridgedeck) decreases. The result is diminished windward ability and bridgedeck pounding. While too much weight and windage and too little bridgedeck clearance may not be a problem in sheltered waters, it can be uncomfortable and even dangerous in the open sea.

Carried to the opposite extreme, the light, over-canvassed and fragile all out racing multihull is the nautical equivalent of a Grand Prix racing car; very fast in capable hands, but not for the average sailor. Most sailors will be able to find a multihull design that blends accommodation and performance in a ratio that suits them.

Catamarans (with the exception of trailerable designs) usually have more interior room than trimarans of similar length. Most large trimarans are either custom built or owner built. Currently,

production built trimarans are available up to about 10 meters (34 ft.) in length. Production catamarans are usually less oriented toward performance and have more cruising amenities than production trimarans.

For long distance or liveaboard cruising I generally recommend a minimum length of about 35 to 40 feet, although many sailors have successfully cruised worldwide on shorter boats. Larger boats have better sea-keeping and load carrying abilities, and they are generally much more expensive to purchase and maintain. Take my advice and don't buy more boat than you need.

How do you as a buyer locate, inspect, make an offer on, finance, survey, sea trial, clear foreign registration, insure, deliver, import and document a vessel that might be halfway around the world? The self-serving but accurate answer is to utilize a good multihull yacht broker. Because of the aforementioned complications, a knowledgeable broker is perhaps even more useful to a multihull buyer than to a monohull buyer. There are a few yacht brokers worldwide with specialized knowledge of and interest in multihulls. A good broker will help answer your questions about the various boat designs and construction methods, and help place you in contact with multihulls well suited to your needs. Spend time researching the multihull of your choice and you will be rewarded many times over.

Those new to multihulls usually find out early on that, unlike many monohulls, the boat they are looking for will likely not be located in their town, or in their state or maybe even in their country. Although the popularity of multihulls has increased dramatically in recent years, they are still rather thinly distributed. Be prepared to travel a considerable distance to find the multihull you want.

A good multihull yacht broker earns his sales commission by reducing his client's time involvement, and by providing standard purchase contracts and insulation between the buyer and seller during the purchase process. A knowledgeable multihull broker can help you to avoid purchasing a boat unsuited to your needs and can often locate a multihull that you would not have found on your own

Some tips on using a broker are:

—Find a broker that you are comfortable working with and who has an in-depth knowledge of multihulls.

—Ask for references. A broker's integrity is his most valuable asset and should be beyond reproach.

—Look for a broker that is a member of one of the recognized associations such as the Yacht Architects and Brokers Association. These organizations have strict codes of ethics that their members must abide by. Their members also use the standard contract forms of the Association.

4. Once you find a broker you are comfortable with, stick with him. A competent broker will have the means to locate virtually any multihull on the market, whether it is listed directly with him or through another broker. It is not necessary to call every broker you can find. Besides, your broker will expend more time and effort working with you if there is a reasonable chance he will eventually conclude a purchase.

Your search for a cruising multihull should be an enjoyable and educational experience. Take your time, make effective use of all the available resources at your disposal, and you'll most likely avoid the potential pitfalls.

Brokers can offer many options
—by Randy Hogen,
California Multihull

We are often asked at our office why we sell so many new multihulls as opposed to used ones. Although the reasons may vary from person to person, there is a common thread among our clients. The boat they purchase is the culmination of a dream and they want to make the best choice possible.

A new multihull is an investment, with popular models maintaining almost their full original purchase price. New designs allow for high performance in an easily handled boat, Owner Version layouts where an entire hull of a catamaran is devoted to the owner's accommodations, and larger engine choices for true motorsail capabilities.

Multihulls, and catamarans in particular, are ideal charter vessels, resulting in a great many released-from-charter vessels now available at reasonable prices. But there can be a toll on a luxurious new boat that 30 to 40 different people have used for a week or so each year. Charter boats get a lot of use and, if you've got a long way to go to view one for purchase, it may be worth the effort to have a qualified surveyor with multihull experience go see it first. In the end, many clients who look at these charter cats decide that with the layouts, engines, and efficient hull shapes of new boats, the work of bringing a charter cat back home and up to standards is not as attractive as it first seemed.

Used boats that have been privately owned and maintained are usually in much better shape than used charter boats, although some charter boats remain in excellent condition and there are many cases of privately owned boats in poor shape. A broker can help you sort out the condition of the boat and its current market value.

Customers looking for a new multihull have several options for how they go about it. They can buy a new production boat, a semi-custom boat built from a stock design, or the stock design itself and build it themselves. Some brokers serve as dealers or agents for a range of new multihull products that tend to complement each other and offer something for almost all clients.

Clients often come to a broker stating that they are simply cruisers and that speed just isn't important, but this attitude quickly fades when they find out that speed can be an important asset when cruising, besides being downright fun! Many of the cruising cats on the market provide great charter or liveaboard potential but don't perform well in light winds with a normal cruising payload. A performance multihull that can sail well into the high 'teens or even low 20's should also sail well when loaded and in light airs—as well or better than many performance cruising monohulls.

Because of the demand for new production catamarans, most production builders will not allow the customer many choices beyond engine options and a choice of layouts. They just don't need to disrupt a back-ordered production line for one boat. A good alternative is to seek out a semi-custom builder producing a good stock design. If you can't find anything on the market that can meet your needs, contract a reputable designer to create a custom boat.

Choose a designer whose ideas most closely match your own, and when the bids go out make sure you select a builder with ample multihull experience. I've seen several people hire a builder with no previous multihull experience to build their

custom multihull. The builder obviously had the lowest bid, inevitably because he had no idea what it takes to build a quality multihull. Before you know it you can end up with a boat way over budget and with some serious flaws in construction or the way it handles under sail. And resale value for this type of craft can be much lower than a similar vessel built by a reputable yard.

A quick word on do-it-yourself building. I've been involved in several multihull projects, starting when I was 15 years old, and it's a lot of work, but can be quite rewarding. You can save money if you do most or all the work yourself. Don't be mislead, however, by the "anyone can do it" claims in design portfolios. Background experience with plans, tools, materials, and procedures go a long way towards the quality of the finished product.

And by all means, use plans from a well-known and respected multihull designer. In addition to ensuring that the boat will sit properly on her lines and sail and handle properly, if you need to get out of the project part way through construction your partially finished boat will be much more marketable.

A brokerage transaction
—by John Sykes, 2Hulls

A properly performed brokerage process often saves both the buyer and seller money, time, and innumerable hours of frustration. Let's assume you've decided to buy a cruising multihull and avail yourself of a yacht broker. Tell the broker what you have in mind, what you want the yacht to do, and how much you are willing to spend. A good broker is going to ask you numerous questions. Answer them as fully and honestly as you can. If you don't intend to buy a boat soon, let the broker know that. That way he need not bother you with "deal-of-the-week" boats; he has a better idea of what information to communicate and when, and will work all the harder for you when you are ready to purchase. It's also a big help if you have been to boat shows and can identify models that you find particularly interesting.

The Purchase & sale agreement. Eventually, through trial and error, and by viewing many different multihulls, you'll find what you are looking for. Make an offer, but do it formally. Most brokers have a fairly standardized contract, usually called a "Purchase and Sale Agreement". The important elements in the contract are:

—The "Deposit", normally 10% of the purchase price.

—The "Acceptance of Offer Date", normally only a day or two from the date of the offer unless there are communications problems involved. A short time lapse between the two is good for the seller since it avoids a prolonged delay of the sale. It's also good for the buyer since it helps prevent his contract being "shopped", or used as a basis to solicit higher offers.

—The "Subject To's", which are many and varied, but usually involve marine survey and sea trial contingencies and may involve personal inspection and/or financing contingencies.

—The "Acceptance or Rejection Date", or the date by which the buyer accepts or rejects the vessel, a process usually in writing. If the contract is properly done, the buyer's deposit will not be forfeited unless he accepts the yacht and then doesn't pay for it.

—The "Closing Date", the date by which the buyer must pay for the boat or forfeit his deposit. Very often, if some snag occurs and there is good reason to delay this date, the buyer and seller will find a way to agree on a new date.

Following preparation of the Purchase & Sale Agreement, the listing broker presents it to the seller. In most cases, the seller makes a counter-offer, suggesting a price somewhere between the original asking price and the offer. This back and forth process may take a while. Some brokers handle this orally, while others insist on a re-executed Purchase & Sale Agreement at every step. In most instances, we've found the oral process easier and perfectly adequate. Ultimately, buyer and seller will have a written agreement stating the terms and final price. Now you have a contract—but you've only just begun!

The Marine survey & sea trial. Next you should schedule the marine survey and sea trial, or trial run. These are normally done on the same day unless you are dealing with a big and very complicated yacht. The buyer pays for the survey and haulout, the seller for the sea trial.

—Marine survey. The marine survey is an extremely important part of the boat purchasing process, thus the need to choose carefully when selecting a surveyor. Most brokers are willing to suggest several, but loath to commit themselves to recommending just one. If you trust your broker, interview his suggested surveyors. You can also ask an insurance agent whom they recommend. A survey is virtually always a prerequisite to securing insurance coverage.

—Sea trial. The purpose of the sea trial is to demonstrate that the boat's parts operate under stress, and it gives you a good chance to take a good look at the sails. A sea trial usually last several hours. Most surveyors charge extra to go along on one, particularly if they think it's going to be more of an outing than a valid sea trial.

Acceptance of vessel. Following your review of the results of the survey and sea trial, you must make your acceptance decision.

Without writing a book about it (and one could certainly be written!), the best guidance we can give involves the following points:

—If there are items in the survey that you feel should be addressed by the seller, you may want to ask for an adjustment in price. When you do this, however, remember that you are not entitled to replacement of items with new items, simply items that work or were similar to those not in working order. Our usual recommendation is that no seller do this work, but rather that the buyer and seller negotiate the probable cost of those items replaced new and allow for an adjustment to the purchase price of 50% of those costs. There is no requirement for the seller to accept any adjustment, but many sellers will be reasonable at this point, especially if a written acceptance subject to the adjustment(s) is presented, since they know that the sale is close to conclusion. Buyers beware—acceptance of a vessel and then failure to close normally results in a forfeiture of your deposit.

Documentation. Now it's time to close the transaction. The first step, in most cases, is to hire a good documentation agent. The documentation agent checks title, prepares the necessary transfer of ownership documents, and registers and/or federally documents the vessel. We can't emphasize the importance of using a documenter enough, particularly as the bureaucracies and the origins of the vessels become more complicated every day. Buyers who attempt to do this process themselves usually become hopelessly frustrated and rarely get the work done properly the first time. The documenter does not usually guarantee title, but simply does his best to verify the title situation. We know of no one at this time actually offering title insurance on yachts.

Closing. You have finally arrived at the closing. Most of our closings these days are not "sit-down" affairs. Generally, the selling

broker or the documenter gathers all the necessary executed documents and proof of ownership. The buyer makes payment by wire transfer or sends a cashiers check(s) to the Trust Account of the broker. When both elements are in place, the money will be transferred to the seller and the documents to the buyer. Congratulations—you now own a cruising multihull!

Brokering—European style
—by Patrick Boyd,
Patrick Boyd Multihulls

They say that the two happiest days of your life are the day you buy your first boat, and the day that you sell it. Yacht Brokers make every effort to keep the process a pleasurable one, both for the buyer and the seller.

As a Broker, I am first approached by the seller to act on his behalf to sell his boat. I make it clear to both parties that I am acting, in law, on behalf of the seller, though a lot of my time is spent acting as an independent consultant.

To this end I require that the seller provide relevant information about the boat, including its age, builder, materials, length, beam, draft, accommodations, engine, sails, electronics, dinghies, and liferafts. I also ask that he list any smaller gear to be sold with the boat, thus avoiding disputes.

If they are available, I like to have a layout drawing (many of which I have in my portfolio) and good color photos of the boat for advertising and to show prospective clients. In England, the seller also provides the broker with a Declaration of Outstanding Debts, if any.

I provide the seller with a Multihull For Sale form, which gives me information about the seller, and authorization to offer the boat on his behalf, and it clearly states what commission the seller will be charged. The owner also receives a small booklet outlining the services that we provide and what we expect from him.

Once the information is gathered, I often visit the boat with the vendor to go through the inventory with him to ensure that I understand which items, if any, are *not* included in the sale. This is particularly important when a boat is still in commission and a prospective buyer needs to know which items will be removed from the boat in the event of a sale. Quite often there are no decent photographs of the boat, so I take a set with my wide-angled lens to illustrate the details being sent out. The owner sometimes has some idea of what the boat will fetch, but often wants advice on this.

I then return to my office, prepare a detail sheet from the information obtained, and send the vendor a copy for him to check and return to me approved, together with a set of photographs. It is quite astonishing how few vendors have a decent sailing photograph of their boat. Some have no photographs at all. If I do manage to obtain one, it almost certainly features in one of my regular advertisements in the leading yacht magazines throughout the world.

Initially, I go through the computer to see who in the last twelve months has been looking for such a boat. A mailshot then goes out to all of them drawing their attention to this latest listing. Some come back immediately to say they have already bought a boat, or that Grandmother didn't die after all, or the wife has bought another mink coat instead! But some respond positively and ask to go and see the boat.

I suppose the main reason why a vendor employs a Broker is not because he is enthusiastic about paying him a commission, but because the Broker spends thousands of dollars a year spreading the word around that

he has his fabulous list of second-hand multihulls. Most importantly, he has built a long mailing list of people actively looking for a boat. The Broker can also take the valuable administrative load off the vendor of sifting out the time-wasters and nut cases.

From the buyer's point of view, the Broker is a vital source of information about the product he is selling. Unless he is employed by one or other of the new boat manufacturers, the broker should have no particular axe to grind about which boat in their listing is best. A Broker is also useful to both seller and buyer since they are typically unused to and shy of financial negotiations, much preferring to deal with a third party.

The buyer will have seen advertisements by the Broker, perhaps over a period of many years, and presumably likes the variety of boats being presented and the style of presentation. He may have met the Broker at a boat show, at a symposium or at his yacht club. It very often takes many years to build up some sort of reputation for honesty and straight dealing which many of us regard as being more important than anything else.

Very often the buyer comes on a personal recommendation from a previous client. Best of all, clients and boats come back time after time to the Broker they like to do business with. To get this reputation needs diligence, hard work, and a great attention to detail. The person making an inquiry needs to feel that he is being taken seriously and often, particularly if he has never bought a boat before, needs a lot of guidance so he does not make a mistake. Occasionally, a reputable Broker will even send a buyer away to get more experience or suggest that they buy a monohull or a condo in Florida instead.

It is most important for the Broker to try to get inside the head of the buyer, asking himself the questions that the buyer should be asking him. Obviously, the buyer must give some idea of how much money is available, then be asked what is he going to use the boat for—family holidays, liveaboard, charter, gunkholing or ocean cruising? Is he sailing solo or with his family? What is his sailing background? Is he looking for speed or accommodation, because certainly the more of the one, the less the other will be available.

Is he prepared to do a little renovation work, or a lot, or does he want to buy a pristine boat? Is he prepared to travel to inspect a boat? This is usually a function of price. Buyers will rarely travel far to inspect a boat selling for less than $15,000, but are usually quite willing to travel modest distances for moderately-priced boats and long distances for boats over $100,000.

All these facts build up a picture upon which the Broker is able to make recommendations. He sends off details of those listings as soon as possible, preferably the same day, together with a complete list of all second-hand multihulls on offer at that time. After these lists have invariably been passed around to friends and acquaintances, it is amazing how often a buyer ends up a long way in size and price from his original specification. More money seems to become miraculously available. A huge percentage are never heard from again, but a number want to inspect boats. Some choose to initially view the boat with the seller, others with just the Broker, and some with both at the same time.

If the buyer is interested he makes an offer based on the asking price, and here a word of warning. Although it is the practice in the States to make initial offers substantially below asking price, this may be treated as an insult in Europe where there is often little negotiating slack in the asking price. The Broker will pass the offer to the vendor and negotiate a fair price acceptable to both parties.

Next, the Broker prepares a Sales Contract which, in England, has been prepared and agreed upon by the British Marine Industry Federation, The Royal Yachting Association, The Yacht Harbours Association, and the Yacht Brokers Designers and Surveyors Association . This is prepared in triplicate for Vendor, Buyer and Broker. The buyer then lodges a 10% deposit and has 14 days to get the boat slipped and surveyed at his expense, plus a further 14 days to consider the survey report, get any repairs priced, renegotiate the price of the boat in light of the survey, or in the worst case reject it because of "Materials Defects".

Many thousands of words have been spoken and written about what is, and what is not, a "Material Defect" and no one seems to agree. In the end, however, if the buyer believes the boat to be unsatisfactory, for any of a variety of reasons, his deposit is normally returned.

At this time the only other condition of sale would be a Sea Trial. In my experience a sea trial on a sailboat is often unsatisfactory—there always seems to be either too much or too little wind, and the buyer often does not know what he should be looking for. It does, however, allow for a test of the engines and a good look at the sails. Afterwards, the vendor usually goes through the boat in some detail with the buyer after the sale has taken place, but not normally as a condition.

No reputable Broker suggests that a buyer finalize a purchase without a marine survey and a visit to the boat unless it is a real bargain. Sometimes, against all advice, it happens and most Brokers dread the inevitable reproachful telephone call from the buyer who has discovered some undeclared defect because nobody, including the vendor and Broker, knew it existed.

While this is all going on, an English Broker yet again checks "Title", ensuring that the person who says he owns the boat does in fact do so, and that there are no debts on the boat. In the United Kingdom, you can pay £25.00 to get a "Transcript of Registry" which will either show an outstanding mortgage or the boat to be clear. If there is a debt, the Broker must clear that debt before letting the vendor sign the Bill Of Sale which declares the boat to be "Without Encumbrances".

As an experienced yacht broker and multihull enthusiast for over 25 years, I have found it to be a most enjoyable job; otherwise I would have retired years ago. I have met numerous interesting clients, designers and builders of multihulls, many of whom have become old friends. So many of the international band of multihull sailors are extremely interesting people, too many to enumerate, but to a man and woman they are singular, outward-looking people, not content to sail an old-fashioned monomaran, but looking for something better. In multihulls they have found it.

Affordable Classics
A host of used boats that won't break the bank

If you feel that a new multihull is out of your price range, set your sights on a used boat that satisfies your needs. Since multihulls hold their value well, you may have to go back a few years to find a boat you can afford. There are some classic older designs that make wonderful cruising boats, though many of the production builders of these classics are no longer in business and the boats themselves vary widely in condition and how well they are outfitted. Also keep in mind that owner-built classics may vary widely in construction and sophistication of finish.

For the most part it's still a seller's market, though there are many good deals to be had, especially if you are patient in your search and capable of some minor repair and cosmetic boat work. When looking at the cost of a used classic you must take into account the equipment she has (most long-time cruising boats have gear worth thousands of dollars on board) and how recently she has been overhauled and refitted.

Classic cats

The most widely available used US cat on the market has to be the *Gemini*, whether one of the older *3000* or *3200* designs, or the more recent *3400* version. The layout for the entire *Gemini* line is similar to that for the present day *105M* shown on page 286. These boats sell in the US $50,000-$85,000 range depending on year and condition.

The *Americat 3014* and the newer *C-Cat 3014* and *Endeavourcat 30* are also readily available at a good market prices. These boats have interior layouts similar to the present day *Endeavourcat 30 MkII* shown on page 184.

The *Heavenly Twins 26* remains one of the most sought after production cruisers for couples or small families on a budget. The layout is similar to the present *Heavenly Twins* shown on page 206. You should be able to find one of these of the MkI to MkIV vintage, from £12,000-£45,000. You'll find other Pat Patterson designs on the European used boat market, including the *Summer Twins 28, Star Twins 31*, and *Ocean Winds 33, and Ocean Twins 38* (see page 246).

The *Catalac 8m* & *9m* production catamarans are also readily available. The *9m* layout is similar to the present day model shown on page 144. The *8m* has one double cabin forward on the bridgedeck and a single berth to port, with galley down to starboard. These stable cruisers don't have a great turn of speed, but they are roomy, comfortable and sail moderately well for their vintage. These boats are available in the £12,000-£46,000 range depending on year and condition. If you like the layout but need something a little larger, you may be able to find one of the *Catalac* 10-, 11-, or 12-meter boats.

There are numerous Prout production catamarans on the used market. The *Sirocco 26* is a sweet pocket cruiser that is perfect for coastal work or going through the canals. She has galley down in the starboard hull and a double berth forward on the bridgedeck, plus three other single berths. You'll see models up to the present day version from £20,000-£40,000. The Prout *Quest 31* was replaced by the *Quest 33*, which was in turn replaced by the *Event 34*. Another popular used Prout is the *Snowgoose*, a solid cruiser that started out as the *34/35* and grew to the *37*, which is still built today as the *Prout 37* (see page 292). Prout boats are typically well built and can be lying in some very interesting places! Expect to pay around £25,000-£45,000 for the *Quest*, around £65,000-£75,000 for the *Event*, and £30,000-£95,000 for the *Snowgoose* depending on year and condition.

The classic Sailcraft production cats such as the *Iroquois 30* and the *Cherokee 35* are almost always available on the used market. Condition may vary, but these fast cruisers can often be a bargain. The *Iroquois* has two doubles aft and two singles forward, while the *Cherokee* has four doubles. Prices range from £12,000-£40,000. The larger version of these boats is the *Apache 45*, often available and usually a lot of boat for the price.

The *Hirondelle 23* pocket cruiser has nice lines and can provide a good base for coastal explorations. Layout is similar to the present day model on page 308. Prices typically range from £7,500-£20,000 depending on model (standard, MkI or Family) and year.

The Solaris line of catamarans were produced for many years in England. Their price on the used market is relatively high, since these boats were made to a high standard. You'll find examples of the entire range of Solaris boats if you look long enough, including the *Sunbeam 24* (in the £20,000-30,000 range), the *Suncat 30* designed by Derek Kelsall, the *Sunstar 32* (still being produced by Blue Water Catalacs, see page 146), the *Sunrise 36*, the *Solaris 42*, and the *Suncrest 46*.

You'll always find a fair number of used Wharram open-bridgedeck cats on the market, mostly owner built and in varying size and condition. Models to look for include the *Tiki*, *Pahi*, *Tanenui*, and *Tangaroa*.

Another vintage cat found on the used market is the *Catfisher 28* (later produced in a 32 foot version), a comfortable motorsailer with completely protected wheelhouse and 8 berths. These boats are usually in the US $45,000-$75,000 range.

Fountaine Pajot is a well know catamaran builder in France, and their production over the years has been prolific. It is disappointing that the *Maldives 32* is no longer produced, although they appear on the used market from time to time. The design of the *Maldives 32* is similar to the *Tobago 35*, with a small galley aft on the bridgedeck, two double berths aft in the hulls, and two singles forward in the hulls. Prices range from FF400,000-FF500,000. The *Louisiane 37* is an older design with the hulls accessed separately from the main cabin. Prices for this boat range from FF300,000-FF400,000. The *Fiji 39*, *Casamance 44*, and more recent *Antigua 37* are other Fountaine Pajot cats worth looking for.

The *Edel 35* (and older *33*) cats are fast and, though produced fairly recently, still offer good value for the money. Some Edels have an open bridgedeck in the Cabrio style and others have bridgedeck accommodations that are accessed separately from the hulls, with layout similar to the present day *Edel Aventure 11m* shown on page 180. These boats are available in the US $65,000-$115,000 range depending on condition and equipment.

Beneteau produced their *Beneteau Blue II* catamaran for a number of years, and you'll find these boats on the lists of most used multihull brokers. With a LOA of 34 feet, 4-6 berths, and twin inboard engines, they can make a good family cruiser. Prices vary dramatically, from US $65,000-$175,000.

Used *Outremer 40* fast cruisers, similar to the present day version on page 140, can be typically be had for $80,000-$130,000.

Seawind technically still makes the *Seawind 850*, which evolved from the older *Seawind 24*. Quite a few of these boats were produced and they are often seen on the used market.

Dean of South Africa produced the *Dean 365*, which later became the *Dean 400*. These boats are similar in concept to Prout's *Snowgoose 37*, only with much more room. They are sometimes seen on the used market for around US $100,000.

Classic Tris

Hundreds of *Telstar 8m* trimarans were produced in the UK in 70s and early 80s. This trailerable pocket cruiser had rigid decks between the main hull and amas, and 1 single and 2 double berths. They are typically priced at $10,000-$20,000.

Used *Dragonfly* folding trimarans are available worldwide. Look for the older *600*, the *25* made in North America, and the *800* made in Denmark, similar in layout to the present day model shown on page 352. Prices range from US $10,000-$40,000.

Tri-Star trimarans designed by Ed Horstman (see page 430), *Searunner* tris designed by John Marples and Jim Brown (see page 434), *Lodestar 35* tris designed by Arthur Piver, and *Cross* tris designed by Norm Cross are rugged and roomy classic cruisers, available in lengths from 24 to over 40 feet. If fast passages are your main concern, look for anything designed by Dick Newick (see pages 440-443), Derek Kelsall, or Lock Crowther. The boats described above are usually owner built, and some may be well over 20 years old, so you should check out the construction and finish before spending your money. Prices vary widely.

Ian Farrier's classic trimaran designs include the *TrailerTri 680 & 720*, trailerable sport cruisers with four berths, and the *Command 10*, a 33 foot high performance long-distance cruiser. Prices for the *TrailerTri* range from $10,000-25,000, while the *Command 10* can be purchased for $50,000-80,000. Farrier's more recent production designs include the *F-series* tris built by Corsair Marine (shown on pages 332-337) and the *F-25* built by Colorado Composites (shown on page 326).

Owner Building A Stock Design

The path less taken may be right for you

If you really want a strong, seaworthy cruising catamaran at a realistic price, it is possible. If you think you are going to equal or better the quality and level of sophistication of a modern production cruiser by building it yourself, you may be in for a disappointment.

If you wish to break free of the herd mentality and move in a different direction to achieve your cruising goals—without spending the family nest egg—there is a way, but it is a thorny path with potential pitfalls. The successful owner builder is one who is properly prepared with the right design, the right materials and construction expertise, and the right attitude.

Not seen too often in the glossy magazines and seldom at upscale yacht clubs and marinas is a class of cruising catamarans that meet every criteria for seaworthiness, safety and economy. They may actually be the largest single class of cruising catamarans in the world.

Before revealing what the class is, pretend you are in the Pacific Ocean back in the year 1000 BC. Spread before you are dozens, perhaps hundreds of serious offshore catamarans. They are built from individual trees hollowed out to form the hulls with plank decks lashed to the hulls with rope made from hemp. They have a "Manu" (wave-breaking stick) on the bows.

Rudders are lashed to the sterns. Masts are short and stayed with rope. Sails are made from cloth woven from native grasses and are fully battened with bamboo sticks.

The boats you are seeing in your mind's eye were built entirely from organic materials. Entire homesteads and conquering armies moved on these swift, seaworthy catamarans as the early Polynesians colonized the entire pacific basin as far south as New Zealand and as far east as Hawaii; this proves these vessels had adequate windward ability, something western ships would lack for another thousand years.

This technology still exists today in the class of boats mentioned above, albeit changed somewhat to make allowances for modern materials. The design simplicity inherent in the technology beckons to all who understand and appreciate the paradigm that true genius is to make complex things simple. The man responsible for keeping this technology alive is James Wharram. Since his Polynesian designs span the entire range of cruising boat sizes, meet every criteria for a reasonably-priced seagoing cruiser, and are immensely popular, I will use Wharram designs as my benchmark for owner-built boats. True to their Polynesian roots Wharram's designs do not have bridgedeck cabins, although some of the newer models provide good bridgedeck protection for the helmsman. This has kept them from appealing to the masses, but then what of an extraordinary nature does?

From the simplicity of James Wharram we advance through a group of more sophisticated designers such as Peter Brady, Ian Farrier, Tony Grainger, Kurt Hughes, John Marples, Dick Newick, Jeff Schionning and others who sell plans for comfortable high-performance cruising multihulls.

As the level of sophistication increases, so does the time, effort and cost involved. Attempting to create a vessel equal to or better than available production vessels can save you money if done properly—otherwise it may end up costing you more in addition to a huge time commitment. It's a little like trying to build your own automobile by purchasing the parts and assembling it yourself. You must really want to owner build for the satisfaction of creating something yourself.

On the other hand, there are many people who truly like building boats, and the cost is a secondary concern. For those of this ilk there are many competent designers ready and eager to help.

Why Building Is Better
—by Kurt Hughes,
Kurt Hughes Sailing Designs
In my opinion the multihull that an owner-builder constructs and finishes can not only be a good boat, it can often be far better and cost much less than some from a production factory.

One of the most useful reasons to build instead of buy a cruising multihull is the quality of the design and how that design fits your life-style. There are hundreds of great multihull designs for builders, but only a handful of designs are available as production boats. The chance of finding a vessel that fits your needs is much greater if you find a design and build it yourself.

Even an existing design that suits the needs of an owner quite well can be modified to better meet his particular requirements. For instance, an owner builder may want a revision to have 6'-9" headroom, and can make it so easily.

An owner-builder can have a boat with the latest technical advances, in contrast to a production boat which will take years from the design being drawn to hull number one going for its first sail. Afterwards, the accountants will insist that as many units as possible be taken off of the mold, even if the design is well past its time.

Many production multis are the result of a market study, something not always done by multihull sailors. A market study can prove to be the death of design excellence for a serious sailor. The features that would make a serious ocean boat often do not stand up to the test of marketing pressure and the imaginary average consumer.

An owner-builder can choose and own a serious ocean multihull without the influence of marketing departments and the leveller of conforming to the average consumer, whoever that is. If using a recent design, a multi built by an owner-builder should be both lighter and stronger than most production boats of equivalent size.

There are many reasons for this, including the use of epoxy instead of lower grade production resins with gel coat, and often better quality fiber structures with more recent engineering. Many production multis are packed with as many features as possible into whatever waterline length is available. Too often the result is a boat that won't point and wallows in bad weather.

An owner-builder has the option of not only choosing a design that has a long enough waterline to be safe, but even extending that waterline if desired. The result can be a multihull that sails better than a production vessel.

The phrase "backyard boat", often applied to owner-built multihulls, suggests rough plywood and house paint, yet often the opposite is true. Many backyard boats are stunning. Because of the care usually taken, an owner-built boat can not only have very high quality where it is expected, but even where it is not expected—in the hidden places.

No one is more careful about preventing voids or making good bonding joints, for example, than an educated owner-builder. With good tools, modern epoxy technology and two-part polyurethane paint, an owner-built multi can look as good as a factory boat or better. One of the most important advantages of being an owner-builder is knowing what the multi is made of and how it was actually built. An owner-builder knows what is under the paint. Just as important is the understanding a builder develops for how boats are made. Most owner-builders become so educated that they could probably be marine surveyors when they are done building. The skills and knowledge stay with an owner-builder for a lifetime.

Repairs to an owner-builder's boat are different. They are less daunting. If a jetski crashes through the side of an owner-builder's cat or tri, it is unpleasant but not a disaster. It was built once and the builder knows how to do that part again. An owner-builder is less dependent on high-priced boatyards for repair. That ability can save thousands of dollars during the bumpy life of a boat. The knowledge acquired from

building also makes cruising to distant isles less daunting—if something goes wrong you can fix it yourself.

Finally, the costs should be much less for building a multihull than buying a production boat. Many people, including myself and many others in the industry, can have the multi they want only by building it. Ignoring the price of shop rent, ruined clothes and bad fast food, the cost to build your own multi should be from a third to a half that of a similar sized production one. Viewed another way, if one had $80,000 to work with, that could be a 30 foot or less production multi, or a 40 to 45 foot multi that you build yourself. That can make a big difference in how and where you cruise.

Where to build. Builders choose many types of building spaces from backyards to space in an industrial park. Obviously, shop space must be dry and lockable. Many multihull builders start with a space slightly longer than the boat and only fifteen or twenty feet wide. In this truncated space they build components—hulls, crossarms, cabin sides and so on. Once these are done, they can be joined in more expensive full-width space nearer the water. Make certain to measure the width and height of the entire trip from boatshop to open water.

A boat project will create great amounts of dust and noise. The epoxy has no fumes, but painting fumes can be an environmental problem. Make sure that your neighbors are willing to put up with boat construction nearby.

What materials to build with. Owner-built multis usually come in three basic types: wood/epoxy, composites, and strip plank (which is a little of both). While wood/epoxy multis tend to be a bit less expensive and a bit faster to build, they are more vulnerable to impact damage. Composite ones, made of foam/glass for example, take a bit more time and have greater materials cost, but are better able to resist impact damage. Unlike framed hulls, composite ones have no stringers to contend with. Strip plank hulls have no stringers either, but they have the same impact resistance as other wood/epoxy hulls. Most designers will sell a design in material of either type depending on the builder's needs, and work with the builder to define those requirements.

Locating the best sources of materials is almost a half-time job in my office. We provide builders with at least 25 pages of sources, information to be updated at least every quarter. Asking the designer to connect you with other builders in your area is a good way to track down what is being used locally. Multihull clubs are sometimes a good resource for finding out where local builders are getting supplies. Some clubs even buy supplies in bulk.

What skills are needed. Naturally, a good set of tools and basic skills are required. Builders who purchase a compressor and air tools usually don't regret it. I have found in many cases that amateur owner-builders have better results with new tools and technologies than professionals do. They don't presume to already know everything about boat building; they listen and read instead of deciding to build it the way the last one was done.

Proper tools, skills and construction information are inseparable. Most designers have very complete and informative plans, and there are important builder's books available on the subject.

What sequence to follow. After selecting a design and a designer, owner-builders either do all the work themselves or they hire professional builders to help with some of the steps. Many times a professional builds the hulls and crossarms; then the owner takes it from there. Professionals typically allow the owner to help with some phases of the construction as well. In that way, the owner gets all the quality advantages with significant price savings over a production boat.

The down side of building. Building your own multi is not for everyone. It puts a big impact on one's life and life-style. For a time period varying from six months to several years, owner-builders must expect to have little free time and a serious countenance.

In years past, owner-built multihulls could expect to sell for only slightly more than the cost of materials. That has changed in the 90's, though they still must be well built and finished to keep resale value. A well built multi by a known and active designer should have the same market value as a production multihull of similar size.

An owner-builder will find that the burden of proof is on him when dealing with surveyors and insurers. Since these professionals usually have no yardstick to gauge the quality and value of an owner-built boat, one has to prepare for what seem to be insulting and ignorant questions about the boat you build.

Building a cruising multihull is not for everyone, but with a good space to build in, the proper tools, skills and construction information, and a positive outlook, building a boat can be a rewarding experience. It also serves as a great alternative for those unable to afford production cruising boats.

Financing a
Cruising Multihull

Charter Management
An affordable option for financing a multihull

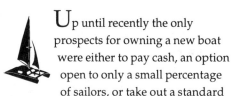Up until recently the only prospects for owning a new boat were either to pay cash, an option open to only a small percentage of sailors, or take out a standard boat loan. Standard loans are similar in nature to car loans, only the qualifications can be more stringent. Buyers must make a downpayment of 20 to 25 percent of the total cost of the boat, and have sufficient income to justify a mortgage on a large purchase used for recreation. The standard term of a boat loan is 15 years, and the interest you'll pay on the loan over that time period is substantial. The positive side of buying a boat in this way is that you will eventually own a boat that has been sailed only by you or the skippers you allow to sail her. The problem with this scenario is that many sailors can't justify the monthly payments and mounting interest, especially if they have only a limited amount of time each year to sail. Over the years a need has existed for some other way for sailors to acquire a new boat.

Charter management, an option now open to anyone buying a new boat, satisfies both the need for more multihulls in the charter business and the financial and practical needs of many private owners. This type of arrangement is ideal for those whose time available for cruising or maintaining their boat is limited, or for

those who want to defray the cost of boat ownership, buy a larger or better-equipped boat than they could otherwise afford, or have their boat substantially paid for by the time they retire. Charter management can also serve to maximize your sailing vacations while minimizing the costs, and to improve your sailing and cruising skills. The beauty of charter management is that you could be building equity while you enjoy gaining experience on your own boat.

The choices for charter management are varied, but the concept is generally the same. You must still pay the necessary downpayment and secure financing for the boat of your choice, a limiting factor for those on a budget. Another consideration is that boats going into a charter fleet must be outfitted to a higher standard than a cruiser on a budget might otherwise choose, including more powerful engine options, rubber dinghies with engines, extra hatches, davits, windlasses, pressurized hot and cold water, inverter, and so on. Once you've purchased the boat, it is then placed in charter service for an agreed upon number of weeks per year. In return, the charter company stores and maintains your boat, gives you a percentage of the charter proceeds, and allows you to use the boat for time periods mutually agreed upon.

Some companies offer total maintenance programs with a smaller percentage of the proceeds going to the owner; others offer larger revenues with the owner assuming more of the burdens of maintenance and operation. Depending on the boat, the financing and the charter management arrangement, the annual revenues going to the owner may or may not cover the annual mortgage payments. The lower the initial cost of your boat, the larger your downpayment, and the longer your term of financing, the more likely the mortgage payments will be met or exceeded.

You can enter into charter management in one of three ways:

Do it yourself. Most charter companies are happy to receive a multihull in good condition into their fleet. The manufacturer or sales agent you purchase from should be able to direct you to charter companies who want your particular model boat. You should investigate carefully and choose one that you trust and that fits your requirements. Try to keep your options open. Don't enter into a long-term commitment as you may want to take the boat to a different cruising ground or change companies sooner than you originally expected.

Pre-packaged Charter Management Program. Select one of the pre-packaged professional programs offered by Allied Yacht Charters, Florida Yacht Charters, The Moorings, Tortola Marine Management, Tropic Island Yacht Management, Sun Yacht Charters, and many others. These programs typically give you good value. Since the flexibility of these programs is limited, however, you must determine if you'll be able to get the boat you want (including your choice of interior layout and outfitting) and make certain that it won't be tied up in the program for too long.

Individualized Yacht Profit Sharing Management Program. You can also set up your new boat as a profit-making business that is professionally managed in a Yacht Profit Sharing Management Program (YPSMP) such as that offered by Bay Yacht Agency. These plans often combine the flexibility of Do-It-Yourself plans with the advantages of a pre-packaged program. In a YPSMP you get the tax advantages of deducting all the expenses of keeping your boat in charter. The business tax advantages and charter income combine to build equity and reduce your cash flow, allowing you to own your boat in much less time while maintaining a higher degree of freedom about when and where your boat is placed in charter. Each case is different, but if you can make the initial investment, on average you'll end up owning your boat in 1/3 the time while paying 1/3 the monthly payment of a standard boat loan.

YPSMPs are set up on an individual basis so they can address the needs of each client. They differ from pre-packaged management programs in other ways, too. You usually have more choice in the type of boat you want to end up owning, including the way it is equipped. You can pre-wire, pre-plumb, and pre-build spaces for adding elaborate live-aboard touches when you have taken the boat over for personal use.

As an example of the process, when you apply for a YPSMP you typically receive a package of information that includes pricing information on your boat of choice, a complete discussion of your options and management alternatives, information on the various charter fleets within the program, and a comprehensive business plan showing cash flow, profit and loss, financing structure, tax advantages, resale value, and normal and worst case scenarios. It's up to you to take the initiative to arrange the plan to suit your needs.

Sample Yacht Profit Sharing Management Program

The following is a sample projection from Bay Yacht Agency, averaged for five years and based on actual data with clients purchasing similar yachts. You may stay in this type of program as long as you like, since it is a flexible, profitable program custom designed for each client. Each case is slightly different, but as an example let's assume the following:

Boat:	Fountaine Pajot Tobago 35
Aquisition cost:	$215,742 *cost with delivery, duty, & all options required for charter)
Loan specs:	standard boat loan, 8.99% interest rate, 15 year term
Payment:	$1,640.19 *per month after standard down payment
Charter location:	Caribbean *boat remains in Caribbean during the entire year

Annual income: $82,553 *assumes 29 weeks of charter as follows:
                 7 wks @ $3800, 4 wks @ $3200, 6 wks @ $2850, 12 wks @ $2300

Annual expenses: $71,481 *assumes the following expenses:

Loan costs:	$19,682.
Dockage total:	3,780.
Insurance:	4,315. *unlimited chartering, $1M liability
Maintenance:	6,895. *based on 10-year averages
Management:	34,739. *total charter services including admin., turn around, check in/out, ice/fuel/propane, water/diesel, daily inspection/weekly run check, dock watch, cleaning, taxi, laundry
Advertising:	350.
Virgin Islands tax:	400.
Utilities:	180.
Delivery:	1,140. *yearly cost, amortized over 5 years

Cash flow (+ /-): $11,072 *income less expenses, compared to -$24,938 for conv. loan
                    Monthly profit/loss: $923 vs. -$2078 for conv. loan/expenses
                    Monthly profit/loss with tax advantages: $1,214

Monthly cost to own in five years, as opposed to conventional 15 years:

5-year amort. cost:	$3,358. *assumes 39% down payment
Less normal pay't:	1,640.
Less profit/loss:	1,214. *with tax advantages
Monthly cash flow:	-504. *with tax advantages

Summary: The monthly cost to own this boat in 5 years with YPSMP is $504, as compared to paying $2,078 per month for 15 years to own the boat with a conventional loan.

It's important to know that any charter management program is only an aid in reaching your financial goals. None of the programs generate enough money to fully fund your boat, as all of the reputable companies will tell you up front, and you'll still need to have the required down payment and be able to qualify for financing. It's unlikely that you'll be given a guarantee of yearly income from charter management companies, since many variables come into play. The best you can do is review the performance of similar boats in a specific location and be prepared for all contingencies, including major repairs that may be needed.

You must also ask yourself if charter management suits your needs and personal situation. Some people can successfully handle a charter management arrangement. Others who tend to have a close emotional attachment to their boat are not good candidates. You must be able to live comfortably with the fact that others are using, or are responsible for, your rather large investment which may be located hundreds or thousands of miles away. If you can look at this as you would a time-share purchase on land, you have a good chance of success.

Charter management programs are mostly geared for the bareboat charter trade.

Larger boats are not suitable for bareboat chartering; the systems and maintenance are just too complex and it takes much more experienced sailors to handle them. The alternative for owners of larger boats is to set the yacht up as a crewed charter business, with a dedicated crew aboard at all times to accommodate guests who plan their own itinerary. A crewed charter arrangement has higher expenses and less income since there is less demand, but it may be a good alternative for wealthier businessmen who wish to take advantage of the tax deductions and be able to entertain their clients.

It's not necessary to think only in terms of charter management in the Bahamas, the Caribbean or the Mediterranean. There may be good opportunities right in your own backyard. Some companies move your boat from summer to winter locations, while others offer reciprocal arrangements with other operators so you can use similar boats in different areas.

The main benefit to charter management is having your boat ready for cruising when and where you want it and have it well-cared for the rest of the year. Purchasing a boat and adding it to a charter fleet is an affordable option that might be right for you.

Co-Owning A Boat
For some, a good approach to getting a multihull

For most co-owners of things, the idea to share ownership springs from necessity. If you are on a limited budget, then co-owning a boat, though perhaps not ideal, can provide an alternative to either charter management, a steep mortgage payment, or owning no boat at all.

A boat placed in charter management, while typically cared for and maintained properly by the management company, will be used by countless individuals of widely varying levels of sailing competence and an inevitable disregard for the welfare of a boat they are only renting for a week or two. The initial investment required for a boat purchased with charter management in mind is low (typically 20 to 30 percent of the purchase price), but the vessel may not become fully accessible to you for years to come and the toll on it can be high by the time it is paid for.

Co-ownership, on the other hand, means the owners have total control over who uses the boat, as well as how and when they use it. The initial investment is higher, up to 50 percent of the purchase price for two co-owners, but chances are the boat will be kept in better condition and for less money when only a few people skipper her.

If the boat you want is still out of reach with only two co-owners, more can be introduced, although the potential for problems with personalities and scheduling rises significantly as the number of owners increases. For most, it makes more sense to limit the partnership to two.

One way to successfully accommodate additional boat owners is to set up a time-sharing company with one person in charge of maintenance and scheduling. As with time-sharing a condominium, you would pay for a set amount of time on the boat each year, plus some amount for yearly maintenance costs. These would be relative to the number of partners. You would be more limited in this type of arrangement as to when and where you sailed, but would have less expense and responsibility. There would also be less chance of misunderstandings and personality clashes. This type of ownership could be a good alternative to chartering each year, especially once you know what boat you like and where you want to sail her. Success would depend on a proper initial ownership structure and having a competent person in charge.

Another cost-cutting strategy is to limit the co-owners to two or three, then place the boat in charter management only during the times the boat is sitting idle. This would generate some charter income while keeping the liability to the boat to a minimum, particularly since the boat would be maintained when it otherwise would be in storage.

Finding someone to co-own with is a delicate endeavor. Co-ownership of anything requires that two people like, respect, trust, and are willing to compromise with each other. With a sailboat the situation is compounded by the very nature of sailing and sailors themselves. Sailors can be among the most determined, independent, opinionated, uncompromising people anywhere. Helpful, friendly and outgoing towards other sailors, they still remain the proverbial "king of the castle" within the confines of their own boat. If you doubt it, try entering a new harbor and dropping anchor for a while. Seemingly friendly cruisers (usually men) will be dashing over in their dinghies to introduce themselves and offer help, news and advice. Don't be deceived. What they are really doing is assessing your boat, your rigging, your gear and gadgetry, going through a mental checklist of what needs improvement. If you stay long enough in the harbor you'll find out exactly where (in their opinion) your shortcomings lie. Co-owning with this breed can be daunting at best.

On the positive side, there are many sailors who successfully co-own a boat. If the boat is based in one place co-ownership should be fairly straightforward, rather like co-owning a condo in ski country; that is, provided you can agree on which anchor tackle works best, whether the mainsail needs replacing, what, if any, high-tech equipment to buy, whether to use oars or an outboard with the dinghy, and so on.

Various options exist for your choice of co-owner. Try to find someone fiscally responsible who you feel you can trust, someone with a similar outlook regarding how to sail and care for a boat and the best locations to cruise in. Family and friends should perhaps be given first consideration,

although you may not wish to jeopardize your relationship with people you are close to. Be forewarned that the most reasonable, even tempered individuals can become transformed when problems arise over co-owned property, and conflicts can have lasting effects. If you end up with a potential co-owner you are unfamiliar with, try to get to know each other before diving into a co-ownership venture. And protect your investment by creating a legal co-ownership document that covers all contingencies.

If you are buying a boat that you or your co-owner(s) have never owned, the proceedure is fairly painless. If you are buying in to a boat already owned by one of the partners, make sure you fully understand what gear is on board and what condition it's in. Kitchen utensils, linens, boat gear, and dinghy can sound nice on paper, but you may find a major disparity between your vision of "equipped" and some else's, particularly a bachelor's.

Before choosing a co-owner, honestly evaluate the chances for it becoming a success. Do you have the same sailing ambitions as the other? If there's more than one woman, can you agree on changes to the boat's interior? With children, are they rowdy and uncontrolled, the kind that make a habit of breaking things? Are there any pets, and if so, are they well behaved? If your co-owner is single, does he or she plan to fill the boat with masses of friends? These are basic issues that should be seriously considered before entering into co-ownership of a boat. Discuss every angle of boat co-ownership, including the boat's name, registration and how you determine when each partner has access to the boat.

Once you enter into a partnership, keep the lines of communication open. Make allowances for how the other person might feel about when and where you plan to sail the boat, and what cosmetic or practical changes you feel are important. Make sure everyone knows what is expected in terms of maintenance and repair. In any partnership, be it marriage or business, one partner will probably be the dominant one, the other more willing to compromise. Bit by bit, issues will be raised, evaluated, and dealt with.

Owning half a boat can be as much fun as owning a whole. By choosing your partner wisely and drawing up an official agreement of terms, unpleasant surprises can be avoided. You'll probably discover that even a co-owned boat can feel completely yours while you are the ones living on it. This is an important attribute to co-owning; the ability to feel all the benefits of full proprietorship while in residence.

For many people, co-ownership offers the only opportunity to experience the adventure of traveling by sailboat. Although, as with most challenging things in life, there is always a risk involved, co-owning can be a chance worth taking.

Just as with single ownership of a boat, the time may come when one partner needs to sell out. Although this is a possibility with any partnership, it shouldn't keep you from co-owning a boat. Even if the worst happens and both shares must be sold, you'll have had the pleasure of cruising on your own boat for a while. Real co-owning is always a compromise.

Sample Co-Ownership Terms

* The names of each partner, the percentage of the boat they officially own, and the date ownership commences.

* In the event of death of one of the partners, that share should pass on to the heirs of the deceased.

* The boat should be surveyed prior to co-ownership and insured as long as the ownership agreement is in effect

* Only the co-owners should be allowed to skipper the boat.

* No non-prescription drugs of any type or other illegal substances should be allowed aboard the boat (there is a high potential for liability here).

* The partners of the boat should agree in writing to any capital expenditures, to when and where the boat is to be located, and what the schedule of use is to be for each year.

* The yearly maintenance costs, such as hauling and bottom painting, engine maintenance, and minor repairs, should be split by the partners according to their percentage of use each year.

* Major boat repairs or improvements should be initiated only by mutual agreement, and the costs should be split by the owners according to their percentage of ownership.

* The partners should keep each other informed of developments concerning the boat.

* The partners should agree to keep the boat in good operating condition while on board, to perform the necessary maintenance required, and to leave the boat in clean and appropriate condition for the next user.

* Provisions for owners selling their share of the boat if desired should be included.

Owning A
Cruising Multihull

Multihull Insurance

Understanding your policy

—by David Williams
Berg-Williams Marine Insurance
Insurance is mandatory for those with outstanding boat loans or with boats in charter management programs, and even those sailors without obligation usually want the security of knowing their yacht, which may also be their primary home, is properly insured. Before purchasing marine insurance, it pays to have a good understanding of what your choices are and the terms and conditions in a typical policy.

New policy holders usually find it difficult to understand the content and intent of the policy after the first paragraph. Most finally give up and file the policy away in an insurance folder somewhere, hoping they won't be unfortunate enough to need a full grasp of the information it contains. While it is tempting to neglect the responsibility of fully understanding your insurance coverage, anyone who does so is courting disaster. Most regions in North America now require that policies be written in plain English, but as is the case with legal documents, boat insurance described in plain English can still be difficult to understand. Let's review some of the essential elements of insurance companies and their policies.

There are two distinct types of insurers, the domestic insurance company and the overseas insurer, both of which are equally capable. The overseas insurer, however, will be more liberal when it comes to extended navigation, whereas the domestic insurer will probably offer lower rates if you navigate close to home. The financial condition of a domestic insurance company is easily investigated as it is documented by several independent authorities. The most recognized of these is in the U.S. is the A.M. Best Company whose insurance company rating guide can be found in every well-stocked library in the country. A.M. Best rates insurance companies on their financial condition as related to their ability to settle claims, with "A" being the highest rating and "C" the lowest. You should always endeavor to insure with an "A" rated company.

Now on to the Overseas Insurer. The best known of these insurers is Lloyds of London, an insuring institution that has been in continuous operation since the 17th Century. There are many overseas insurers which do not have the record nor the integrity of Lloyds of London, and they should be investigated thoroughly before trusting your yacht to them. While overseas insurers are not rated by the A.M. Best company, the Standard & Poor Index does rate them on financial size & deposits on hand in U.S. trust accounts. Similar ratings are available in most other countries.

In many instances an overseas insurer may be your best choice since they have traditionally been less conservative regarding multihulls, vessel design, and extended navigation. Your concerns can be laid to rest by dealing with an insurance agent who understands marine insurance and who would not want you sailing to far off destinations with an insurance policy he would not buy for his own boat.

When looking for marine insurance, I strongly advise the following:

—Always chose an "A"-rated domestic insurance company or a well-respected overseas insurer.

—Check their references.

—Understand the policy wording.

—Don't believe rumors; investigate them for yourself.

—Most importantly of all, make an informed decision.

Stop and think for a minute—the wording of your insurance policy may be the only thing standing between you and a denied claim. Don't let that happen. Marine insurance is like a life raft. You never expect to use it, but when you really need it you hope it will come to your rescue without hesitation. Just as you wouldn't buy the least expensive canister labeled "life raft" without knowing all about the contents, don't buy an insurance policy without first inspecting it in the minutest detail. Let's review some of the major headings in a typical insurance policy.

Insuring agreement

Remember that an insurance policy is a contract. Ask yourself under what conditions does the insurance company agree to insure you? This is usually straightforward, but watch for words like " reasonable care" and "due diligence". If you find discourag-

ing words like that in the Insuring Agreement, don't continue—it can only get worse.

Causes of loss

The best way to look at this section is to ask what can happen to your boat that the policy does *not* cover? You should be buying an "All Risk" yacht policy. An All Risk policy does not give you a list of what is covered (Named Perils) but rather it literally covers you for all risks.

If you bought a "Named Perils" policy after it was explained to you that it did not cover your cruising catamaran for collision with a motor vehicle and a few other innocuous things, you may have laughed at the concept of your boat in an automobile accident. But what if you're hauled out for annual maintenance and the boat yard fork lift backs into the braces holding your boat, it falls over and causes considerable damage. Are you covered? With an All Risk policy you would be, with a Named Perils policy as described above you wouldn't be.

Of course, there are going to be a few things your "All Risk" policy does not cover. These are listed in the section called "Exclusions" and you should read this section carefully. Every marine insurance policy has standard exclusions on damage that is confined to, or results directly from wear and tear, gradual deterioration, marring, denting, and scratching. What this means is the company will not buy you a new engine when the old one wears out, replace your through-hull fittings that are eaten away by electrolysis, nor compensate you for having someone clean your hulls or buff out the scratches.

The thing you want to be on the lookout for in the exclusions is the use of the word "indirectly"; if you find it then I advise you read the rest very, very carefully, since that wording can eliminate coverage that could be vital to your peace of mind. Other exclusions to look for and avoid are "damage caused by mechanical breakdown" and, believe it or not, "damage by water"!

Your policy *must* include coverage for "Subsequential Loss." What this means is that you will be covered for damage resulting from one part of your boat failing which causes damage to another part of the boat. For example, let's say a swage fitting failed and the mast collapsed onto your boat. Many policies will only cover the cost of the swage fitting and not the subsequent damage since it wasn't the mast that failed. Demand Subsequential Loss wording!

Payment For Loss

This is the hardest section to understand, as well as the one with the greatest shock potential. The language you should demand in this section agrees to pay you the "Insured Value" listed on the "Declarations" page in the event of a total loss. Accept nothing less. What if you have a partial loss? This is where it gets tricky. There are two basic forms, "Replacement Cost", and "Actual Cash Value".

In the first case (the one you want), with few exceptions the company agrees to pay you for the cost of replacing damaged equipment, rigging, machinery, and other permanent fittings with new gear. In the latter case, equipment may be replaced with used gear, the cost of used gear, or the actual value of the gear when it was lost or destroyed.

Liability

If your boat is afloat in the waters of the U.S., then she (as a legal entity) and you (as the owner) are subject to the body of

maritime law which has developed over the centuries and, although it was never intended to, currently applies to recreational vessels. The form of liability coverage in a proper yacht policy is referred to as "Protection & Indemnity". What you should look for here is language that says something like "...to indemnify the insured (that's you) for any liability he may incur as a result of the ownership, use, maintenance, or operation of the boat."

Make sure that "Removal of Wreck" is also covered under this section. It is your responsibility to pay to remove your boat from the waters of the U.S. if she sinks, and you could pay dearly for this service. The cost to remove vessels sunk by Hurricane Andrew was $500 per foot; $20,000 to remove your damaged 40 foot trimaran which the insurance company paid you $45,000 for after the hurricane is a big bite out of a small pie.

Declarations

The next thing you ask is, "Who, What, Where and When is she covered?" This is found on the Declarations page which details all the information specific to your boat. Make absolutely sure that it is correct in every detail and that you understand exactly what conditions it places upon you. Check the spelling of your name and the boat details. Are the navigation limits correct? Is the period of coverage correct? What are you required to do in case of a hurricane? How much is your boat insured for? Is this enough coverage?

How important is the Insurance Agent? If you look hard enough you will come across a Marine Insurance professional who will bore you with difficult questions about your boat and your cruising plans in an effort to customize your marine insurance policy and get you the correct coverage. If your insurance agent starts asking questions such as "Where will you stop at night on your trans-Atlantic voyage?" or "Is your *Privilege 39* used for water skiing?", then it's time to excuse yourself to find one who knows the difference between a Rhumb Line and a dock line, or more importantly a catamaran from a trimaran and a cruising boat from a racing machine. Imagine the problems you could encounter explaining a starboard tack/port tack collision to an adjuster from a large insurance company that also insures cars, tractors and homes.

Conclusion

Is all this attention to detail really necessary? Yes, unless you're one of the few who strongly believe that all insurance companies are kind, benevolent, and humanitarian (in which case, I wish you *lots* of luck).

For the rest of you here's a condensed version of what to look for in the U.S.:

—"A-Rated" insurers or highly-rated, respected overseas insurers.

—All Risk policies are better than Named Peril policies.

—Replacement Cost polices are much better than Actual Cash Value policies.

—Understand the wording of your policy without exception.

—a Marine Insurance professional. Ask him or her what a Rhumb Line is.

—Price should not be the only consideration. My father always told me, "Son, there are three things in life you should not buy based solely on price. The first is brain surgery, the second is a parachute, and the third is insurance." I did not always agree with my father, but on this he was right.

Now that you have the right boat and insurance policy, go sailing and remember, "The Lord does not deduct from a man's allotted time, that time he spends at sea."

A Marine Survey

A must for every prospective multihull owner

Before purchasing a boat, it is always best to get an independent evaluation of its condition from a competent, experienced marine surveyor. While a survey of a used boat will pinpoint its flaws and trouble spots, a survey of a new boat can be equally valuable by helping avoid potential warranty problems. Many people do choose to buy a boat without a survey, deeming the cost too great and relying on friends, acquaintances, sales agents, or the previous owners for advice and counsel. They often find to their chagrin that they have made a mistake, one that costs them far more than the fee of a knowledgeable surveyor would have been.

The survey report is often used as a bargaining chip between buyer and seller, with "Subject to Survey" the clause most often found in contracts for sale of a vessel. A number of contracts contain a clause allowing for a percentage differential in price based on the survey. A common clause, for instance, states that the buyer will absorb any repair and replacement costs up to five percent of the purchase price of the yacht. Beyond five percent, the difference is either split between the parties or absorbed by the seller. It's easy to see how important a Report of Survey is to both parties before buying or selling a boat. In addition to using a survey for insurance or financing, it can also be used to take advantage of professional expertise, not only to diagnose what needs repair, but also in evaluating the vessel's capability to satisfy the prospective owners and their cruising situation.

A good surveyor can often save many times the initial cost of the survey by pointing out potential problems, since even experienced sailors rarely know the true condition of their yacht. Surveyors are trained to spot the less obvious flaws that routinely remain hidden to prospective buyers or owners, things like rot in the aft crossbeam transom, hull blistering penetrating into the laminate, or jury rigged and unsafe engines and fuel tanks.

A survey can also be a useful document to add to the vessel's permanent log. Together with an inventory list, it will often satisfy customs officials concerning the origins and ownership of the ship's equipment. In their endless quest to quell the drug trade, U.S. Customs officials have been known to cut into concealed compartments with drills and chain saws, sometimes finding compartments you didn't even know existed. A surveyor can not only locate such compartments, but can also recommend ways to make them more visible or accessible in order to satisfy customs regulations, preventing damage in the event of a boarding inspection.

The basics of a survey

Once a survey is completed, you will receive a clearly written, concise report of findings about the condition and state of repair of the vessel, including its systems, subsystems, equipment, and all of its parts. Most reports will also include an appraisal and statement of financing and insurability risk. Rather like a personal physical examination, the boat survey report will list in detail the condition of every aspect of the boat, items such as its weaknesses and lack of proper or required equipment. Within certain constraints and guidelines, it will describe recommendations for repair, replacement, or redesign. A repair estimate, however, will not be inclusive, as repair costs are beyond the scope of survey.

In the final analysis, a boat does not "pass" or "fail" a survey, except in a predetermined sense of suitability, or in its confirmation of a seller's claims. For instance, suppose you want to buy a boat for circumnavigation. The surveyor can evaluate the scantlings, construction and equipment and note them accordingly in his report, then give his opinion as to the vessel's suitability for its intended use, including the capabilities of the intended buyer. Or perhaps the seller has made a claim of being "free of rot", something the survey can confirm or deny, thus "passing" or "failing" the survey.

Recommendations for additional equipment, modifications, refit and redesign are normally beyond the scope of a prepurchase survey. If you want them, negotiate these things into the survey prior to engaging the surveyor, making sure your chosen surveyor has the appropriate acumen to properly undertake the responsibility. Services like these usually require a Naval Architect or Marine Engineer.

A survey report will also confirm or deny claims made by owners, brokers and other parties with vested interests. With no vested interest of his own, the surveyor in effect represents the boat, allowing him to make the most impartial, unbiased judgement when it comes to the boat's true condition. With respect to this inherent objectivity, a Report of Survey is usually the basis for both financing and insurance acquisition. Both institutions rely heavily upon such documentation and generally accept the surveyor's opinion as to the value and insurance or financial risk involved in a given boat.

Since most survey reports contain an appraisal, it's important to choose a surveyor who is familiar and experienced with the type of boat you plan to purchase. This is particularly important when buying a multihull, as the surveyor must know how to obtain comparable sales pricing information beyond the BUC and NADA listings. These services often possess little information concerning multihull yachts. Any experienced multihull surveyor should already know where to research and document multihull pricing and appraisal information.

Finding a surveyor

One problem most first-time multihull sailboat purchasers have is finding a suitable surveyor, and a surveyor with a working knowledge of multihulls in particular. Before contracting a surveyor, find out what knowledge they have of your particular boat and which professional organizations they belongs to, if any. In the U.S. there are several professional organizations: the Society of Accredited Marine Surveyors (SAMS), the National Association of Marine Surveyors (NAMS), and the

Marine Surveyors Guild. SAMS and NAMS have strict entry requirements. The Society of Naval Architects and Marine Engineers (SNAME) is another professional group which has been around for over a century and screens its members thoroughly. The American Boat and Yacht Council (ABYC) and the National Fire Protection Association (NFPA) are solely informational and standard setting organizations, ones which surveyors are encouraged to belong and contribute to although they have no accreditation. BOAT/US has a list of surveyors from whom its insurance underwriters will accept surveys, making this probably the most practical reference and cross-check available. Other countries have their equivalent organizations for professional marine surveyors.

A multihull surveyor should be an independent, experienced, knowledgeable professional who has an unbiased view of your prospective boat and will competently examine every square inch of it and issue a comprehensive report on his findings. If done properly, a survey could be likened to a premarital physical, a transcript of school records, and a CIA investigation all combined, with the surveyor taking the role of diagnostician, educator, and sleuth in the course of a survey. He should be capable of finding any evidence of previous damage and repair, and any weak, inadequate, or wrongly applied materials or installations.

Making a contract

It's always best to have a written "contract for survey" before proceeding, explaining the exact terms, conditions and expectations of the survey to the purchaser of the service. As most survey contracts end up being last minute rush affairs, more often than not undertaken over the phone, it is important that you have an idea about questions a surveyor will ask before agreeing to do your survey.

The following is a sample list of questions you can expect:

1. The kind of boat it is and the name of the manufacturer. The length, beam, draft, year of manufacture, construction, equipment, rig type, and so on.

2. The boat's name and description, plus the name and phone number of the present owner.

3. Details of sale, including the price agreed upon.

4. Legal details such as import duties paid, documentation numbers, and mortgages or other liens.

5. Location of the boat.

6. What arrangements, if any, have been made for haulout, and a statement of who is responsible for haulout, along with where and when it is to take place. With most surveys, the owner arranges and directs the haulout, while the purchaser pays.

7. Who will be present when the survey is performed and who will take care of the yard bills.

8. What is going to be covered or excluded under the survey. In most cases, engines, electronics and specialty equipment such as air conditioning or SCUBA compressors are not covered, but are handled by other specialists.

The cost of a survey

Survey costs vary depending upon the type of boat, the experience of the surveyor and the geographical area of the survey. Rates in the industry are typically based upon the length of the boat plus add-ons. For instance, a twin screw luxury catamaran may cost $12 to $15 dollars per foot depending upon location. An outboard powered medium-size catamaran will most likely cost $10 per foot from an experienced surveyor. Many surveyors have a 30 foot minimum fee. Fees normally do not include travel or out-of-pocket expenses.

Add-ons to the standard survey can be gear such as sails, dinghies, electronics, and extra engines or generators, or special travel or survey considerations. Special circumstances might include surveying a boat on the beach or in a sling using a dinghy to check the bottom. Basic survey rates for most surveyors cover a standard diagnostic evaluation for the vessel. Anything beyond that is an extra to be negotiated.

Survey basics

Hauling the boat. You should always have the boat hauled for the survey inspection, even if the owner can show you paid bills for having the bottom done last week. This avoids unpleasant surprises like osmotic blistering and guarantees a thorough examination of such critical underwater features as hull-fairness, zincs, through-hull fittings, shafts, props, pintels, gudgeons, rudders, distortion, paint condition, hogging and the like.

Because the underwater parts represent the most difficult, costly and inherently dangerous areas of the boat, they should never be glossed over or taken for granted. The assessment of a boatyard is different from the assessment of a surveyor and the needs of the purchaser, making it a less than reliable source in the event of a boat sale.

The walk-around. A good surveyor prefers to be present, if possible, when the boat is hauled, for this is the best time to conduct the initial walk-around portion of his survey. As the boat is lifted in the slings or on a railway, he specifically watches for excess mobility, flexing, bending, hogging

and other signs of structural inadequacy, weakness or damage. Once the boat is out of the water, before he touches a mallet or probe, the surveyor should carefully study the boat's lines from a distance, walking around and observing it from all angles. What he is looking for are bumps, hollows, bulges, unfairness, hogging, signs of delamination, broken frames, poor construction, inadequate scantling, and repaired, damaged or over-stressed rigging. Spotting any suspicious areas, he will usually mark them with chalk for later comparison from inside the hull.

Hull inspection. Next, the surveyor sounds the entire hull with a mallet, pausing to scrutinize every through-hull fitting. He will carefully inspect the rudder(s), pintels, gudgeons, rudder post and bearings, often finding both excessive wear and electrolytic damage overlooked by both owner and boatyard. Poking around the centerboard or daggerboard trunk(s), he looks for stress cracks, damage, pivot pin wear, or leakage, and notes the shape and fairness of the boards. Then he sounds the propeller, inspecting the shaft, struts, bearings and fittings, taking careful note of their condition, composition and size. If he knows anything about multihulls at all, he will know exactly where to check for stress cracking of the boat's structure at the major joints. Even the best surveyor, however, may not be able to distinguish between cosmetic cracking of faring compound and actual laminate damage. In that case, destructive testing or special expertise may be called for.

Finally, he will meticulously inspect the hull-deck joint, the place where many problems occur, of which leakage is only one. Upon completion, a surveyor should have examined every square inch of the vessel, run his hands over the rigging (although probably not the mast above deck level which, unless specifically agreed beforehand, is the job of a rigger), checked the halyards, sheaves, furled or bagged sails and all the myriad other parts, and examined all equipment and safety gear.

Checking papers. After checking the entire boat, the surveyor will ask about the ship's papers, including registration, title, USCG document, import duty receipts, receipts for equipment, instruction books, warranties, owners manuals, etc. This is entirely for your protection, as you would not be the first person to buy a boat only to discover it had a lien on or was missing some vital document.

Finished with the "hands on" part of his inspection, the surveyor still has the most demanding part of his survey ahead of him: preparing the report. Many surveyors specify delivery of the report within a certain time period, an important aspect as other parties, such as finance institutions, are usually awaiting its outcome.

Additional survey techniques

Electronic testing. Depending on inclination, testing with a Moisture Meter or an Electronic Sounding Device may or may not be part of a survey. Many people have become infatuated with these instruments and insist upon their use. Surveyors are usually more than willing to comply since not only does it transfer some of their judgement with its concomitant responsibility to a machine, but it allows them to charge more for their service. For most applications, a good surveyor doesn't need special equipment. There are times, however, when they are indispensable and the purchaser should understand the cost involved for specialized testing

Destructive testing. Thus far, we have only discussed survey using "nondestructive testing", or testing by observation, sound or radio frequencies. Destructive testing is quite another matter. Before a surveyor can probe a single blister, he must first get permission from the owner of the boat. Often, permission for such superficial destructive testing as probing blisters is implied, as the owner may benefit as much as the prospective buyer.

Destructive testing is used when there is outward evidence of some inward problem that can only be assessed through this method of examination. For instance, the cracking of fairings in high stress areas or the condition of suspect fuel tanks might only be discovered through destructive testing. A surveyor will often want to reserve judgment of an area until he sees what it looks like inside. Destructive testing for specialty items is usually contracted for separately.

Conclusion

By now it should be clear why a pre-purchase survey is as necessary to the success of buying a boat as a physical examination is to maintaining your health. Understand that a surveyor is a diagnostician, not a practitioner, and is only there to discover problems and make recommendations. Also remember that as a professional trained to find every possible flaw, he might make the boat that once charmed you suddenly seem like a lame duck. No boat, not even a new one, is perfect. It's simply the surveyor's job to help you chose wisely, avoid unpleasant surprises, and ultimately secure a fair price.

Yacht Delivery
What to know before having your boat delivered

Delivery is a service often used by yacht owners and production builders. Yacht deliveries are performed by either professionals or amateurs, and occasionally by a combination of the two. Having a stranger sail your yacht is not an experience to be taken lightly. It is a very special kind of relationship and should be carefully considered.

Professional delivery

There are many well-established professional yacht delivery firms capable of delivering your boat from the point of purchase to your desired new location. Since their rates and services vary, they should be consulted directly. Most arrange for their own crew and many will quote a net price that includes out-of-pocket costs such as food and fuel, though not air-fares. Some ask for a stipulated rate of pay based upon either mileage or time plus out-of-pocket costs. Some delivery firms insist upon having full control of the vessel, while others may agree to take the owner along with them. The latter scenario is fraught with difficulties that arise from differing priorities and personality clashes.

Forewarned is forearmed. Most clashes have to do with the agenda that the owner has for being on-board during the delivery. For example, say the owner wants to combine a delivery with a cruise. He has insufficient experience to undertake the passage himself, so he hires a delivery skipper. The owner is interested in learning the trade, having a good time, and not working too hard. Those are the very things that are at variance with most professionals. Professionals have to earn a living, so any extra time or effort can cut into their profit unless the owner is willing to provide compensation . Discussing the priorities and payment prior to signing a contract will cure most of those problems.

Amateur delivery

Amateur delivery is most often undertaken by friends or family of the owner, people the owner knows and trusts. Most amateur delivery revolves around the delivery crew's desire for a vacation and the adventure of the delivery. There have been numerous incidences of amateur crews not completing deliveries, the most prevalent reason being underestimating the difficulty of the delivery and the time involved.

Except in rare circumstances, a delivery trip is not a cruise and problems are bound to occur if it's treated as such. In a delivery situation the objective is to get the boat delivered within the time specified. Many inexperienced delivery skippers underestimate the difficulties involved in delivery, even though they may have sufficient sailing experience to do the job. Unfortunately for both them and the yacht owners, sailing experience alone is not sufficient.

A delivery skipper must be tenacious, wily, mechanically-inclined, and able to direct the activities of others. He must have an inordinate sense of responsibility and of financial priority. On a trans-ocean delivery, he must show leadership and generate confidence and loyalty in his crew. Transocean deliveries are invariably undertaken short-handed. If one crew is seasick, the others must cover the watch.

A delivery trip by definition rules out leisurely sails. Reality forces you to be up before dawn, press on until dark, anchor in less-than-desirable anchorages and keep going no matter what the wind or weather. Time off is only to make emergency repairs. The number of aborted deliveries and boats damaged by amateur crews is what keeps the professional companies in business.

Delivery costs

You should figure about US$225 per day for a licensed professional captain. Crew arrangements depend upon the nature of the delivery, the season of the year and waters traversed. For instance, a delivery from Boston to Miami may take longer but be less demanding than a delivery from Boston to London. Therefore, there are different rates and different crew arrangements. Present rates begin at US$200 per day or US$2 per mile base for the captain, plus crew and out-of-pocket costs.

The delivery of a 36 foot cat from Clearwater, FL to San Juan, Puerto Rico is:
—Captain's fee. US$2 per mile, 2000 miles = US$4000
—Two crew. One free, in training, the second @ US$50 per day, 20 day est. = US$1000.

—Air-fares, three persons, San Juan, Tampa = US$900.
—Food, fuel, customs fees, misc. = US$1000.
—Total Estimate = US$6900 (this does not include a special insurance rider required by certain carriers).

The contract

Written contracts should clearly stipulate the terms, such as:
—Date the vessel is to be picked up.
—Full amounts of charges to be billed.
—A list of crew members.
—What safety and communications equipment will be supplied by the delivery team and what equipment must be on-board at the time crew accepts the vessel.
—What preparations the owner must make prior to crew acceptance for delivery.
—The route and estimated time of arrival.
—Any communications arrangements.
—Arrangements for emergency repairs.
—A pro-forma invoice and estimate of expenses.

The length of delivery

Sailboats are not noted for their speed, especially in the direction of most deliveries, to windward. Our theoretical delivery above allows twenty days to get two-thousand miles. That is an average of one hundred miles per day. The cruising cat in our example is a fast boat, so why estimate such a long time? The reason is the route. It is two thousand miles, all to windward, against the prevailing currents, and it is a circuitous route, needing to take into consideration two island chains, reefs and shoal water.

On routes like the U.S. East Coast Intracoastal Waterway, skippers figure for low-power sailboats about 50 miles per day in autumn and 60 miles per day in spring. It is too dangerous to travel the ICW in darkness.

What to expect

You should expect a thoroughly professional relationship, one in which the captain is straightforward, honest and spells out the possibilities and pitfalls. He should not gloss over any potential problem and should answer all your questions with his best estimate. The crew should be respectful of your property and maintain it as though it were their own. Professional captains have a good reputation for taking care of an owner's vessel safely and in good time. Your vessel shouldn't receive worse wear than you would give it yourself.

The alternatives

There are often alternatives to crewed delivery, including trucking, railway and shipping. In the U.S., there are specialized carriers that will deliver boats up to fourteen feet wide for far less than a professional crew could deliver them. Between fourteen and twenty feet, options drop dramatically as prices rise in proportion. Over twenty feet, all land options, including railway, are lost.

Freighters represent a good alternative. While it is prohibitively expensive to ship from one coastal U.S. city to another, in many parts of the world you can ship for less than a delivery. Americans have avoided excessive freight charges by sailing first to Mexico, Canada, Cuba and other Antilles nations and shipping from there. On board a freighter a multihull, unlike keel boats or power boats that need cradles, will sit serenely on its own bottom with a minimum of dunnage. Rates are favorable,

especially for the smaller boats. Delivery costs are usually figured by distance, not size, so a thirty-foot boat can cost the same to deliver as a sixty-footer.

Preparing for delivery

In most cases, the owner of the boat knows more about the boat and its idiosyncrasies than any other person. There are always little things that only the owner understands: getting the throttle in just the right position to engage the starter, holding the cabin door key in that certain way so it will turn, removing a certain storage case to gain easy access to the engine dipstick. I am sure you can supply a list of such items that apply to your boat. A credible list prepared ahead of time helps captain and crew enormously and can quite possibly save damage to your boat.

Included with that list should be a map of exactly where all the through-hull fittings are located and what they operate. There should be an emergency closure of some sort for each fitting. Most often these are tapered soft-wood plugs that are tied directly to the fitting for which their use is intended. It is vital that each through-hull fitting be tested for proper operation, and lubricated if necessary prior to the arrival of the delivery crew.

A diagram of the lockers and cupboards showing the location of emergency equipment and necessary stores, tools and replacement parts should be prepared or updated. Before a delivery you should test, repair or replace the following:

    —Personal flotation devices (PFD's).
    —Bilge pumps.
    —All through-hull fittings.
    —Hatches or ports. Make sure that they seal well and any fore-deck hatches can be secured.

—Drains. Especially check foredeck sail-locker and anchor-locker drains. These are notorious for becoming plugged with items stored in the lockers, preventing the locker from draining.

—Steering system, cables, rods, quadrants and all hinge and pivot points. Provide spares and a proper emergency steering method.

—Lubricants and lots of spare filter cartridges. This can be critical in parts of the world where contaminated fuel might be encountered.

—US and other national requirements for safety equipment, including flares and signalling equipment.

—Life-raft if on board; have it inspected prior to delivery. If no inflatable life-raft is to be provided, create an alternate plan and designate equipment and strategies.

—Life-lines and stanchions.

—Dinghy, davits, dinghy outboard and the method of securing them for safety.

Legal preparation

Notify your insurance company before the delivery, and provide the Captain with a letter stating that you authorize him to be in possession of the vessel. Be sure that the letter is identical in format to that on the legal documents. For example, if the document reads: Gerald R. Smith, make sure your letter is not signed Jerry Smith, or Gerald Smith or G. Smith. If the vessel is owned by a corporation, the letter should be signed exactly as it is on the document and the corporate seal affixed. Bureaucrats are notorious for picking up such variances and detaining folks while they verify the right of the persons on-board to be in possession of the vessel. A notary seal is helpful.

—Be absolutely certain that all necessary documents, registrations and licenses are current and will remain so during the delivery. Don't forget the dinghy registration. Ship's radio station licenses must show all the frequencies of the equipment on board, including EPIRB's.

—All major equipment should be listed on a customs declaration and paid receipts kept aboard with that declaration. While seldom called for, these papers establish ownership of the equipment on the vessel and prevent problems with customs officials.

—Prepare a complete inventory and attach it to the ship's log. Include in the inventory the serial numbers of all equipment. Especially important are electronic equipment, camera equipment, binoculars, and other valuable items.

—Remove all firearms. Do not burden a delivery crew with the legal requirement of your firearms. Many countries and some states in the U.S. will confiscate your vessel for illegal firearms. The chances of a thorough search when a delivery crew is aboard are far greater than when the owner is aboard. In some jurisdictions, like New York City, flare pistols are considered firearms. The states of Connecticut, Massachusetts and New York have tough variations of standard firearms regulations. Most of these variant regulations are available by contacting BOAT/US.

—Make sure all your radios are properly licensed. Restricted radio operator permits are required in most ITU signatory nations. If you are a HAM operator, you need the proper reciprocal licensing for the countries you pass through. Check with the overseas operator about the requirements for high-seas telephone licensing in your destination countries.

In & Out Of The Water

Hauling and storing your cruising multihull

As a cruising multihull owner you'll be faced with the decisions of how and where to keep your boat, both during the cruising season and when the boat is not in use. Let's take a brief look at some of the options and their implications.

Trailerable cruisers

Trailerable sport trimarans represent an exceptional opportunity for sailors who want a seaworthy vessel that can be quickly and easily transported. Being relatively lightweight for their length, they are able to be trailered by most passenger cars. They can also be stored in your backyard or other convenient, safe, out-of-the-water location, eliminating the cost of marina and storage yard fees. Trailerability doesn't seem to affect the performance of these fast multihulls; they are without a doubt the hottest sailboats on the market.

There are also some trailerable cruising cats, each with their own advantages and differences. By and large they represent an exhilarating breed of day sailors or coastal cruisers, whereas the larger sport trimarans displayed in this book have captured the field of bluewater trailerable cruisers.

Moorings & harbors

If your boat isn't trailerable, chances are you'll be keeping it in the water during the cruising season or, if the boat is in the tropics, during the times when the boat is in use. Storing a cruising multihull "on the hard" is generally only an option for routine maintenance or making repairs, or for long-term storage.

Some lucky sailors have their own waterfront dock; it's hard to imagine anything more convenient for cruising enthusiasts. The rest of us, however, must find a safe, secure and convenient location for in-the-water storage.

Anchoring or mooring your multihull is the least expensive in-the-water storage method. Most countries now have harbor dues for anchored boats; in some countries boats are charged based upon their square footage—their length times their width—a concern for multihull owners. In America it is rare for anchoring or mooring fees to penalize for excess beam. A few places such as south Florida do have certain facilities that charge extra for beam. In fact one south Florida sailing club restricts its mooring field to monohull yachts exclusively. As prime mooring grounds become more crowded, it is to be expected that prices will reflect the total area a boat consumes.

Offsetting any potential disadvantage of anchoring or mooring restrictions is the ability of most multihulls to utilize areas too shallow for the modern monohull. This rather large expanse of water open only to multihulls is a definite plus in places like the Chesapeake Bay and its tributaries, an area with forty percent of its navigable waters four feet deep or less.

Slip rents vary widely depending upon that old arbiter, supply and demand. In many waterfront communities there are slips at private homes going begging, while slips at the upscale condo association docks bring premium prices.

Marinas and their ambiance vary widely. They range from a sort of laid-back nautical junkyard through the most posh places imaginable. There are live-aboard marinas and marinas that specialize in charter boats. Marinas can be fascinating places to live and offer endless life-style possibilities. Though multihulls are often wider than average, they often find slips that are too shallow for most craft and, therefore, often wind up with the slips closest to shore.

For multihull owners who can only use their boat a small portion of each year, charter management offers the combination of a safe berth, usually at a marina or other secured facility, and a professional maintenance package. This type of program isn't for everyone, but it does provide a worry-free place to store your boat in the water, and the boat will be ready to go when you arrive for your cruise.

Hauling and servicing

There was a time in the recent past when it was difficult to find a marine service facility that could lift a vessel over 16 feet wide. That era is rapidly drawing to close—many marinas now have travel lifts that can accommodate boats to 22 feet in width. Occasionally, you'll find a marine railway in service; they usually have no problem hauling boats with excessive beam.

Down in the islands there are numerous floating dry-docks in use. Since the majority of yachts in many island locations are multihulls, there are typically plenty of wide dry-docks to go around. Hardly ever seen in monohull circles but quite common with the 26 to 36 foot range of multihulls is lifting them by fork lift. Many designs, especially certain popular catamaran designs, are routinely lifted by fork lift.

A definite multihull advantage is their ability to beach and dry out on the tide. While many monohulls do this in certain areas of high tide range using special "legs" to keep them from falling over, most multihulls can use the nominal tide ranges of the Caribbean and South Pacific on hidden little beaches in paradise. Three to four feet of tidal range is adequate to do most chores on a multihull. The tropical areas in which most of us dream of cruising have about that range.

Catamaran owner's are rarely penalized by boatyards when it comes time for bottom painting. The fact that they must strike two waterlines is offset by the ease of painting a shallow-draft vessel—there's a lot less blocking and moving of scaffolding. Don't expect to use less paint, however, as multihulls usually have a similar or greater surface area than a comparable monohull.

Marinas traditionally charge by the foot of overall length for hauling and storage. Your multihull will be charged at that same rate in the vast majority of marinas and boatyards, although it pays to shop around; discriminatory charges based upon hull type are beginning to appear.

Real or imagined difficulties in owning a multihull sailboat should not deter you. For every disadvantage to keeping your boat in or out of the water, there is an advantage.

Multihull
Seamanship

Sailing A Cruising Multihull I
Basic moderate weather sailing techniques

 What is sailing and sail trim like on a cruising cat or tri? To a large extent that depends on your level of sailing expertise, on the boat you sail, and your perspective. Since the basic sailing concepts apply to multihulls as well, you'll find the experience similar to monohull sailing with subtle but important differences.

Those new to sailing have few preconceptions about how a multihull should perform. They find multihulls relatively easy, forgiving boats to learn on, as they aren't trying to subdue years of monohull sailing instincts. Becoming proficient at sailing and at sailing a multihull become one and the same. While experienced monohull sailors have a firm grounding in the basics of sailing, they need to get over the mindset of always comparing multihull sailing to sailing one-hulled ballasted boats. Once they can do that the process is easy.

The boat you learn on tends to become your benchmark for what multihull sailing is all about, though performance and handling varies remarkably between various designs. Despite the huge strides in market acceptance over the past few years, there is still a tendency to lump all multihulls together. Some sailors learn on a true cruising multihull, quite a different experience from sailing a high-performance model.

Your perspective on what sailing is all about also influences your approach to multihulls. Some sailors feel you really aren't sailing unless you are cold, wet and tired. If you can relate to those sentiments, you'll probably be disappointed with sailing a multihull. I personally couldn't disagree more, having always taken great pleasure in the comfortable, protected sailing conditions and quick passages a multihull affords.

Sailing fast and on the level

One of the first things you notice is the lack of heeling on a cruising multihull. There's no need for constantly bracing yourself and your gear at unnatural angles. Sailing is more comfortable and less tiring, which should translate into more enjoyment and safer operating conditions.

Searching for a downside to level sailing, I'd say there's a lack of feedback that heeling provides the helmsman. With no appreciable heel and a reduced tendency for weather or lee helm on a multihull, it's more difficult to tell when it's time to reduce sail. You have to rely on boat speed and boat motion relative to the seas. Multihulls have no real ability to spill a gust of wind by heeling; they typically translate excess wind energy into acceleration, something that takes a little getting used to. Rapid acceleration is most noticeable on light displacement multihulls with high-performance rigs. I thought I knew what boat acceleration was until I sailed a 31 foot trimaran sport cruiser. She went from 6-7 knots to 12-13 knots in the blink of an eye, quite normal, I later discovered, for high-performance cruisers.

Cruising multihulls not only accelerate quickly, they maintain higher average speeds than monohulls. Slower cruising multihulls sail about like fast monohulls, only with higher top speeds, so sailing and sail trim is comparable. High-performance cruising multihulls, however, can attain speeds of 20 knots or more. Sailing at those speeds is quite different, partly because everything happens much faster and partly because the apparent wind is brought far forward, to the point where a broad reach on a monohull becomes a close reach on a fast multihull, and a beam reach becomes close-hauled sailing. Most cruising multihulls on the market fall somewhere in between, so as a rule you can expect to maintain smaller sheeting angles and flatter sails for a given true windspeed.

The multihull motion

While multihulls sail faster, the sensation of speed can be less than on a monohull due to the wide decks and virtually no heeling. Multihulls don't plunge and rise through the waves like a heavy displacement boat. They stay on the surface of the water, so their motion is lighter, quicker, less sustained in one direction. Some long-time monohull sailors miss the steadiness and responsiveness of a keelboat, but most have an easier time with the multihull motion. Others find it just as easy to be seasick on a multihull.

Light displacement sailing

Multihulls have no use for heavy ballast, since their comfort and safety depends on their ability to remain perched on top of the waves. Good performance is linked to the designer's recommended payload, which is usually relatively light compared to the boat's displacement. This is one reason many live-aboard and charter multihulls lack sparkling performance, because they've been loaded in excess of the designer's recommendations.

You'll need to get used to the handling of a light displacement boat. Multihulls can accelerate rapidly, and similarly they lose their way rapidly upon heading into the wind, much to the chagrin of neophyte sailors as they attempt to anchor, shoot moorings, close with docks, and come about. In general you'll need to head up closer to your desired stopping point than you would in a ballasted boat (a little unnerving in the beginning), and maintain boat momentum to make good gains to windward and to bring the boat smoothly through a tack.

Shallow draft

Most cruising catamarans have either low profile fixed keels (draft typically ranges between 2'4" to 3'6") or daggerboards where the draft can vary from less than 2'0" with boards up to over 6'0" with boards down (trimarans typically have one centerboard or daggerboard in the main hull). It's a major adjustment for monohull sailors to cruise on a shallow draft multihull. It's not unusual for monohull sailors to hyper-ventilate the first time they sail fast in five to six foot deep, crystal-clear Bahamian water.

Room with a view

Multihulls have lots of room topsides for sail handling and crew maneuvering. Catamarans usually have full-width travelers for the mainsail, and those designs with bridgedeck cabins have the added advantage of a saloon area almost on level with the cockpit providing good visibility of the surrounding water. This allows crew members to stay in touch with the those in the cockpit and with the course being steered. It's not unusual for one crew member to help navigate while tending to some domestic chore "below" in the main cabin.

You may find it difficult initially to steer a straight course over the wide foredeck of a catamaran. The secret is to sight over some point up forward that keeps your line of sight parallel with the boat's centerline, and make sure you always steer with that point as a reference.

Upwind sailing

Years ago multihulls were considered to have poor windward ability, but modern cruising multihull designs exhibit very respectable upwind performance. Those boats with sleek topside profiles, efficient hull shapes, and daggerboards or center-boards will point the best, but even on a cat with bridgedeck accommodations and integral keels you can make better way to windward than equivalent monohulls if you know what you're doing. One trick is to not pinch a multihull as close to the luff line as you would a heavy-displacement monohull. By falling off just a bit and keeping your sails full, you'll maintain momentum and higher average speeds, and avoid making excessive leeway.

Maintaining speed is especially important when getting ready to come about, since good momentum helps take you through a tack smoothly. All tris and most high-performance cruising cats with daggerboards tack with little effort. The

balance of the cruising cats now on the market come about less quickly (especially if they have excessive windage), but usually without problem. Vintage cruising cats tend to come about in a rather stately fashion. Light winds with choppy seas is always a bit of a challenge, since it's hard to gather the momentum needed to overcome the seas in those conditions. You might occasionally have to backwind the jib to avoid being caught in irons, but the technique should only be employed if necessary since it tends to slow your progress.

When you're ready to come about on a multihull, do it decisively, and make sure you are close to the wind but still maintaining good speed. Trim the main hard before tacking. This allows the main to act like the aft section of a windvane, helping swing the boat into the wind. Find a lull in the waves and bring the helm over smoothly, and keep it there until you approach 45 degrees off the wind on the new tack. At that point slowly reverse the helm to bring the boat onto your new heading. As you pass through the wind, ease the main a bit to reduce the windvane effect, which is no longer needed, and to allow the main to fill and provide power on the new tack. If you lose momentum during the tack and need to backwind the jib, delay the release of the headsail sheet until the back side of the jib has filled and is pushing the boat off the wind. As soon as you're well through the wind, but no farther than necessary, release the windward sheet and haul the leeward sheet in quickly to get the boat moving forward again. Always trim the jib first and then the main. Allow the boat to pick up speed before moving close to the wind again.

When close-hauled in a monohull in windy conditions, standard practice is to head up when hit with a gust. This prevents excessive heeling that can result in a knockdown. On a high-performance cruisng multihull luffing up is still the best course of action when you're temporarily overpowered; falling off can make the boat accelerate rapidly. Another way to cope with gusts is to use a square-top mainsail; the square top blows off in a gust, serving as an automatic first reef.

You'll have to allow for additional leeway when going to windward in any shallow draft boat. Daggerboards help reduce leeway by reaching down into deeper water. Recommendations from the builder or designer and your own experience under sail will tell you how much to allow in various sea conditions.

On catamarans with a daggerboard in each hull, use both boards down in light winds to give you the most lift. In moderate winds, use the leeward board since it will be in slightly deeper water. As you gain speed or fall off the wind, the daggerboard can be gradually raised; experience on your boat will tell you how much you can comfortably raise the board under various sea and wind conditions. High speeds can make it difficult to raise the board; you may find you have to reduce speed temporarily to ease the pressure on the board trunk.

Downwind sailing

Sailing downwind in a multihull is a breeze, with reaching typically a perfect point of sail. When sailing from a close reach to a beam reach or from a beam reach to a broad reach in a multihull, trim the sails as you would for a monohull—ease the sheets until the leeward telltales flow aft evenly. The main difference from monohull sailing is that fast multihulls bring the apparent wind farther forward, so that for a

lot of downwind sailing the sails are set as though for a beam reach. Fast cruisng multihulls are often seen flying asymmetrical spinnakers with the headsail up, an advantage for racing. Slower cruising multihulls differ less from monohulls when sailing downwind, although flatter sheeting angles are typically needed to maintain proper sail trim.

When the destination is dead downwind, fast cruising multihulls usually "tack" on a broad reach course and jibe 90 degrees through the wind, the opposite of sailing to windward. This technique produces the fastest speeds and best distance made good. Slower multihulls usually sail closer to dead downwind, but with little heel the typical rolling motion of a monohull is all but eliminated and the tendency to broach is greatly reduced.

Cruising multihull sailors favor asymmetrical spinnakers for downwind sailing in light winds. The tack of an asymmetrical spinnaker is supported by a line from each of the outward bows and one from the main bow of a tri or forward beam of a cat. Asymmetrical spinnakers can be set without a pole due to the wide beam of a multihull, although a short pole permanently mounted on the main bow of a tri or the forward beam of a cat allows the tack to be tightened using only one line. When flying a spinnaker on a multihull you need to be aware of when it's time to reduce sail. Higher boat speed means lighter apparent winds, and it's easy to get caught in true winds too strong for spinnakers. Get recommendations from your boat designer or sailmaker on maximum windspeeds for your boat and sailplan. On a fast multihull, heading downwind temporarily depowers the sails just as luffing up does when going to windward.

When sailing downwind in light winds, trim the spinnaker first by sheeting it in until the sail begins to stall, then easing the sheet until the leeward telltales flow aft evenly. If the headsail can be carried, trim that next in the same manner, then set the main traveler and trim the main.

If your boat has daggerboards, keep the board(s) down partially for a beam reach to minimize leeway, then raise the board(s) gradually as you sail farther off the wind. Experience will tell you exactly where to place the board(s) in various conditions; it's best to keep a foot or so of board down when running to improve steerage.

Jibing on a monohull is done under controlled conditions to avoid rigging damage to gear or personal injury. Boat speed is usually low compared to the apparent wind, so the boom and mainsail can swing across with considerable force. Jibing on a multihull can be quite different because of the reduced apparent wind, a wide mainsheet track to control the mainsail, and the reduced chance of broaching. When jibing a fast cruising multihull from a broad reach, don't steer down near the wind before the jibe. This reduces boat speed and makes the conditions more similar to a monohull. It's better to bring the helm over steadily and "tack" through about 90 degrees until you are sailing on the opposite broad reach course. On slower multihulls you'll need to jibe in a more controlled fashion. Take the slack out of the main as you steer downwind and pull the traveler amidships. Bear away to jibe the mainsail. As the headsail becomes blanketed by the main, jibe the headsail. Ease the traveler and trim the mainsail on your new heading.

Jibing with an asymmetrical spinnaker complicates the process slightly. As the boat passes through the jibe, release the working sheet and allow the sail to be blown outboard. When the wind is on the opposite quarter haul in the new sheet. On the new heading make sure the sheets as well as the lines bracing the tack are free and clear.

Downwind Surfing

Light-displacement multihulls occasionally surf down the backside of waves under normal sailing conditions. They can sometimes surf at speeds approaching true wind speed, which brings the apparent wind to zero and causes the headsail or spinnaker to temporarily collapse. A spinnaker in this situation may wrap itself around the headstay; if it wraps tightly, you may need to jibe the mainsail to allow it to release itself. When released, jibe back to your original course. You can help prevent spinnaker wrap by temporarily oversheeting until the apparent wind picks up again. Repeated surfing might indicate that you have too much sail up for the wind and sea conditions.

Maneuvering under sail

Maneuvering a multihull under sail in tight anchorages or around docks requires some practice, particularly with cruising cats that lack good crisp response to the helm. Give yourself some additional time and distance to turn, and be aware of how quickly a multihull can accelerate in a gust or come to a stop once headed into the wind. Play your main and jib just as you would with a monohull.

Sailing A Cruising Multihull II

Basic heavy weather sailing techniques

 First, let us make the distinction between heavy weather sailing and survival sailing. Heavy weather sailing is done in full control of your circumstances and ability to manage your vessel. Survival is when you pass that point and must take action to preserve life and property, a topic discussed later in this article under the heading of Drag Devices.

Historically, many situations that would have been survival situations in other craft were just heavy weather sailing for cruising catamarans. A classic story by Robin Knox-Johnston was published in *Cruising World*. It is his account of sailing his catamaran through force 12 winds. There are other similar experiences that support the notion that keeping the vessel underway is a good survival tactic.

Little has been written specifically for survival situations in multihulls. The basic reason for this lack of literature is the astonishing safety record compiled by ordinary sailors in "off-the-shelf" catamarans. At the time of the famous Fastnet disaster, of which volumes have been written, there were two Prout catamarans in the vicinity. They were shadowing the fleet as unofficial entries when the racing fleet sailed into a serious storm. The carnage caused by the storm was so great that a "Committee On Safety From Capsizing"

was formed. Their purpose was to design a minimum stability formula for ocean racing monohull yachts. The weather that was a disaster to the Fastnet fleet was considered merely "beastly weather for sailing" by the two adjacent catamarans.

During the tragic "Queen's Birthday" typhoon off New Zealand, the two catamarans showed that even with aging and somewhat handicapped short crew they could provide predictable and adequate safety. There are numerous stories of catamaran crews simply furling all sails, lashing the helm amidships and going below to wait out the storm while their cat bobbed around looking after herself.

Basic tactics

Knowing when to reef is the most important skill to develop for heavy weather sailing; next comes sail shape and sheeting angle. There are a few generalities that will help you get started learning about heavy weather sailing tactics:

—As the wind increases, move the sheeting point to leeward. This is one of the best features of multihull sailing. Multihulls have a wide sheeting base which allows a greater angular choice for sail trim than narrow boats. Ease off the traveller to move the main to leeward and use an outside rail attachment point, stanchion base or toe track and car to move the jib to leeward.

—Allow more twist in the sails as the wind strengthens and reduce camber (flatten) the sails. This is achieved in the main by slacking the main-sheet and in the jib by moving the sheeting point aft.

—Reduce sail. Most multihulls are just as happy with reduced sail and you will be surprised how little speed you really lose.

—Learn to use a barber-hauler (see glossary) to control your jib. A barber-hauler does not need to be a fancy multi-part tackle, but can be made from most anything, including just a length of line from the clew of your jib to an appropriate turning point and to a winch.

—Slow down to a more moderate speed. Think of it as similar to slowing down your car when you come to a rough road.

—Choose a sail combination according to direction. Downwind, reduce the main area first, then the jib. Upwind, reduce jib area first, then the main. This is just a rule-of-thumb. It must be tailored to the individual vessel.

—Expect to hand-steer downwind in big waves. Your auto pilot will not be able to react fast enough, nor can it anticipate waves. The trick is never to allow yourself to be perpendicular to the wave, but always to be at an angle to it. That way you are always sailing downhill and you reduce the chance of pooping or pitchpoling (pooping is unheard of in cruising catamarans and pitchpoling comes from excessive speed perpendicular to the waves).

Getting to windward

If you seriously feel the need to maximize your heavy-weather windward ability under sail, then you must be prepared to change headsails for the purpose. Roller-reefing sails are good to a certain

point. It must be remembered that a sail is sewn to pull against the head, the tack and the clew with the luff supported by a stay. When a sail is partially rolled, it is no longer pulling against the designed strong points, it is pulling against the luff and the foot where they roll around the stay. While it is possible to do reasonably well with a partially rolled jib, it is without doubt much better to have a sail specifically cut for that purpose, such as a good storm jib.

On the other hand, if you do what most cruisers do and simply run your engine about one third your normal cruising speed you will go to windward just fine. This motor-sailing concept is almost the universal choice of cruisers for going to windward in heavy weather. In a catamaran with twin engines, it is usually necessary to run only one of the engines to gain the desired effect.

Knowing when to reef

This is the most often asked question concerning multihull safety. The answer is deceptively simple: "It is time to reef when you first think about it." This is not meant to belittle the importance of knowing that "time". As you acquire more experience with your particular boat, the more feel you will get for the process.

Let us compare learning how to "feel" your boat with how you learned to "feel" your car. When you first learned to drive, how did you know when to start slowing for a stop? If you started slowing too soon, you created a traffic hazard. If you started too late, you wound up with a panic stop or a rear-end collision. How did you learn this subjective judgmental skill? How did this judgmental process become habitual? The "feel" just developed with experience.

Subjective sailing. From the subjective point of view, when you begin to feel uneasy, apprehensive or concerned, it is time to reef. When the boat no longer has its feather light touch at the helm, it is time to reef. When the boat's motion changes from its normal light, resilient feeling to one of petulant obedience, it is time to reef. When the lee bow seems to want to plunge and bury, it is time to reef.

Objective sailing. From the objective point of view, when the apparent wind speed goes over 15 knots, it is time to reef on most boats. When you are heeled 2 degrees more than normal, it is time to reef. When you are no longer strong enough to crank in the sails, it's time to reef.

Reefing, as referred to in this section, includes both headsail and mainsail. As a rule for masthead boats going upwind, reef the jib first; downwind, reef the main first. It is hard to generalize about fractional rigs. Sailing under main alone is typically far more controllable and the main can be reefed as necessary. The fully battened mainsail has the most sail controls, is held on two sides by spars, and can be given optimum size and shape.

Experience counts!

There is no substitute for experience, so take your boat out in a controlled environment in strong winds with some capable crew. If you have a cruising catamaran, sail it as hard as you can and try to lift a hull. You probably won't be able to do it, but you will learn a lot about how your cat feels when you begin to reach the realistic usable limits. Then never sail your boat that hard again if you can help it!

Trimarans

A trimaran is far easier to judge when overpressed than a catamaran. The extreme initial stability of the cat muddies both sensory and visual clues. A trimaran initially heels almost like a monohull, and you can visually see the lee float being depressed. Since there is more heel, there is more familiarity for those used to monohulls. As with any multihull, however, the wide beam of a trimaran allows you trimming angles not available to monohulls, thus you can have far more control and can keep your power up longer. A good multihull also requires less power to move at speed because it is lighter and does not have the hull speed limitation factor of a monohull.

Drag devices

—by Victor Shane
Para-Anchors International

The multihull configuration has proved itself to be more seaworthy than even the most ardent of its proponents anticipated. The proverbial fly in the ointment has to do with what many people perceive as the multihull's Achilles' heel: *capsize.* The argument goes that ballasted monohulls are more likely to capsize, and they sink while multihulls don't. On the other hand, a monohull's ballast will right the boat if she is capsized (even though she may be dismasted or have sustained other damage), while in the unlikely event a multihull is capsized she will need outside assistance to right herself (a ship with a crane, for instance). If that outside assistance is not forthcoming, the multihull will remain upside down indefinitely and may have to be written off altogether.

The dynamics that lead to capsize are complicated. Entire books have been written on the subject. Although simply lying ahull (broadside to the waves) is a technique that has been employed successfully on many cruising catamarans, as a general rule boats are far less likely to capsize when they are properly aligned with the seaway (parallel to the direction in which the wind and the seas are running). Many experts feel that the ability to survive a severe storm, whether on a monohull or multihull, is closely related to alignment, and therefore boats should be forcefully brought into alignment by some sort of a drag device. There are two classes of drag devices: 1) Parachute Sea Anchors used off the bow, and 2) Drogues towed off the stern.

A sea anchor forcefully holds your boat's bow(s) into the seaway. A drogue keeps your boat aligned with the seaway if you choose to run downwind with the storm. According to experts, a sea anchor and drogue are two items that enable a multihull to be respected as a fully seawor-thy, sail-anywhere yacht.

Parachute sea anchors. All boats are designed to penetrate the waves with their bows. This is especially true of multihulls which, as a rule, have knife-like bows. A parachute sea anchor is used to keep those knife edges pointed into the waves offshore, where the water is too deep to use a regular anchor. It aligns the boat by "anchoring" it bow-on to the surface of the ocean. More importantly, it provides sufficient drag to pull those knife-like bows through large breaking waves without allowing the capsize or pitchpole cycle to begin.

Small cone-type sea anchors have proven to be ineffective and unstable; what are needed are parachute-type devices. As a general rule, the diameter of the parachute sea anchor should be large enough (A) to maintain stable inflation without being tumbled by surface action, (B) to overcome the lateral resistance of any keels involved, (C) to hold the bow/s into the seas and keep side-to-side yaw to a minimum, and (D) to

reduce drift so as to protect the rudder and its fitting. As a general guideline the diameter of the parachute sea anchor should be *at least* 35% of the LOA for both monohull and multihull yachts. When in doubt select a bigger chute.

Modern parachute sea anchors must be used in conjunction with a long nylon rode to allow the boat to yield to the seas and not stand up against them. The long nylon rode is integral to the parachute anchoring system to prevent excessive dynamic loads. For both monohulls and multihulls it is suggested that this rode be equal to *at least* ten times LOA of the boat when in survival conditions (for example, a 40 ft. multihull will need a nylon tether that is *at least* 400 feet long).

Rode diameters should be the same as ground tackle rode. A bridle is essential for multihulls. It is recommended that the arms of this bridle be equal to 2.5 times the beam of the multihull (for example, a multihull with a 20 foot beam will have a bridle whose arms are about 50 feet each. A swivel is required at the parachute terminal and it is recommended that all other unions be in the form of spliced thimbles (no knots) utilizing shackles of equal strength which are wired shut.

Centerboards and daggerboards should be lowered (or partially lowered) when using a parachute sea anchor off the bow. This has the effect of keeping the CLR (center of lateral resistance) well forward which, in turn, minimizes the extent of side-to-side yaw.

Bow rollers used for conventional anchors can be used for the para-anchor; however these must have retaining pins to keep the rode in place (otherwise the rode will jump off the roller when the bow of the vessel dips down into a trough). Heavy-duty chafing gear must be used where the anchor line meets the boat. Never underestimate what chafe can do to your equipment, to your boat and to the lives of those on board. Chafe is the bane of any storm anchoring system. Never take it for granted that the protective rubber or leather sleeve is going to stay put; it's going to migrate, and sooner than you think. Post anchor watch and keep a sharp eye on the gear.

The safest method of deploying a parachute sea anchor in heavy weather is known as the *standing set*. This method allows the boat's drift to pay out the rode. The procedure is as follows:

1) Head up into the wind, allow sails to luff and the boat to stall.

2) Lower/furl all sail.

3) Secure the rudder amidships, lower all boards.

4) Heave the float.

5) Slam-dunk the para-anchor ON THE WINDWARD SIDE (and never on the lee side, where the boat may drift over and foul with it).

6) As the boat drifts away from the sea anchor, snub the line to help the canopy open under water (only half a turn is required on the cleat; do not fully cleat until adequate "scope" has been payed out.)

7) Secure the rode; put on chafe gear.

An alternative method, commonly used by commercial fishermen and requiring a great deal of practice, is known as the *flying set*. In this case the vessel is placed on a downwind course and the para-anchor is jettisoned off the stern while quartering the seas on storm jib or bare poles (mainsail has to be furled). With all but the last coils of the line slipped, the helm is put down hard. As the slack goes out of the system the rode will pull the bow around into the wind. *A WORD OF CAUTION: Because of the*

dynamic and/or shock loads involved in attempting to stop a heavy boat that is moving downwind at some speed, the author does NOT recommend the flying set in heavy weather situations.

Parachute sea anchors can be retrieved by means of full or partial trip-line. I favor attaching the trip-line to the crown of the parachute, since it enables the crew to invert the canopy and retrieve it with relative ease. A partial trip-line doesn't come all the way back to the boat (unlike the full trip-line) and hence reduces chance of nasty foul-ups. The procedure is fairly straightforward; simply winch (or power) the boat up to the second float and retrieve it with a boat-hook. Haul in the trip-line and bring the chute on deck. Even so, it is best to wait for calmer weather before retrieving a large parachute sea anchor.

Drogues. Drogues generate much less drag than parachute sea anchors and require considerable sea room for use. They are towed off the stern in order to limit the speed of the vessel when running before strong following seas. Speed-limiting drogues are, for all intents and purposes, steering assist devices, requiring a man at the helm. They may simply consist of a warp (length of line), or warps, with bights of chain attached. They may consist of any number of on-board items towed off the stern, or they may be purpose-made devices.

Drogues must track straight as they are being towed through the sea. If the drogue configuration is unstable it may "squid", "kite" and "zig-zag" in a seaway, allowing the tow-line to go slack and boat to possibly broach and capsize. Stable tracking is critical in association with the drogue concept. Whereas large diameter parachute sea anchors are designed to block the flow of water outright, small drogues must be designed to allow for very stable flow configurations. They may be solid plastic devices shaped like torpedoes, as is the case with the two-stage Australian *Sea Brake*, or they may be parabolic baskets fabricated from strong nylon webbing, as is the case with the American *Galerider*. Other devices may work, including those associated with defense and aerospace recovery systems (ballute, guide-surface, hemisflow, ringslot and ribbon chutes used mainly for aircraft deceleration).

Speed-limiting drogues are used in conjunction with several hundred feet of nylon or Dacron towline (consult the manufacturer's instructions). In general, it is necessary to use some chain next to the drogue. This helps to keep the drogue submerged. Any speed-limiting device may lose its bite if it is allowed to surface, and/or be pulled out of a wave face. In this connection it is important to position the drogue *behind* its wave when the boat is beginning to surge down the face of another wave. This pulls the drogue through the meaty part of the wave (and not into thin air).

Drogues used with bridles will take more control of the whole situation. Even so, they are not designed to take total control of the situation, as sea anchors are. If the boat needs to be steered, on the other hand, no bridle should be used. By bringing a single towline to a winch well forward of the rudder the helmsman may be able to steer the boat freely, even with the drogue in tow. Raising and lowering the boards will give additional control, either to the drogue or to the helmsman.

Drogue or sea anchor? Speed-limiting drogues are designed for low drag. The associated "Catch 22" is as follows: the same low drag that allows the boat to be steered may allow the boat to be pitchpoled in the ultimate storm. The forces that pitchpole a boat are so great that they will yank the drogue through the sea while throwing the boat end over end. You need the higher drag of a sea anchor to be physically pulled through the breaking sea (and not be thrown by it). It goes without saying, therefore, that the prudent sailor will have both items on board, and know when to use which. If he is towing a speed-limiting drogue off the stern, for instance, the prudent sailor will keep an eye on the barometer in anticipation of making the transition from drogue to sea anchor. And if that transition becomes imminent the prudent sailor will go to the sea anchor early on in the game, long before he is irrevocably committed to the dread toboggan ride to oblivion.

Conclusion

You will be able to remain under sail in many heavy weather situations on a cruising multihull—as long as you reef when you should. You will probably find when the wind is up you can go just as fast reefed down. Besides, most times you will want to slow down a bit to remain comfortable—yes, a bit like slowing your car down when you come to a rough stretch of road.

There is one other basic rule of thumb associated with reefing: on a monohull you typically reef to the strength of the gusts, while on a multihull you reef to the strength of the lulls.

Maneuvering Under Power
Docking and handling in tight quarters

This section describes a few of the major handling techniques and explains how they differ. In general, multihulls respond better and faster to their auxiliary power sources than do comparable keel boats. The reason is a simple matter of the horsepower-to-weight ratio. On the other hand, multihulls often have higher windage than comparable keel boats and are more prone to be maneuvered like powerboats rather than heavy displacement boats. While wetted surface and windage is of some consequence, the primary difference in technique is due to the multihull's lack of momentum and increased beam.

Two of the most common maneuvers under power on a cruising multihull are docking or turning in tight quarters, and handling powerboat wakes. A brief discussion of each is given below.

Docking twin-screw cats

Many of you are familiar with maneuvering twin-screw power boats. As easy as they are to maneuver, twin-screw catamarans are even better because their wide beam creates options not available in a narrow boat. Twin screws provide confidence in docking. Knowing the procedures and the theory behind those procedures allows you to quickly master the techniques and build the skills to handle most situa-tions. If you can handle docking, you can handle any other maneuvering situation including tying to pilings, approaching and leaving slips and other situations you may encounter.

The helm. The helm is not normally used in these maneuvers; all maneuvering is done with the throttles. Simply leave your wheel with the rudders centered and perform all steering operations with the two throttles. There are some caveats, however. This article assumes an "average" produc-tion twin-screw catamaran with spade rudders and three-blade fixed propellers. Two-blade props, folding props and feathering props will change the amount of thrust available. A single engine with twin hydraulic drives has different operating characteristics, since you cannot create greater and lesser thrusts at the individual props. With certain propeller options there is precious little reverse thrust to use. We are also assuming the use of single-lever engine controls. Occasionally you'll come across dual lever controls, or the transmis-sion and throttle on separate levers. While dual lever control may be routine on single engine installations, it tends to complicate twin-screw installations.

The theory and the practice. On most twin-screw power boats, when you put one engine in forward and the other in reverse and apply equal throttle to both engines, you spin on a centerline point. In a twin-screw catamaran, you can pivot the boat on any one of three pivot points depending upon how you apply the power to the engines. Using equal engine thrust you will pivot from the center of the boat. Using greater and lesser power, you will pivot from the side applying the lesser power (see figure 1). For instance, if you want to pivot to the left on your port hull, you would put your port engine in reverse and your starboard engine in forward. Then you would apply a lesser amount of power to the port engine, just enough power to keep the boat from moving forward. With the greater thrust coming from the starboard engine, the boat will literally swing around the port hull.

Let's say you didn't have enough room on the right side to clear an obstacle, making it is necessary to pivot on the starboard hull. In that case you would put greater thrust on the port engine in reverse, which would literally pull the port side of the boat away from the forward moving starboard side, thus pivoting on the outside, or in this case starboard hull.

Not every case is identical or calls for the use of thrust exactly the way it is portrayed in the following diagrams. With a little practice and the use of prudent judgement you will be an expert in no time.

The same techniques described here apply to being underway, at rest or docking. They are related to techniques used to operate a track vehicle such as a tank or a bulldozer. The concept of greater and lesser thrust is similar, except that in a track vehicle the inside, or pivoting side, is held in place by a brake.

When using engines for maneuvering the terms are defined as:

—Lesser Thrust: enough thrust to keep

that hull from going forward or aft, or relatively stationary.

—Greater Thrust: enough thrust to make that hull go forward or aft. Thus the hull with greater thrust pivots around the center of lateral resistance of the stationary hull. Equal and opposite thrust pivots the boat around its center point.

Figure 1. This shows a twin-screw catamaran applying equal thrust forward and aft and spinning at the center point of the vessel's center of lateral resistance.

Figure 2. This shows a catamaran in a tight docking situation with strong current coming from ahead. To prevent abrasion with the dock, a fender is placed in the stern quarter. To prevent rolling the fender out, the technique is to literally pull the starboard hull around until the bows are clear of the forward boat. At that point, the starboard engine is taken out of reverse and put in forward, more power is applied to the port engine and the boat moves quickly out of the slip, the current keeping the vessel clear of the docked boat.

Figure 3. This shows the identical technique as above except that the current is reversed, making it expedient to go out backwards. Twin-screw catamarans are equally maneuverable forwards or backwards, with the exception of boats with folding two-bladed props.

Figure 4. This shows the most difficult situation for any sailboat, being pinned to the dock by current, wind or both. The technique is similar to figure 2, but you must be prepared to either walk the fender forward or have several fenders available. Preventing fenders from tangling or jamming in pilings is the major problem. Use more thrust on the port side engine as the cat turns into the current. Once the bows are clear of the boat ahead of you and

Figure 1

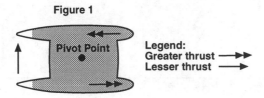

Pivot Point

Legend:
Greater thrust →→
Lesser thrust →

Current

Figure 2

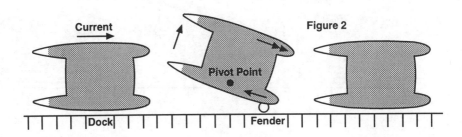

Pivot Point

Dock   Fender

Figure 3   Current   Current

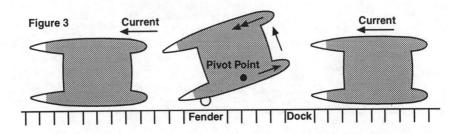

Pivot Point

Fender   Dock

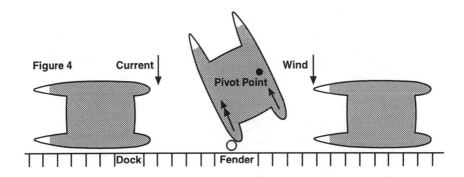

Figure 4   Current   Pivot Point   Wind

Dock   Fender

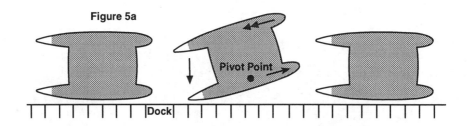

Figure 5a   Pivot Point

Dock

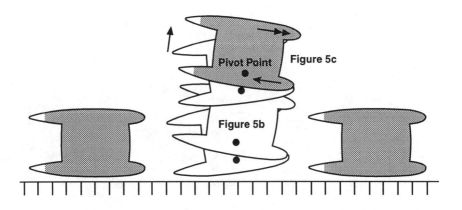

Pivot Point   Figure 5c

Figure 5b

the stern is clear of the dock, continue enough reverse thrust on the starboard engine to assure the bows continuing to turn into the current but not so much that you force the boat backwards. Often, you can just slip the engine out of gear at this point so as to lessen the aft-pulling force. It's a judgement call depending upon the strength of the current or wind.

As soon as the port bow passes clear of the boat ahead of it, give more power on the port engine and less on the starboard to pivot the boat into facing directly up current. Keep pivoting until you are facing into the current to make sure you do not get swept into the boat ahead of you. The figure shows the final position when both engines are in forward but the port (lee-ward) engine is using greater thrust to compensate for the current and bias the boat towards the favored side.

Figure 5. 5a through 5c show a proce-dure to leave a crowded dock when there is no significant wind or current. This is a skill to practice at every opportunity. It is possible to do this maneuver without any fenders against the dock as you literally "walk" the boat into or out of a tight slip sideways. As shown in the diagram, first tip the bows in towards the dock to pull the stern out. Then reverse the engine direc-tions to pull the bows away. If your first try pulled the stern far enough away so you can clear the dock, just keep turning until clear. Otherwise, repeat the first procedure to "walk" the boat out a little farther.

Single screw multihulls

Most cruising multihull single-screw vessels are either outboard powered or have a single diesel with a sonic drive leg. Both are handled the same, which is the classic single screw technique. For instance,

assume the same situation as above. You must back away from a tightly packed dock, backwards, up-current.

With a single-screw vessel you need a spring-line and a fender. You attach the spring-line from the dockside forward cleat to the dock (use a method that you can quickly detach). Place the fender forward where the bow will contact the dock. Place your engine in forward, turn your rudder hard in the direction of the dock. The force of the engine against the spring-line will push the stern out. When your boat is forty-five degrees to the dock, put the engine in reverse and back straight out against the current as you release the spring line. The current will keep you from sweeping back into the dock. Once out, steer off onto your desired course.

In general, catamarans with single-screw systems handle almost identically to any other outboard-powered boat. Since you actually turn the propulsion unit, be it outboard or sonic leg, you have the distinct advantage of being able to maneuver the boat without being underway, that is not having water flow across the rudders as required in any fixed propeller drive. This feature allows cruising catamarans to be among the most maneuverable of all cruising boats.

Powerboat wakes

Powerboat wakes are the nemesis of many sailboaters. When traveling in waterways or other marked channels, your vessel will encounter irritating wakes thrown by the parade of powerboats. Powerboat wakes represent one of the major challenges of inland waterway cruising. They are quite different from the storm-generated waves or the shallow chop and wind against the current waves of some notorious bodies of water. There are two types of wakes to contend with, those from vessels passing you and those from vessels going in the opposite direction. The antidote for these waves is very similar in both cases. Theoretically, try to take the waves at approximately a forty-five degree angle to your centerline. This will vary somewhat depending upon your type of boat.

Wakes from astern. Wakes coming from astern represent the lesser problem. You can often surf on them under complete control if you catch them right. Different powerboats throw wakes at different angles. Some come almost parallel to your boat, while others come perpendicular or directly abeam. The beam-on wakes are the most difficult to handle.

If the wakes come up from behind you at a forty-five degree angle or less, hold your course. If the waves come anywhere from forty-five degrees to beam on, hold your course to the last possible minute, when the wave is only inches from your boat, then fall off and head down until your stern is at forty-five degrees to the wave. Hold that course until the last wake-wave, then return to your original course, compensating to regain any distance lost.

In the event you do not have sufficient sea-room for this maneuver, you can steer each individual wave or you can use the standard tactic plus throttling back on the engine. By throttling back you allow the waves to pass under you without giving you any forward motion. If you are under sail, make sure to keep enough room to leeward to complete these tactics.

Most keel boats do not do this maneuver because of the possibility of pooping, broaching, or having water splash up into the cockpit. You will sometimes see them spin around and head into the wakes bow-on. This creates problems on a crowded waterway. On a multihull, if you allow the waves to hit beam-on your boat will roll, but not nearly so badly as a keel boat in similar circumstances. Multihulls tend to have a quick snapping roll.

Wakes from ahead. Wakes from boats passing in the opposite direction are a little easier to judge. Again, try for a forty-five degree angle. Experiment with closing that angle to less than forty-five degrees. The closer you can get that angle, the less under-deck slapping you will get. A little practice and you will be able to arrive at a good angle that will neither roll the boat nor slap underneath.

Hobby-horsing. After crossing a wake you will often wind up hobby-horsing. This is especially so in narrow channels where you get reverberation from the sea-walls. All boats may do this to some degree, but some catamarans are worse than others. The quick and easy way to stop this motion is to again turn forty-five degrees into the wave train. Turn quickly to break the pattern, then return to your course quickly in order not to pick the harmonics back up again.

Sailor's Multihull Guide

Color Photo Section

Center Photo: *A lovely shot of two cruising catamarans from the BareCat Charters charter fleet down in the Virgin Islands. To reserve your place aboard one of their PDQ or Privilege cruising cats, contact BareCat Charters at 1-800-296-5287, or 1-520-575-6566 outside U.S., email: XSNW38b@prodigy.com*

Upper Left: *A stern view of a Dufour Nautitech 435 sailing in light winds under main and spinnaker. For a full description of this boat see page 176.* **Upper Right:** *A picturesque view of a Dufour Nautitech 475. Note the distinctive cabintop overhang of the Nautitech line. For a full description of this boat see page 178.* **Lower Left:** *Echo, one of Dick Newick's lovely performance cruising trimarans. For a full description of this boat see page 440.* **Lower Right:** *A Peter Brady designed Saracen 13.2 meter cat lying peacefully at anchor down under. For a full description of this boat see page 372.*

Upper Left: *A reefed Catana 44 sailing comfortably and on the level in a stiff breeze. For a full description of this boat see page 154.*
Upper Right: *A stately Catana 531 pulled up to a beach somewhere in paradise. For a full description of this boat see page 158.*
Lower Left: *A Maine Cat 30 open bridgedeck catamaran, complete with a rigid hardtop protective cover, under full sail on the coast of Maine. For a full description of this boat see page 250.* **Lower Right:** *The unique, state-of-the-art Zefyr 43 trimaran from Walker Wingsail Systems. For a full description of this boat see page 362.*

Upper Left: *A well built Norseman 430 working hard at the charter trade in the Caribbean. For a full description of this boat see page 320.* **Upper Right:** *The luxurious and functional main cabin of a Lagoon 57. For a full description of this boat see page 236.* **Lower Left:** *A spacious Tasman Elite 4000 on a close reach under full sail. For a full description of this boat see page 312.* **Lower Right:** *A Seawind 1000 in a scenic anchorage on the Chesapeake. For a full description of this boat see page 302.*

Upper Left: *A Gold Coast 44C high-performance cruiser sailing effortlessly in light winds. For a full description of this boat see page 200.* **Upper Right:** *A Gold Coast 53 Daycharter catamaran providing an exhilerating ride for her guests. For a full description of this boat see page 376.* **Lower Left:** *An Atlantic 42 performance catamaran from Chris White, with its center cockpit and protected aft wheelhouse. For a full description of this boat see page 242.* **Lower Right:** *A comfortable PDQ 32 MkII cruising catamaran from PDQ Yachts. For a full description of this boat see page 280.*

Upper Left: *The stable and comfortable Endeavourcat 30 MkII cruising catamaran. For a full description of this boat see page 184.*
Upper Right: *An Endeavourcat 34 doing some downtown sailing in southern Florida. For a full description of this boat see page 186.* **Lower Left:** *A view forward from the stern of an Endeavourcat. For a full description of these boats see pages 184-189.* **Lower Right:** *A shot of the elegant interior of an Endeavourcat cruising catamaran. For a full description of these boats see pages 184-189.*

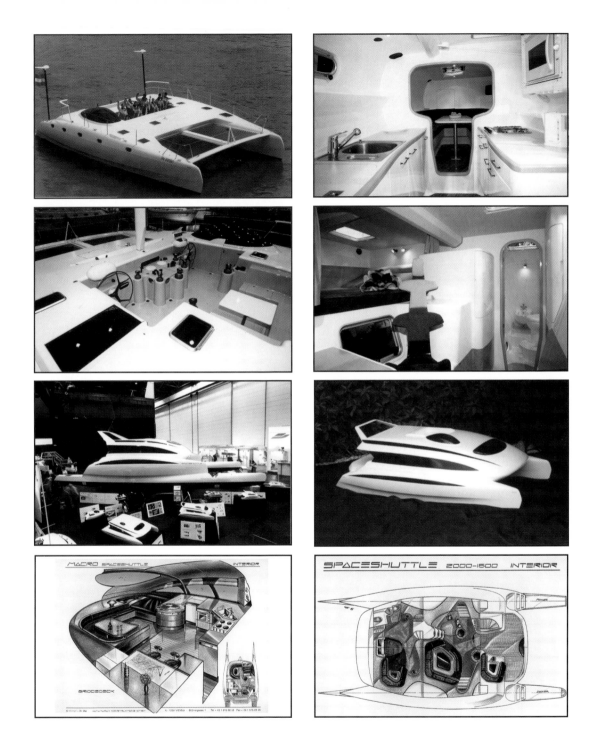

KKG Photos, Clockwise From Upper Left: *1. A crew of hearty sailors enjoying a test cruise aboard a Novara catamaran from KKG. 2. A sample shot of the elegant galley and dining area of a KKG open bridgedeck cat. 3. An example of the livable interior of catamarans from KKG. 4. The futuristic concept of the Macro Spaceshuttle cruising cat from KKG. 5. An interior layout of the state-of-the-art Spaceshuttle 1800-1300 from KKG. 6. The main cabin design of the Macro Spaceshuttle from KKG. 7. A Spaceshuttle catamaran on display with the entire KKG line of performance multihulls. 8. The sleek topsides of a KKG open bridgedeck cat.*

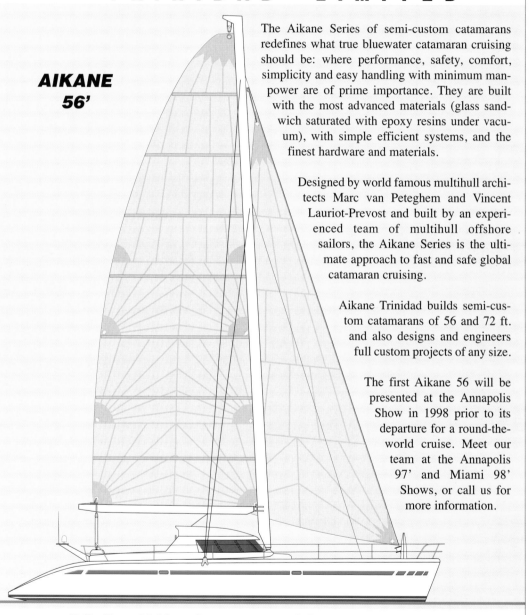

A I K A N E
T R I N I D A D • L I M I T E D

**AIKANE
56'**

The Aikane Series of semi-custom catamarans redefines what true bluewater catamaran cruising should be: where performance, safety, comfort, simplicity and easy handling with minimum manpower are of prime importance. They are built with the most advanced materials (glass sandwich saturated with epoxy resins under vacuum), with simple efficient systems, and the finest hardware and materials.

Designed by world famous multihull architects Marc van Peteghem and Vincent Lauriot-Prevost and built by an experienced team of multihull offshore sailors, the Aikane Series is the ultimate approach to fast and safe global catamaran cruising.

Aikane Trinidad builds semi-custom catamarans of 56 and 72 ft. and also designs and engineers full custom projects of any size.

The first Aikane 56 will be presented at the Annapolis Show in 1998 prior to its departure for a round-the-world cruise. Meet our team at the Annapolis 97' and Miami 98' Shows, or call us for more information.

P.O. Box 3163 • Carenage • Trinidad • West Indies
tel: 868-634-4060 • fax: 868-634-4061 • e-mail: aikane@wow.net

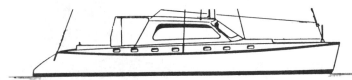
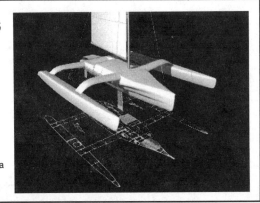

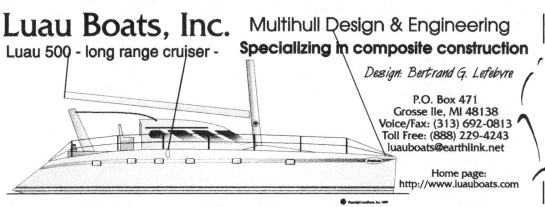
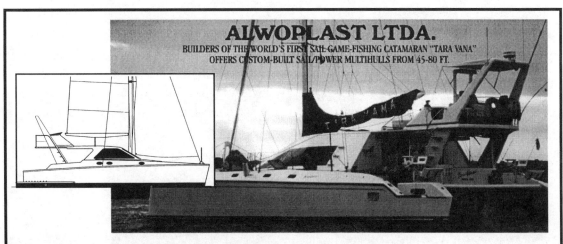

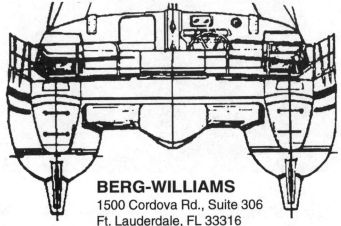

Production &
Semi-Custom
Catamarans

SAVANNAH 26

GENERAL INFORMATION

Classification   Production catamaran,
Trailerable sport cruiser

Approx. Cost   US $60-70,000

Designer   Woods Design

Builder   Advanced Cruising Designs
64 Peninsula Dr.
Hilton Head Island, SC
29926 USA
Tel: (800) 230-9532
         (803) 837-3885
Fax: (803) 837-3880
email: KSMontor@aol.com

Year Introduced   1997

Number of boats built   1 (as of Sep 97)

N. American Dealers   Buy factory direct

Other Cruising Multihulls By Builder
   None at present

KEY FEATURES

Hull & Sail Plan
- Round-bilge hull with flare and knuckle in topsides, daggerboards, reverse transoms
- Forespar AeroRig provides self-tacking, simple sail handling

Deck Layout
- Folding design has trampoline foredeck
- Central bridgedeck pod with hull access hatches, cozy U-shaped cockpit
- Kick-up rudders for beaching/trailering

Standard Accommodations
- Galley aft, table/settees convert to a double berth, hull access through deck hatches
- Port and starboard hulls have single berths fore & aft, with space for a portable toilet aft, a dressing area and sink midships, and storage under the berths

Mechanical
- Tiller steering, tiller bar with extension
- Single 9.9 hp or twin 4 hp outboards

DESCRIPTION

The Savnnah 26 is a trailerable performance catamaran with both cruising and racing capabilities. She has been designed for coastal and lake sailing by one to two couples or a family. Single handed sailing is also quite easy due to the AeroRig, which is controlled by one sheet and has a self-tacking, roller-furling jib. A round bilge hull with flare and knuckle in the topsides was selected for low resistence at speed and increased seakindliness. Other design features include a trampline netting foredeck, wide side decks, daggerboards, semi-balanced rudders that kick-up for beaching and trailering, and tiller bar steering. Interior layout has been kept simple to reduce weight and maintenance. The bridgedeck area has comfortable table seating that converts to a large double berth, plus a small galley with standing headroom. Four single berths are located in the hulls.

SPECIFICATIONS

Displacement	2,200 lbs, 1000 kg	
Standard Auxiliary	1 x 9.9 hp outboard	
Overall Length	26'0"	7.93 m
Waterline Length	25'4"	7.73 m
Bridgedeck Length	16'6"	5.03 m
Wing Deck Clearance	1'6"	0.46 m
Beam (max.)	15'4"	4.68 m
Draft (boards up)	0'10"	0.25 m
Draft (boards down)	4'4"	1.32 m
Mast Hgt. Off Water	41'6"	12.66 m

SAIL AREA

Mainsail	215 sf	20 sm
Genoa	91 sf	8 sm
Total Area	306 sf	28 sm
Spinnaker		

CAPACITY

Berths	4 sgle, 1 dble
Staterooms	none
Heads	2 (portable)
Fuel	4 gal + (portable)
Fresh Water	25 gal 95 ltr
Payload	800 lbs, 363 kg

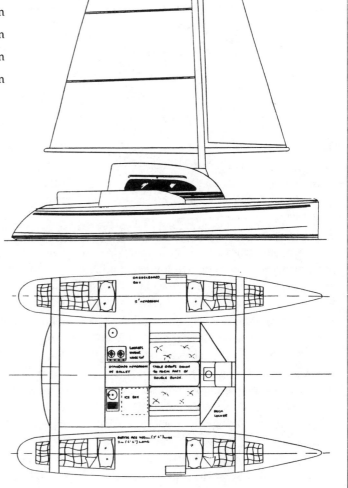

AIKANE 56

GENERAL INFORMATION

Classification Semi-custom catamaran, Cruiser/charter cruiser

Approx. Cost US $585,000

Designer Marc Van Peteghem & Vincent Lauriot-Prevost

Builder Aikane Trinidad Ltd.
Address P.O. Box 3163
Carenage, Trinidad
West Indies
Tel: (868) 634-4060
Fax: (868) 634-4061
email: aikane@wow.net

Year Introduced 1997

Number of boats built 1 in progress
(as of Sep 97)

N. American Dealers Buy factory direct

Other Cruising Multihulls By Builder
Aikane 72, Aikane 72 Day Charter, Aikane 95

KEY FEATURES

Hull & Sail Plan
- Integral keels, daggerboards, long reverse transoms with molded boarding steps
- Fractional sloop rig, fully roached main, roller-furling genoa

Deck Layout
- Trampoline forward w/ central walkway
- Cabin top overhangs for window shading
- Large cockpit with U-shaped seating
- Twin sundecks aft, dual helms forward

Standard Accommodations
- Galley up to port forward, nav area center forward, large settee/dining area to starboard
- Starboard hull has guest staterooms fore and aft with central common head
- Port hull owner's stateroom w/ berth aft, lockers/head midships, workshop forward

Mechanical
- Wheel steering, dual cockpit helms forward
- Twin inboards, access from aft decks

DESCRIPTION

The Aikane 56 is a semi-custom catamaran designed for bluewater cruising. A compromise has been struck between high performance and comfort/safety, with a hull construction of glass sandwich saturated with epoxy resins under vacuum. Boat design features include watertight bulkheads fore and aft, daggerboards, fully-battened mainsail, and fractional rig. Cockpit layout features a full U-shaped settee aft, two teak tables, two sun bathing areas, plus two separate steering stations. The spacious interior provides one hull reserved for owner use with aft double berth, en suite head and shower, and workshop with bench and storage bins. The starboard hull for guests or family has 2 additional double berth cabins. Bridgedeck saloon includes a U-shaped settee with folding table, navigation station, bar with stool, and well-equipped galley.

SPECIFICATIONS

Displacement	19,750 lbs, 9000 kg	
Standard Auxiliary	2 x 38 hp inboards	
Overall Length	56'4"	17.15 m
Waterline Length	51'4"	15.60 m
Bridgedeck Length	26'6"	8.05 m
Wing Deck Clearance	3'0"	0.90 m
Beam (max.)	26'7"	8.07 m
Draft (boards up)	4'0"	1.18 m
Draft (boards down)	8'8"	2.60 m
Mast Hgt. Off Water	73'8"	22.42 m

SAIL AREA

Mainsail	890 sf	84 sm
Genoa	585 sf	55 sm
Total Area	1475 sf	139 sm
Spinnaker	1530 sf	142 sm

CAPACITY

Berths	3 doubles	
Staterooms	3	
Heads	2	
Fuel	132 gal	500 ltr
Fresh Water	155 gal	600 ltr
Payload	variable	

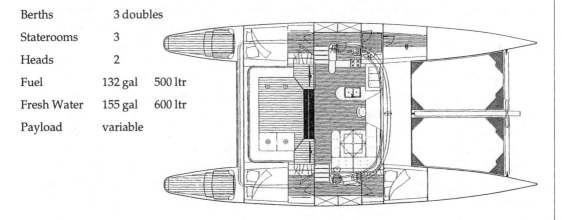

AIKANE 72

GENERAL INFORMATION

Classification   Semi-custom catamaran,
Cruiser/charter cruiser

Approx. Cost   US $1,500,000 (cruiser)
US $700,000 (day charter)

Designer   Marc Van Peteghem &
Vincent Lauriot-Prevost

Builder   Aikane Trinidad Ltd.
P.O. Box 3163 Carenage,
Trinidad, West Indies
Tel: (868) 634-4060
Fax: (868) 634-4061
email: aikane@wow.net

Year Introduced   1998

Number of boats built   none at present
(as of Sep 97)

N. American Dealers   Buy factory direct

Other Cruising Multihulls By Builder
Aikane 56, Aikane 72 Day Charter,
Aikane 95

KEY FEATURES

Hull & Sail Plan
- Integral keels, daggerboards, long reverse transoms with molded boarding steps
- Fractional sloop rig, fully roached main, roller-furling genoa

Deck Layout
- Trampoline forward w/ central walkway
- Cabin top overhangs for window shading
- Large cockpit with U-shaped seating
- Twin sundecks aft, dual helms forward

Standard Accommodations
- Galley up starboard forward, nav area center forward, living/dining areas to port
- Starboard hull has large staterooms fore and aft with two heads, storage areas
- Port hull has large staterooms fore and aft with two heads, storage areas

Mechanical
- Wheel steering, dual cockpit helms forward
- Twin inboards, access from aft decks

DESCRIPTION

The Aikane 72 is a semi-custom performance catamaran designed for either crewed charter or private ownership.   Similar to the smaller Aikane 56, a compromise has been struck between high performance and comfort/safety, with a hull construction of glass sandwich saturated with epoxy resins under vacuum. On deck are sunbathing areas and dual helm stations. The immense interior provides one hull for owner and crew, the other for guests. Aft starboard is a master suite with queen-size berth, plus bathroom with twin wash basins, shower and fully-enclosed head. Forward are the crew's quarters with double berth, head/shower, and all-weather galley. Two double berth cabins with en suite head serve as guests quarters to port. The spacious saloon features a comfortable seating area, navigation center, bar, entertainment center, and large galley.

SPECIFICATIONS

Displacement	37,300 lbs, 17,000 kg	
Standard Auxiliary	2 x 100 hp inboard	
Overall Length	72'3"	21.95 m
Waterline Length	65'7"	20.30 m
Bridgedeck Length	35'8"	10.88 m
Wing Deck Clearance	4'0"	1.20 m
Beam (max.)	33'9"	10.25 m
Draft (boards up)	4'5"	1.18 m
Draft (boards down)	9'6"	2.60 m
Mast Hgt. Off Water	92'8"	28.10 m

SAIL AREA

Mainsail	1615 sf	150 sm
Genoa	790 sf	73 sm
Total Area	2405 sf	139 sm
Spinnaker	1780 sf	165 sm

CAPACITY

Berths	4 doubles	
Staterooms	4	
Heads	4	
Fuel	264 gal	1000 ltr
Fresh Water	316 gal	1200 ltr
Payload	variable	

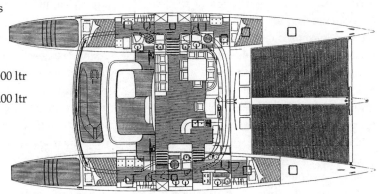

RENAISSANCE 320
MkII

GENERAL INFORMATION

Classification   Production catamaran,
Cruiser

Approx. Cost   US $125,000

Designer   American Multihulls

Builder   American Multihulls
6675 Landings Drive
Lauderhill, FL 33319
Tel: (954) 735-1133
Fax: (904) 325-0199
email:

Year Introduced   1993
(as the Renaissance 32)

Number of boats built

N. American Dealers   Buy factory direct

Other Cruising Multihulls By Builder
None at present

KEY FEATURES

Hull & Sail Plan
- Integral keels, inboard rudders, reverse transoms with molded boarding steps
- Fractional sloop rig, fully roached main, roller-furling, self-tacking jib

Deck Layout
- Trampoline forward with walkway, lockers just aft, wide side decks, good foot space
- large cockpit with hardtop and stern arch
- Cockpit lockers and storage areas

Standard Accommodations
- Galley up to port with nav area nearby, large dining area to starboard
- Starboard hull has comfortable staterooms fore and aft with central common head
- Port hull has the master stateroom with berth aft and large head forward

Mechanical
- Wheel steering, helm forward in cockpit
- Twin inboards, access from aft cabins

DESCRIPTION

The Renaissance 320 is a cruising catamaran designed to optimize comfort while still offering an exciting boat to sail. Waterline length-to-beam is ten to one and her beam greater than one half of her waterline length. The addition of low-aspect-ratio keels and a 452 square foot sail plan make the Renaissance a good choice for easy cruising due to her interior comfort, simple sail handling, and good performance. Her appearance is unique, with numerous rounded edges that give her a pleasing look: a circular trampoline netting, semi-circular cockpit and hatch opening, oval ports and curved cabin roof. Reverse transoms with molded steps and hand rails make boarding easy. Interior layout features two forward private cabins with queen size berths, a small aft double berth, spacious saloon with seating for six, and a well-equipped galley.

SPECIFICATIONS

Displacement	7,800 lbs, 3538 kg	
Standard Auxiliary	2 x 9.9 hp outboard	
Overall Length	32'0"	9.76 m
Waterline Length	29'7"	9.07 m
Bridgedeck Length	22'4"	6.81 m
Wing Deck Clearance		
Beam (max.)	16'3"	4.96 m
Draft (max.)	2'10"	0.88 m
Mast Hgt. Off Deck		
Mast Hgt. Off Water	48'0"	14.64 m

SAIL AREA

Mainsail		
Genoa		
Total Area	651 sf	61 sm
Spinnaker		

CAPACITY

Berths	2 doubles	
Staterooms	2	
Heads	1	
Fuel	56 gal	212 ltr
Fresh Water	64 gal	242 ltr
Payload		

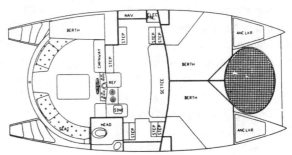

OUTREMER 40

GENERAL INFORMATION

Classification   Semi-custom catamaran, Cruiser/racer

Approx. Cost   FF 1,200,000

Designer   Gérard Danson

Builder   Atelier Outremer
Address   ZA rue de l'Industrie
34280 La Grande Motte,
France
Tel: (33) 67 56 02 63
Fax: (33) 67 56 15 47
email:

Year Introduced

Number of boats built

N. American Dealers   Buy factory direct

Other Cruising Multihulls By Builder
Outremer 50 and other cruising multihulls

KEY FEATURES

Hull & Sail Plan
- Glass epoxy hulls, daggerboards, reverse transoms with molded boarding steps
- Fractional sloop rig, fully roached main, roller-furling genoa

Deck Layout
- Trampoline forward, lockers just aft
- Sleek cabin top, large walkways
- Large cockpit with aft seating
- Tiller steering with dual helms aft

Standard Accommodations
- Galley up to port aft, nav area center to starboard, large settee/dining area forward
- Starboard hull has single berth/storage aft, head, double berth midships, 2 single for'd
- Port hull has single berth/storage aft, head, double berth midships, 2 single for'd

Mechanical
- Tiller steering, dual cockpit helms aft
- Single engine w/ twin drives, cockpit access

DESCRIPTION

The Outremer 40 is fast and efficient. She combines a competitive turn of speed with good cruising potential. Available in both cruising and day charter versions, her interior layout can be customized to the owner's liking. The most unusual aspect of the Outremer 40 is that she combines the desirable characteristics of hulls accessed separately through deck hatches with the option of accessing them through low headroom walkways from the bridgedeck saloon cabin. The result is a sleek, low profile boat with a very functional interior layout, including a comfortable bridgedeck cabin complete with galley, lounge area, and navigation center. The standard engine layout is a single inboard mounted aft in the cockpit with twin hydraulic drives. Twin inboards mounted one each hull, aft, are also available.

SPECIFICATIONS

Displacement	9,923 lbs, 4500 kg
Standard Auxiliary	1 x 30 hp inboard
Overall Length	39'8" 12.10 m
Waterline Length	39'4" 12.00 m
Bridgedeck Length	19'7" 5.97 m
Wing Deck Clearance	
Beam (max.)	22'4" 6.81 m
Draft (boards up)	1'7" 0.50 m
Draft (boards down)	6'7" 2.00 m
Mast Hgt. Off Water	49'3" 15.02 m

SAIL AREA

Mainsail	538 sf	50 sm
Genoa	538 sf	50 sm
Total Area	1076 sf	100 sm
Spinnaker	1614 sf	150 sm

CAPACITY

Berths	4-6 sgls, 2 dbls	
Staterooms	4	
Heads	2	
Fuel	26 gal	100 ltr
Fresh Water	53 gal	200 ltr
Payload		

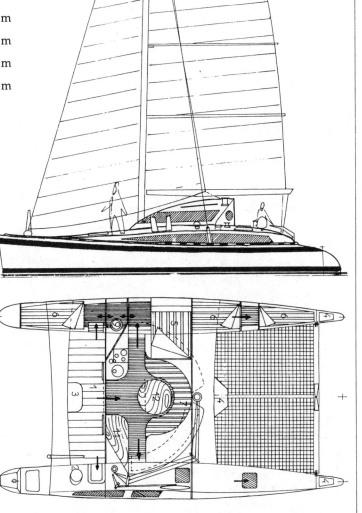

OUTREMER 50

GENERAL INFORMATION

Classification   Semi-custom catamaran,
Cruiser/racer

Approx. Cost   FF 1,200,000

Designer   Gérard Danson

Builder   Atelier Outremer
ZA rue de l'Industrie
34280 La Grande Motte,
France
Tel: (33) 67 56 02 63
Fax: (33) 67 56 15 47
email:

Year Introduced

Number of boats built

N. American Dealers   Buy factory direct

Other Cruising Multihulls By Builder
   Outremer 40, other cruising catamarans

KEY FEATURES

Hull & Sail Plan
- Glass epoxy hulls, daggerboards, reverse transoms with molded boarding steps
- Fractional sloop rig, fully roached main, roller-furling genoa

Deck Layout
- Trampoline forward, lockers just aft
- Sleek cabin top, large walkways
- Large cockpit with aft seating
- Tiller steering with dual helms aft

Standard Accommodations
- Galley up to port aft, nav area center to starboard, large settee/dining area forward
- Starboard hull has 2 heads & 3 staterooms fore, midships, and aft
- Port hull has 2 heads & 3 staterooms fore, midships, and aft

Mechanical
- Tiller steering, dual cockpit helms aft
- Twin inboards, access from aft decks

DESCRIPTION

The Outremer 50 is a racer/cruiser capable of high performance on all points of sail. The larger sistership to the Outremer 40, she brings a greater degree of luxury and elegance to cruising with her light, airy and immensely spacious interior accessed completely through the main bridgedeck cabin. An excellent boat for the charter business, the Outremer 50 has four double-berth staterooms plus two additional double berths midships on the bridgedeck accessed from each hull. She also boasts a well-equipped galley and saloon table seating for ten. The fine hull design, fractional sloop rig, daggerboards, and low cabin profile result in a sleek, fast boat that is still easily sailed by a small crew. This boat is a good choice for racing/cruising, long distance cruising, or luxury accommodations in the charter trade.

SPECIFICATIONS

Displacement	16,500 lbs, 7500 kg	
Standard Auxiliary	2 x 30 hp inboard	
Overall Length	49'6"	15.10 m
Waterline Length	49'2"	15.00 m
Bridgedeck Length	29'6"	9.00 m
Wing Deck Clearance		
Beam (max.)	25'7"	7.8 m
Draft (boards up)	2'3"	0.70 m
Draft (boards down)	9'10"	3.00 m
Mast Hgt. Off Water	65'7"	20.00 m

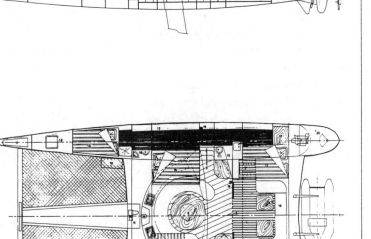

SAIL AREA

Mainsail	807 sf	75 sm
Genoa	807 sf	75 sm
Total Area	1614 sf	150 sm
Spinnaker	2152 sf	200 sm

CAPACITY

Berths	6 doubles	
Staterooms	4	
Heads	4	
Fuel	79 gal	300 ltr
Fresh Water	211 gal	800 ltr
Payload	4,400 lbs, 2000 kg	

CATALAC 900

GENERAL INFORMATION

Classification   Production catamaran,
                       Cruiser

Approx. Cost   Call for current price

Designer   J. Winterbotham, T. Lack

Builder   Blue Water Catalacs
                       160 rue Montmartre
                       75002 Paris
                       Tel: (33) 01 40 26 63 32
                       Fax: (33) 01 40 26 63 34
                       email:

Year Introduced

Number of boats built

N. American Dealers   Buy factory direct

Other Cruising Multihulls By Builder
   Solaris Sunstar 32, many other old Solaris
designs, from the Sunbeam 24 to the
Suncrest 46

KEY FEATURES

Hull & Sail Plan
- V-shaped hulls with integral keels,
- Masthead sloop rig, main with reef points,
  roller-furling genoa

Deck Layout
- Rigid foredeck with self-draining lockers
- high cabin roof with good foot space
- Large cockpit with U-shaped seating
- Twin sundecks aft, single helm forward

Standard Accommodations
- Bridgedeck has U-shaped settee with table
- Starboard hull has double berth stateroom
  forward, nav area and single berth
  midships, and head aft
- Port hull has single stateroom foreward,
  galley midships, and single stateroom aft

Mechanical
- Wheel steering, helm forward to port
- Twin inboards or single outboard engine
  options

DESCRIPTION

Originally called the Catalac 9m, Blue Water
Catalacs now produces this grand old design
as the Catalac 900. She is similar in layout to
her smaller sistership, the 8m, and by all
means an all-out cruiser with a decent turn of
speed and very livable accommodations. The
interior layout is excellent for living aboard,
particularly if one modifies the bulkhead
between the two forward cabins to create one
huge stateroom with his and her dressing
areas on either side. This is a stable, comfortable 30 foot boat, with considerable room
below and plenty of uncluttered cockpit space
above. She has leak-resistant, operable ports
and a protected steering station inset into the
main cabin forward in the cockpit. Sailing
performance is best off the wind. This boat is
an affordable choice for comfortable cruising.

SPECIFICATIONS

Displacement	8,000 lbs, 3629 kg	
Standard Auxiliary	twin inboard or outboard	
Overall Length	29'3"	8.92 m
Waterline Length	24'6"	7.47 m
Bridgedeck Length	26'8"	8.13 m
Wing Deck Clearance	3'0"	0.90 m
Beam (max.)	14'0"	4.27 m
Draft (max.)	2'6"	0.76 m
Mast Hgt. Off Deck		
Mast Hgt. Off Water	44'0"	13.42 m

SAIL AREA

Mainsail		
Genoa		
Total Area	450 sf	42 sm
Spinnaker		

CAPACITY

Berths	3 sgls, 1 dble	
Staterooms	3	
Heads	1	
Fuel	20 gal	76 ltr
Fresh Water	50 gal	190 ltr
Payload		

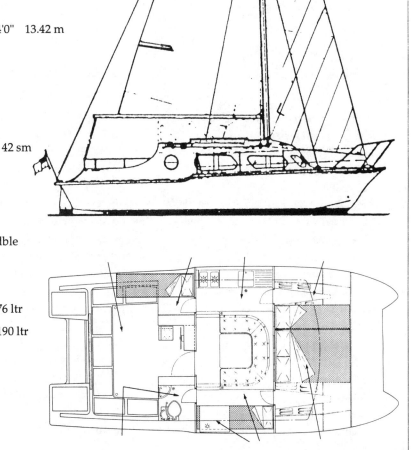

SUNSTAR 32

GENERAL INFORMATION

Classification Production catamaran,
Cruiser

Approx. Cost Call for current price

Designer Erik Lerouge

Builder Blue Water Catalacs
Address 160 rue Montmartre
75002 Paris
Tel: (33) 01 40 26 63 32
Fax: (33) 01 40 26 63 34
email:

Year Introduced

Number of boats built

N. American Dealers   Buy factory direct

Other Cruising Multihulls By Builder
   Catalac 900, many other old Solaris designs,
from the Sunbeam 24 to the Suncrest 46

KEY FEATURES

Hull & Sail Plan
- Integral keels, long reverse transoms with molded boarding steps
- Fractional sloop rig, fully roached main, roller-furling genoa

Deck Layout
- Trampoline forward, rigid deck just aft
- Cabin top overhangs for window shading
- Large cockpit with U-shaped seating
- Swim platform aft, single helm

Standard Accommodations
- Large saloon seating area with table to starboard, nav area aft to port
- Starboard hull has stateroom aft, workshop and storage midships, and head forward
- Port hull has stateroom aft, galley midships, and stateroom forward

Mechanical
- Wheel steering, single cockpit helm
- Twin inboards, access from aft staterooms

DESCRIPTION

This is one of the newer catamaran designs built by Solaris Yachts before going out of business. Blue Water Catalacs now produces this boat along with other former Solaris models. An outright cruiser, the Sunstar 32 incorporates speed and comfort in an affordable, modest-sized craft. Designed to be easily handled, she has a fractional sail plan, fully-roached and battened mainsail, roller-furling headsail, and all control lines leading to the cockpit. Cruising comfort is a priority, with a very livable layout and a touch of luxury. Two queen-size cabins aft and a smaller double forward provide ample space for a family. A four cabin plan with a reduced head compartment is available, as are other custom layouts. The navigation area is located on the bridgedeck out of the way of traffic instead of in the hull as on other cats of similar size.

SPECIFICATIONS

Displacement	8,360 lbs, 3800 kg	
Standard Auxiliary	2 x 9 hp inboard	
Overall Length	31'10"	9.72 m
Waterline Length	31'5"	9.59 m
Bridgedeck Length	20'6"	6.23 m
Wing Deck Clearance		
Beam (max.)	17'3"	5.26 m
Draft (boards up)	4'0"	1.18 m
Mast Hgt. Off Deck	39'0"	11.89 m
Mast Hgt. Off Water	47'8"	14.53 m

SAIL AREA

Mainsail	332 sf	31 sm
Genoa	208 sf	19 sm
Total Area	540 sf	50 sm
Spinnaker	660 sf	61 sm

CAPACITY

Berths	3 doubles	
Staterooms	3	
Heads	1	
Fuel	24 gal	91 ltr
Fresh Water	64 gal	242 ltr
Payload	2,500 lbs, 763 kg	

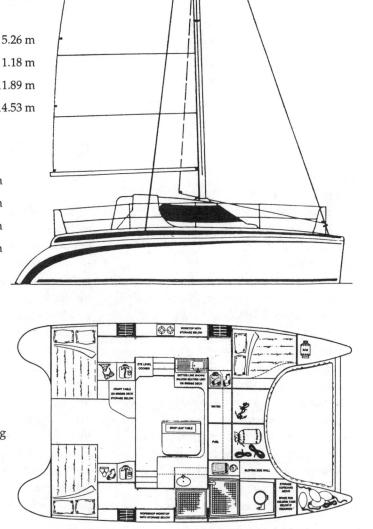

OASIS 380

GENERAL INFORMATION

Classification	Semi-custom catamaran Luxury motorsailer
Approx. Cost	AUS $250,000
Designer	Grainger Designs
Builder	Catamaran Developments 8 Pomona Terrace, Labrador, Gold Coast, Qld 4215 Australia Tel: (61) 7 5573 4581 Fax: (61) 7 5573 4581 email:

Year Introduced   1997

Number of boats built   3 (as of Sep 97)

N. American Dealers   None at present

Other Cruising Multihulls By Builder
   Oasis 380 motoryacht

KEY FEATURES

Hull & Sail Plan
- Semi-displacement hull, integral keels, reverse transoms with boarding steps
- Fractional sloop rig, fully roached main, roller-furling genoa

Deck Layout
- Rigid foredeck with locker storage
- Large cockpit ample seating, open access between the swim decks and the cockpit
- Twin sundecks aft, single or dual helms

Standard Accommodations
- Large main saloon area with L-shaped settee and dining table midships
- Starboard hull has stateroom aft, galley midships, and stateroom forward with head
- Port hull has aft stateroom, central head, and large forward stateroom

Mechanical
- Wheel steering, single/dual cockpit helms
- Twin inboards, access from cabin sole

DESCRIPTION

This new production catamaran from southern Australia offers a choice between motorsailor and motoryacht versions. As with all Grainger designs, she has good bridge deck clearance, generous payload, and efficient hull shapes for long range cruising in open ocean conditions. Designed primarily for charter operation, she is also well suited to private use as a blue water cruiser. The semi-displacement hull shape have been optimized for efficiency and comfort under motor while still allowing for respectable sailing perfor-mance. The cockpit features open transoms for easy access between the swim deck and main cockpit area, plus a raised helm position for good visibility forward. Twin helm stations may be fitted on the sailing version and an internal helm station added if desired. Standard accommodations include four double cabins.

SPECIFICATIONS

Displacement	21,723 lbs, 9874 kg	
Standard Auxiliary	2 x 27 hp inboard	
Overall Length	38'5"	11.70 m
Waterline Length	35'7"	10.85 m
Bridgedeck Length	33'0"	10.11 m
Wing Deck Clearance	2'6"	0.75 m
Beam (max.)	21'8"	6.60 m
Draft (max.)	2'9"	0.86 m
Mast Hgt. Off Deck	51'10"	15.83 m
Mast Hgt. Off Water	59'8"	18.20 m

SAIL AREA

Mainsail	544 sf	51 sm
Jib	234 sf	22 sm
Total Area	778 sf	73 sm
Reacher	406 sf	38 sm

CAPACITY

Berths	4 doubles	
Staterooms	4	
Heads	2	
Fuel	238 gal	900 ltr
Fresh Water	132 gal	500 ltr
Payload	5852 lbs, 2654 kg	

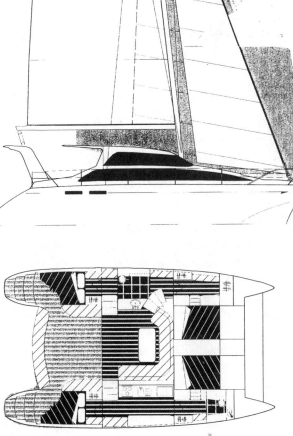

CATANA 381

GENERAL INFORMATION

Classification   Production catamaran,
                       Cruiser/racer

Approx. Cost   FF 1,345,000

Designer   Christophe Barreau

Builder   Catana
                       Zone Technique du Port,
                       66140 Canet en Roussillon
                       France
                       Tel: (33) 4 68 80 13 13
                       Fax: (33) 4 68 73 00 40
                       email:

Year Introduced   1996

Number of boats built   19   (as of Sep 97)

N. American Agent
  Navigator Yachts
  301B 53rd St., West Palm Beach, FL 33407
  Tel: (561) 845-8581 Fax: (561) 845-9027
  email: navigator@flinet.com

Other Cruising Multihulls By Builder
  Catana 411, Catana 44, Catana 471, and
Catana 531

KEY FEATURES

Hull & Sail Plan
- 10-year structural warranty on hulls using Twaron®, daggerboards, reverse transoms
- Fractional sloop rig, fully roached main, roller-furling jib

Deck Layout
- Trampoline forward with large lockers just aft, wide side decks w/ good foot space
- large cockpit with circular seating, table to port, helm center aft on raised platform

Accommodations
- Galley up to port aft, nav area to starboard aft, large circular dining area forward
- Starboard hull same as port or optional master suite with large head aft
- Port hull has large staterooms fore and aft with central common head

Mechanical
- Wheel steering, central helm aft in cockpit
- Twin inboards, access from aft decks

DESCRIPTION

Formally the Catana 38, the new 381 incorporates numerous design and layout changes. More streamlined in appearance, her standard layout now offers four large double-berth cabins fore and aft in the hulls and a large head midships each hull. The optional owner's version offers a private stateroom in the starboard hull. There's an attractive bridgedeck galley to port with double sinks and stove aft and a large counter with built-in refrigeration unit forward. The slim hulls, fractional rig, daggerboards, and light construction—familiar Catana trademarks—all result in high performance under sail. Sail handling is easy for one or two people, with all controls located in the cockpit. The raised central helm station at the stern allows for good visibility to port and starboard under sail. Comfortable yet fast, the Catana 381 is good for extended cruising or charter work.

SPECIFICATIONS

Displacement	12,362 lbs, 5600 kg	
Standard Auxiliary	2 x 20 hp inboard	
Overall Length	38'8"	11.79 m
Waterline Length	38'8"	11.79 m
Bridgedeck Length	21'0"	6.40 m
Wing Deck Clearance	2'8"	0.80 m
Beam (max.)	21'7"	6.60 m
Draft (boards up)	2'3"	0.70 m
Draft (boards down)	6'6"	2.00 m
Mast Hgt. Off Water	55'9"	17.00 m

SAIL AREA

Mainsail	441 sf	41 sm
Genoa	452 sf	42 sm
Total Area	893 sf	83 sm
Spinnaker	969 sf	90 sm

CAPACITY

Berths	3-4 doubles	
Staterooms	3-4	
Heads	2	
Fuel	53 gal	200 ltr
Fresh Water	106 gal	400 ltr
Payload	3,307 lbs, 1500 kg	

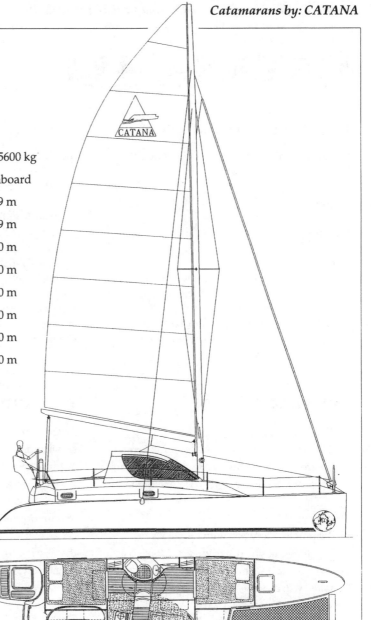

CATANA 411

GENERAL INFORMATION

Classification	Production catamaran, Cruiser/racer
Approx. Cost	FF 2,020,000
Designer	Christophe Barreau
Builder	Catana Zone Technique du Port, 66140 Canet en Roussillon France Tel: (33) 4 68 80 13 13 Fax: (33) 4 68 73 00 40 email:

Year Introduced 1995

Number of boats built 27 (as of Sep 97)

N. American Dealers
Navigator Yachts
301B 53rd St., West Palm Beach, FL 33407
Tel: (561) 845-8581 Fax: (561) 845-9027
email: navigator@flinet.com

Other Cruising Multihulls By Builder
Catana 381, Catana 44, Catana 471, and Catana 531

KEY FEATURES

Hull & Sail Plan
- 10-year structural warranty on hulls using Twaron®, daggerboards, reverse transoms
- Fractional sloop rig, fully roached main, roller-furling jib

Deck Layout
- Trampoline forward with large lockers just aft, wide side decks w/ good foot space
- large cockpit with seat to starboard and table with seating to port, dual helms aft

Accommodations
- Galley up to port forward, nav area to starboard, large circular dining area between
- Starboard hull same as port or optional master suite with large head forward
- Port hull has large staterooms fore and aft with central common head

Mechanical
- Wheel steering, dual helms aft in cockpit
- Twin inboards, access from aft decks

DESCRIPTION

Large enough to offer maximum comfort yet small enough to be single-handed, the Catana 411 is an excellent middle-range boat. As with her sisterships, she has been proven in bluewater conditions. The high performance and luxurious touches characteristic of all Catana yachts make this a very livable boat that is exciting to sail. Designed for both private ownership and the charter trade, she can sleep up to eight people or provide ample space for a large family. Both cockpit and saloon seating can accommodate a large group. Similar to the Catana 381, the optional owner's version provides private, spacious starboard hull accommodations for the owner; the port hull is configured for guests, with two cabins (fore and aft) and a common central head. Handling under sail or power is easy with all sail and daggerboard controls leading to the cockpit.

SPECIFICATIONS

Displacement	14,569 lbs, 6600 kg	
Standard Auxiliary	2 x 30 hp inboard	
Overall Length	40'8"	12.40 m
Waterline Length	40'4"	12.30 m
Bridgedeck Length	24'8"	7.50 m
Wing Deck Clearance	2'8"	0.80 m
Beam (max.)	22'3"	6.80 m
Draft (boards up)	2'3"	0.70 m
Draft (boards down)	6'1"	2.10 m
Mast Hgt. Off Water	59'1	18.00 m

SAIL AREA

Mainsail	527 sf	49 sm
Genoa	495 sf	46 sm
Total Area	1022 sf	95 sm
Spinnaker	1076 sf	100 sm

CAPACITY

Berths	3-4 doubles
Staterooms	4
Heads	2
Fuel	106 gal 400 ltr
Fresh Water	106 gal 400 ltr
Payload	4,409 lbs, 2002 kg

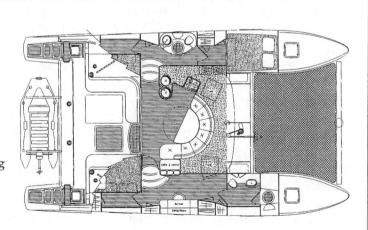

CATANA 44

GENERAL INFORMATION

Classification   Production catamaran, Cruiser/racer

Approx. Cost   FF 2,515,000

Designer   Lock Crowther/C. Barreau

Builder   Catana
Zone Technique du Port,
66140 Canet en Roussillon
France
Tel: (33) 4 68 80 13 13
Fax: (33) 4 68 73 00 40
email:

Year Introduced   1993

Number of boats built   17 (as of Sep 97)

N. American Dealers
Navigator Yachts
301B 53rd St., West Palm Beach, FL 33407
Tel: (561) 845-8581 Fax: (561) 845-9027
email: navigator@flinet.com

Other Cruising Multihulls By Builder
Catana 381, Catana 411, Catana 471, and Catana 531

KEY FEATURES

Hull & Sail Plan
- 10-year structural warranty on hulls using Twaron®, daggerboards, reverse transoms
- Fractional sloop rig, fully roached main, roller-furling jib

Deck Layout
- Trampoline forward with large lockers just aft, wide side decks
- large cockpit with seat to starboard and table with seating to port, dual helms aft

Accommodations
- Galley up to port aft, nav area to starboard forward, large u-shaped dining forward
- Starboard hull same as port or optional master suite with large head forward
- Port hull has large staterooms fore and aft, each with its own private head

Mechanical
- Wheel steering, dual helms aft in cockpit
- Twin inboards, access from aft decks

DESCRIPTION

The Catana 44 incorporates all the speed, comfort and stability so characteristic of all cruising boats designed by Lock Crowther. Performance is excellent without sacrificing a high degree of liveaboard comfort, including standing headroom throughout the interior, well-appointed bridgedeck area and four spacious private double staterooms with adjoining heads. This boat is well suited for the crewed or bareboat charter trade. Dual helm stations offer excellent visibility. Boat handling is simple with cockpit controls and twin diesel engines. The spacious semi-circular saloon seating incorporates a panoramic view and easy access from the bridgedeck galley. As with all the Catana boats, an owner's version reserves the starboard hull for private use (large stateroom, work or storage area, and head), leaving the port hull for guests.

SPECIFICATIONS

Displacement	16,777 lbs, 7600 kg	
Standard Auxiliary	2 x 40 hp inboard	
Overall Length	44'0"	13.40 m
Waterline Length	43'4"	13.20 m
Bridgedeck Length	25'0"	7.63 m
Wing Deck Clearance	2'9"	0.84 m
Beam (max.)	23'0"	7.00 m
Draft (boards up)	2'7"	0.80 m
Draft (boards down)	7'2"	2.20 m
Mast Hgt. Off Water	63'11"	19.50 m

SAIL AREA

Mainsail	570 sf	53 sm
Genoa	592 sf	55 sm
Total Area	1162 sf	108 sm
Spinnaker	1292 sf	120 sm

CAPACITY

Berths	3-4 dbls, 0-2 sgls
Staterooms	3-4
Heads	3-4
Fuel	106 gal 400 ltr
Fresh Water	106 gal 400 ltr
Payload	6,614 lbs, 3002 kg

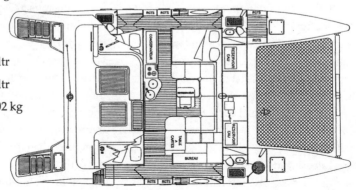

CATANA 471

GENERAL INFORMATION

Classification   Production catamaran,
Cruiser/racer

Approx. Cost   FF 2,835,000

Designer   Christophe Barreau

Builder   Catana
Zone Technique du Port,
66140 Canet en Roussillon
France
Tel: (33) 4 68 80 13 13
Fax: (33) 4 68 73 00 40
email:

Year Introduced   1997

Number of boats built   8   (as of Sep 97)

N. American Dealers
Navigator Yachts
301B 53rd St., West Palm Beach, FL 33407
Tel: (561) 845-8581 Fax: (561) 845-9027
email: navigator@flinet.com

Other Cruising Multihulls By Builder
Catana 411, Catana 44, Catana 471, and
Catana 531

KEY FEATURES

Hull & Sail Plan
- 10-year structural warranty on hulls using Twaron®, daggerboards, reverse transoms
- Fractional sloop rig, fully roached main, roller-furling jib

Deck Layout
- Trampoline forward with large lockers just aft, wide side decks w/ good foot space
- large cockpit with ample seating, table to port, dual helm stations aft

Accommodations
- Galley up to port aft, nav area to starboard aft, large circular dining area forward
- Starboard hull has master suite with berth aft, storage midships, large head forward
- Port hull has large staterooms fore and aft with central common head

Mechanical
- Wheel steering, dual helms aft in cockpit
- Twin inboards, access from aft decks

DESCRIPTION

The new Catana 471 replaces the former Catana 48 and continues the Catana tradition of speed, comfort and stability. Similar to the 44, she can accommodate up to eight people with her four double-berth staterooms and four separate head compartments. Bridgedeck layout is elegant, with comfortable semi-circular saloon seating for up to twelve people, an all around panoramic view, and a spacious galley. Extra-large ports in both hulls guarantee excellent ventilation throughout the boat. The optional owner's version provides an aft stateroom with bed, settee, vanity, desk and vast storage, plus a huge forward head with separate shower, wash basin and WC compartments. On deck there is plenty of room for sunbathing or lounging, ideal for charter guests. All sail, daggerboard and engine controls lead to the cockpit for out-of-the-way handling.

SPECIFICATIONS

Displacement	19,646 lbs, 8900 kg	
Standard Auxiliary	2 x 40 hp inboard	
Overall Length	46'1"	14.30 m
Waterline Length	45'3"	13.80 m
Bridgedeck Length	25'5"	7.75 m
Wing Deck Clearance	2'11"	0.90 m
Beam (max.)	24'7"	7.50 m
Draft (boards up)	2'7"	0.80 m
Draft (boards down)	7'6"	2.30 m
Mast Hgt. Off Water	63'1"	19.50 m

SAIL AREA

Mainsail	807 sf	75sm
Genoa	538 sf	50 sm
Total Area	1345 sf	125 sm
Spinnaker	1507 sf	140 sm

CAPACITY

Berths	3 doubles
Staterooms	3
Heads	3
Fuel	104gal 400 ltr
Fresh Water	156 gal 600 ltr
Payload	7,716 lbs, 3503 kg

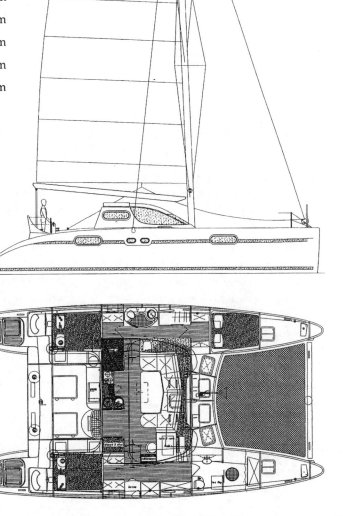

CATANA 531

GENERAL INFORMATION

Classification   Production catamaran,
                      Luxury cruiser

Approx. Cost   FF 3,750,000

Designer   Christophe Barreau

Builder   Catana
                      Zone Technique du Port,
                      66140 Canet en Roussillon
                      France
                      Tel: (33) 4 68 80 13 13
                      Fax: (33) 4 68 73 00 40
                      email:

Year Introduced   1994

Number of boats built   5   (as of Sep 97)

N. American Dealers
  Navigator Yachts
  301B 53rd St., West Palm Beach, FL 33407
  Tel: (561) 845-8581 Fax: (561) 845-9027
  email: navigator@flinet.com

Other Cruising Multihulls By Builder
  Catana 381, Catana 411, Catana 44, and
Catana 471

KEY FEATURES

Hull & Sail Plan
- 10-year structural warranty on hulls using Twaron®, daggerboards, reverse transoms
- Fractional sloop rig, fully roached main, roller-furling jib

Deck Layout
- Trampoline forward with lockers, sun area just aft, wide side decks w/ good foot space
- large cockpit with circular seating, table to port, dual helms aft in cockpit

Accommodations
- Galley up to port aft, nav area to starboard aft, dual circular seating areas forward
- Starboard hull 3 staterooms with twins singles forward and heads fore and aft
- Port hull has large staterooms fore and aft each with private heads

Mechanical
- Wheel steering, dual helms aft in cockpit
- Twin inboards, access from aft decks

DESCRIPTION

The new Catana 531 is the largest and most luxurious of the popular Catana line of catamarans. Ideal for the charter trade, she offers supreme comfort for up to eight people without sacrificing any of the speed and stability of the smaller Catana boats. The familiar fractional rig, stream-lined hull configuration and ease of sailing all guarantee a high level of performance. Saloon seating is enormous, with a panoramic view and easy access to the bridgedeck galley and bar. All four staterooms, two in each hull, come with their own private head and shower compartment. The optional owner's version incorporates the usual starboard hull reserved for the owner, with the port hull laid out for guests in two double cabins and private heads. Like the Catana 471, this boat is best suited for the crewed charter trade or luxury private ownership.

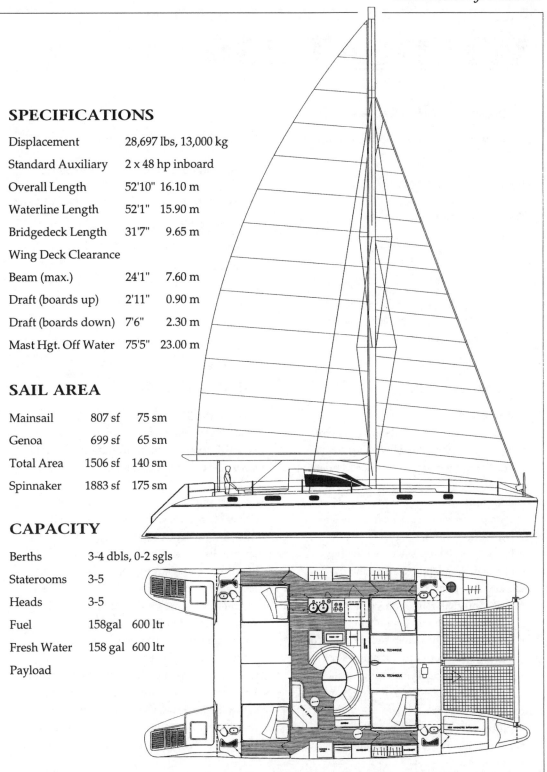

SPECIFICATIONS

Displacement	28,697 lbs, 13,000 kg	
Standard Auxiliary	2 x 48 hp inboard	
Overall Length	52'10"	16.10 m
Waterline Length	52'1"	15.90 m
Bridgedeck Length	31'7"	9.65 m
Wing Deck Clearance		
Beam (max.)	24'1"	7.60 m
Draft (boards up)	2'11"	0.90 m
Draft (boards down)	7'6"	2.30 m
Mast Hgt. Off Water	75'5"	23.00 m

SAIL AREA

Mainsail	807 sf	75 sm
Genoa	699 sf	65 sm
Total Area	1506 sf	140 sm
Spinnaker	1883 sf	175 sm

CAPACITY

Berths	3-4 dbls, 0-2 sgls	
Staterooms	3-5	
Heads	3-5	
Fuel	158gal	600 ltr
Fresh Water	158 gal	600 ltr
Payload		

WILDCAT 350

GENERAL INFORMATION

Classification	Production catamaran, Cruiser/racer
Approx. Cost	US $135,000
Designer	Jeff Schionning
Builder	Prime Boating
Agent	Charter Cats SA
	P.O. Box 5590
	Durban 4000, S. Africa
	Tel: (27) 31 304-2994
	Fax: (27) 31 301-6600
	email: kims@iafrica.com

Year Introduced	1996
Number of boats built	3 (as of Sep 97)
N. American Dealers	Buy factory direct

Other Cruising Multihulls By Builder
Wildcat 930, Royal Cape Cat 45

KEY FEATURES

Hull & Sail Plan
- Integral keels or daggerboards, reverse transoms with molded boarding steps
- Fractional sloop rig, fully roached main, roller-furling genoa

Deck Layout
- Trampoline forward w/ central walkway with locker storage just aft.
- Large cockpit with U-shaped seating
- Single helm midships, arch at stern

Standard Accommodations
- Galley up center aft or down in starboard hull, large saloon area with table forward
- Starboard hull has double staterooms fore and aft, galley option, and single forward
- Port hull has double stateroom or head aft, double and single berth or storage forward

Mechanical
- Wheel steering, single cockpit helm aft
- Twin outboards, inboards optional

DESCRIPTION

The Wildcat 350 is the latest in a range of modern catamarans designed by Schionning Boats of Australia, built in South Africa, and marketed by International Yacht Brokers. Wildcats are reknowned for their safety, comfort and speed, making them an excellent choice for charter work or private ownership. Boat design features fast, easily-driven hulls, tough balsa core construction, a simply handled rig, and large cockpit with built-in dive platform. A range of options are offered for interior layout, with the possibility of sleeping up to ten. Most popular is the "heads up front" option, allowing for complete cabin privacy while including a spacious shower, head and sink for everyone. The 2m headroom through both hulls and saloon makes this a very liveable boat. Auxiliary power options include one or two outboards (in a covered bay) or two inboards.

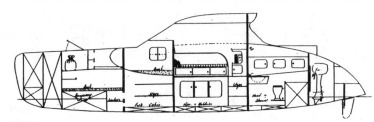

SPECIFICATIONS

Displacement	9,922 lbs, 4500 kg	
Standard Auxiliary	2 x 8 hp outboard	
Overall Length	34'5"	10.50 m
Waterline Length	32'10"	10.00 m
Bridgedeck Length	20'0"	6.12 m
Wing Deck Clearance	2'7"	0.80 m
Beam (max.)	26'7"	8.07 m
Draft (fixed keels)	2'7"	0.88 m
Mast Hgt. Off Deck	43'5"	13.25 m
Mast Hgt. Off Water	55'9"	17.00 m

SAIL AREA

Mainsail	527 sf	49 sm
Genoa	280 sf	26 sm
Total Area	807 sf	75 sm
Spinnaker	785 sf	73 sm

CAPACITY

Berths	3-4 dbls, 0-2 sgls	
Staterooms	3-4	
Heads	2	
Fuel	53 gal	200 ltr
Fresh Water	106 gal	400 ltr
Payload		

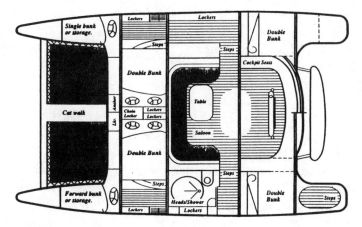

ROYAL CAPE 45

GENERAL INFORMATION

Classification   Production catamaran,
Luxury cruiser

Approx. Cost   US $218,000

Designer   Kim & Eric Schoeman

Builder   Prime Boating
Agent   Charter Cats SA
P.O. Box 5590
Durban 4000, S. Africa
Tel: (27) 31 304-2994
Fax: (27) 31 301-6600
email: kims@iafrica.com

Year Introduced   1994

Number of boats built   12 (as of Sep 97)

N. American Dealers   Buy factory direct

Other Cruising Multihulls By Builder
  Wildcat 930, Wildcat 350

KEY FEATURES

Hull & Sail Plan
- Integral keels, reverse transoms, molded boarding steps
- Fractional sloop rig, fully roached main, roller-furling genoa

Deck Layout
- Small trampoline area forward
- Raised forward cabin, ample foot space
- Expansive cockpit with U-shaped seating
- Swimdeck aft, helm forward

Standard Accommodations
- Huge galley up to port forward, large settee/dining area to starboard
- Starboard hull has 3 double staterooms (2 for guests and one for crew), 2-3 heads
- Port hull has 3 double staterooms (2 for guests and one for crew), 2-3 heads

Mechanical
- Wheel steering, cockpit helms forward
- Twin inboards, access from aft deck

DESCRIPTION

The Royal Cape Cat is a comfortable cruising catamaran, ideal for charter or private ownership. Design and sail plan have been selected for comfort, stability and ease of sailing. Abovedecks feature a spacious cockpit, aft swim deck, and molded transom steps for easy boarding. Forward of the cabin is a sunning platform, plus two trampoline areas divided by a gang-plank for providing solid footing when anchoring or doing foredeck work. Accommodations include two doubles aft, two forward of the saloon on the bridgedeck, and two in the bows, all en suite, allowing plenty of space for eight guests and two crew members. The saloon offers full guest seating at the dining table, an entertainment center, and bridgedeck galley. Spacious and ideally suited for charter work, the large galley has stove, sink, refrigerator/freezer, plus ample counter & storage space.

SPECIFICATIONS

Displacement	17,637 lbs, 8,000 kg	
Standard Auxiliary	2 x 18 hp inboard	
Overall Length	45'0"	13.72 m
Waterline Length	42'0"	12.80 m
Bridgedeck Length	34'5"	10.50 m
Wing Deck Clearance	2'9"	0.85 m
Beam (max.)	25'6"	8.38 m
Draft (max)	3'0"	0.91 m
Mast Hgt Off Deck		
Mast Hgt. Off Water	62'4"	19.01 m

SAIL AREA

Mainsail	581 sf	54 sm
Geno	689 sf	64 sm
Total Area	1270 sf	118 sm
Spinnaker	1400 sf	130 sm

CAPACITY

Berths	6 doubles	
Staterooms	6	
Heads	6	
Fuel	264 gal	1000 ltr
Fresh Water	396 gal	1500 ltr
Payload		

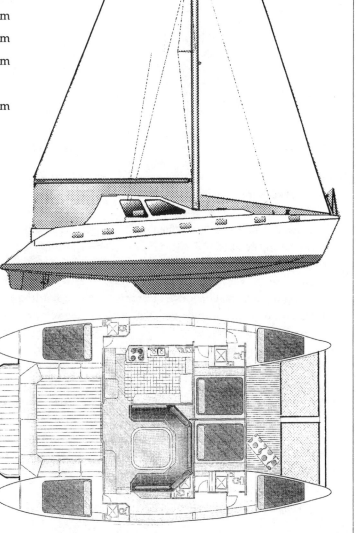

CHINCOGAN 520

GENERAL INFORMATION

Classification   Semi-custom catamaran, Cruiser/racer

Approx. Cost   AUS $355,000

Designer   Tony Grainger

Builder   Chincogan Catamarans
Lot 20 Hayley Place
Murwillumbah NSW 2484
Australia
Tel: (61) 66 72 6377
Fax: (61) 66 72 6377
email:

Year Introduced   1997

Number of boats built   1 (as of Sep 97)

N. American Dealers   Buy factory direct

Other Cruising Multihulls By Builder
Chincogan 40

KEY FEATURES

Hull & Sail Plan
- Integral keels, reverse transoms with molded boarding steps
- Fractional sloop rig, fully roached main, roller-furling genoa

Deck Layout
- Trampoline forward with central walkway, wide rigid foredeck with lockers just aft
- Large cockpit with hardtop overhang, stern arch, single or dual helms

Standard Accommodations
- Galley up to starboard, lounge/table area to port, nav station and bar aft
- Starboard hull has large staterooms fore & aft, common head midships
- Port hull large staterooms fore & aft, with common head midships

Mechanical
- Wheel steering, single/dual helms forward
- Twin inboards, access from aft decks

DESCRIPTION

The Chincogan 520 is a newly designed, high performance ocean cruiser/racer. Featuring the latest in hull design and construction technology, she is built in foam/glass composite. Standard sailplan is a fractional sloop rig with fully battened main and roller-furling jib. Mast height, however, can vary according to which of the various size rigs is selected. Fuel and water carrying capacity can also be tailored to suit the individual owner. Interior layout is spacious, with a fully-equipped galley, bar, navigation station, and saloon seating located on the bridgedeck. Each hull includes two double-berth cabins with a shared head. Designed for offshore cruising, the Chincogan 520 continues the Grainger tradition of offering a fast, comfortable cruiser.

SPECIFICATIONS

Displacement	19,448 lbs, 8840 kg	
Standard Auxiliary	1 x 45 hp outboard	
Overall Length	51'7"	15.75 m
Waterline Length	48'2"	14.68 m
Bridgedeck Length	28'9"	8.76 m
Wing Deck Clearance	3'0"	0.92 m
Beam (max.)	24'0"	7.32 m
Draft (max.)	3'7"	1.10 m
Mast Hgt. Off Deck	64'0"	19.48 m
Mast Hgt. Off Water	72'0"	22.00 m

SAIL AREA

Mainsail	677 sf	63 sm
Genoa	420 sf	39 sm
Total Area	1097 sf	102 sm
Spinnaker		

CAPACITY

Berths	4 doubles
Staterooms	4
Heads	2
Fuel	variable
Fresh Water	variable
Payload	6,334 lbs, 2880 kg

CONSER 47

GENERAL INFORMATION

Classification   Semi-custom catamaran, Cruiser/racer

Approx. Cost   US $300,000

Designer   John Conser

Builder   Conser Catamaran
1995 Irvine Ave.
Costa Mesa, CA 92627 USA
Tel: (714) 645-0272
Fax: (714) 645-0272
email:

Year Introduced   1992

Number of boats built   4 (as of Sep 97)

N. American Dealers   Buy factory direct

Other Cruising Multihulls By Builder
None at present

KEY FEATURES

Hull & Sail Plan
- Triaxial cloth/foam core/resin hulls with daggerboards, reverse transoms, buoyancy
- Fractional sloop rig, fully roached main, self-tending jib

Deck Layout
- Trampoline forward with central walkway and integral swim ladder, lockers aft
- Large cockpit with T-shaped seating
- Good visibility, dual helms forward

Standard Accommodations
- Galley up to port aft, nav area to starboard
- Hull access from cockpit only
- Starboard hull has head aft, access to cockpit, double berth with storage forward
- Port hull layout is the same as starboard, with a head aft and large double forward

Mechanical
- Wheel steering, dual cockpit helms forward
- Single outboard accessed from cockpit

DESCRIPTION

The Conser 47 is designed as a comfortable cruising/racing catamaran, equally suited to relaxed family outings or exciting day sails. Blending high performance characteristics with liveaboard comfort, she sails like a race boat, yet carries amenities suitable for serious offshore cruising. The Conser 47 is capable of averaging 12-15 knots under sail, even when loaded with cruising gear. The powerful fractional rig with fully battened mainsail and jib is simple enough to be handled by one or two people. Deck and cockpit space are immense, while the three interior cabins, accessed separately, comfortably cater to several couples. Dual steering consoles to port and starboard in the cockpit offer good visibility and protection under sail. The main saloon cabin has a table with settees forward, a galley to port and navigation area to starboard.

SPECIFICATIONS

Displacement	10,000 lbs, 4536 kg	
Standard Auxiliary	1 x 45 hp outboard	
Overall Length	47'0"	14.34 m
Waterline Length	45'0"	13.73 m
Bridgedeck Length	20'0"	6.10 m
Wing Deck Clearance	2'6"	0.79 m
Beam (max.)	24'0"	7.32 m
Draft (boards up)	1'8"	0.52 m
Draft (boards down)	6'8"	2.04 m
Mast Hgt. Off Water	58'0"	17.70 m

SAIL AREA

Mainsail	650 sf	61 sm
Genoa	325 sf	30 sm
Total Area	975 sf	91 sm
Spinnaker	1565 sf	146 sm

CAPACITY

Berths	2 doubles	
Staterooms	2	
Heads	2	
Fuel	30 gal	114 ltr
Fresh Water	90 gal	341 ltr
Payload	3,000 lbs, 1360 kg	

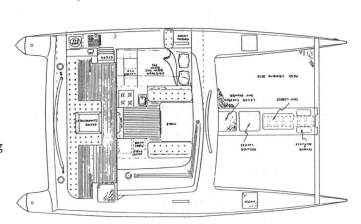

CORSAIR 3600

GENERAL INFORMATION

Classification   Semi-custom catamaran, Cruiser/racer

Approx. Cost   Call for current price

Designer   OSTAC Yachts

Builder   Corsair Marine
150 Reed Court
Chula Vista, CA 91911 USA
Tel: (619) 585-3005
Fax: (714) 585-3092
email: corsair33@aol.com

Year Introduced   1997

Number of boats built   1 (as of Sep 97)

N. American Dealers
Contact Corsair Marine

Other Cruising Multihulls By Builder
F-24, F-28, & F-31 trimarans

KEY FEATURES

Hull & Sail Plan
- Integral keels, reverse transoms wth molded boarding steps, buoyancy compartments
- Fractional sloop rig, fully roached main, roller-furling genoa

Deck Layout
- Trampoline forward with central walkway, lockers aft, lounge area seats four
- Comfortable cockpit with seating port & starboard, stern arch

Standard Accommodations
- Bridgedeck has U-shaped seating with table forward, access to heads and hulls
- Starboard hull has stateroom/shower aft, galley midships, large sail locker forward
- Port hull has double stateroom/head aft, nav/storage midships, stateroom forward

Mechanical
- Wheel steering, helm forward in cockpit
- Twin inboards, access from aft cabins

DESCRIPTION

The Corsair 3600 is a modern cruising catamaran that nicely straddles the line between luxury and high-performance. It is designed for short-handed sailing with simple sail controls and an efficient layout. This boat, built of high-tech materials to exacting standards, is equally at home long-distance cruising or weekend racing where she will acquit herself very well. When cruising under normal conditions, speeds of 7 to 9 knots to windward and 10 to 15 knots reaching are comfortably achieved. This boat sails well to windward and she reportedly tacks with ease. Her accommodations are spacious, with three private double cabins, two complete head compartments, a large saloon seating area with panoramic views, and a large navigation area. This boat is a good choice for performance bluewater cruising.

SPECIFICATIONS

Displacement	9,400 lbs, 4270 kg	
Standard Auxiliary	2 x 18 hp inboard	
Overall Length	36'1"	11.00 m
Waterline Length	35'5"	10.80 m
Bridgedeck Length	20'0"	6.10 m
Wing Deck Clearance		
Beam (max.)	20'2"	6.15 m
Draft (max.)	2'11"	0.90 m
Mast Hgt. Off Deck	47'0"	14.34 m
Mast Hgt. Off Water	55'5"	16.93 m

SAIL AREA

Mainsail	456 sf	42 sm
Genoa	383 sf	36 sm
Total Area	839 sf	78 sm
Reacher	992 sf	92 sm

CAPACITY

Berths	3 doubles	
Staterooms	3	
Heads	1-2	
Fuel	40 gal	150 ltr
Fresh Water	132 gal	500 ltr
Payload		

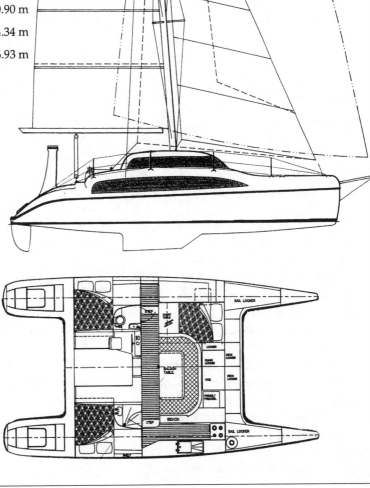

SHUTTLECAT 31

GENERAL INFORMATION

Classification	Semi-custom catamaran, Cruiser/racer
Approx. Cost	US $169,000 (finished boat)
Designer	John Shuttleworth
Builder:	Dale Schneider, Inc. 7000 Barrancas Avenue Bokeelia, FL 33922 USA Tel: (941) 283-1653 Fax: (941) 283-0426 email:

Year Introduced

Number of boats built   Many of these designs have been built worldwide

N. American Dealers   Buy factory direct

Other Cruising Multihulls By Builder
Shuttlecat 40 Open & Bridgedeck versions, other custom multihulls

KEY FEATURES

Hull & Sail Plan
- hulls have flared design for smaller beam at waterline than above; daggerboards
- Fractional sloop rig, raked wing mast, fully roached main, self-tacking jib

Deck Layout
- Trampoline forward with open bridgedeck just aft, sleek cabin roof lines
- Large cockpit with circular seating all around a central cockpit table
- Ample bridgedeck locker and storage space

Standard Accommodations
- Open bridgedeck design; optional soft cover creates weathertight bridgedeck "cabin".
- Starboard hull has comfortable staterooms fore and aft with central common head
- Port hull has large dinette aft, galley midships, and stateroom forward

Mechanical
- Rudders connected to tillers; wheel opt'l.
- Single outboard engine in cockpit well

DESCRIPTION

The Shuttlecat 31 is a fast cruising catamaran that is very similar to another successful Shuttleworth production cat, the Tektron 35. She represents one of many designs originating from Shuttleworth's Spectrum 42. The unusual yet well-proven flared hull form creates a small waterline imprint for speed and a wider form above waterline for increased interior accommodations and additional buoyancy when reaching. Bridgedeck accommodations have been eliminated, although a bimini with roll-down curtains provides privacy in port. Dale Schneider offers the boat finished or in various stages of construction for the amateur builder. Her sistership, the Shuttlecat 40, is available from Dale Schneider in open bridgedeck and full bridgedeck versions.

SPECIFICATIONS

Displacement	4,840 lbs, 2200 kg	
Standard Auxiliary	1 or 2 outboards	
Overall Length	31'0"	9.45 m
Waterline Length	29'1"	8.87 m
Bridgedeck Length	16'9"	5.11 m
Wing Deck Clearance	1'0"	0.92 m
Beam (max.)	22'3"	6.78 m
Draft (boards up)	1'4"	0.41 m
Draft (boards down)		
Mast Hgt. Off Water	52'0"	15.86 m

SAIL AREA

Wing mast	54 sf	5 sm
Mainsail	384 sf	36 sm
Jib	209 sf	19 sm
Total Area	647 sf	60 sm
Spinnaker	variable	

CAPACITY

Berths	3-4 doubles
Staterooms	3
Heads	1
Fuel	variable
Fresh Water	variable
Payload	2,750 lbs, 1250 kg

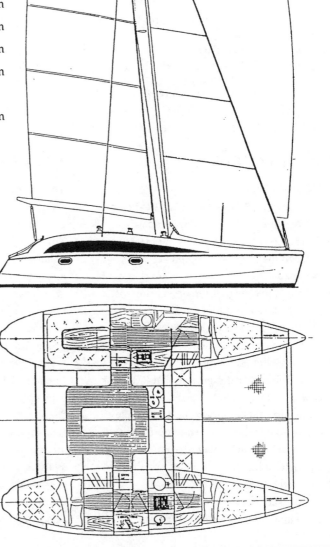

SHUTTLECAT 40

GENERAL INFORMATION

Classification   Semi-custom catamaran,
Cruiser/racer

Approx. Cost   US $325,000 (finished boat)

Designer   John Shuttleworth

Builder: Dale Schneider, Inc.

Address: 7000 Barrancas
Bokeelia, FL 33922 USA
Tel: (941) 283-1653
Fax: (941) 283-0426
email:

Year Introduced

Number of boats built   Many of these
designs have been
built worldwide

N. American Dealers   Buy factory direct

Other Cruising Multihulls By Builder
Shuttlecat 40 Bridgedeck version,
Shuttlecat 31, custom multihulls

KEY FEATURES

Hull & Sail Plan
- hulls have flared design for smaller beam at waterline than above; daggerboards
- Fractional sloop rig, raked wing mast, fully roached main, self-tacking jib

Deck Layout
- Trampoline forward with open bridgedeck just aft, sleek cabin roof lines
- Circular cockpit seating w/central table
- Ample bridgedeck locker and storage space

Standard Accommodations
- Open bridgedeck design; optional soft cover creates weathertight bridgedeck "cabin"
- Starboard hull has large dinette aft, galley and head midships, and stateroom forward
- Port hull has stateroom aft, head, nav area and berth midships, and stateroom forward

Mechanical
- Rudders connected to tillers; wheel opt'l
- Twin inboards, access from aft berths

DESCRIPTION

The Shuttlecat 40 is a larger version of the Shuttlecat 31. A high-performance cruising catamaran, she features the same unusual hull form that typifies Shuttleworth designs: a small waterline for speed and wider form above the waterline for additional buoyancy and increased interior space. Like the Shuttlecat 31, the 40 is available in kit form, intended for use by skilled amateur builders. In kit form the hulls and decks are already made, with the owner making the finishing touches. A full set of drawings comes with each kit. Accommodations include two sizeable hull areas with standing headroom, twin forward double-berth staterooms, one aft double, head and galley. Two versions are available, one with an open bridgedeck design and starboard hull saloon, similar to the Shuttlecat 31, and the other a bridgedeck saloon version.

SPECIFICATIONS

Displacement	12,155 lbs, 5500 kg	
Standard Auxiliary	2 x 18 hp inboard	
Overall Length	40'0"	12.15 m
Waterline Length	39'0"	11.89 m
Bridgedeck Length	22'6"	6.85 m
Wing Deck Clearance	2'10"	0.88 m
Beam (max.)	27'0"	8.25 m
Draft (boards up)		
Draft (boards down)		
Mast Hgt. Off Water	60'8"	18.50 m

SAIL AREA

Mainsail		
Genoa		
Total Area	970 sf	90.1 sm
Spinnaker	variable	

CAPACITY

Berths	4-5 doubles
Staterooms	3
Heads	2
Fuel	variable
Fresh Water	variable
Payload	5,950 lbs, 2700 kg

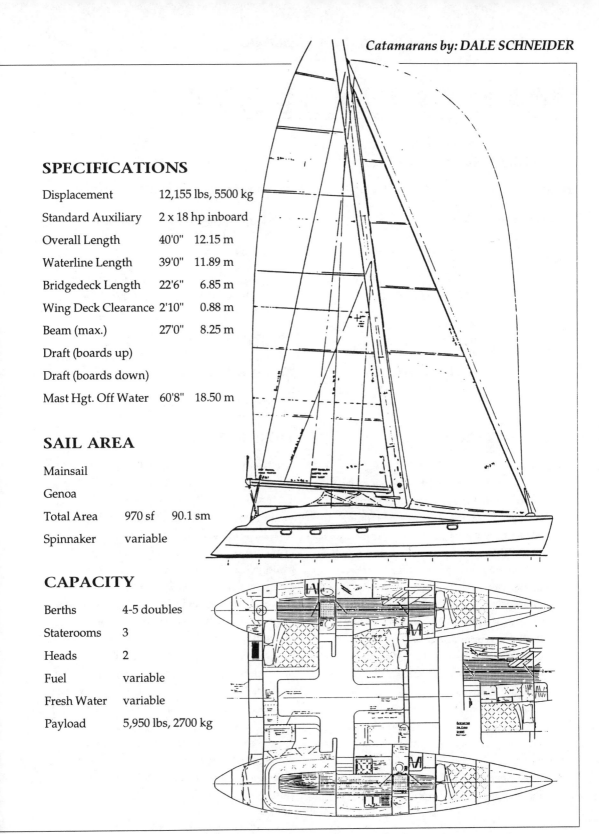

NAUTITECH 395

GENERAL INFORMATION

Designer Mortain & Mavrikios

Approx. cost US $235,000

Classification Production catamaran, Cruiser/racer

Builder Dufour & Sparks
1 rue Blaise Pascal, 17185
Périgny La Rochelle, France
Tel: (33) 05 46 30 07 60
Fax: (33) 05 46 45 46 96
email: dwalsh@abs.net

Year introduced 1996

Number of boats built 14 (as of Sep 97)

N. American Agent
Dufour USA
1 Chelsea Court, Annapolis, MD 21403
Tel: (410) 268-6417   Fax: (410) 268-9739
email: dwalsh@abs.net

Other Cruising Multihulls By Builder
Nautitech 435, Nautitech 475, Nautitech 60, Nautitech 82, and Nautitech 98

KEY FEATURES

Hull & Sail Plan
- Integral keels, inboard rudders, reverse transoms with molded boarding steps
- Fractional sloop rig, fully roached main, roller-furling genoa

Deck Layout
- Trampoline forward with large lockers just aft, wide side decks w/ good foot space
- Large cockpit with hardtop overhang, table to starboard, dual helms, locker storage

Standard Accommodations
- Galley up to starboard aft, nav area to port aft, large circular dining area forward
- Starboard hull has comfortable staterooms fore and aft with central common head
- Port hull same as starboard or optional master suite with large head forward

Mechanical
- Wheel steering, dual helms aft in cockpit
- Twin inboards, access from aft berths

DESCRIPTION

The Nautitech 395 is the smallest of the line of catamarans developed and built by Dufour Yachts. The overall look is streamlined and modern, with a fine entry at the bows, reverse transoms, and sufficient beam for good upwind ability. Stiffness has been achieved through the use of laminated epoxy cross beams and vacuum-bagged sandwich construction. One innovative design feature is the rigid hardtop extension over the forward part of the cockpit. This hardtop can easily be converted into full bimini coverage in hot climates, extending over the whole cockpit. The interior is light, airy and modern in appearance, with semi-circular saloon seating, elegant bridgedeck galley, and two options for sleeping arrangements—four double berth cabins with a head in each hull, ideal for chartering, or a complete owner's suite in the port hull.

SPECIFICATIONS

Displacement	14,550 lbs, 6591 kg	
Standard Auxiliary	2 x 20 hp inboard	
Overall Length	39'3"	11.98 m
Waterline Length	37'1"	11.30 m
Bridgedeck Length	25'0"	7.63 m
Wing Deck Clearance	2'5"	0.75 m
Beam (max.)	21'0"	6.40 m
Draft (max.)	4'0"	1.20 m
Mast Hgt. Off Deck	43'2"	13.15 m
Mast Hgt. Off Water	49'3"	15.02 m

SAIL AREA

Mainsail	520 sf	47 sm
Genoa	290 sf	26 sm
Total Area	810 sf	73 sm
Spinnaker	710 sf	64 sm

CAPACITY

Berths	3-4 dbls, 2 sgls	
Staterooms	3-4	
Heads	2	
Fuel	53 gal	200 ltr
Fresh Water	132 gal	500 ltr
Payload	4,410 lbs, 2000 kg	

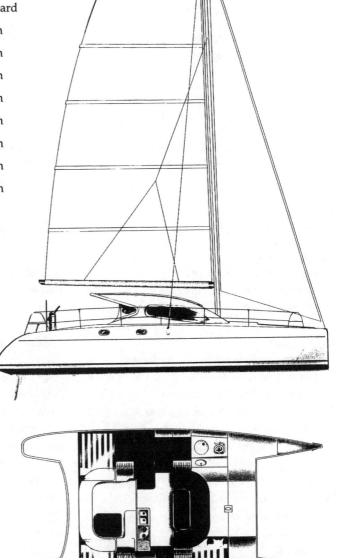

NAUTITECH 435

GENERAL INFORMATION

Designer   Mortain & Mavrikios

Approx. cost   US $280,000

Classification   Production catamaran,
Luxury cruiser

Builder: Dufour & Sparks
1 rue Blaise Pascal, 17185
Périgny La Rochelle, France
Tel: (33) 05 46 30 07 60
Fax: (33) 05 46 45 46 96
email: dwalsh@abs.net

Year introduced   1995

Number of boats built   30 (as of Sep 97)

N. American Agent
Dufour USA
1 Chelsea Court, Annapolis, MD 21403
Tel: (410) 268-6417   Fax: (410) 268-9739
email: dwalsh@abs.net

Other Cruising Multihulls By Builder
Nautitech 395, Nautitech 475, Nautitech 60,
Nautitech 82, and Nautitech 98

KEY FEATURES

Hull & Sail Plan
- Integral keels, inboard rudders, reverse transoms with molded boarding steps
- Fractional sloop rig, fully roached main, roller-furling jib

Deck Layout
- Trampoline forward with large lockers just aft, wide side decks w/ good foot space
- Large cockpit with hardtop overhang, table to starboard, dual helms, locker storage

Standard Accommodations
- Galley up to starboard aft, nav area to port aft, large circular dining area forward
- Starboard hull has spacious staterooms fore and aft, each with a private head
- Port hull same as starboard or optional master suite with berth & settee aft

Mechanical
- Wheel steering, dual helms aft in cockpit
- Twin inboards, access from aft berths

DESCRIPTION

The Nautitech 435 has the same ultra-modern look of the smaller 395. The wide beam, fine bow entry, stream-lined cabin roof with hardtop extension, moderate wetted area of the hulls, and fractional rig all point to comfortable sailing with good windward ability. As with all the Dufour catamarans, construction is vacuum-bagged sandwich and laminated epoxy plywood bulkheads for sufficient stiffness. Twin steering consoles aft offer good visibility. Two interior layouts are offered: one is an owner's version with a private, port hull suite; the other is ideal for the charter trade, with four double-berth cabins, each with its own private head and shower compartment. The attractive alcove galley is conveniently located on the bridgedeck, adjacent to the spacious saloon seating area. The overall feeling is one of style and comfort in an easily sailed yacht.

SPECIFICATIONS

Displacement	16,500 lbs, 7491 kg	
Standard Auxiliary	2 x 20 or 30 hp inboard	
Overall Length	43'5"	13.25 m
Waterline Length	40'4"	12.30 m
Bridgedeck Length	28'6"	8.69 m
Wing Deck Clearance	2'7"	0.80 m
Beam (max.)	21'8"	6.60 m
Draft (max.)	4'0"	1.20 m
Mast Hgt. Off Deck	48'3"	14.72 m
Mast Hgt. Off Water	54'5"	16.61 m

SAIL AREA

Mainsail	550 sf	51 sm
Jib	350 sf	33 sm
Total Area	900 sf	84 sm
Spinnaker	1000 sf	93 sm

CAPACITY

Berths	4 doubles
Staterooms	4
Heads	4
Fuel	72 gal 273 ltr
Fresh Water	195 gal 739 ltr
Payload	4,850 lbs, 2200 kg

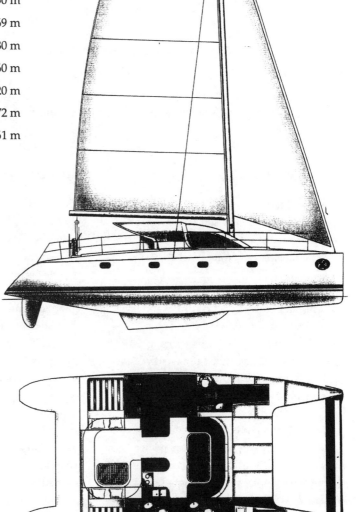

NAUTITECH 475

GENERAL INFORMATION

Designer	Mortain & Mavrikios	**Year introduced**	1995
Approx. cost	US $396,000	**Number of boats built**	35 (as of Sep 97)

Classification   Production catamaran, Luxury cruiser

Builder: Dufour & Sparks
1 rue Blaise Pascal, 17185
Périgny La Rochelle, France
Tel: (33) 05 46 30 07 60
Fax: (33) 05 46 45 46 96
email: dwalsh@abs.net

N. American Agent
Dufour USA
1 Chelsea Court, Annapolis, MD 21403
Tel: (410) 268-6417 Fax: (410) 268-9739
email: dwalsh@abs.net

Other Cruising Multihulls By Builder
Nautitech 395, Nautitech 435, Nautitech 60, Nautitech 82, and Nautitech 98

KEY FEATURES

Hull & Sail Plan
- Integral keels, inboard rudders, reverse transoms with molded boarding steps
- Fractional sloop rig, fully roached main, roller-furling jib

Deck Layout
- Trampoline forward w/ central walkway, large lockers just aft, wide side decks
- Large cockpit with hardtop overhang, large table midships, and dual saloon entrances

Standard Accommodations
- Galley up midships aft; nav area to port, large circular dining area forward
- Starboard hull has one single and two double staterooms, and two private heads
- Port hull the same as starboard; both hulls have abundant locker and storage space

Mechanical
- Wheel steering, dual helms aft in cockpit
- Twin inboards, access from aft berths

DESCRIPTION

The Nautitech 475 is ideally suited for the charter trade or as a well-appointed private yacht. Accommodations below assure ultimate privacy in four cabins with large double berths and private heads. The galley, located aft on the bridgedeck, is a charter cook's dream, with a double sink, four-burner stove, extensive counter space, and overhead cupboards, all located out of the line of traffic. The spacious saloon seating area, conveniently situated beside the galley, provides easy access for feeding large numbers, plus an impressive view through the over-sized, all-around windows. Abovedecks, the large cockpit and extensive deck space seem capable of accommodating any number of sunbathers or sailing enthusiasts. The hull configuration, over-all beam, smaller waterline area, and fractional rig are intended to provide ease of sailing and windward ability.

SPECIFICATIONS

Displacement	18,500 lbs, 8391 kg	
Standard Auxiliary	2 x 30 or 40 hp inboard	
Overall Length	47'0"	14.30 m
Waterline Length	45'8"	13.90 m
Bridgedeck Length	32'0"	9.76 m
Wing Deck Clearance	2'7"	0.80 m
Beam (max.)	25'0"	7.60 m
Draft (max.)	4'0"	1.20 m
Mast Hgt. Off Deck	54'4"	16.57 m
Mast Hgt. Off Water	60'6"	18.45 m

SAIL AREA

Mainsail	806 sf	75 sm
Jib	309 sf	29 sm
Total Area	1115 sf	104 sm
Spinnaker	1400 sf	130 sm

CAPACITY

Berths	2 sgls, 4 dbls	
Staterooms	6	
Heads	4	
Fuel	106 gal	402 ltr
Fresh Water	195 gal	738 ltr
Payload		

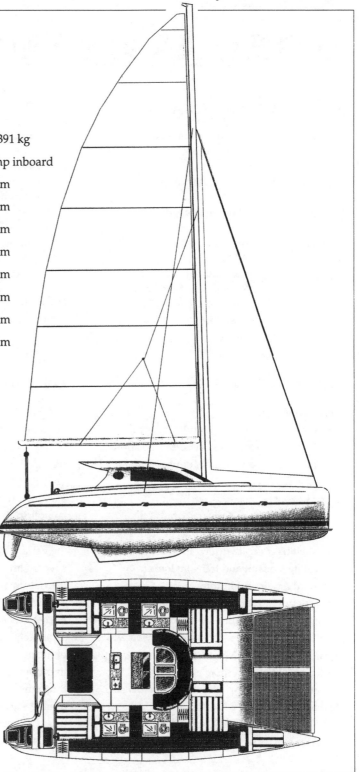

EDEL AVENTURE 11m

GENERAL INFORMATION

Classification   Production catamaran,
Cruiser/racer

Approx. Cost   Call for current price

Designer   Maurice Edel

Builder: Bateaux Edel
Z.I. du Pont Neuf,
rue Touboulic
Rochefort s/Mer, France
Tel: (33) 46 87 58 90
Fax: (33) 46 87 58 93
email:

Year Introduced   1996

Number of boats built   4   (as of Sep 97)

N. American Dealers   None at present
UK dealer:
Multihull World, Thornham Marina,
Emsworth, Hants, UK
tel: (44) 1243 377333 fax: (44) 1243 377378
email: sales@multihullworld.co.uk

Other Cruising Multihulls By Builder
None at present

KEY FEATURES

Hull & Sail Plan
- Slim, high-performance hulls, integral keels, inboard rudders, reverse transoms
- Fractional sloop rig, fully battened main, roller-furling jib

Deck Layout
- Large trampoline forward, central main cabin on bridgedeck, side access to hulls
- Spacious cockpit with wrap-around seating, cockpit and transom lockers

Standard Accommodations
- Bridgedeck cabin has galley and nav area aft, U-shaped seating with table forward
- Starboard hull has stateroom aft, head with large shower midships, stateroom forward
- Port hull has stateroom aft, head with large shower midships, stateroom forward

Mechanical
- Wheel steering, helm forward in cockpit
- Twin inboards, access from aft cabins

DESCRIPTION

The Edel Aventure 11m, a new version of the popular Edel Cat 35, continues the Edel tradition of combining high-performance sailing with comfortable accommodations. This boat is sleek and fast, with pleasing lines and uncluttered decks. There are three layouts to choose from: the Traditional, with separate bridgedeck accomodation module; the Family, with conventional coachroof and covered intercourse between the hulls; and the Cabrio, with open bridgedeck. In the Traditional version shown in the layout, the bridgedeck accommodations are accessed separately from the hulls, reducing the profile of the main cabin while providing ample living space. Entry to the hulls is midships through sliding hatches. Down below are double staterooms fore and aft, with a full head between. The forward staterooms can have one double berth or two singles.

SPECIFICATIONS

Displacement	8,140 lbs, 3700 kg	
Standard Auxiliary	2 x 12 hp inboard	
Overall Length	35'8"	10.89 m
Waterline Length	32'10"	10.00 m
Bridgedeck Length	21'4"	6.50 m
Wing Deck Clearance	1'8"	0.50 m
Beam (max.)	19'10"	6.05 m
Draft (max)	3'2"	0.95 m
Mast Hgt. Off Deck	44'7"	13.60 m
Mast Hgt. Off Water	50'2"	15.30 m

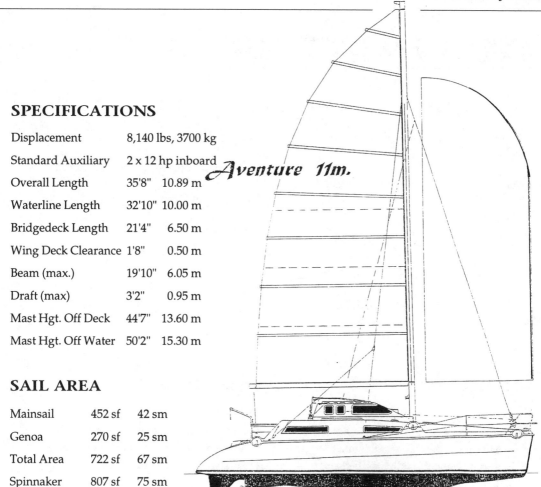

Aventure 11m.

SAIL AREA

Mainsail	452 sf	42 sm
Genoa	270 sf	25 sm
Total Area	722 sf	67 sm
Spinnaker	807 sf	75 sm

CAPACITY

Berths	4 doubles	
Staterooms	4	
Heads	1	
Fuel	48 gal	180 ltr
Fresh Water	48 gal	180 ltr
Payload	3,960 lbs, 1800 kg	

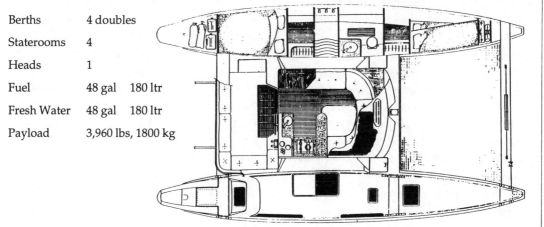

QUADCAT 28

GENERAL INFORMATION

Classification   Production catamaran, Cruiser

Approx. Cost   Call for current price

Designer   J. Kostanski

Builder   Encore Intern'l Multihulls
4281 Madele Rd.
N. Vancouver, BC V7N 4EI
Canada
Tel: (604) 980-3324
Fax: (604) 980-1207
Cell: (604) 618-0359

Year Introduced   1997

Number of boats built   1 (as of Sep 97)

N. American Dealers   Buy factory direct

Other Cruising Multihulls By Builder
None at present

KEY FEATURES

Hull & Sail Plan
- Unique 4-hull design, two main hulls plus two folding hulls that nest in main hulls
- Fractional sloop rig, fully roached and battened main, roller-furling jib

Deck Layout
- Trampoline forward, dual lockers just aft, netting between main hull and amas
- Comfortable cockpit with seating port & starboard, raised seats at stern

Standard Accommodations
- Bridgedeck has L-shaped seating with table forward, access to hulls
- Starboard hull has berth aft, galley midships, large sail locker forward
- Port hull has double stateroom/head aft, nav/storage midships, stateroom forward

Mechanical
- Wheel steering, helm forward in cockpit
- Single outboard at stern

DESCRIPTION

The Quadcat 28 is a new variable beam auxiliary sailing catamaran that is turning heads in the industry. Considered a breakthrough design by her builders, she is based on a tunnel-hull catamaran platform which is narrow enough to fit easily into any marina berth. This boat features unique retractable secondary floats port and starboard which give extra stability and sail-carrying capacity. The floats fold neatly into the side of each main hull. The folding and unfolding of the floats takes only 15 seconds (and is operated from the cockpit), draft is only 15 inches, and the boat sails at 15 knots! If the wind fails, the 25 hp engine can power the boat in the 12-knot range, greatly extending weekend sailing horizons. The Quadcat 28 is trailerable by any vehicle with 5,000 lbs capacity. This boat should be great for fast cruising on weekend or coastal explorations.

SPECIFICATIONS

Displacement	3,600 lbs, 1632 kg	
Standard Auxiliary	1 x 25 hp inboard	
Overall Length	28'6"	8.69 m
Waterline Length	27'0"	8.24 m
Bridgedeck Length	20'0"	6.10 m
Wing Deck Clearance	1'0"	0.31 m
Beam (max.)	18'0"	5.49 m
Beam (min.)	9'6"	2.90 m
Draft (max.)	1'3"	0.38 m
Mast Hgt. Off Water	42'6"	12.96 m

SAIL AREA

Mainsail	310 sf	29 sm
Jib	175 sf	16 sm
Total Area	485 sf	45 sm
Screacher	275 sf	26 sm
Spinnaker	350 sf	33 sm

CAPACITY

Berths	3 sgls, 1 dble	
Staterooms	none	
Heads	1	
Fuel	12 gal	45 ltr
Fresh Water	15 gal	57 ltr
Payload		

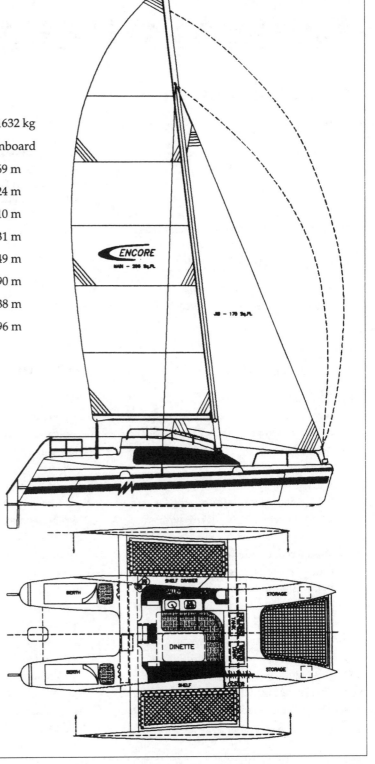

ENDEAVOURCAT 30
MkII

GENERAL INFORMATION

Classification	Production catamaran, Cruiser
Approx. Cost	US $99,500
Designer	Endeavour Design
Builder:	Endeavour Catamarans 3703 131st. Ave. North Clearwater, FL 33762 Tel: (813) 573-5377 Fax: (813) 573-5190 email: endeavcats@aol.com

Year Introduced 1995

Number of boats built

N. American Dealers
Contact Endeavour Catamarans

Other Cruising Multihulls By Builder
Endeavourcat 34 & 36

KEY FEATURES

Hull & Sail Plan
- Integral keels, reverse transoms with molded boarding steps, built-in buoyancy
- Masthead sloop rig, fully battened main, self-tending jib with Camber Spar™

Deck Layout
- Full rigid foredeck, self-draining lockers
- Aft cabins create cozy cockpit with ample seating and lockers

Standard Accommodations
- Bridgedeck salon has L-shaped settee with dining table and additional seat
- Starboard hull has stateroom aft, lockers midships, and large head forward
- Port hull has stateroom aft, long galley midships and forward

Mechanical
- Wheel steering, helm forward in cockpit
- Outboard mounted off stern, optional 10 hp twin diesels

DESCRIPTION

The Endeavourcat 30 MkII version is a dependable cruiser in a small, workable size. A pleasant compromise has been struck between providing a well-built, safe craft and incorporating a liberal number of comfortable touches. The sail plan and running rigging have been kept simple—this boat can easily be single-handed. The mainsail is fully battened, the jib self-tending, and all sail controls lead to the cockpit. Belowdecks, the layout includes an airy main cabin with comfortable saloon seating, an ample galley in the port hull, and twin queen-sized double berth cabins, providing generous space for one or two couples, or a small family. Extra features like hot and cold pressurized water, 110 Volt power, ice box and separate shower stall are standard. The Endeavourcat 30 MkII is best suited to those with an eye for comfort and ease of sailing.

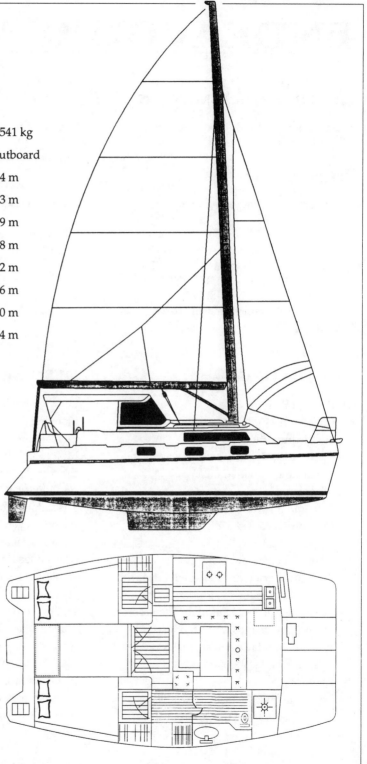

SPECIFICATIONS

Displacement	7,800 lbs, 3541 kg	
Standard Auxiliary	1 x 25 hp outboard	
Overall Length	30'0"	9.14 m
Waterline Length	27'8"	8.43 m
Bridgedeck Length	28'6"	8.69 m
Wing Deck Clearance	1'10"	0.58 m
Beam (max.)	14'6"	4.42 m
Draft (max.)	2'10"	0.86 m
Mast Hgt. Off Deck	40'0"	12.20 m
Mast Hgt. Off Water	47'0"	14.34 m

SAIL AREA

Mainsail	367 sf	34 sm
Jib	118 sf	11 sm
Total Area	485 sf	45 sm
Spinnaker		

CAPACITY

Berths	2 doubles	
Staterooms	2	
Heads	1	
Fuel	60 gal	227 ltr
Fresh Water	60 gal	227 ltr
Payload		

ENDEAVOURCAT 34

GENERAL INFORMATION

Classification   Production catamaran, Cruiser

Approx. Cost   US $139,000

Designer   Endeavour Design

Builder: Endeavour Catamarans
3703 131st. Ave. North
Clearwater, FL 33762
Tel: (813) 573-5377
Fax: (813) 573-5190
email: endeavcats@aol.com

Year Introduced   1996

Number of boats built

N. American Dealers
Contact Endeavour Catamarans

Other Cruising Multihulls By Builder
Endeavourcat 30 & 36

KEY FEATURES

Hull & Sail Plan
- Integral keels and skegs, reverse transoms, built-in buoyancy
- Masthead sloop rig, fully battened main, self-tacking jib with Camber Spar™

Deck Layout
- Full rigid foredeck, self-draining lockers
- Cozy center cockpit with ample seating, large locker aft

Standard Accommodations
- Bridgedeck salon has L-shaped settee with dining table, stateroom forward
- Starboard hull has comfortable stateroom aft, locker midships, and head forward
- Port hull has stateroom aft, galley midships, and stateroom forward

Mechanical
- Wheel steering, helm aft in cockpit
- Twin diesels, engine access from aft staterooms

DESCRIPTION

Long known for manufacturing cruising monohulls, Endeavour developed the Endeavourcat 34 as well as the smaller 30 MkII to satisfy a growing interest in cruising catamarans. Emphasis has been placed on providing a comfortable, safe family cruiser. The sailplan and rig are simple and easily handled, even by one person, with fully battened mainsail, self-tacking jib, and all controls leading to the cockpit. The layout is similar to the Mk II, with twin queen-berth aft staterooms, port side galley, large head with separate shower stall, and large saloon seating area. She has an additional stateroom forward of the saloon cabin. Extra touches like hot and cold pressurized water, 110 volt power and ice box are standard. The Endeavour 34 works well as a charter vessel or as a dependable private cruiser for a family.

SPECIFICATIONS

Displacement	8,950 lbs, 4064 kg	
Standard Auxiliary	2 x 10 hp inboard	
Overall Length	34'0"	10.37 m
Waterline Length	32'10"	10.01 m
Bridgedeck Length	32'4"	9.86 m
Wing Deck Clearance	1'10"	0.58 m
Beam (max.)	15'0"	4.58 m
Draft (max.)	2'10"	0.86 m
Mast Hgt. Off Deck	40'0"	12.20 m
Mast Hgt. Off Water	47'0"	14.34 m

SAIL AREA

Mainsail	367 sf	34 sm
Jib	158 sf	15 sm
Total Area	525 sf	49 sm
Spinnaker		

CAPACITY

Berths	3 doubles	
Staterooms	3	
Heads	1	
Fuel	60 gal	227 ltr
Fresh Water	60 gal	227 ltr
Payload		

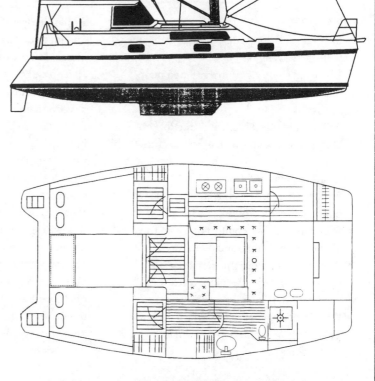

ENDEAVOURCAT 36

GENERAL INFORMATION

Classification   Production catamaran, Cruiser

Approx. Cost   US $149,000

Designer   Endeavour Design

Builder: Endeavour Catamarans
3703 131st. Ave. North
Clearwater, FL 33762
Tel: (813) 573-5377
Fax: (813) 573-5190
email: endeavcats@aol.com

Year Introduced   1997

Number of boats built

N. American Dealers
   Contact Endeavour Catamarans

Other Cruising Multihulls By Builder
   Endeavourcat 30 & 34

KEY FEATURES

Hull & Sail Plan
- Integral keels and skegs, reverse transoms, built-in buoyancy
- Masthead sloop rig, fully battened main, self-tacking jib with Camber Spar™

Deck Layout
- Full rigid foredeck, self-draining lockers
- Cozy center cockpit with ample seating, large locker aft

Standard Accommodations
- Bridgedeck salon has L-shaped settee with dining table, stateroom forward
- Starboard hull has comfortable stateroom aft, locker midships, and head forward
- Port hull has stateroom aft, galley midships, and stateroom forward

Mechanical
- Wheel steering, helm forward in cockpit
- Twin diesels, engine access from aft staterooooms

DESCRIPTION

Similar in design and layout to the Endeavourcat 34, the new 36 features increased headroom and an additional 4 ft by 10 ft aft deck that is ideal for fishing, diving, or simply lounging. Otherwise the two boats have the same fine entry bows, relatively narrow beam by modern standards, easily handled rig, and elegant accommodations for up to three couples. The large cockpit includes port and starboard seating, a central dining table, and a helm station to port. The standard layout offers three double staterooms, a spacious saloon area with seating, dining table and navigation station, and a generous galley with double sinks, stove, full-size oven, and lots of counter space. A good boat for either the charter trade or private use, the Endeavourcat 36 is ideal for those who value their comfort on board and who enjoy entertaining and water sports.

SPECIFICATIONS

Displacement	9,250 lbs, 4200 kg	
Standard Auxiliary	2 x 10 hp inboard	
Overall Length	36'0"	10.98 m
Waterline Length	33'0"	10.06 m
Bridgedeck Length	32'4"	9.86 m
Wing Deck Clearance	1'10"	0.58 m
Beam (max.)	15'0"	4.58 m
Draft (max.)	2'10"	0.86 m
Mast Hgt. Off Deck	40'0"	12.20 m
Mast Hgt. Off Water	47'0"	14.34 m

SAIL AREA

Mainsail	367 sf	49 sm
Jib	158 sf	15 sm
Total Area	525 sf	49 sm
Spinnaker		

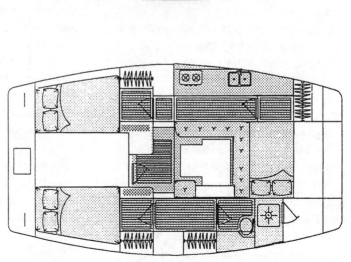

CAPACITY

Berths	3 doubles	
Staterooms	3	
Heads	1	
Fuel	60 gal	227 ltr
Fresh Water	90 gal	340 ltr
Payload		

TOBAGO 35

GENERAL INFORMATION

Classification Production catamaran, Cruiser

Approx. Cost Call for current price

Designers M. Joubert & B. Nivelt

Builder: Fountaine Pajot
Zone Industrielle
17290 Aigrefeuille, France
Tel: (33) (05) 46 35 70 40
Fax: (33) (05) 46 35 50 10
email: fountain@club-internet.fr

Year Introduced   1993

Number of boats built

N. American Dealers
  Contact Fountaine Pajot for dealer list

Other Cruising Multihulls By Builder
  Athena 38, Venezia 42, Bahia 46
Marquises 56, Taïti 75 Daycharter

KEY FEATURES

Hull & Sail Plan
- Integral low asect ratio keels
- Plumb bow, reverse transoms
- Fractional sloop rig
- Fully roached main, roller-furling jib

Deck Layout
- Large trampoline area forward, wide rigid deck just aft with self-draining lockers
- Wrap-around seating & table in cockpit
- Good foot rests, hand-holds

Standard Accommodations
- Galley up on starboard bridgedeck, with large seating area and nav station to port
- Starboard hull has stateroom forward, common head midships, stateroom aft
- Port hull has stateroom with head forward, locker midships, stateroom with head aft

Mechanical
- Wheel steering to starboard in cockpit
- Twin inboards, access from aft cabins

DESCRIPTION

The Tobago 35, now Fountaine Pajot's smallest production cruising catamaran, is equally at home on relaxed family cruises or tough bluewater passages. Based on the same concepts as the larger Venezia 42, she strives to combine superior performance and comfort through the use of state-of-the-art construction techniques. Safety features include stronger hull, high bridgedeck clearance, wide beam and easily driven hulls. The bridgedeck accommodations on the Tobago 35 are superb, with a modern galley, comfortable settee and navigation area arranged in a sweeping arc. The hull accommodations are equally comfortable, with two doubles and a single berth in the starboard hull and a large stateroom with double and single berth to port. An insulated cabin roof and saloon window shading keep the boat interior cool. This yacht is a serious modest-size cruiser.

SPECIFICATIONS

Displacement	8,820 lbs, 4000 kg	
Standard Auxiliary	2 x 10 hp inboard	
Overall Length	35'0"	10.60 m
Waterline Length	32'3"	9.84 m
Bridgedeck Length	22'6"	6.86 m
Wing Deck Clearance		
Beam (max.)	19'0"	5.80 m
Draft (max.)	3'1"	0.96 m
Mast Hgt. Off Deck	45'4"	13.82 m
Mast Hgt. Off Water	50'9"	15.48 m

SAIL AREA

Mainsail	430 sf	40 sm
Genoa	301 sf	28 sm
Total Area	731sf	68 sm
Spinnaker		

CAPACITY

Berths	2 sgls, 3 dbls	
Staterooms	3	
Heads	1	
Fuel	37 gal	140 ltr
Fresh Water	66 gal	250 ltr
Payload	5,000 lbs, 2268 kg	

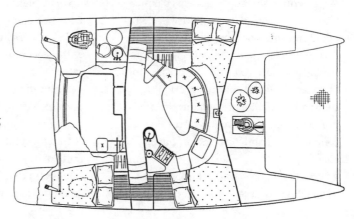

ATHENA 38

GENERAL INFORMATION

Classification Production catamaran, Cruiser

Approx. Cost Call for current price

Designers M. Joubert & B. Nivelt

Builder: Fountaine Pajot
Zone Industrielle
17290 Aigrefeuille, France
Tel: (33) (05) 46 35 70 40
Fax: (33) (05) 46 35 50 10
email: fountain@club-internet.fr

Year Introduced

Number of boats built

N. American Dealers
   Contact Fountaine Pajot for dealer list

Other Cruising Multihulls By Builder
   Tobago 35, Venezia 42, Bahia 46
   Marquises 56, Taïti 75 Day Charter

KEY FEATURES

Hull & Sail Plan
- Integral low asect ratio keels
- Plumb bow, reverse transoms
- Fractional sloop rig
- Fully roached main, roller-furling jib

Deck Layout
- Large trampoline area forward, wide rigid deck just aft with self-draining lockers
- Wrap-around seating & table in cockpit
- Good foot rests and hand-holds

Standard Accommodations
- Bridgedeck has galley to starboard, large seating area forward, and nav area to port
- Starboard hull has stateroom forward, common head midships, stateroom aft
- Port hull has stateroom forward, common head midships, stateroom aft

Mechanical
- Wheel steering to starboard in cockpit
- Twin inboards, access from aft deck/cabin

DESCRIPTION

This middle-range yacht with a touch of elegance replaces the Antigua 37 Maestro in the Fountaine Pajot line. It is intended primarily for family cruising or the bareboat charter trade. All the creature comforts have been catered to, with easy sail-handling, generous accommodations, a light, airy interior, stream-lined decor, and numerous luxury options. Design features include a wide beam, fractional rig, and low aspect ratio keels. Sailing performance is good without jeopardizing comfort. The spacious saloon cabin has been completely redesigned, incorporating a modern galley and serving counter, a comfortable lounge area and dining table, and a navigation area all set in a sweeping arc that is now Fountaine Pajot's trade mark. Four separate double-berth cabins and two large heads provide ample accommodations.

SPECIFICATIONS

Displacement	12,128 lbs, 5500 kg	
Standard Auxiliary	2 x 20 hp inboard	
Overall Length	38'1"	11.60 m
Waterline Length		
Bridgedeck Length	23'9"	7.24 m
Wing Deck Clearance		
Beam (max.)	20'8"	6.30 m
Draft (max.)	3'1"	0.95 m
Mast Hgt. Off Deck		
Mast Hgt. Off Water		

SAIL AREA

Mainsail	538 sf	50 sm
Genoa	376 sf	38 sm
Total Area	914 sf	88 sm
Spinnaker		

CAPACITY

Berths	4 doubles	
Staterooms	4	
Heads	2	
Fuel	40 gal	180 ltr
Fresh Water	80 gal	360 ltr
Payload		

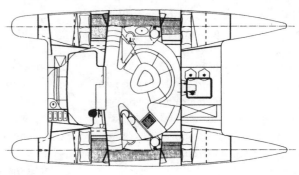

VENEZIA 42

GENERAL INFORMATION

Classification   Production catamaran, Cruiser

Approx. Cost   Call for current price

Designers   M. Joubert & B. Nivelt

Builder: Fountaine Pajot
Zone Industrielle
17290 Aigrefeuille, France
Tel: (33) (05) 46 35 70 40
Fax: (33) (05) 46 35 50 10
email: fountain@club-internet.fr

Year Introduced

Number of boats built

N. American Dealers
Contact Fountaine Pajot for dealer list

Other Cruising Multihulls By Builder
Tobago 35, Athena 38, Bahia 46
Marquises 56, Taïti 75 Day Charter

KEY FEATURES

Hull & Sail Plan
- Integral low asect ratio keels
- Plumb bow, reverse transoms
- Fractional sloop rig
- Fully roached main, roller-furling jib

Deck Layout
- Large trampoline area forward, wide rigid deck just aft with self-draining lockers
- Wrap-around seating & table in cockpit
- Good foot rests and hand-holds

Standard Accommodations
- Galley up on starboard bridgedeck, with large seating area and nav station to port
- Starboard hull has stateroom forward, common head midships, stateroom aft
- Port hull has stateroom forward, common head midships, stateroom aft

Mechanical
- Wheel steering to starboard in cockpit
- Twin inboards, access from aft deck

DESCRIPTION

Almost futuristic in design as are all modern Fountaine Pajot catamarans, the Venezia 42 brings a new sleekness to the look of cruising catamarans. Pronounced features include narrow, fine-entry bows, a streamlined profile, modern fractional rig, and and an innovative roof "cap", which lets light and air into the saloon cabin. The boat has been set up for short-handed sailing, with all controls leading to the cockpit. Performance is high on all points of sail due to an efficient underbody and sail plan. Accommodations are comfortable and practical. Single berths have been added to the two forward staterooms, making them ideal for crew members or families with children. With the Venezia 42, every effort has been made to produce a craft that combines cruising comfort and stability with good performance and ease of handling.

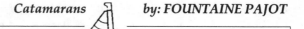

SPECIFICATIONS

Displacement	14,960 lbs, 6800 kg	
Standard Auxiliary	2 x 28 hp inboard	
Overall Length	42'0"	12.60 m
Waterline Length	41'0"	12.51 m
Bridgedeck Length	27'3"	8.30 m
Wing Deck Clearance		
Beam (max.)	23'0"	6.95 m
Draft (max.)	3'11"	1.20 m
Mast Hgt. Off Deck	56'10"	17.32 m
Mast Hgt. From WL	62'0"	18.91 m

SAIL AREA

Mainsail	653 sf	60 sm
Genoa	326 sf	30 sm
Total Area	978 sf	90 sm
Spinnaker		

CAPACITY

Berths	2 sgls, 4 dbls
Staterooms	4
Heads	2
Fuel	92 gal 350 ltr
Fresh Water	132 gal 500 ltr
Payload	10,000 lbs, 4536 kg

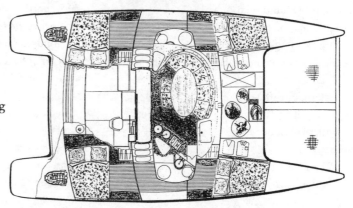

BAHIA 46

GENERAL INFORMATION

Classification   Production catamaran,
Luxury cruiser

Approx. Cost   Call for current price

Designers   M. Joubert & B. Nivelt

Builder: Fountaine Pajot
Zone Industrielle
17290 Aigrefeuille, France
Tel: (33) (05) 46 35 70 40
Fax: (33) (05) 46 35 50 10
email: fountain@club-internet.fr

Year Introduced   1996

Number of boats built

N. American Dealers
Contact Fountaine Pajot for dealer list

Other Cruising Multihulls By Builder
Tobago 35, Athena 38, Venezia 42,
Marquises 56, Taïti 75 Daycharter

KEY FEATURES

Hull & Sail Plan
- Integral keels, plumb bow, reverse transoms
- Fractional sloop rig
- Fully roached main, roller-furling jib

Deck Layout
- Large trampoline area forward, wide rigid deck just aft with self-draining lockers
- Wrap-around seating & table in cockpit
- Good foot rests and hand-holds

Standard Accommodations
- Spacious galley up on starboard bridgedeck, large seating area and nav station to port
- Starboard hull has stateroom forward with double and single berth, head midships, staterooom aft
- Port hull has staterooms fore and aft, each with private head

Mechanical
- Wheel steering to starboard in cockpit
- Twin inboards, access from aft deck

DESCRIPTION

The Bahia 46, the latest luxury cruising catamaran from Fountaine Pajot, is well designed and superbly crafted. She does a nice job of filling the gap between the Venezia 42 and the Marquises 56. Her exterior features include fine-entry bows, a stream-lined profile, modern fractional rig, and an innovative roof "cap", which lets light and air into the saloon cabin. As with her sister ships, performance is high on all points of sail due to an efficient underbody and sail plan. The inboard engines are accessible from the deck aft of the cockpit. Her balance under sail is accentuated by an easy-to-handle sailplan. The cockpit is large and well protected for extended cruising. The Bahia is available in three configurations: an Owners layout where one entire hull is a private suite; a Bareboat Charter layout with four double staterooms, and a Crewed Charter version.

SPECIFICATIONS

Displacement	20,950 lbs, 9500 kg
Standard Auxiliary	2 x 38 hp inboard
Overall Length	46'0" 14.00 m
Waterline Length	
Bridgedeck Length	28'4" 8.62 m
Wing Deck Clearance	
Beam (max.)	24'1" 7.30 m
Draft (max.)	4'3" 1.30 m
Mast Hgt. Off Deck	
Mast Hgt. From WL	

SAIL AREA

Mainsail	775 sf	72 sm
Genoa	548 sf	51 sm
Total Area	1323 sf	123 sm
Spinnaker		

CAPACITY

Berths	2 sgls, 4 dbls
Staterooms	4
Heads	3-4
Fuel	105 gal 400 ltr
Fresh Water	226 gal 860 ltr
Payload	

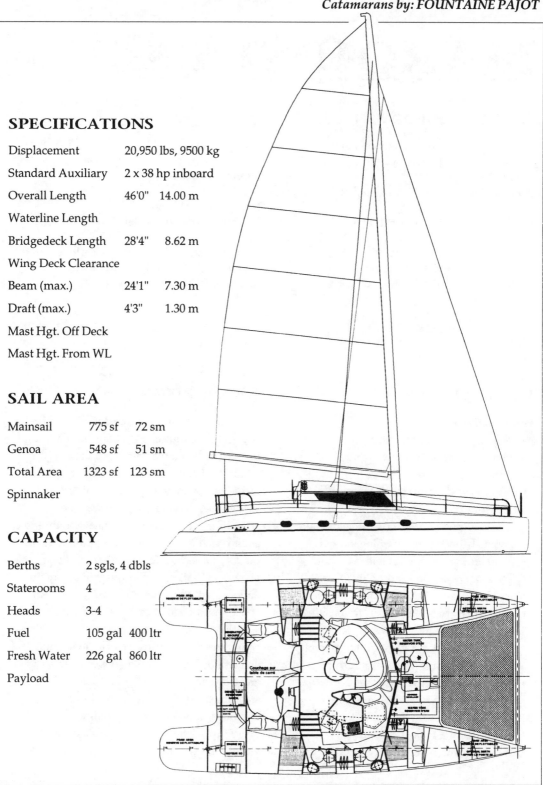

MARQUISES 56

GENERAL INFORMATION

Classification   Production catamaran,
                      Luxury cruiser

Approx. Cost   Call for current price

Designers   M. Joubert & B. Nivelt

Builder: Fountaine Pajot
                      Zone Industrielle
                      17290 Aigrefeuille, France
                      Tel: (33) (05) 46 35 70 40
                      Fax: (33) (05) 46 35 50 10
                      email: fountain@club-internet.fr

Year Introduced

Number of boats built

N. American Dealers
    Contact Fountaine Pajot for dealer list

Other Cruising Multihulls By Builder
    Tobago 35, Athena 38, Venezia 42,
Bahia 46, Taïti 75 Daycharter

KEY FEATURES

Hull & Sail Plan
- Integral low asect ratio keels
- Plumb bow, reverse transoms
- Fractional sloop rig
- Fully roached main, roller-furling jib

Deck Layout
- Large trampoline area forward, wide rigid deck just aft with self-draining lockers
- Wrap-around seating & table in cockpit
- Good foot rests and hand-holds

Standard Accommodations
- Galley forward to starboard, large seating areas with tables both fore and aft
- Starboard hull has staterooms fore and aft with private heads, nav area midships
- Port hull has staterooms fore and aft with private heads, storage midships

Mechanical
- Wheel steering to port in cockpit
- Twin inboards, access from aft deck

DESCRIPTION

The Marquises 56, an updated version of the successful Marquises 53, is a spectacular luxury yacht and the flagship of the Fountaine Pajot line. Her new features include an overhanging cabin roof that shades the saloon cabin windows, extended aft hulls that create her additional length, and a renovated interior decor. As with the 53, the Marquises 56 offers the discriminating owner or charter company elegant accommodations that include four large double-berth staterooms (the forward staterooms have additional single berths) with en suite head compartments, crew quarters aft in the hulls, and a saloon cabin with dual lounge areas aft and a spacious galley to port. There is full standing headroom throughout bridgedeck and hulls, and luxurious appointment at every turn. The Marquises 56 is truly a world class cruising yacht.

SPECIFICATIONS

Displacement	28,600 lbs, 13000 kg	
Standard Auxiliary	2 x 48 hp inboard	
Overall Length	56'0"	17.20 m
Waterline Length	52'3"	15.93 m
Bridgedeck Length	36'6"	11.12 m
Wing Deck Clearance		
Beam (max.)	26'7"	8.15 m
Draft (max.)	4'6"	1.4 m
Mast Hgt Off Deck	65'6"	19.98 m
Mast Hgt. From WL	71'10"	21.92 m

SAIL AREA

Mainsail		
Genoa		
Total Area	1722 sf	160 sm
Spinnaker		

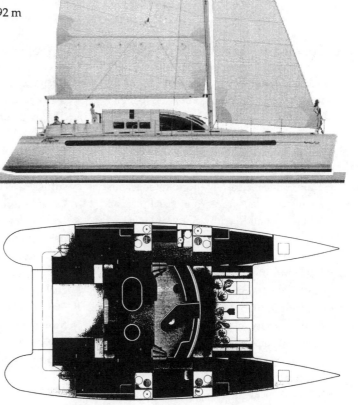

CAPACITY

Berths	2 sgls, 4-5 dbls	
Staterooms	4-5	
Heads	4	
Fuel	158 gal	600 ltr
Fresh Water	317 gal	1200 ltr
Payload		

GOLD COAST 44C

GENERAL INFORMATION

Classification   Semi-custom catamaran,
                     Cruiser/racer

Approx. Cost   US $375,000

Designer   R. Hatfield, D. Branch

Builder: Gold Coast Yachts
                     P.O. Box 1980, Kingshill,
                     St. Croix, USVI 00851
                     Tel: (809) 778-1004
                     Fax: (809) 778-2859
                     email:

Year Introduced   1991

Number of boats built   1 (as of Sep 97)

N. American Dealers   Buy factory direct

Other Cruising Multihulls By Builder
   Gold Coast 53C cat & 56C tri
Gold Coast 46, 53, 62, & 70 day charter cats
Gold Coast 55 (worlds fastest motor-sailer)

KEY FEATURES

Hull & Sail Plan
- wood/epoxy hull, daggerboards, sugar scoop transoms, watertight compartments
- Fractional sloop rig, wing mast, fully roached main, roller-furling genoa

Deck Layout
- Trampoline forward w/ rigid foredeck just aft, wide decks, wrap-around cockpit seats
- Mid helm station with comfortable seat
- Cockpit seating for 12, ample storage areas

Standard Accommodations
- Galley up aft with long counter, settee with table forward, nav area to port
- Starboard hull has mech. room aft, double berth midships, single berth & head forward
- Port hull has stateroom aft, storage midships, large head compartment forward

Mechanical
- Wheel steering, helm forward midships
- Inboards, full headroom access to starboard

DESCRIPTION

Designed as a fast, efficient bluewater cruiser, the Gold Coast 44C incorporates all the design features of the popular 53C in a smaller craft. Comfortable and spacious, her layout is well-suited to liveaboard cruising, with everything kept as simple and self-sufficient as possible. The characteristic Gold Coast hull configuration, sail plan, rotating wing spar and daggerboards provide high performance, while the wood/epoxy hull is durable, lightweight and moisture resistant. Built to order, the interior layout can be custom-designed to suit individual needs. Standard features include standing headroom throughout, a bridgedeck galley and navigation area, comfortable saloon seating, and a real king-size berth on the bridgedeck.

Catamarans by: GOLD COAST YACHTS

SPECIFICATIONS

Displacement	15,000 lbs,	6804 kg
Standard Auxiliary	2 x 37 hp inboard	
Overall Length	44'3"	13.67 m
Waterline Length	41'7"	12.85 m
Bridgedeck Length	20'0"	6.10 m
Wing Deck Clearance	2'9"	0.84 m
Beam (max.)	24'9"	7.60 m
Draft (min.)	3'0"	0.91 m
Draft (max.)	6'0"	2.14 m
Mast Hgt. Off Water	62'0"	18.91 m

SAIL AREA

Wing Mast	85 sf	8 sm
Mainsail	540 sf	50 sm
Genoa	373 sf	35 sm
Total Area	998 sf	93 sm
Spinnaker	1100 sf	102 sm

CAPACITY

Berths	1 sgle, 2 dbls
Staterooms	3
Heads	1 full, 1 half
Fuel	60 gal 227 ltr
Fresh Water	120 gal 454 ltr
Payload	6,000 lbs, 2722 kg

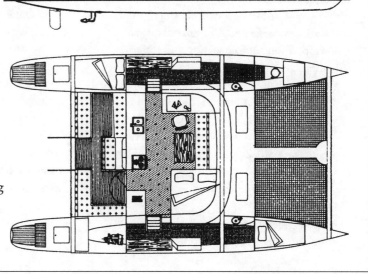

GOLD COAST 53C

GENERAL INFORMATION

Classification	Semi-custom catamaran, Cruiser/racer	**Year introduced**	1994
Approx. Cost	Call for current price	**Number built**	
Designer	Gold Coast Design Group	**N. American dealers**	Buy factory direct
Builder	Gold Coast Yachts P.O. Box 1980, Kingshill, St. Croix, USVI 00851 Tel: (809) 778-1004 Fax: (809) 778-2859 email:	**Other Cruising Multihulls By Designer** Gold Coast 44C cat & 56C tri (cruisers) Gold Coast 46, 53, 62, & 70 (day charters) Gold Coast 55 (worlds fastest motor-sailer)	

KEY FEATURES

Hull & Sail Plan
- wood/epoxy hull, daggerboards, sugar scoop transoms, watertight compartments
- Fractional sloop rig, wing mast, fully roached main, roller-furling genoa

Deck Layout
- Trampoline forward with central rigid walkway, wide decks, huge cockpit with wrap-around ample seating and storage

Standard Accommodations
- Galley up aft, U-shaped table and seating forward, navigation area to starboard
- Starboard hull has staterooms aft and midships with private heads; doule crew berth forward, access from forward hatch
- Port hull same as starboard, with staterooms aft, midships, and forward

Mechanical
- Wheel steering, helm forward midships
- inboard engines, access from aft deck

DESCRIPTION

One of Gold Coast Yachts' popular designs, the 53C cruiser shows the same high-performance characteristics as the day charter version on a comfortable, luxurious cruising catamaran. Ideal for the crewed charter business, her accommodations include four double staterooms with private baths, separate crew quarters accessed from the forward deck, spacious cockpit and saloon table seating, and a full-size galley located on the bridgedeck. With her efficient hull design, adjustable daggerboards, aft steering console, and Gold Coast's standard rotating wing mast, handling under sail is simple work, even for a short-handed crew. A fast cruiser, the 53C can satisfy private owners and crewed-charter operators alike.

SPECIFICATIONS

Displacement	22,000 lbs, 9979 kg	
Standard Auxiliary	2 x 45 hp inboards	
Overall Length	53'5"	16.27 m
Waterline Length	49'0"	15.00 m
Bridgedeck Length	21'0"	6.41 m
Wing Deck Clearance	2'11"	0.92 m
Beam (max.)	28'9"	8.75 m
Draft (min.)	3'0"	0.90 m
Draft (max.)	7'0"	2.13 m
Mast Hgt. Off Water	70'6"	21.50 m

SAIL AREA

Wing Mast	120 sf	11 sm
Mainsail	727 sf	68 sm
Genoa	440 sf	41 sm
Total Area	1287 sf	120 sm
Spinnaker	1016 sf	95 sm

CAPACITY

Berths	1 sgle, 5 dbls	
Staterooms	6	
Heads	5	
Fuel	80 gal	303 ltr
Fresh Water	250 gal	946 ltr
Payload	10,000 lbs, 4536 kg	

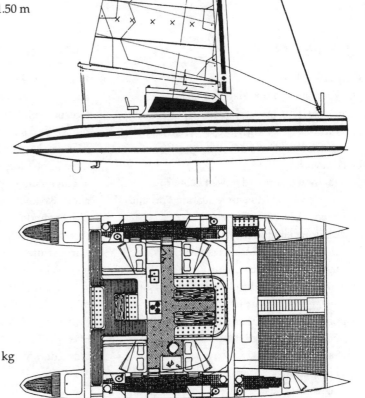

EVEN KEEL 37

GENERAL INFORMATION

Classification   Semi-custom catamaran,
                     Cruiser/racer

Approx. Cost   Call for current price

Designer   Walter Greene

Builder: Greene Marine
                     RR 1, PO Box 343
                     Yarmouth, ME 04096 USA
                     Tel: (207) 846-3184
                     Fax: (207) 846-1485

Year Introduced   1993
                           (as the Even Keel 35)

Number of boats built 4 (as of Sep 97)

N. American Dealers   Buy factory direct

Other Cruising Multihulls By Builder
   Custom multihulls

KEY FEATURES

Hull & Sail Plan
- Wood-epoxy hulls, daggerboards, reverse transoms with molded steps
- Fractional sloop rig, fully-battened main, self-tacking jib with Camber Spar™

Deck Layout
- Trampoline forward, raised cabin roof
- Large cockpit with ample seating port and starboard

Standard Accommodations
- Bridgedeck has table and settees forward, with forward berths on the bridgedeck
- Starboard hull has head aft, galley midships, and large stateroom forward
- Port hull has engine and locker aft, nav area midships, and large stateroom forward

Mechanical
- Tiller steering at console aft in cockpit
- Single inboard, access from port aft cabin

DESCRIPTION

Formerly the Even Keel 35, the new 37 is another cruiser/racer designed by Walter Greene, well-known multihull designer, builder and sailor. Similar to Greene Marine's larger commercial catamarans, the Even Keel is intended to handle easily at average sailing speeds of 10 to 15 knots, and run at 8.5 knots under diesel power. Capable of accommodating four adults comfortably, this is a good choice for owners seeking a stable cruiser that also performs well on the racing circuit. The Even Keel has been specifically designed with home builders in mind, with both plans and kit boat parts available in addition to complete boats. The Even Keel 37 is also available in an open bridgedeck version.

SPECIFICATIONS

Displacement	5,500 lbs, 2498 kg	
Standard Auxiliary	1 x 18 hp inboard	
Overall Length	37'4"	11.41 m
Waterline Length	35'0"	10.68 m
Bridgedeck Length	19'0"	5.80 m
Wing Deck Clearance	2'6"	0.76 m
Beam (max.)	19'0"	5.80 m
Draft (boards up)	1'7"	0.49 m
Draft (boards down)	5'7"	1.74 m
Mast Hgt. Off Water	44'0"	13.40 m

SAIL AREA

Mainsail	437 sf	41 sm
Jib	276 sf	26 sm
Total Area	713 sf	67 sm
Spinnaker	700 sf	65 sm

CAPACITY

Berths	2 doubles	
Staterooms	2	
Heads	1	
Fuel	30 gal	114 ltr
Fresh Water	60 gal	227 ltr
Payload	2,000 lbs, 907 kg	

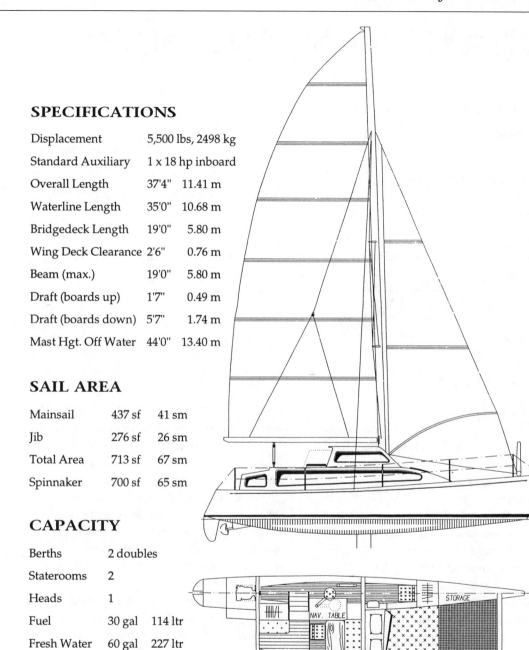

HEAVENLY TWINS 27

GENERAL INFORMATION

Classification   Production catamaran,
Cruiser

Approx. Cost   US $85,000

Designer   Pat Patterson

Builder   Heavenly Cruising Yachts,
Multihull World
Thornham Marina,
Emsworth, Hants,
PO10 8DD, UK
Tel: 44 (0) 1243 377333
Fax: 44 (0) 1243 377378
email: sales@multihullworld.co.uk

Year Introduced   1972
(as the Heavenly
Twins 26)

Number of boats built   400   (as of Sep 97)

N. American Dealers   Buy factory direct

Other Cruising Multihulls By Builder
Heavenly Twins 36

KEY FEATURES

Hull & Sail Plan
- Integral low-aspect-ratio keels and skegs, central nacelle and built-in buoyancy
- Masthead sloop rig, fully battened main with reefing points, roller-furling jib

Deck Layout
- Full rigid foredeck, self-draining lockers, cozy center cockpit with ample seating, central engine compartment, and lockers

Standard Accommodations
- Bridgedeck has port and starboard settees, dining table that converts to queen berth
- Starboard hull has comfortable stateroom aft, nav area midships, and head forward
- Port hull has aft stateroom aft, galley midships, and storage forward

Mechanical
- Wheel steering, helm forward in cockpit
- Optional twin diesels or single inboard in cockpit compartment with hydraulic drives

DESCRIPTION

One of the oldest and most popular production cruising catamarans in the business, the Heavenly Twins has long proven its dependability. Very seaworthy and strongly built, she has made numerous ocean crossings and several circumnavigations. Her cozy yet ample cockpit provides security at sea, while allowing for two comfortable cabins aft. The new 27 foot design incorporates a host of improvements over the original 26 foot version, including improved rig, sails, and sheeting arrangements; better windward performance; and lighter yet stronger construction. She also incorporates stoop-through passages so the aft cabins can be accessed from the main cabin (only available with a single engine option). Easily handled, she is an ideal choice for families and couples new to sailing, or those seeking an affordable, comfortable ocean-going cruiser.

SPECIFICATIONS

Displacement	5,600 lbs, 2851 kg	
Standard Auxiliary	1 x 9.9 hp outboard	
Overall Length	27'0"	8.20 m
Waterline Length	21'6"	6.60 m
Bridgedeck Length	25'10"	7.89 m
Wing Deck Clearance	varies with nacelle	
Beam (max.)	13'9"	4.20 m
Draft (max.)	2'3"	0.70 m
Mast Hgt. Off Deck	29'6"	9.00 m
Mast Hgt. Off Water	38'0"	11.59 m

SAIL AREA

Mainsail	140 sf	13 sm
Genoa	240 sf	22 sm
Staysail	32 sf	3 sm
Total Area	412 sf	38 sm
Spinnaker	550 sf	51 sm

CAPACITY

Berths	2-3 doubles
Staterooms	2
Heads	1
Fuel	20 gal 90 ltr
Fresh Water	52 gal 234 ltr
Payload	1,650 lbs, 750 kg

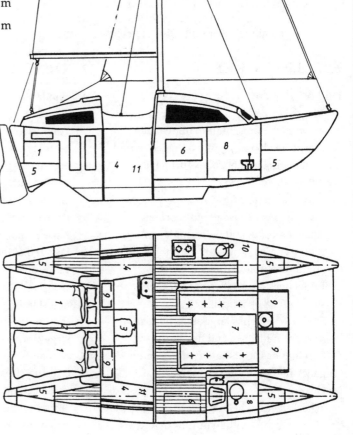

HEAVENLY TWINS 36

GENERAL INFORMATION

Classification   Production catamaran,
                       Cruiser

Approx. Cost   US $180,000

Designer   Pat Patterson

Builder: Heavenly Cruising Yachts,
                       Multihull World
Address: Thornham Marina,
                       Emsworth, Hants,
                       PO10 8DD, UK
                       Tel: 44 (0) 1243 377333
                       Fax: 44 (0) 1243 377378
                       email: sales@multihullworld.co.uk

Year Introduced   1996

Number of boats built   2 (as of Sep 97)

N. American Dealers   Buy factory direct

Other Cruising Multihulls By Builder
   Heavenly Twins 27

KEY FEATURES

Hull & Sail Plan
- Integral low-aspect ratio keels and skegs, reverse transoms, built-in buoyancy
- Masthead sloop rig, fully battened main with reefing points, roller-furling jib

Deck Layout
- Small trampoline forward with center walkway, rigid deck just aft with lockers
- Cozy center cockpit with ample seating, central engine compartment and lockers

Standard Accommodations
- Bridgedeck has U-shaped settee with table seating for 8-10 persons
- Starboard hull has large stateroom aft, nav area midships, and head forward
- Port hull has large stateroom aft, long galley midships, and storage forward

Mechanical
- Wheel steering, helm forward in cockpit
- Single inboard with hydraulic drives

DESCRIPTION

Similar to her smaller sistership, the Heavenly Twins 36 is designed to sail safely and comfortably in all conditions. Numerous features are similar, including the familiar centre cockpit where all sail handling can be carried out, conservative sail area, large aft sleeping cabins, and graceful lines. Despite her expanded size, accommodations below have been kept similar to the 27, resulting in a layout that feels spacious and uncluttered. Large aft double-berth cabins, a long fully-equipped galley, comfortable, airy saloon, and standing headroom throughout all make this an extremely livable boat. She also has large storage lockers and high payload capability for liveaboard or long-range cruising. Designed by someone with vast ocean sailing experience, the Heavenly Twins 36 offers an excellent choice for safe bluewater cruising.

SPECIFICATIONS

Displacement	8,400 lbs, 3814 kg	
Standard Auxiliary	1 x 28 hp inboard	
Overall Length	36'0"	10.98 m
Waterline Length		
Bridgedeck Length	27'0"	8.24 m
Wing Deck Clearance	2'6"	0.76 m
Beam (max.)	19'0"	5.80 m
Draft (max.)	3'0"	0.92 m
Mast Hgt. Off Deck	42'0"	12.81 m
Mast Hgt. Off Water	50'0"	15.25 m

SAIL AREA

Mainsail	243 sf	23 sm
Genoa	218 sf	20 sm
Total Area	461 sf	43 sm
Spinnaker	850 sf	79 sm

CAPACITY

Berths	2-3 doubles	
Staterooms	2	
Heads	1	
Fuel	30 gal	114 ltr
Fresh Water	60 gal	227 ltr
Payload	5,600 lbs, 2545 kg	

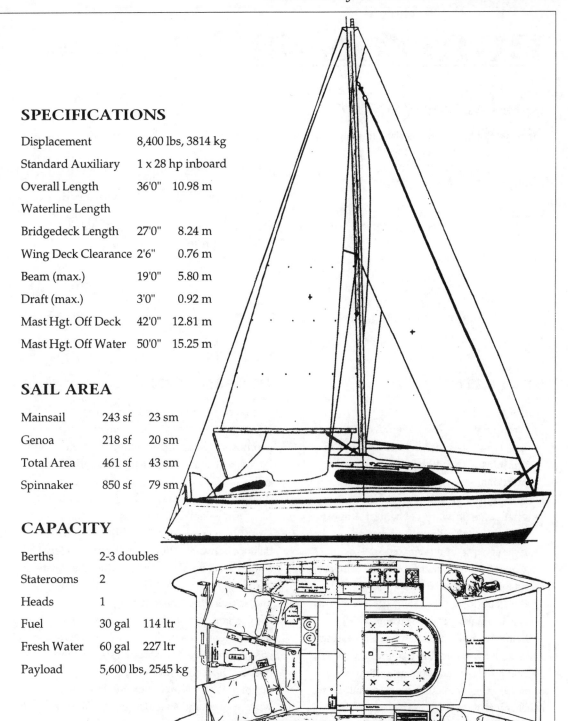

HORIZON 48

GENERAL INFORMATION

Classification Semi-custom catamaran,
Cruiser/racer

Approx. Cost US $495,000

Designer Marc Van Peteghem &
Vincent Lauriot Prevost

Builder: Horizon Boats
4210 Highway 165
Hollywood, SC 29449 USA
Tel: (803) 889-3191
Fax: (803) 889-8788
email:

Year Introduced 1997

Number of boats built 1 (as of Sep 97)

N. American Dealers Buy factory direct

Other Cruising Multihulls By Builder
None at present

KEY FEATURES

Hull & Sail Plan
- Strip-planked, epoxy laminated hulls, daggerboards, inboard rudders, reverse transoms with molded steps
- Fractional sloop rig, roller-furling jib

Deck Layout
- Trampoline forward w/ central support, lockers just aft, wide side decks
- large cockpit with table to port, ample seating, lockers and storage areas

Standard Accommodations
- Bridgedeck has table and settees to port, settee and nav area to starboard
- Starboard hull has stateroom aft, head with large shower midships, stateroom forward
- Port hull has stateroom aft with private head, galley midships, workroom forward

Mechanical
- Wheel steering, dual helms aft in cockpit
- Twin inboards, access from aft cabins

DESCRIPTION

The Horizon 48 is designed as an easy-to-handle blue water cruiser. Construction is of composite cedar strip-planking, with all laminates vacuum-bagged and materials chosen to meet the requirements of weight, durability and strength. Daggerboards, a high bridgedeck clearance, 25-foot beam, large hulls, and watertight bulkheads strike a balance between sailing performance, safety, stability and comfort. Sail handling has been kept simple with a fully battened mainsail and self-tending, roller-furling jib. The comfortable interior layout features three double cabins (including the owner's stateroom with private washroom, shower and head), a workshop and storage cabin (or optional fourth sleeping cabin), large head with shower, and spacious galley. She is a well built craft with many state-of-the-art features characteristic of her designers.

SPECIFICATIONS

Displacement	18,740 lbs, 8500 kg
Standard Auxiliary	2 x 38 hp inboard
Overall Length	47'7" 14.50 m
Waterline Length	44'0" 13.40 m
Bridgedeck Length	27'2" 8.28 m
Wing Deck Clearance	2'4" minimum
Beam (max.)	24'11" 7.60 m
Draft (boards up)	3'7" 1.10 m
Draft (boards down)	6'3" 1.90 m
Mast Hgt. Off Water	62'0" 18.90 m

SAIL AREA

Mainsail	753 sf	70 sm
Genoa	430 sf	40 sm
Total Area	1138 sf	110 sm
Spinnaker	1300 sf	121 sm

CAPACITY

Berths	3-4 doubles
Staterooms	3-4
Heads	2
Fuel	120 gal 500 ltr
Fresh Water	185 gal 700 ltr
Payload	5,500 lbs, 2495 kg

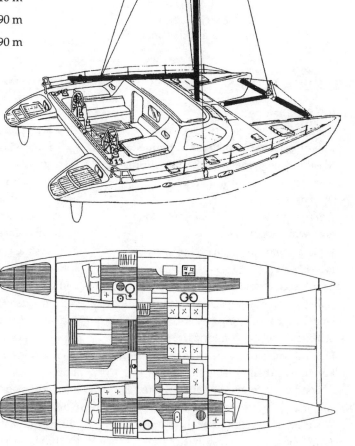

PACKET CAT 35

GENERAL INFORMATION

Classification   Production catamaran,
                     Luxury cruiser

Approx. Cost   US $239,950

Designer   Bob Johnson

Builder: Island Packet Yachts
                    1979 Wild Acres Road
                    Largo, FL 33771 USA
                    Tel: (800) 828-5678
                          (813) 535-6431
                    Fax: (813) 530-5806
                    email: islndpckty@aol.com

Year Introduced   1993

Number of boats built   42 (as of Sep 97)

N. American Dealers   Contact factory
                           for listings

Other Cruising Multihulls By Builder
    None at present

KEY FEATURES

Hull & Sail Plan
- Integral keels, inboard rudders, reverse transoms, DeltaPod under bow bridgedeck
- Masthead sloop rig, in-mast roller-furling main and roller-furling genoa

Deck Layout
- Full rigid foredeck with cushioned lounge area, wide side decks
- Wrap-around seating in cockpit, ample locker space

Standard Accommodations
- Galley up aft midships, nav area to port, large living and dining area forward
- Starboard hull has comfortable stateroom forward with storage area and private head
- Port hull has comfortable stateroom forward with storage area and private head

Mechanical
- Wheel steering, helm center in cockpit
- Twin inboards, aft access in each hull

DESCRIPTION

Built by Island Packet Yachts, one of America's premier sailboat builders, the Packet Cat 35 is a comfortably compact luxury cruiser with a great layout for two couples. A number of innovative touches have been incorporated, comforts unusual in a boat this size: 6'4" headroom throughout, bridgedeck location for the galley, two large private staterooms with adjoining heads, spacious cockpit, and a large built-in padded lounge area on the foredeck. Sail area has been increased for 1997, with a masthead rig and larger genoa area. Sail-handling has been kept simple with a new in-mast roller furling main, while twin diesels provide more than ample power. Everything about the boat has been designed for owner comfort on a workable scale. As the number of boats sold during the past four years implies, the Packet Cat has been a successful venture.

SPECIFICATIONS

Displacement	12,500 lbs, 5793 kg	
Standard Auxiliary	2 x 27 hp inboard	
Overall Length	35'0"	10.68 m
Waterline Length	31'0"	9.46 m
Bridgedeck Length	34'4"	10.47 m
Wing Deck Clearance	varies	
Beam (max.)	15'0"	4.58 m
Draft (max.)	3'0"	0.92 m
Mast Hgt. Off Deck	42'3"	12.89 m
Mast Hgt. Off Water	49'6"	15.10 m

SAIL AREA

Mainsail	230 sf	21 sm
Genoa	535 sf	50 sm
Total Area	765 sf	71 sm
Spinnaker	1014 sf	94 sm

CAPACITY

Berths	2-3 doubles
Staterooms	2
Heads	2
Fuel	55 gal	190 ltr
Fresh Water	140 gal	530 ltr
Payload	2,500 lbs, 1135 kg

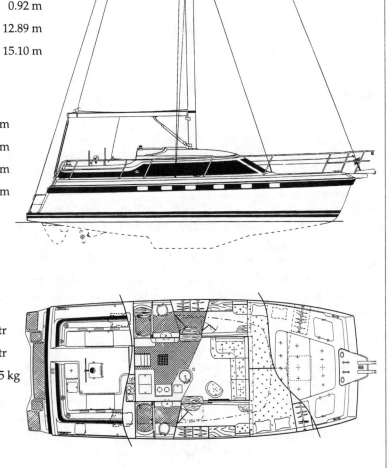

PRIVILEGE 37

GENERAL INFORMATION

Classification   Production catamaran,
Luxury cruiser

Approx. Cost   US $230,000

Designer   Marc Lombard

Builder: Jeantot Marine
Boulevard de l'Ile Vertime
BR 231 - 85106
Les Sables d'Ollone Cedex,
France
Tel: (33) (02) 51 21 05 38
Fax: (33) (02) 51 96 91 95
email:

Year Introduced   1996

Number of boats built

N. American Agent
The Catamaran Company
141 Alton Rd. Miami Beach, FL 33139
Tel: (305) 538-9600 Fax: (305) 538-1556

Other Cruising Multihulls By Builder
Privilege 42, Privilege 45, Privilege 51,
Privilege 65

KEY FEATURES

Hull & Sail Plan
- Integral low asect ratio keels
- Plumb bows, reverse transoms
- Fractional sloop rig, fully roached main, roller-furling jib

Deck Layout
- Dual trampolines with rigid central deck forward, wide rigid deck just aft
- T-shaped seating with table in cockpit
- Twin aft swim/sunbathing decks

Standard Accommodations
- Bridgedeck has large seating area with table, spacious nav area, and stateroom forward
- Starboard hull has stateroom aft, storage areas midships, and large head forward
- Port hull has stateroom aft, galley midships, steps to bridgedeck stateroom and head

Mechanical
- Wheel steering aft in cockpit
- Twin inboards, access from cockpit

DESCRIPTION

The Privilege 37 is one of the newest additions to the Jeantot Marine line of ocean cruising catamarans. Designed to be stable and comfortable, she has a simple, easily-handled rig with fully battened mainsail and roller-furling genoa. Three layouts are available: the standard layout with three cabins and one head with shower; an optional version with an additional head and shower (this is the layout shown on the following page), and an owner's version with a spacious two cabin suite layout with attached private head and shower compartments. Additional luxury touches include wild cherry cabinetry, pressurized hot and cold water, an aft transom handshower, teak cockpit table, and 12-volt refrigeration in the galley. As with all the Privilege yachts, the 37 is ideal for the charter trade as well as private ownership.

SPECIFICATIONS

Displacement	14,330 lbs, 6506 kg	
Standard Auxiliary	2 x 18 hp inboard	
Overall Length	36'8"	11.18 m
Waterline Length	34'2"	10.42 m
Bridgedeck Length	31'4"	9.60 m
Wing Deck Clearance		
Beam (max.)	21'6"	6.56 m
Draft (max.)	3'11"	1.19 m
Mast Hgt. Off Deck	48'0"	14.64 m
Mast Hgt. Off Water	55'0"	16.78 m

SAIL AREA

Mainsail	474 sf	44 sm
Genoa	345 sf	32 sm
Total Area	819 sf	76 sm
Spinnaker		

CAPACITY

Berths	3 doubles	
Staterooms	3	
Heads	2	
Fuel	47 gal	178 ltr
Fresh Water	80 gal	303 ltr
Payload		

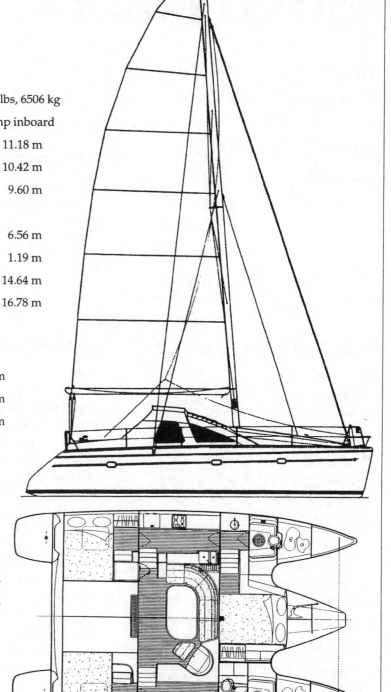

PRIVILEGE 42

GENERAL INFORMATION

Classification Production catamaran, Luxury cruiser

Approx. Cost US $355,000

Designer Marc Lombard

Builder Jeantot Marine
Boulevard de l'Ile Vertime
BR 231 - 85106
Les Sables d'Ollone Cedex,
France
Tel: (33) (02) 51 21 05 38
Fax: (33) (02) 51 96 91 95
email:

Year Introduced 1996

Number of boats built

N. American Agent
The Catamaran Company
141 Alton Rd. Miami Beach, FL 33139
Tel: (305) 538-9600 Fax: (305) 538-1556

Other Cruising Multihulls By Builder
Privilege 37, Privilege 45, Privilege 51, Privilege 65

KEY FEATURES

Hull & Sail Plan
- Integral low asect ratio keels
- Near-plumb bows, reverse transoms
- Fractional sloop rig
- Fully roached main, roller-furling jib

Deck Layout
- Dual trampolines forward, wide rigid deck just aft with lounge area
- Wrap-around seating with table in cockpit
- Swim platforms aft

Standard Accommodations
- Bridgedeck has large seating area with table, spacious nav area, staterooms forward
- Starboard hull has staterooms fore & aft with private heads, storage midships
- Port hull has staterooms fore & aft with private heads, comfortable galley midships

Mechanical
- Wheel steering, dual helms aft in cockpit
- Twin inboards, access from cockpit

DESCRIPTION

The Privilege 42 replaces the very successful Privilege 39, a popular boat in the bareboat charter trade. She continues the tradition of a luxury craft designed for families and friends or charter work. The new design is much faster than the 39, making her an exciting, yet safe boat to sail. The new hulls add three additional feet of length and one additional foot in width, while the interior space has also been enlarged and features 6'5" headroom in the saloon and 6'4" in the hulls. The interior accommodations include four double cabins, each with its own head, shower and sink, or a private cruiser version with three cabins. Abovedecks, the spacious cockpit has suntanning mattresses on each side, seven lockers located underneath the seating areas, dual helm stations, and a teak cockpit table designed to fit eight.

SPECIFICATIONS

Displacement	20,900 lbs, 9488 kg	
Standard Auxiliary	2 x 27 hp inboard	
Overall Length	42'0"	11.29 m
Waterline Length	36'10"	10.68 m
Bridgedeck Length	35'0"	6.13 m
Wing Deck Clearance		
Beam (max.)	23'0"	5.95 m
Draft (max.)	3'11"	0.99 m
Mast Hgt. Off Deck	54'10"	14.90 m
Mast Hgt. Off Water	62'0"	16.71 m

SAIL AREA

Mainsail	646 sf	60 sm
Genoa	442 sf	41 sm
Total Area	1088 sf	101 sm
Spinnaker		

CAPACITY

Berths	4 doubles	
Staterooms	4	
Heads	4	
Fuel	107 gal	405 ltr
Fresh Water	132 gal	500 ltr
Payload		

P42'

PRIVILEGE 45

GENERAL INFORMATION

Classification	Production catamaran, Luxury cruiser	

Approx. Cost   US $455,000

Designer   Marc Lombard

Builder   Jeantot Marine
Boulevard de l'Ile Vertime
BR 231 - 85106
Les Sables d'Ollone Cedex,
France
Tel: (33) (02) 51 21 05 38
Fax: (33) (02) 51 96 91 95
email:

Year Introduced

Number of boats built

N. American Dealers
The Catamaran Company
141 Alton Rd. Miami Beach, FL 33139
Tel: (305) 538-9600 Fax: (305) 538-1556

Other Cruising Multihulls By Builder
Privilege 37, Privilege 42, Privilege 51,
Privilege 65

KEY FEATURES

Hull & Sail Plan
- Integral low asect ratio keels
- Near-plumb bows, reverse transoms
- Fractional sloop rig
- Fully roached main, roller-furling jib

Deck Layout
- Dual trampolines forward, wide rigid deck just aft with lounge area
- Wrap-around seating with table in cockpit
- Swim platforms aft

Standard Accommodations
- Bridgedeck has large seating area with table, spacious nav area, staterooms forward
- Starboard hull has staterooms fore & aft with private heads, storage midships
- Port hull has staterooms fore & aft with private heads, comfortable galley midships

Mechanical
- Wheel steering, dual helms aft in cockpit
- Twin inboards, access from cockpit

DESCRIPTION

Like all the Privilege yachts, the interior of the 45 surrounds you with the luxury of fine joinery and furnishings. Streamlined tinted Lexan windshields offer both an attractive look and excellent visibility. Ideal for the charter trade or a liveaboard family, accommodations are offered in two versions: the standard option features five double-berth cabins (two aft, two forward, and one in the central forepeak accessed from the foredeck), generous galley, four heads, and a spacious saloon dining area with adjoining navigation station; for the charter trade, two single-berth cabins can be added forward as crew quarters. The large cockpit has two tables, ample bench seating, generous storage in eight cockpit lockers, and access to each watertight engine room. Redesigned transoms come equipped with recessed swim ladders and a swimming/diving platform.

SPECIFICATIONS

Displacement	23,100 lbs,	10,500 kg
Standard Auxiliary	2 x 27 hp inboard	
Overall Length	44'10"	13.67 m
Waterline Length	40'8"	12.60 m
Bridgedeck Length	35'0"	10.75 m
Wing Deck Clearance		
Beam (max.)	23'10"	7.28 m
Draft (max.)	3'11"	1.20 m
Mast Hgt. Off Deck	56'5"	17.20 m
Mast Hgt. From WL	64'0"	19.50 m

SAIL AREA

Mainsail	646 sf	60 sm
Genoa	506 sf	47 sm
Total Area	1152 sf	107 sm
Spinnaker		

CAPACITY

Berths	0-2 sgls, 5 dbls	
Staterooms	5	
Heads	4	
Fuel	106 gal	400 ltr
Fresh Water	160 gal	606 ltr
Payload		

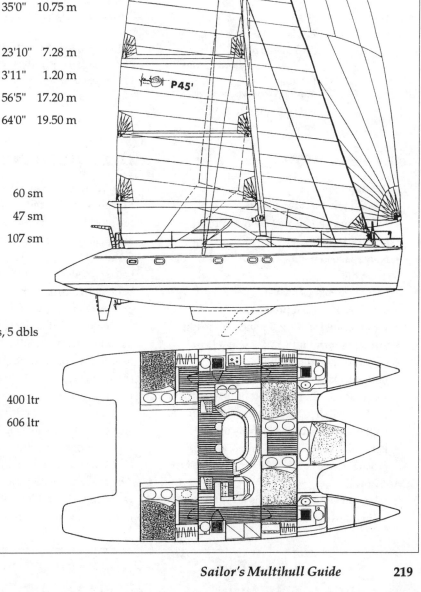

PRIVILEGE 51

GENERAL INFORMATION

Classification   Production catamaran,
Luxury cruiser

Approx. Cost   US $554,000

Designer   Marc Lombard

Builder   Jeantot Marine
Boulevard de l'Ile Vertime
BR 231 - 85106
Les Sables d'Ollone Cedex,
France
Tel: (33) (02) 51 21 05 38
Fax: (33) (02) 51 96 91 95
email:

Year Introduced

Number of boats built

N. American Dealers
The Catamaran Company
141 Alton Rd. Miami Beach, FL 33139
Tel: (305) 538-9600 Fax: (305) 538-1556

Other Cruising Multihulls By Builder
Privilege 37, Privilege 42, Privilege 45,
Privilege 65

KEY FEATURES

Hull & Sail Plan
- Integral low asect ratio keels
- Near-plumb bows, reverse transoms
- Fractional sloop rig
- Fully roached main, roller-furling jib

Deck Layout
- Dual trampolines forward, wide rigid
  deck just aft with lounge area
- Wrap-around seating, 2 tables in cockpit
- Swim platforms aft

Standard Accommodations
- Bridgedeck has 2 seating areas with tables,
  spacious nav area, staterooms forward
- Starboard hull has staterooms fore & aft
  with private heads, head midships
- Port hull has staterooms fore & aft with
  private heads, comfortable galley midships

Mechanical
- Wheel steering, dual helms aft in cockpit
- Twin inboards, access from cockpit

DESCRIPTION

An updated version of the Privilege 482, the
51 continues the tradition of offering one of
the most luxurious yachts afloat. Both mast
height and sail area have been increased,
featuring the same rigging only with
backstays eliminated. She sports a fully
battened, full-roach main and roller-furling
genoa, plus a bowsprit extension for carrying
a spinnaker. Other design improvements
include better ventilation, higher saloon
headroom, and a striking sense of space and
luxury throughout. Designed principally for
the charter trade, accommodations include a
captain's quarters (children's playroom or
study on the private version), 8 ft long galley,
plus four double-berth guest staterooms with
closet, dresser, drawer and storage space.
Abovedecks are dual swim platforms,
recessed swim ladders, and a new cockpit
design with seating for ten to twelve guests.

SPECIFICATIONS

Displacement	25,353 lbs,	11,500 kg
Standard Auxiliary	2 x 27 hp inboard	
Overall Length	51'7"	15.72 m
Waterline Length	46'7"	14.20 m
Bridgedeck Length	39'8"	12.16 m
Wing Deck Clearance		
Beam (max.)	26'5"	8.05 m
Draft (max.)	4'6"	1.37 m
Mast Hgt. Off Deck	63'6"	19.37 m
Mast Hgt. From WL	72'2"	22.01 m

SAIL AREA

Mainsail	797 sf	74 sm
Genoa	624 sf	58 sm
Total Area	1421 sf	132 sm
Spinnaker		

CAPACITY

Berths	1 sgle, 5 dbls	
Staterooms	5	
Heads	4	
Fuel	152 gal	575 ltr
Fresh Water	230 gal	871 ltr
Payload		

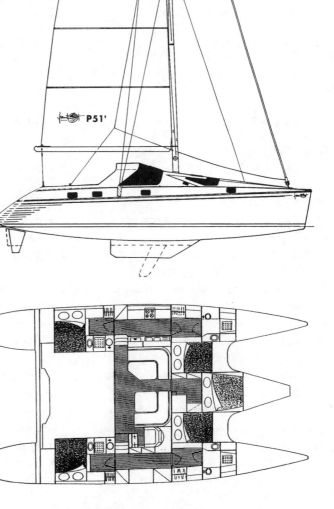

P51'

PRIVILEGE 65

GENERAL INFORMATION

Classification   Production catamaran,
                       Luxury cruiser

Approx. Cost   US $1,900,000

Designer   Marc Lombard

Builder   Jeantot Marine
                       Boulevard de l'Ile Vertime
                       BR 231 - 85106
                       Les Sables d'Ollone Cedex,
                       France
                       Tel: (33) (02) 51 21 05 38
                       Fax: (33) (02) 51 96 91 95
                       email:

Year Introduced

Number of boats built

N. American Dealers
   The Catamaran Company
   141 Alton Rd. Miami Beach, FL 33139
   Tel: (305) 538-9600 Fax: (305) 538-1556

Other Cruising Multihulls By Builder
   Privilege 37, Privilege 42, Privilege 45,
Privilege 51

KEY FEATURES

Hull & Sail Plan
- Integral low asect ratio keels
- Near-plumb bows, reverse transoms
- Fractional cutter rig
- Fully roached main, roller-furling jibs

Deck Layout
- Dual trampolines forward, wide rigid
  deck just aft with lounge area
- Dual seating areas with tables in cockpit
- Huge aft deck for sunbathing, swimming

Standard Accommodations
- Bridgedeck has bar/lounge areas aft, 2
  seating/tables areas, staterooms forward
- Starboard hull has staterooms fore & aft
  with private heads, storage midships
- Port hull has staterooms fore & aft with
  private heads, spacious galley midships

Mechanical
- Wheel steering, dual helms aft in cockpit
- Twin inboards, access from cockpit

DESCRIPTION

The Privilege 65 is a mega-yacht designed
with every luxury and comfort in mind. The
almost 150 sm of deck surface make this an
ideal yacht for the charter trade with room for
numerous passengers, scuba diving,
windsurfing or waterskiing. Despite her size,
sailhandling has been kept easy and smooth.
Deck and cockpit layout include a combination rigid and trampoline foredeck, large
lockers, spacious T-shaped cockpit with
abundant seating, two tables, lateral sunbathing decks, and aft swim platforms. Below are
two aft double-berth cabins with hanging
lockers, bridgedeck galley and saloon seating
on two U-shaped settees, two heads with sink
and shower, and two private forward
staterooms with en suite heads and shower
compartments. Two crew quarters with dual
single beds and separate heads with showers
are also located in the bow.

SPECIFICATIONS

Displacement	55,000 lbs,	25,000 kg
Standard Auxiliary	2 x 80 hp inboard	
Overall Length	65'0"	19.85 m
Waterline Length	52'3"	17.80 m
Bridgedeck Length	50'6"	15.40 m
Wing Deck Clearance		
Beam (max.)	34'0"	10.50 m
Draft (max.)	5'0"	1.53 m
Mast Hgt Off Deck	79'8"	24.30 m
Mast Hgt. From WL	89'3"	27.2 m

SAIL AREA

Mainsail	1238 sf	115 sm
Genoa	990 sf	92 sm
Staysail	463 sf	43 sm
Total Area	2691 sf	250 sm
Spinnaker		

CAPACITY

Berths	4 sgls, 6 dbls	
Staterooms	6	
Heads	6	
Fuel	400 gal	1514 ltr
Fresh Water	581 gal	2200 ltr
Payload	13,200 lbs,	6000 kg

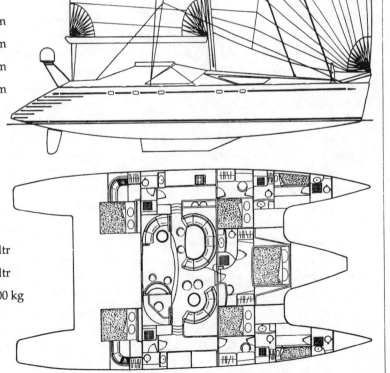

P65'

NOVARA 50RC

GENERAL INFORMATION

Classification   Semi-custom catamaran,
Cruiser/racer

Approx. Cost   US $800,000

Designer   Dr. Mai, Phil Morrison

Builder   KKG
Buttnergasse 1
A - 1230 Vienna, Austria
Tel: (43) 1 615 6666
Fax: (43) 1 615 6699
email:

Year Introduced   1997

Number of boats built

N. American Agent
California Multihull Yacht Sales & Charters
1235 Scott St., San Diego, CA 92106
Tel: (619) 222-9694
Fax: (619) 222-9693
email: cm@ginko.com

Other Cruising Multihulls By Builder
Novara 52SC and other boats in the Novara series, Macro Spaceshuttle, Spaceshuttle 1800-1300, Spaceshuttle 2000-1500

KEY FEATURES

Hull & Sail Plan
- Flared hulls, 1 or 2 daggerboards, inboard rudders, reverse transoms with steps
- Fractional sloop rig, rotating wing mast, fully battened main, self-tacking jib

Deck Layout
- Trampoline forward w/ central support, lockers just aft, open bridgedeck design
- large cockpit, wide span aft deck with barbecue terrace and dinghy bay

Standard Accommodations
- Bridgedeck is open abovedecks creating wide cockpit; aft berths are on bridgedeck
- Starboard hull has owner's stateroom aft with head, nav area, stateroom forward
- Port hull has dining area/double berth aft, galley midships, stateroom/head forward

Mechanical
- Wheel steering, dual helms aft in cockpit
- Twin inboards, access from aft decks

DESCRIPTION

The Novara 50RC is designed for high performance. Low weight and sleek hulls guarantee extended fast cruising, with speeds of up to 30 knots and good windward ability. The complete boat, as well as the light weight inner liners, are built in high quality female epoxy molds in vacuum bagged carbon foam sandwich composite. A double wave-piercing arrow bow leads to a long waterline with spray-reducing sharp entry angle and aerodynamic optimization for upwind performance. Accommodations are spacious due to the flared sleek hulls, with three double berth sleeping cabins (including an owner's suite), galley, navigation center, and large seating area with an additional double berth. Other unique features include an anti-mosquito system, aft barbecue terrace, inner helm and navigation center with head up display, and starboard fighter-style canopy.

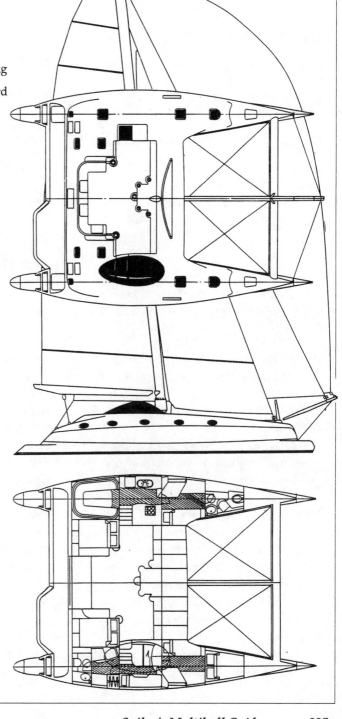

SPECIFICATIONS

Displacement	9,900 lbs, 4500 kg	
Standard Auxiliary	2 x 47 hp inboard	
Overall Length	50'0"	15.25 m
Waterline Length	49'6"	15.10 m
Bridgedeck Length	25'3"	7.70 m
Wing Deck Clearance	3'5"	1.05 m
Beam (max.)	34'9"	10.60 m
Draft (boards up)	1'6"	0.45 m
Draft (boards down)	10'8"	3.25 m
Mast Hgt. Off Water	79'4"	24.20 m

SAIL AREA

Wing Mast	106 sf	10 sm
Mainsail	1125 sf	105 sm
Jib	490 sf	45 sm
Total Area	1721 sf	160 sm
Spinnaker	2000 sf	180 sm

CAPACITY

Berths	5 sgls, 3 dbls
Staterooms	3
Heads	2
Fuel	60 gal 230 ltr
Fresh Water	100 gal 380 ltr
Payload	5,500 lbs, 2500 kg

NOVARA 52C

GENERAL INFORMATION

Classification   Semi-custom catamaran,
Cruiser/racer

Approx. Cost   US $780,000

Designer   Dr. Mai, Phil Morrison

Builder   KKG
Buttnergasse 1
A - 1230 Vienna, Austria
Tel: (43) 1 615 6666
Fax: (43) 1 615 6699
email:

Year Introduced   1997

Number of boats built

N. American Agent
California Multihull Yacht Sales & Charters
1235 Scott St., San Diego, CA 92106
Tel: (619) 222-9694
Fax: (619) 222-9693
email: cm@ginko.com

Other Cruising Multihulls By Builder
Novara 50RC and other boats in the Novara series, Macro Spaceshuttle, Spaceshuttle 1800-1300, Spaceshuttle 2000-1500

KEY FEATURES

Hull & Sail Plan
- Flared hulls, hydrodynamic keels dagger-board optional) reverse transoms w/ steps
- Free standing rotating Swing Rig with fully battened main and self-tacking jib

Deck Layout
- Trampoline forward w/ central support, lockers just aft, sleek cabintop design
- large cockpit, wide span aft deck with barbecue terrace and swim plaforms

Standard Accommodations
- Bridgedeck has galley to port, seating for 12, nav station, entertainment center aft
- Starboard hull has double stateroom aft, owner's cabin with private head forward
- Port hull has staterooms fore & aft, head with shower and single berth midships

Mechanical
- Wheel steering, dual helms aft in cockpit
- Twin inboards, access from aft decks

DESCRIPTION

The Novara 52C represents the more traditional design concepts of KKG, with sleek bridgedeck lines and a trampoline foredeck. All four cabins open up into the coachhouse, offering better viewing and good ventilation. The bridgedeck layout is functional and ergonomic, with a large navigation area, comfortable seating, and "galley up". The unique galley equipment incorporates a storage cylinder with three rotating carousel-like turn tables. Above, an aft deck extension provides plenty of space for sunbathing, sitting, and a drop down surfboard box and dinghy storage area, while the aft pontoons allow easy dinghy boarding and access to lower floating platforms. Under sail, the Swing Rig is safe and user friendly when reefing due to the weather cocking effect of a balanced main and self tacking jib. The boom is designed to collect rain water.

SPECIFICATIONS

Displacement	16,500 lbs, 7500 kg	
Standard Auxiliary	2 x 47 hp inboard	
Overall Length	52'5"	15.98 m
Waterline Length	52'1"	15.88 m
Bridgedeck Length	31'6"	9.60 m
Wing Deck Clearance	3'4"	1.00 m
Beam (max.)	33'0"	10.00 m
Draft (maximum)	4'5"	1.35 m
Mast Hgt. Off Deck	70'0"	21.40 m
Mast Hgt. Off Water	77'0"	23.50 m

SAIL AREA

Mainsail	1075 sf	100 sm
Jib	345 sf	32 sm
Total Area	1420 sf	132 sm
Spinnaker		

CAPACITY

Berths	3 sgls, 4 dbls	
Staterooms	4	
Heads	2	
Fuel	122 gal	460 ltr
Fresh Water	200 gal	760 ltr
Payload	6,600 lbs, 3000 kg	

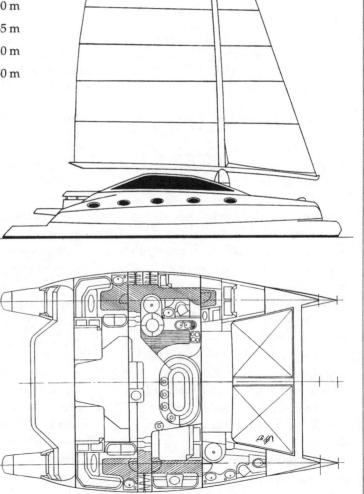

MACRO SPACESHUTTLE

GENERAL INFORMATION

Classification   Semi-custom catamaran,
                     Cruiser/racer

Approx. Cost   US $395,000

Designer   Dr. Mai, Phil Morrison

Builder   KKG
                     Buttnergasse 1
                     A - 1230 Vienna, Austria
                     Tel: (43) 1 615 6666
                     Fax: (43) 1 615 6699
                     email:

Year Introduced   1997

Number of boats built

N. American Agent
   California Multihull Yacht Sales & Charters
   1235 Scott St., San Diego, CA 92106
   Tel: (619) 222-9694
   Fax: (619) 222-9693
   email: cm@ginko.com

Other Cruising Multihulls By Builder
   Novara 50RC, 52C and other boats in the
   Novara series, Spaceshuttle 1800-1300,
   Spaceshuttle 2000-1500

KEY FEATURES

Hull & Sail Plan

- Flared hulls, hydrodynamic keels
  (daggerboard optional), reverse transoms
- Fractional sloop rig, rotating Swing Rig,
  fully battened main, self-tacking jib

Deck Layout

- Trampoline is replaced by large owner's
  suite in cabin with futuristic shape
- large aft sunbathing area with bimini, wide-
  span aft deck, swim platforms

Standard Accommodations

- Bridgedeck has galley, nav area, owner's
  suite forward with seating, queen berth
- Starboard hull has large stateroom aft and
  midships, head with shower forward
- Port hull has large stateroom aft and
  midships, head with shower forward

Mechanical

- Wheel steering, helm forward in cockpit
- Twin inboards, access from aft deck

DESCRIPTION

   The Macro Spaceshuttle is a high performance craft featuring a length to beam ratio
of 1:18.5, lightweight construction, and 50 ft
super slender hulls. The futuristic and
functional bridgedeck layout offers accommodations in the two chined 1.80m wide hulls,
with double berths and head/shower
compartments. Full headroom throughout
characterizes this floating "spaceship" design.
The wave-cutting concept of the hulls reduces
pitching and ensures excellent performance,
while creating a higher payload capacity due
to a larger water plane area. In the super-fast
motorsailer version, the aft pontoons are
kicked up (thus reducing marine berth fees)
and the SARO Tunnel-drive employed.
Under sail, all drive units are retracted for
less drag in the water. Other features include
inner helm options, a hardtop with solar
panels, and an anti-mosquito system.

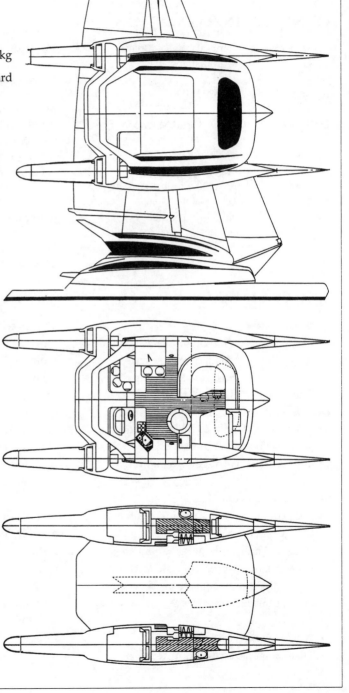

SPECIFICATIONS

Displacement	6,600 lbs, 3000 kg	
Standard Auxiliary	2 x 47 hp inboard	
Overall Length	42'9"	15.00 m
Waterline Length	48'10"	14.90 m
Bridgedeck Length	26'7"	8.10 m
Wing Deck Clearance	3'2"	0.95 m
Beam (max.)	23'0"	7.00 m
Draft (maximum)	4'5"	1.35 m
Mast Hgt. Off Deck	49'2"	15.00 m
Mast Hgt. Off Water	59'0"	17.95 m

SAIL AREA

Mainsail	575 sf	54 sm
Jib	190 sf	17 sm
Total Area	765 sf	71 sm
Spinnaker		

CAPACITY

Berths	2 sgls, 3 dbls
Staterooms	3
Heads	1-2
Fuel	48 gal 180 ltr
Fresh Water	80 gal 300 ltr
Payload	4,400 lbs, 2000 kg

SPACESHUTTLE 1800/1300

GENERAL INFORMATION

Classification   Semi-custom catamaran, Motorsailer cruiser/racer

Approx. Cost   US $800,000

Designer   Dr. Mai, Phil Morrison

Builder   KKG
Buttnergasse 1
A - 1230 Vienna, Austria
Tel: (43) 1 615 6666
Fax: (43) 1 615 6699
email:

Year Introduced   1997

Number of boats built

N. American Agent
California Multihull Yacht Sales & Charters
1235 Scott St., San Diego, CA 92106
Tel: (619) 222-9694
Fax: (619) 222-9693
email: cm@ginko.com

Other Cruising Multihulls By Builder
Novara 50RC, 52C and other boats in the Novara series, Macro Spaceshuttle, Spaceshuttle 2000-1500

KEY FEATURES

Hull & Sail Plan
- Flared hulls, hydrodynamic keels (daggerboard optional), reverse transoms
- Fractional sloop rig, rotating Swing Rig, fully battened main, self-tacking jib

Deck Layout
- Trampoline is replaced by large owner's suite in cabin with futuristic shape
- large cockpit, flybridge with int'r & ext'r helms, wide-span aft deck, swim platforms

Standard Accommodations
- Bridgedeck has galley, nav area with helm, lounge seating, owner's suite forward
- Starboard hull has large stateroom aft and midships, dressing room/head forward
- Port hull has stateroom aft, head midships, owner's head forward, his & hers showers

Mechanical
- Wheel steering, 3 helm locations
- Twin inboards, access from aft decks

DESCRIPTION

The Spaceshuttle 1800-1300 is the newest and most revolutionary of the KKG boats. By replacing the trampoline-front crossbeam elements with a composite shell structure, a unique owners suite is created that has a double berth, seating corner, entertainment centre, hanging lockers and huge window. Similar cabin space can only be found on monohulls double the length. Her "bullet" type aerodynamic bridgedeck also creates a flybridge-sunbathing deck with excellent all round visibility. Different interior layouts are possible, including an owner's version featuring a spacious split-level head in the port forward hull. Charter versions (more cabins and berths) and wheelchair versions (a continuous level bridgedeck) are also possible with the KKG modular concept used. She has a free standing, 360 degree rotating carbon-fibre Swing Rig for easy sail-handling.

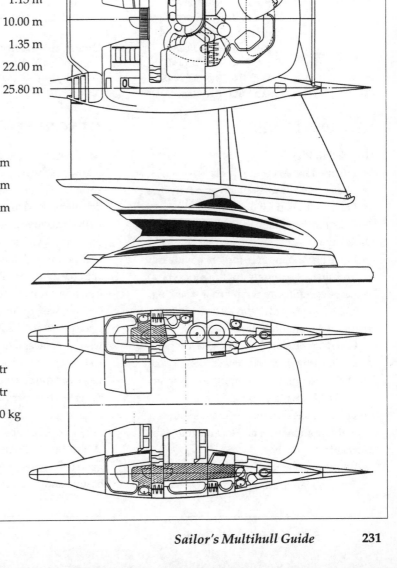

SPECIFICATIONS

Displacement	17,600 lbs, 8000 kg	
Standard Auxiliary	2 x 100 hp inboard	
Overall Length	59'0"	18.00 m
Waterline Length	58'8"	17.90 m
Bridgedeck Length	40'0"	12.20 m
Wing Deck Clearance	3'9"	1.15 m
Beam (max.)	33'0"	10.00 m
Draft (max.)	4'5"	1.35 m
Mast Hgt. Off Deck	72'2"	22.00 m
Mast Hgt. Off Water	84'7"	25.80 m

SAIL AREA

Mainsail	1310 sf	122 sm
Jib	410 sf	38 sm
Total Area	1720 sf	160 sm
Spinnaker		

CAPACITY

Berths	3 sgls, 4 dbls
Staterooms	4
Heads	3
Fuel	122 gal 460 ltr
Fresh Water	200 gal 760 ltr
Payload	7,500 lbs, 3400 kg

LAGOON 410

GENERAL INFORMATION

Classification   Production catamaran,
                     Cruiser

Approx. Cost   Call for current price

Designers   Van Peterghem,
                     Lauriot-Prévost

Builder   Lagoon/Jeanneau
                     Rue de l'Ile Pointiere, ZI
                     de Cheviré-BP 40120, 44101
                     Nantes Cedex 4, France
                     Tel: (33) (02) 40 32 00 17
                     Fax: (33) (02) 40 32 00 02
                     email: cata-lagoon.com

Year Introduced   1998

Number of boats built   none (as of Sep 97)

N. American Agent
     Lagoon America
     105 Eastern Ave., Suite 202
     Annapolis, MD 21403
     Tel: (410) 280-9400   Fax: (410) 280-9401
     email: lagoonam@aol.com

Other Cruising Multihulls By Builder
     Lagoon 470, Lagoon 57, Lagoon 67

KEY FEATURES

Hull & Sail Plan
- Integral low-asect-ratio keels
- Near-plumb bows, long reverse transoms
- Fractional sloop rig
- Fully roached main, roller-furling jib

Deck Layout
- Large trampoline area forward, wide rigid deck just aft with self-draining lockers
- Large cockpit with wrap-around seating, table to starboard, helm forward to port

Standard Accommodations
- Galley up on starboard bridgedeck, with large seating area and nav station to port
- Starboard hull has stateroom aft, storage midships, and large head forward
- Port hull has staterooms fore and aft, with common head and lockers midships

Mechanical
- Wheel steering forward to port in cockpit
- Twin inboards, access from aft cabins

DESCRIPTION

Another new design from Lagoon, the 410 maintains the traditions from which it springs. The standard model includes three double-berth cabins and two large heads, with a spacious galley-living area on the bridgedeck which opens directly to the cockpit through a wide, sliding door. The starboard forward stateroom can also function as an office or workroom. The cockpit, well protected by the cabin roof, has a starboard side table which can seat up to ten. The placement of the helm station at the roof's rear provides a wider view as well as more cockpit space. The forward section of the cabin roof provides some shading for the cabin windows. In the bow the transverse net offers a comfortable, secure seating area. With a fully-battened main and roller furling genoa, the Lagoon 410 promises to be an easily handled boat with high performance.

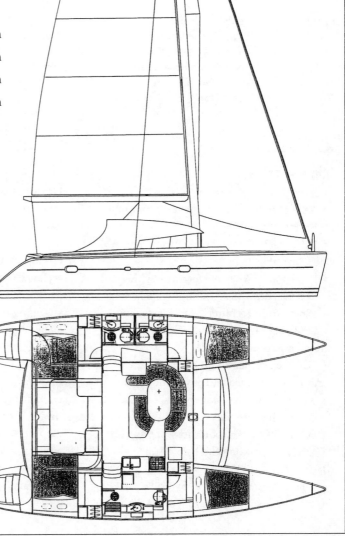

SPECIFICATIONS

Displacement	15,653 lbs,	7100 kg
Standard Auxiliary	2 x 28 hp inboard	
Overall Length	40'5"	12.37 m
Waterline Length	38'5"	11.70 m
Bridgedeck Length	24'0"	7.35 m
Wing Deck Clearance		
Beam (max.)	23'6"	7.09 m
Draft (max.)	3'11"	1.20 m
Mast Hgt. Off Deck	52'0"	15.86 m
Mast Hgt. From WL	60'0"	18.30 m

SAIL AREA

Mainsail	570 sf	53 sm
Genoa	388 sf	36 sm
Total Area	958 sf	89 sm
Spinnaker	1292 sf	120 sm

CAPACITY

Berths	2-4 doubles	
Staterooms	2-4	
Heads	2	
Fuel	68 gal	260 ltr
Fresh Water	158 gal	600 ltr
Payload		

LAGOON 470

GENERAL INFORMATION

Classification   Production catamaran, Cruiser

Approx. Cost   Call for current pricing

Designers   Van Peterghem, Lauriot-Prévost

Builder   Lagoon/Jeanneau
Rue de l'Ile Pointiere, ZI
de Cheviré-BP 40120, 44101
Nantes Cedex 4, France
Tel: (33) (02) 40 32 00 17
Fax: (33) (02) 40 32 00 02
email: cata-lagoon.com

Year Introduced   1998

Number of boats built   none (as of Sep 97)

N. American Agent
Lagoon America
105 Eastern Ave., Suite 202
Annapolis, MD 21403
Tel: (410) 280-9400 Fax: (410) 280-9401
email: lagoonam@aol.com

Other Cruising Multihulls By Builder
Lagoon 410, Lagoon 57, Lagoon 67

KEY FEATURES

Hull & Sail Plan
- Integral low-asect-ratio keels
- Near-plumb bows, long reverse transoms
- Fractional sloop rig
- Fully roached main, roller-furling jib

Deck Layout
- Large trampoline area forward, wide rigid deck just aft with self-draining lockers
- Wrap-around seating & table in cockpit
- Sleek cabin top with shading overhang

Standard Accommodations
- Galley up on starboard bridgedeck, with large seating area and nav station to port
- Starboard hull has staterooms fore and aft, each with private heads
- Port hull has staterooms forward and aft, each with private head compartments

Mechanical
- Wheel steering to port in cockpit
- Twin inboards, access from aft decks

DESCRIPTION

The Lagoon 470 is the latest creation from Lagoon/Jeanneau. She has all the standard features sailors have come to expect from the Lagoon line, plus a new cabin roof design incorporating a shading overhang and elegant yet practical interior layout and styling. The Lagoon 470 has an efficient fractional rig, fully battened mainsail, and sweeping reverse transoms with boarding steps. Accommodations include two large aft double staterooms with hanging lockers and bureaus, two slightly smaller double cabins up forward, and a total of four private head compartments midships. The bridgedeck design is unmistakenly French, with gently curving settees and galley countertops. The galley and lounge areas are large enough to comfortably handle eight charter guests or a large family.

SPECIFICATIONS

Displacement	19,842 lbs, 9000 kg	
Standard Auxiliary	2 x 38 hp inboard	
Overall Length	46'3"	14.10 m
Waterline Length	42'8"	13.00 m
Bridgedeck Length	31'6"	9.59 m
Wing Deck Clearance		
Beam (max.)	25'11"	7.90 m
Draft (max.)	3'11"	1.20 m
Mast Hgt. Off Deck	59'0"	18.01 m
Mast Hgt. From WL	66'9"	20.40 m

SAIL AREA

Mainsail	710 sf	66 sm
Genoa	376 sf	35 sm
Total Area	1086 sf	101 sm
Spinnaker	1292 sf	120 sm

CAPACITY

Berths	4 doubles	
Staterooms	4	
Heads	4	
Fuel	160 gal	600 ltr
Fresh Water	130 gal	480 ltr
Payload		

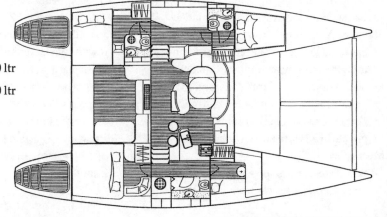

LAGOON 57

GENERAL INFORMATION

Classification   Production catamaran, Luxury cruiser

Approx. Cost   Call for current price

Designers   Van Peterghem, Lauriot-Prévost

Builder   Lagoon/Jeanneau
Rue de l'lle Pointiere, ZI
de Cheviré-BP 40120, 44101
Nantes Cedex 4, France
Tel: (33) (02) 40 32 00 17
Fax: (33) (02) 40 32 00 02
email: cata-lagoon.com

Year Introduced   1993

Number of boats built   7   (as of Sep 97)

N. American Agent
Lagoon America
105 Eastern Ave., Suite 202
Annapolis, MD 21403
Tel: (410) 280-9400   Fax: (410) 280-9401
email: lagoonam@aol.com

Other Cruising Multihulls By Builder
Lagoon 410, Lagoon 470, Lagoon 67

KEY FEATURES

Hull & Sail Plan
- Integral low-asect-ratio keels
- Near-plumb bows, long reverse transoms
- Fractional cutter rig
- Fully roached main, roller-furling jib

Deck Layout
- Large trampoline area forward, wide rigid deck just aft, wide side decks
- Wrap-around seating & table in cockpit
- Large door to saloon cabin, aft sundecks

Standard Accommodations
- Spacious lounge area to starboard, dinette to starboard, nav area forward midships
- Starboard hull has large staterooms with private heads fore and aft, galley midships
- Port hull has large staterooms with private heads fore and aft, storage midships

Mechanical
- Wheel steering, dual helms aft in cockpit
- Twin inboards, access from aft decks

DESCRIPTION

The Lagoon 57 is one of the largest of the Lagoon/Jeanneau catamarans. Her dynamic design is the product of the Grande Prix multihull experience of her designers, Marc Van Peteghem and Vincent Lauriot-Prévost. Conceived as a sea-friendly performance cruiser, she is built with sophisticated materials and craftsmanship. From her stylish appearance to her luxury accommodations, the Lagoon 57 is destined to appeal to the well-heeled private owner as well as crewed charter operators. Standard interior layout features four private staterooms with en suite heads, well equipped galley, and spacious saloon with dual seating areas, one primarily a lounge area and the other a large dining area. Easy to handle under sail, the Lagoon 57 frequently reaches speeds of up to 22 knots.

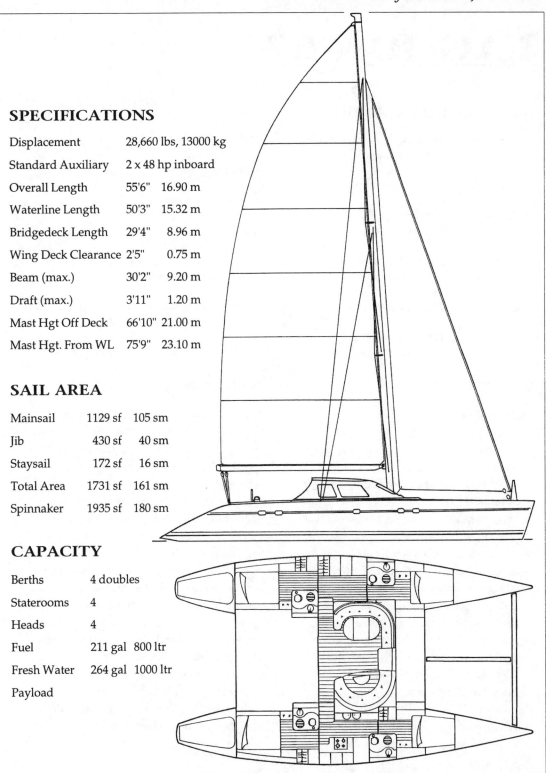

SPECIFICATIONS

Displacement	28,660 lbs, 13000 kg	
Standard Auxiliary	2 x 48 hp inboard	
Overall Length	55'6"	16.90 m
Waterline Length	50'3"	15.32 m
Bridgedeck Length	29'4"	8.96 m
Wing Deck Clearance	2'5"	0.75 m
Beam (max.)	30'2"	9.20 m
Draft (max.)	3'11"	1.20 m
Mast Hgt Off Deck	66'10"	21.00 m
Mast Hgt. From WL	75'9"	23.10 m

SAIL AREA

Mainsail	1129 sf	105 sm
Jib	430 sf	40 sm
Staysail	172 sf	16 sm
Total Area	1731 sf	161 sm
Spinnaker	1935 sf	180 sm

CAPACITY

Berths	4 doubles	
Staterooms	4	
Heads	4	
Fuel	211 gal	800 ltr
Fresh Water	264 gal	1000 ltr
Payload		

LAGOON 67

GENERAL INFORMATION

Classification   Production catamaran, Luxury cruiser

Approx. Cost   Call for current price

Designers   Van Peterghem, Lauriot-Prévost

Builder   Lagoon/Jeanneau
Rue de l'Ile Pointiere, ZI
de Cheviré-BP 40120, 44101
Nantes Cedex 4, France
Tel: (33) (02) 40 32 00 17
Fax: (33) (02) 40 32 00 02
email: cata-lagoon.com

Year Introduced   1996

Number of boats built   1 (as of Sep 97)

N. American Agent
Lagoon America
105 Eastern Ave., Suite 202
Annapolis, MD 21403
Tel: (410) 280-9400 Fax: (410) 280-9401
email: lagoonam@aol.com

Other Cruising Multihulls By Builder
Lagoon 410, Lagoon 470, Lagoon 57

KEY FEATURES

Hull & Sail Plan
- Integral low-asect-ratio keels
- Near-plumb bows, long reverse transoms
- Fractional cutter rig
- Fully roached main, roller-furling jibs

Deck Layout
- Large trampoline area with central walkway forward, wide rigid deck just aft
- U-shaped seating with table in cockpit
- Expansive deck space, sundecks aft

Standard Accommodations
- Bridgedeck has two large seating areas and spacious central nav station or office
- Starboard hull has huge staterooms with private heads fore & aft, crew quarters
- Port hull has huge staterooms with private heads fore & aft, home-size galley midships

Mechanical
- Wheel steering, dual helms aft in cockpit
- Twin inboards, access from aft decks

DESCRIPTION

The Lagoon 67 is the grandest yacht in the Lagoon catamaran fleet. Despite her size, she is easy to handle. She frequently reaches speeds of up to 26 knots, making her an exciting yacht under sail. From a choice of layout to the style of decoration, the Lagoon 67 can be customized to suit each individual owner. The standard interior layout offers four double-berth, well-appointed state-rooms, each with its own writing desk and seat, large hanging locker, and en suite head/shower compartment. The spacious saloon provides two seating areas, two teak tables, and elegant yet functional navigation station, while the galley area, located in the hull, comes equipped with stove, refrigeration, double sink, hot and cold pressurized water, and ice box. For the crewed charter trade, a crew cabin with two berths and private head can replace the aft starboard cabin.

SPECIFICATIONS

Displacement	39,000 lbs, 19,500 kg	
Standard Auxiliary	2 x 100 hp inboard	
Overall Length	67'7"	20.60 m
Waterline Length	61'0"	18.60 m
Bridgedeck Length	34'0"	10.33 m
Wing Deck Clearance	2'11"	0.90 m
Beam (max.)	35'1"	10.70 m
Draft (max.)	5'3"	1.60 m
Mast Hgt Off Deck		
Mast Hgt. From WL	92'1"	28.09 m

SAIL AREA

Mainsail	1453 sf	135 sm
Jib	915 sf	85 sm
Staysail	398 sf	37 sm
Total Area	2766 sf	257 sm
Spinnaker	2476 sf	230 sm

CAPACITY

Berths	4-5 doubles	
Staterooms	4	
Heads	4	
Fuel	264 gal	1000 ltr
Fresh Water	316 gal	1200 ltr
Payload		

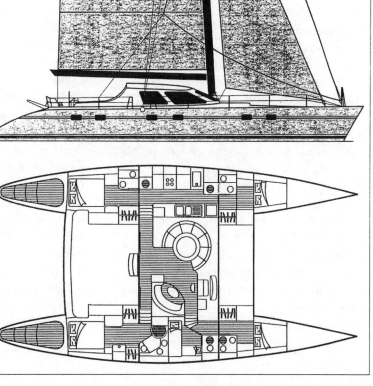

SUNCHASER 58

GENERAL INFORMATION

Classification   Semi-custom catamaran, Cruiser/charter cruiser

Approx. Cost   Call for current pricing

Designer   Kurt Hughes

Builder: Lightspeed Marine Corp
895 Harris St.
Bellingham, WA 98225
USA
Tel: (360) 725-2747
Fax: (360) 725-4697
email: khughes@isomedia.com

Year Introduced   1995

Number of boats built

N. American Dealers   Buy factory direct

Other Cruising Multihulls By Builder
Daycharter version of the Sunchaser 58

KEY FEATURES

Hull & Sail Plan
- Full round hulls, daggerboards, near plumb bows, wide reverse transoms
- Fractional sloop rig, fully battened main, roller-furling headsail, asym. spinnaker

Deck Layout
- Trampoline forward, wide deck just aft, wide side decks, sleek cabin lines, aft decks
- Cockpit has port seating with table, unique raised pilothouse helm station

Standard Accommodations
- Bridgedeck has galley aft to port, huge lounge area & nav station/library forward
- Starboard hull has large aft stateroom, central head, large stateroom forward
- Port hull has large aft stateroom, central head, large stateroom/head forward

Mechanical
- Wheel, helms in cockpit and in saloon area
- Twin inboards, access from aft cabins

DESCRIPTION

The Sunchaser 58 is another high performance cruising multihull from the design office of Kurt Hughes, and now being built on a semi-custom basis by Richard Elder of Lightspeed Marine. The hulls, constructed of triaxial and unidirectional roving on pvc foam using vinylester resin, have a minimum wetted surface, wide transoms for power reaching, and low drag at high speed. The cockpit helm is protected by a raised pilothouse which allows 360-degree visibility. The main saloon cabin is immense, with wet lockers at the cockpit door, an office-size navigation station and library, an entertainment area aft, a sweeping lounge and dining area forward, and a galley aft that is out of the way of foot traffic. Many other boats have four double-berth cabins, but these staterooms are large and comfortable. Storage areas abound on this livable world cruiser.

SPECIFICATIONS

Displacement	29,500 lbs, 13,381 kg	
Standard Auxiliary	2 x 170 hp inboard	
Overall Length	58'2"	17.73 m
Waterline Length	57'0"	17.52 m
Bridgedeck Length	32'3"	9.82 m
Wing Deck Clearance	3'11"	9.40 m
Beam (max.)	23'4"	7.12 m
Draft (min.)	2'0"	0.60 m
Draft (max.)	8'6"	2.59 m
Mast Hgt. Off Water	77'5"	21.62 m

SAIL AREA

Mainsail	1052 sf	98 sm
Jib	380 sf	34 sm
Total Area	1432 sf	133 sm
Spinnaker	1510 sf	140 sm

CAPACITY

Berths	4 doubles	
Staterooms	4	
Heads	2-3	
Fuel	40 gal	151 ltr
Fresh Water	60 gal	227 ltr
Payload	8,000 lbs, 3630 kg	

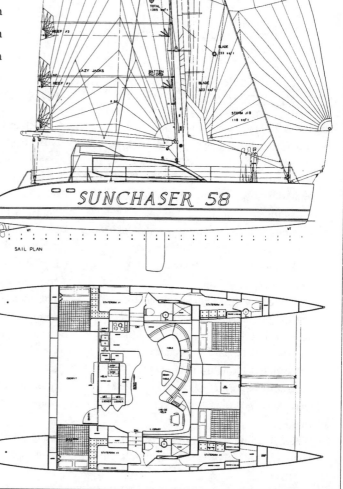

SUNCHASER 58

ATLANTIC 42

GENERAL INFORMATION

Classification   Production catamaran, Cruiser/racer

Approx. Cost   US $359,000

Designer   Chris White

Builder   Lombardi Yachts
Marina Road, North, VA
23128 USA
Tel: (804) 725-2747
Fax: (804) 725-4697
email: cwdesign@ma.ultranet.com

Year Introduced   1996

Number of boats built   3 (as of Sep 97)

N. American Dealers   Buy factory direct

Other Cruising Multihulls By Builder
None at present

KEY FEATURES

Hull & Sail Plan
- Epoxy resin hulls, daggerboards, near-plumb bows, long reverse transoms
- Fractional sloop rig, raked mast, fully battened main and roller-furling genoa

Deck Layout
- Trampoline forward, unique center cockpit layout with protected pilothouse aft
- Cockpit has port & starboard seating

Standard Accommodations
- Bridgedeck has pilothouse with helm and nav station forward, seat and table aft
- Starboard hull has 1 single & 1 double stateroom, head, and long galley aft
- Port hull has 1 single and 1 double stateroom, head, shower/workshop aft forward with storage area and private head

Mechanical
- Wheel steering, helm center in cockpit
- Twin inboards, aft access in each hull

DESCRIPTION

The Atlantic 42 is designed to provide high-performance sailing along with safe, all-weather cruising comfort for up to seven occupants. She's built with high quality materials, and the builder claims she has the highest strength-to-weight ratio of any production catamaran on the market. Her most striking feature is the central cockpit layout, with the mast stepped at the forward end and a pilothouse placed aft of the cockpit. This makes all sheets, halyards, daggerboard controls and reefing lines within easy reach of the helmsman, plus gives unobstructed visibility. An inside steering/nav station is located forward in the pilothouse, which also offers a large dining table with comfortable seating. Other accommodations include a well-equipped galley adjacent to the pilot-house, four separate sleeping cabins and two single berths, plus an optional pilot berth.

SPECIFICATIONS

Displacement	14,500 lbs, 6583 kg	
Standard Auxiliary	2 x 18 hp inboard	
Overall Length	42'0"	12.81 m
Waterline Length	41'0"	12.51 m
Bridgedeck Length	22'0"	6.71 m
Wing Deck Clearance	2'5"	0.72 m
Beam (max.)	23'4"	7.12 m
Draft (min.)	2'8"	0.81 m
Draft (max.)	7'0"	2.14 m
Mast Hgt. Off Water	63'0"	19.22 m

SAIL AREA

Mainsail	625 sf	58 sm
Genoa	370 sf	34 sm
Total Area	995 sf	92 sm
Spinnaker	1250 sf	116 sm

CAPACITY

Berths	2-3 sgle, 2 dble	
Staterooms	4	
Heads	2	
Fuel	54 gal	204 ltr
Fresh Water	80 gal	303 ltr
Payload		

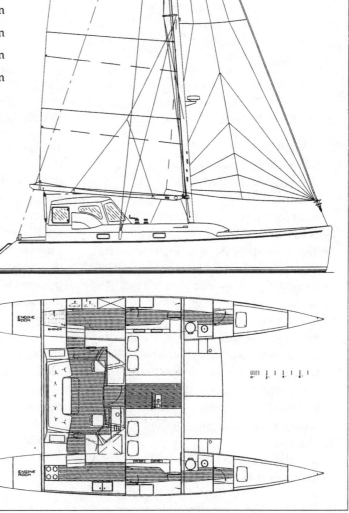

LUAU 350

GENERAL INFORMATION

Classification   Production catamaran, Cruiser

Approx. Cost   US $155,900 (complete)
US $68,000 (kit)

Designer   Bertrand LeFebvre

Builder   Luau Boats, Inc.
PO Box 471
Grosse Ile, MI 48138 USA
Toll-free: (888) 229-4543
Tel/Fax: (313) 693-0813
email:luauboats@earthlink.net

Year Introduced   1996

Number of boats built   3 (as of Sep 97)

N. American Dealers   Buy factory direct

Other Cruising Multihulls By Builder
38 ft. cruising catamaran, other custom multihulls, stock plans available

KEY FEATURES

Hull & Sail Plan
- Integral keels, inboard rudders, reverse transoms with molded boarding steps
- Fractional sloop rig, fully roached main, roller-furling jib

Deck Layout
- Trampoline forward, large lockers just aft
- Wide side decks, good foot space
- Large cockpit offers ample seating and storage lockers

Standard Accommodations
- Bridgedeck has storage lockers aft and semi-circular settee with table, nav area forward
- Starboard hull has stateroom aft, storage/berth forward, head midships
- Port hull has stateroom aft, smaller stateroom forward, galley midships

Mechanical
- Wheel steering, forward to starboard
- Twin inboards, access from aft cabins

DESCRIPTION

The Luau 350 is a well-conceived, fast cruising catamaran. Built in the U.S. by Luau Boats, this 35 footer reflects the French heritage of her designer/builder, Bertrand Lefebvre. Wide beam, shallow draft, flat and stable surfaces, ease of handling and maintenance, comfortable accommodations with lots of headroom, and a reasonable price combine to make this a good choice for family cruising. The Luau 350 is built entirely of strong, blisterproof epoxy resins to emphasize strength, durability and light weight. Accommodations below can sleep up to seven (depending on the layout selected) with at least two queen-size berths; a head with shower; large, well-equipped galley; navigation center; saloon seating for six; and ample ventilation. Other layout options include a workshop, office space, extra sleeping quarters or additional stowage.

SPECIFICATIONS

Displacement	7,800 lbs, 3538 kg	
Standard Auxiliary	2 x 9.9 hp inboard	
Overall Length	35'0"	10.67 m
Waterline Length	32'6"	9.91 m
Bridgedeck Length	22'4"	6.80 m
Wing Deck Clearance	2'0"	0.60 m
Beam (max.)	19'0"	5.79 m
Draft (max.)	2'9"	0.84 m
Mast Hgt. Off Deck	43'0"	13.12 m
Mast Hgt. Off Water	48'6"	14.78 m

SAIL AREA

Mainsail	472 sf	44 sm
Genoa	202 sf	19 sm
Total Area	674 sf	63 sm
Spinnaker	650 sf	60 sm

CAPACITY

Berths	1-2 sgls, 2-3 dbls	
Staterooms	3	
Heads	1	
Fuel	31 gal	117 ltr
Fresh Water	66 gal	250 ltr
Payload	1300 lbs, 590 kg	

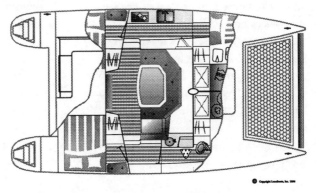

OCEAN TWINS 38

GENERAL INFORMATION

Classification   Semi-custom catamaran
Cruiser

Approx. Cost   £170,000

Designer   Pat Patterson

Builder   Maikara Manufacturing
Agent   Ocean Sales
Thornham Marina,
Emsworth, Hants,
PO10 8DD England
Tel: (44) 1243 377333
Fax: (44) 1243 377378
email: sales@multihullworld.co.uk

Year Introduced   1993

Number of boats built

N. American Dealers   None at present

Other Cruising Multihulls By Builder
The Heavenly Twins 27 and 36 are also
marketed by Ocean Sales and Multihull
World UK

KEY FEATURES

Hull & Sail Plan
- Integral keels & rudder skegs, high-
buoyancy hulls, transoms w/ molded steps
- Masthead cutter rig, battened mainsail,
roller-furling genoa, staysail

Deck Layout
- Fully rigid foredeck with lockers, large
central cockpit with wrap-around seating
- Aft double cabins create protected cockpit

Standard Accommodations
- Bridgedeck area has large settee/dining
area forward, nav area and lockers aft
- Starboard hull has large aft stateroom,
common head midships, stateroom forward
- Port hull has large stateroom aft, common
head midships, long galley forward

Mechanical
- Wheel steering, helm forward in cockpit
- Twin inboards, access from aft cabins

DESCRIPTION

Similar to the former Ocean Winds 33 in
design and layout, the Ocean Twins 38
continues the Patterson tradition of cruising
comfort and dependable performance on an
exceptionally seaworthy, ocean-going craft.
Accommodations are spacious, with a
minimum of three separate staterooms,
standing headroom throughout, and a huge
galley over 12 feet long in the port hull. Her
balanced cutter rig and mast with all sail-
handling control lines accessible from the
cockpit makes performance under sail a
breeze. Her design allows for a truly impressive carrying and storage capacity for a boat
her size, a Patterson trademark evidenced on
his Heavenly Twins series. Well built with
some touches of luxury, the Ocean Twins is
perfect for coastal cruising, ocean passages or
living aboard.

SPECIFICATIONS

Displacement	8,840 lbs, 4000 kg	
Standard Auxiliary	2 x 18 hp inboard	
Overall Length	38'0"	11.70 m
Waterline Length	31'9"	9.71 m
Bridgedeck Length	35'4"	10.80 m
Wing Deck Clearance		
Beam (max.)	19'6"	5.95 m
Draft (max.)	4'0"	1.18 m
Mast Hgt. Off Deck	47'0"	14.33 m
Mast Hgt. Off Water	54'2"	16.51 m

SAIL AREA

Mainsail	250 sf	23 sm
Geno	350 sf	33 sm
Staysail	80 sf	7 sm
Total Area	680 sf	63 sm
Spinnaker		

CAPACITY

Berths	3-4 doubles	
Staterooms	3	
Heads	2	
Fuel	38 gal	173 ltr
Fresh Water	70 gal	318 ltr
Payload	4,420 lbs, 2000 kg	

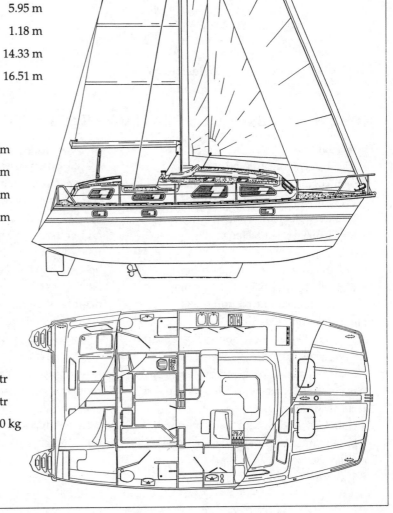

MAINE CAT 22

GENERAL INFORMATION

Classification	Production catamaran, Performance daysailer	**Year Introduced**	1994
Approx. Cost	US $25,950	**Number of boats built**	18 (as of Sep 97)
Designer	Dick Newick	**N. American Dealers**	Buy factory direct

Builder: Maine Cat
Address: P.O. Box 645
Waldoboro, ME 04572 USA
Toll Free: (888) 832-CATS
Tel: (207) 832-6678
Fax: (207) 832-6678
email: mecat@biddeford.com

Other Cruising Multihulls By Builder
Maine Cat 30, other custom multihulls

KEY FEATURES

Hull & Sail Plan
- Kick-up centerboards and rudders
- Semi-circular sections forward, flat run, very fine entry; built-in buoyancy
- Fractional sloop rig w/ moderate roach
- Roller-furling, self-tacking 100% jib

Deck Layout
- Trampoline forward of cross beam
- Rigid bridgedeck w/ hinged folding system aft including cockpit soles

Standard Accommodations
- 3 to 4 adults can sleep comfortably under a bridgedeck tent arrangement
- Cockpit seating is provided by adjustable wood-caned chairs with full back support

Mechanical
- Outboard rudders with tillers connected by aluminum crossbar and telescoping tiller extention
- Transom-hung outboard motor

DESCRIPTION

This boat is one of the only production folding catamarans on the market. Stable 13 foot beam and solid bridgedeck provide a comfortable, dry ride for the whole family. The Maine Cat 22 is a performance day cruiser that can keep 5 or 6 adults dry and relaxed while under sail. This is a real sea boat that can handle a breeze without "flying" a hull—maximum angle of heel is 5 degrees. Watertight compartments fore and aft in each hull provide storage areas for extended camper cruising. All sail controls are double ended to both port and starboard helmsman seats. Pivoting centerboards and rudders allow for shallow water exploring and beaching. Simple single-handed folding system reduces the beam to 8'6" for easy trailering.

SPECIFICATIONS

Displacement	2,340 lbs, 1064 kg	
Standard Auxiliary	3 to 6 hp outboard	
Overall Length	22'0"	6.71 m
Waterline Length	21'8"	6.63 m
Bridgedeck Length	7'6"	2.29 m
Wing Deck Clearance	1'6"	0.46 m
Beam (max.)	13'0"	3.97 m
Beam (folded)	8'6'	2.59 m
Draft (boards up)	0'11"	0.27 m
Draft (boards down)	2'10"	0.88 m
Mast Hgt. Off Water	33'0"	10.07 m

SAIL AREA

Mainsail	196 sf	18 sm
Jib	71 sf	7 sm
Total Area	267 sf	25 sm

CAPACITY

Berths (in tent)	3-4 adults
Storage	65 cubic feet
Heads	1 portable
Fuel (portable)	3 gal 11 ltr
Water (portable)	5 gal 19 ltr
Payload	950 lbs, 432 kg

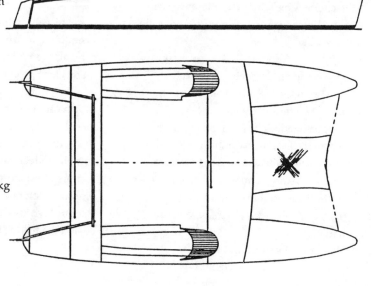

MAINE CAT 30

GENERAL INFORMATION

Classification   Production catamaran,
Cruiser/racer

Approx. Cost   US $79,900

Designer   Maine Cat Design Team

Builder: Maine Cat
Address: P.O. Box 645
Waldoboro, ME 04572 USA
Toll Free: (888) 832-CATS
Tel: (207) 832-6678
Fax: (207) 832-6678
email: mecat@biddeford.com

Year Introduced   1996

Number of boats built   2 (as of Sep 97)

N. American Dealers   Buy factory direct

Other Cruising Multihulls By Builder
Maine Cat 22, custom multihulls

KEY FEATURES

Hull & Sail Plan
- Inboard rudders and custom keels or centerboards; semi-circular sections forward, moderate rocker, fine entry
- Fractional sloop rig w/ moderate roach main, roller-furling/self-tacking 100% jib

Deck Layout
- Trampoline forward w/ central walkway
- Open bridgedeck combines cockpit and open salon, seats 8 adults under bimini

Standard Accommodations
- Open bridgedeck has flexible cover and table that converts to double berth
- Starboard hull has head forward in master stateroom; storage midships, dble berth aft
- Port hull has double berth forward, galley midships, dinette that seats 5 aft

Mechanical
- Wheel steering in central cockpit
- Twin outboards under cockpit seats

DESCRIPTION

The Maine Cat 30 is an affordable open bridgedeck catamaran designed for comfortable, non-heeling family relaxation for a weekend get-away or an extended cruise in the Islands. She can be easily single-handed from the central helm station, with excellent visibility in all directions. All sail and engine controls are within easy reach of the helmsman. Her fine entry, buoyant ends and excellent underwing clearance produce an easy motion in a seaway. Her hulls have a nice flare to the topsides, which yields a very pleasant and open interior. The 7 ft x 12 ft combined deck salon and cockpit areas can be completely enclosed with side curtains and bimini, or left open to enjoy the breeze. Interior layouts and underwater foils can be customized to individual requirements.

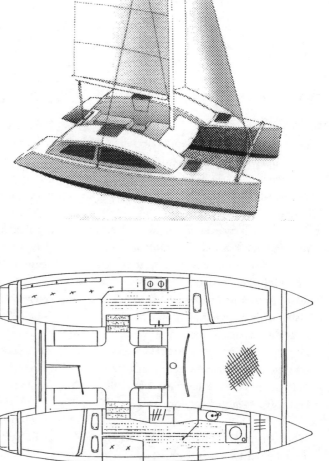

SPECIFICATIONS

Displacement	6,000 lbs, 2724 k₅	
Standard Auxiliary	2 x 9.9 hp outboa	
Overall Length	30'0"	9.15 m
Waterline Length	29'3"	8.92 m
Bridgedeck Length	12'6"	3.81 m
Wing Deck Clearance	2'2"	0.67 m
Beam (max.)	16'0"	4.88 m
Draft (boards up)	2'0"	0.61 m
Draft (boards down)	4'7"	1.40 m
Mast Hgt. Off Water	43'0"	13.12 m

SAIL AREA

Mainsail	350 sf	33 sm
Jib	120 sf	11 sm
Total Area	470 sf	44 sm
Spinnaker	580 sf	54 sm

CAPACITY

Hull Berths	2 dbls, 1 sgle	
Bridgedeck berth	1 double	
Staterooms	2	
Heads	1	
Fuel (portable)	14 gal	53 ltr
Fresh Water	26 gal	98 ltr
Payload	2,400 lbs, 1090 kg	

MANTA 40

GENERAL INFORMATION

Classification   Production catamaran, Cruiser

Approx. Cost   US $200,000

Designer   Manta Enterprises

Builder   Manta Enterprises
7855 126th Ave. N.
Largo, FL 34643 USA
Tel: (813) 536-8446
Fax: (813) 536-8545
email:

Year Introduced   1994
(as the Manta 38)

Number of boats built   31 (as of Sep 97)

N. American Dealers   Buy factory direct

Other Cruising Multihulls By Builder
None at present

KEY FEATURES

Hull & Sail Plan
- Integral keels, inboard rudders, reverse transoms with molded boarding steps
- Fractional sloop rig, fully roached main, roller-furling, self-tacking jib

Deck Layout
- Trampoline forward with walkway, lockers just aft, wide side decks, good foot space
- large cockpit with hardtop and stern arch
- Cockpit lockers and storage areas

Standard Accommodations
- Galley up to port with nav area nearby, large dining area to starboard
- Starboard hull has comfortable staterooms fore and aft with central common head
- Port hull has the master stateroom with berth aft and large head forward

Mechanical
- Wheel steering, helm forward in cockpit
- Twin inboards, access from aft cabins

DESCRIPTION

Formerly the Manta 38, the Manta 40 represents a nice blend of performance, aesthetics, accommodation, and value in a cruising catamaran. Hull, deck, and structural bulkheads are composite construction, utilizing isopthalic and vinylester resins, multiaxial and unidirectional E-glass, polypropylene honeycomb core, and vacuum bagging. The hull is solid fiberglass below the waterline. Both hull and deck are constructed in one piece and bonded together. Standard equipment includes twin 29 hp diesels with S-drives and folding propellers, and electric winch. The accommodation plan has been developed from customer feedback, offering spacious galley up, one complete hull dedicated to the owner's stateroom and head, large separate shower stalls, large refrigerator and freezer compartments, and queen-size berths.

SPECIFICATIONS

Displacement	13,000 lbs, 5900 kg	
Standard Auxiliary	2 x 29 hp inboard	
Overall Length	39'8"	12.00 m
Waterline Length	39'0"	11.80 m
Bridgedeck Length	22'8"	6.91 m
Wing Deck Clearance	2'4"	0.71 m
Beam (max.)	21'0"	6.40 m
Draft (max.)	3'0"	0.92 m
Mast Hgt. Off Deck	50'0"	15.25 m
Mast Hgt. Off Water	59.5"	18.13 m

SAIL AREA

Mainsail	490 sf	46 sm
Genoa	300 sf	28 sm
Total Area	798 sf	74 sm
Spinnaker		

CAPACITY

Berths	3 doubles
Staterooms	3
Heads	2
Fuel	100 gal 379 ltr
Fresh Water	100 gal 379 ltr
Payload	3,500 lbs, 1590 kg

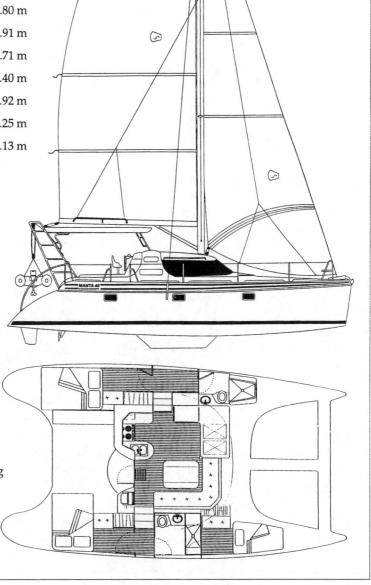

FEATHERLIGHT 43

LIVEABOARD CRUISER

GENERAL INFORMATION

Classification   Semi-custom catamaran,
Cruiser/racer kit

Approx. Cost   US $72,000 kit price

Designer   Jace Hobbs

Builder   Mastermold Composite
Services
PO Box 1392 Key West, FL
33041 USA
Tel: (305) 294-4576
Fax: (305) 294-4576
email:

Year Introduced   1995

Number of boats built

N. American Dealers   Buy factory direct

Other Cruising Multihulls By Builder
Featherlight 38, Featherlight 50,
Mastermold 40 & 50 power cats

KEY FEATURES

Hull & Sail Plan
- Performance daggerboards, kick-up rudders, reverse transoms
- Fractional sloop or cutter rig, fully battened main, roller-furling jibs

Deck Layout
- Small trampoline netting foredeck with central walkway, large lockers just aft
- Aft cabins create protected central cockpit with port & starboard seats and table

Standard Accommodations
- Galley up aft to port, nav area to starboard, large settee & table forward, double berth
- Starboard hull has studio area/guest cabin aft, head/storage midships, berth forward
- Port hull has stateroom aft, storage/shop area midships, berth forward

Mechanical
- Wheel steering, helm forward in cockpit
- Engine options either outboard or inboard

DESCRIPTION

The Featherlight 43 is a light, swift, relatively inexpensive catamaran designed for the owner-builder. Available in kit form, it employs aerospace quality componentry to make this all-composite vessel lighter and less expensive than most production catamarans. The kit price includes hulls, decks, beams, keels and rudder blades. Built of vacuum-bagged composite construction, the Featherlight 43 features hulls designed for speed and load-carrying capacity, modern fractional sailplans, and performance daggerboard/kick-up rudder options. Cabin layout maximizes bridgedeck living and easy access from the cockpit and allows for large privat aft cabins. Other layout features include a large queen-size aft cabin, a studio that converts to a guest cabin, a combination galley/lounge/dining area on the bridgedeck, and a shop area in the port hull.

SPECIFICATIONS

Displacement	8,500 lbs, 3860 kg	
Standard Auxiliary	outboard or inboard	
Overall Length	43'6"	13.27 m
Waterline Length	41'0"	12.51 m
Bridgedeck Length	27'3"	8.30 m
Wing Deck Clearance	2'4"	0.71 m
Beam (max.)	25'0"	7.62 m
Draft (boards up)	2'2"	0.61 m
Draft (boards down)	6'0"	1.83 m
Mast Hgt. Off Water	61'0"	18.61 m

SAIL AREA

Mainsail	557 sf	52 sm
Jib	280 sf	26 sm
Total Area	837 sf	78 sm
Spinnaker	1000 sf	93 sm

CAPACITY

Berths	2 sgls, 3 dbls
Staterooms	2
Heads	1
Fuel	30 gal 114 ltr
Fresh Water	100 gal 379 ltr
Payload	4,500 lbs, 2043 kg

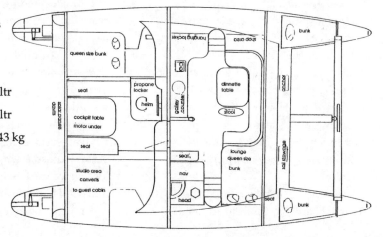

Featherlight Charter Cruiser 43

NIMBLE 39.3

GENERAL INFORMATION

Classification   Semi-custom catamaran, Cruiser

Approx. Cost   Call for current price

Designer   Alexander's Yacht Design

Builder   Mono & Multihull Boatbuilders
Tussendiepen 61c
9206 AC Drachten
The Netherlands
Tel: (31) 512 523599
Fax: (31) 512 523599
email:mmboat@pi.net

Year Introduced   1994

Number of boats built

N. American Dealers   Buy factory direct

Other Cruising Multihulls By Builder
  Nimble 39.9, Nimble 49.4, other custom multihulls

KEY FEATURES

Hull & Sail Plan
- Integral keels, inboard rudders, plumb bows, reverse transoms with steps
- Fractional sloop rig, fully roached main, self-tacking jib

Deck Layout
- Trampoline forward with central walkway, large lockers just aft, wide side decks
- Large cockpit with J-shaped seating and storage lockers, aft swim decks on hulls

Standard Accommodations
- Bridgedeck has L-shaped galley aft to port, settee/table and nav area forward
- Starboard hull has office or stateroom aft, head midships, stateroom forward
- Port hull has stateroom aft, storage midships, and galley forward

Mechanical
- Wheel steering, helm forward to port
- Twin inboards, access from aft cabins

DESCRIPTION

The Nimble 39.3 is a comfortable, lightweight cruising catamaran built in a foam-sandwich-epoxy composite with multiaxial glass, using vacuum-bagging where possible. A major advantage of epoxy composite is that it's virtually maintenance free with the boat painted with linear polyurethane inside and out. Single-handing is easy, with the mast placed in the cockpit and all sheets leading to a single electric winch. Accommodations include two double-berth cabins, an office and workshop, plus two separate head compartments, ideal for living and working aboard. The bridgedeck features a comfortable seating area, galley, and navigation station located close to the cockpit steering console. Large storage areas are located forward of the mast bulkheads in both hulls. All Nimble catamarans are built to order, with owner input and many options.

SPECIFICATIONS

Displacement	10,387 lbs, 4700 kg	
Standard Auxiliary	2 x 20 hp inboard	
Overall Length	39'1"	11.93 m
Waterline Length	36'8"	11.19 m
Bridgedeck Length	26'5"	8.08 m
Wing Deck Clearance	2'5"	0.75 m
Beam (max.)	20'0"	6.10 m
Draft (max.)	3'1"	0.95 m
Mast Hgt. Off Deck		
Mast Hgt. Off Water		

SAIL AREA

Mainsail	350 sf	33 sm
Genoa	339 sf	32 sm
Total Area	689 sf	65 sm
Spinnaker	968 sf	90 sm

CAPACITY

Berths	2-3 doubles	
Staterooms	3	
Heads	2	
Fuel	66 gal	250 ltr
Fresh Water	79 gal	300 ltr
Payload	3,315 lbs, 1500 kg	

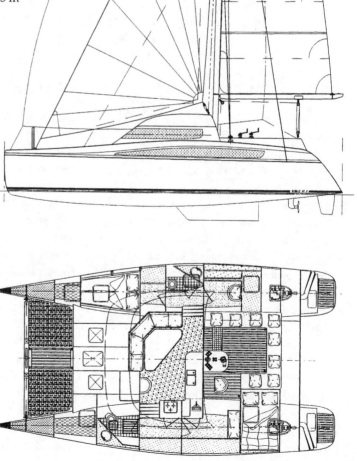

NIMBLE 39.9

GENERAL INFORMATION

Classification   Semi-custom catamaran, Cruiser

Approx. Cost   Call for current price

Designer   Alexander's Yacht Design

Builder   Mono & Multihull
Boatbuilders
Tussendiepen 61c
9206 AC Drachten
The Netherlands
Tel: (31) 512 523599
Fax: (31) 512 523599
email:mmboat@pi.net

Year Introduced   1994

Number of boats built

N. American Dealers   Buy factory direct

Other Cruising Multihulls By Builder
  Nimble 39.3, Nimble 49.4, other custom multihulls

KEY FEATURES

Hull & Sail Plan
- Integral keels, inboard rudders, reverse transoms with molded boarding steps
- Fractional sloop rig, fully roached main, roller-furling jib

Deck Layout
- Trampoline forward with central walkway, large lockers just aft, wide side decks
- Large cockpit with J-shaped seating and storage lockers, aft swim decks on hulls

Standard Accommodations
- Bridgedeck has U-shaped settee and table to port and nav area to starboard
- Starboard hull has stateroom aft, galley midships, large head forward
- Port hull has stateroom aft, storage midships, and large head forward

Mechanical
- Wheel steering, helm forward to port
- Twin inboards, access from aft cabins

DESCRIPTION

As with the smaller Nimble 39.3, the Nimble 39.9 is designed to offer a fast, safe, spacious and affordable catamaran which is easy to handle and maintain. Based on the 39.3, she features longer bows, a higher deck line, and more conventional rig than her smaller sistership. Each boat has its own distinct character due to individual owner input. Standard layout includes two large cabins, two separate heads with shower, a small workshop, and galley in the starboard hull. Storage is plentiful in each bow and on the bridgedeck forward of the mast bulkhead. All electrics are located under the saloon settee, thus placing all heavy equipment on the center of flotation. Twin engines make maneuvering a dream, and sail-handling is kept simple with most controls leading to the cockpit. The Nimble 39.9 promises to provide a livable, high performance cruising choice.

SPECIFICATIONS

Displacement	10,608 lbs, 4800 kg	
Standard Auxiliary	2 x 20 hp inboard	
Overall Length	40'6"	12.35 m
Waterline Length	39'6"	12.05 m
Bridgedeck Length	24'5"	7.45 m
Wing Deck Clearance	2'9"	0.85 m
Beam (max.)	21'9"	6.64 m
Draft (max.)	3'1"	0.95 m
Mast Hgt. Off Deck		
Mast Hgt. Off Water		

SAIL AREA

Mainsail	463 sf	43 sm
Genoa	366 sf	34 sm
Total Area	829 sf	77 sm
Spinnaker	1184 sf	110 sm

CAPACITY

Berths	2-3 doubles	
Staterooms	2	
Heads	2	
Fuel	92 gal	350 ltr
Fresh Water	79 gal	300 ltr
Payload	3,647 lbs, 1650 kg	

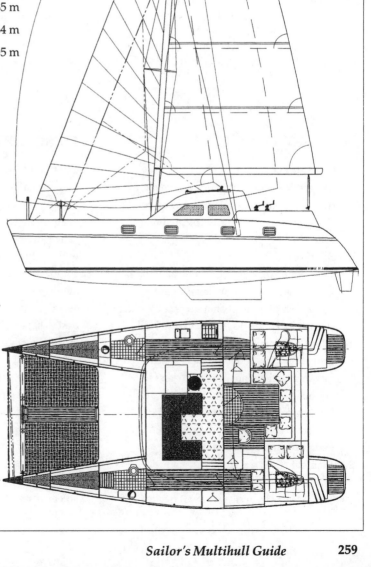

NIMBLE 399

NIMBLE 49.4

GENERAL INFORMATION

Classification   Semi-custom catamaran, Cruiser

Approx. Cost   Call for current price

Designer   Alexander's Yacht Design

Builder: Mono & Multihull
Boatbuilders
Tussendiepen 61c
9206 AC Drachten
The Netherlands
Tel: (31) 512 523599
Fax: (31) 512 523599
email:mmboat@pi.net

Year Introduced   1994

Number of boats built

N. American Dealers   Buy factory direct

Other Cruising Multihulls By Builder
Nimble 39.3, Nimble 39.9, other custom multihulls

KEY FEATURES

Hull & Sail Plan
- Integral keels, inboard rudders, reverse transoms with molded boarding steps
- Fractional sloop rig, fully roached main, roller-furling jib

Deck Layout
- Trampoline forward with central walkway, large lockers just aft, wide side decks
- Large cockpit with U-shaped seating and storage lockers, aft swim decks on hulls

Standard Accommodations
- Bridgedeck has settee/table and nav area forward, galley and storage lockers aft
- Starboard hull has large stateroom aft, head midships, stateroom forward
- Port hull has stateroom aft, storage/head midships, and stateroom forward

Mechanical
- Wheel steering, helm forward to port
- Twin inboards, access from aft decks

DESCRIPTION

The Nimble 49.4 is a large, comfortable cruising catamaran built in a foam-sandwich-epoxy composite with multiaxial glass, using vacuum-bagging where possible. The interior can be finished to the owner's specifications, with up to ten berths and two head compartments, while still giving high daily average speeds when cruising. The Nimble 49.4 is designed for the sailor who wants the best in space, comfort and speed. The original design has one hull reserved for the owner and the other hull for up to four guests, with privacy for all. Storage capacity is huge, and standing headroom of 2.3m is found throughout both hulls. Battery capacity of 600 amp-hour with inverter and watermaker ensure the yacht can be completely self-contained, while twin engines make maneuvering easy. The cockpit has two levels of seating and an optional bimini.

SPECIFICATIONS

Displacement	18,122 lbs,	8200 kg
Standard Auxiliary	2 x 20 hp inboard	
Overall Length	48'3"	14.70 m
Waterline Length	47'9"	14.55 m
Bridgedeck Length	29'5"	8.97 m
Wing Deck Clearance	2'9"	0.85 m
Beam (max.)	26'6"	8.10 m
Draft (max.)	3'7"	1.10 m
Mast Hgt. Off Deck		
Mast Hgt. Off Water		

SAIL AREA

Mainsail	710 sf	66 sm
Genoa	334 sf	31 sm
Total Area	1044 sf	97 sm
Spinnaker	1184 sf	110 sm

CAPACITY

Berths	1 sgle, 3 dbls
Staterooms	4
Heads	2
Fuel	106 gal 400 ltr
Fresh Water	132 gal 500 ltr
Payload	4,310 lbs, 1950 kg

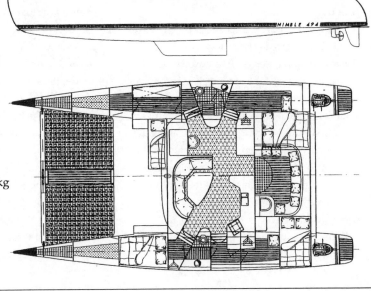

MOORINGS 4500

GENERAL INFORMATION

Classification	Production catamaran, Luxury charter cruiser	**Year Introduced**	1997
		Number of boats built	5 (as of Sep 97)
Approx. Cost	US $400,000		
		N. American Dealers	Buy direct from The Moorings
Designer	Alexander Simonis		

Builder Robertson & Caine
Agent The Moorings
7855 126th Ave. N.
Largo, FL 34643 USA
Toll Free: (800) 521-1126
Tel: (813) 530-5651
Fax: (813) 530-9747
email: yacht@moorings.com

Other Cruising Multihulls By Builder
  None at present

KEY FEATURES

Hull & Sail Plan
- Integral keels, inboard rudders, reverse transoms with molded boarding steps
- Fractional sloop rig, fully roached main, roller-furling genoa

Deck Layout
- Trampoline forward, lockers just aft, wide side decks, large aft sundeck
- large cockpit accessed from transoms, custom cockpit table and arch at the stern

Standard Accommodations
- Galley up to port, large dining area to starboard, nav area to starboard facing aft
- Starboard hull has comfortable staterooms fore and aft, each with a private head
- Port hull has comfortable staterooms fore and aft, each with a private head

Mechanical
- Wheel steering, helm forward in cockpit
- Twin inboards, access from aft deck

DESCRIPTION

The Moorings 4500 was designed to be the ultimate charter/cruiser, with performance, looks, ease of handling and maintenance given equal priority. Drawing on his many years of design experience, Alexander Simonis adjusted overall beam-to-length ratio, hull entry and rig geometry for increased performance and comfort under sail. Intended principally for the luxury charter trade, the standard layout includes four double-berth suites with private head and shower. The bridgedeck saloon features a spacious seating and dining area, navigation station, and well-equipped galley. Topsides, the wide transoms and aft deck offer easy access to the large cockpit with its custom table and ample seating. An ideal yacht for the charter trade, the Moorings 4500 could also easily be converted to private ownership with a master stateroom and workshop.

SPECIFICATIONS

Displacement	21,600 lbs, 9890 kg	
Standard Auxiliary	2 x 50 hp inboard	
Overall Length	44'8"	13.63 m
Waterline Length	39'8"	12.10 m
Bridgedeck Length	35'6"	10.83 m
Wing Deck Clearance	2'3"	0.71 m
Beam (max.)	24'3"	7.40 m
Draft (max.)	4'1"	1.25 m
Mast Hgt. Off Deck	64'6"	19.67 m
Mast Hgt. Off Water	71'0"	21.66 m

SAIL AREA

Mainsail	860 sf	80 sm
Genoa	604 sf	56 sm
Total Area	1464 sf	136 sm
Spinnaker	1560 sf	145 sm

CAPACITY

Berths	4-5 doubles
Staterooms	4
Heads	4
Fuel	120 gal 454 ltr
Fresh Water	200 gal 757 ltr
Payload	10,500 lbs, 4800 kg

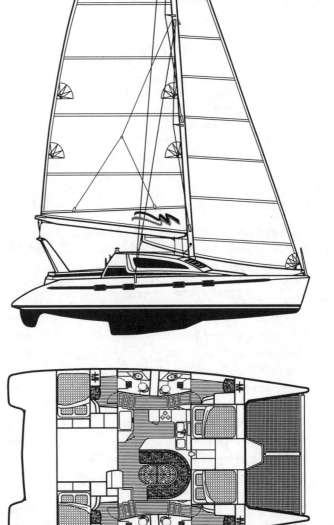

THE MOORINGS - 45'CAT INTERIOR 7/23/96
Revised 3/21/97 by Kim Maguire

ELAN EXTREME 36

GENERAL INFORMATION

Classification	Semi-custom catamaran, Cruiser/charter cruiser
Approx. Cost	US $115,000 (cruiser) US $175,000 (charter)
Designer	Multi-Winds Design
Builder:	Multi-Winds International 655 Maid Marion Hill Sherwood Forest, MD 21405 USA Tel: (410) 849-3316 Fax: email:

Year Introduced 1997

Number of boats built 1 (as of Sep 97)

N. American Dealers Buy factory direct

Other Cruising Multihulls By Builder
Elan 26 and Elan 7.7 Swing-Wing tris

KEY FEATURES

Hull & Sail Plan
- Hull shape precludes keels or daggerboards
- Plumb transoms, outboard rudders
- Fractional sloop rig, fully roached main, self-tacking jib

Deck Layout
- Trampoline forward, open bridgedeck design with wide deck
- Large cockpit offers ample seating and storage space

Standard Accommodations
- Bridgedeck has seating and storage aft through midships, open deck forward
- Starboard hull has single berths fore & aft, hull access and storage midships
- Port hull has storage or single berth aft, head with shower midships & forward

Mechanical
- Wheel steering, helm center of cockpit
- Single outboard, access from cockpit

DESCRIPTION

The Elan Extreme 36 is an open bridgedeck, performance-oriented cruising catamaran that can be easily single handed. Sail handling is a breeze with the fully battened main and self-tending jib. The hull design eliminates the need for fixed keels or daggerboards, allowing the boat to sail in shallow waters without effort. Accommodations in the hulls are simple, with several berths, a head with sink and shower, and room for a cozy galley. There are separate access steps to each hull from the open bridgedeck. Up on deck there is a large open seating area for lounging, with a comfortable helm area with good visibility midships. An outboard engine provides adequate power to move the boat nicely. The Elan Extreme 36 is a practical choice for day charter work or private coastal cruising on a budget.

SPECIFICATIONS

Displacement	6,200 lbs, 2815 kg
Standard Auxiliary	1 x 25 hp outboard
Overall Length	36'0" 10.98 m
Waterline Length	33'6" 10.22 m
Bridgedeck Length	23'6" 7.17 m
Wing Deck Clearance	
Beam (max.)	17'0" 5.19 m
Draft (max.)	2'6" 0.76 m
Mast Hgt. Off Deck	42'2" 12.86 m
Mast Hgt. Off Water	47'6" 14.49 m

SAIL AREA

Mainsail		
Genoa		
Total Area	570 sf	53 sm
Spinnaker		

CAPACITY

Berths	3 singles
Staterooms	none
Heads	1
Fuel	variable
Fresh Water	variable
Payload	

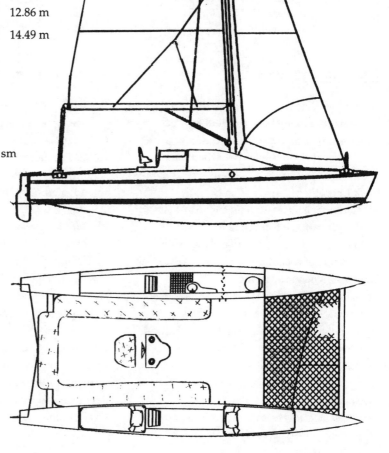

KENNEX 380

GENERAL INFORMATION

Classification	Production catamaran, Cruiser	**Year Introduced**	
Approx. Cost	Call for current price	**Number of boats built**	
Designer	Group GRAAL	**N. American Dealers**	Buy factory direct

Builder Naval de Cordouan
1 quai Verical de Port Bloc,
33123 Le Verdon-Sur-Mer
France
Tel: (33) 5 56 09 69 06
Fax: (33) 5 56 09 69 06
email:

Other Cruising Multihulls By Builder
   Kennex 445
New for 1998: Kennex 395 and Kennex 555

KEY FEATURES

Hull & Sail Plan
- Integral keels, inboard rudders, reverse transoms with steps, plumb bows
- Fractional sloop rig, fully roached main, roller-furling jib

Deck Layout
- Trampoline forward; rigid foredeck just aft with large self-draining lockers
- Large cockpit with sunning platforms on each side of cockpit area

Standard Accommodations
- Galley up to port, large settee and table forward, navigation area to starboard
- Starboard hull has large stateroom aft, head midships, stateroom forward
- Port hull has large stateroom aft, storage midships, head forward

Mechanical
- Wheel steering, helm forward in cockpit
- Twin inboards, access from aft cabins

DESCRIPTION

Formerly the Kennex 380 *Destiny*, this boat is now being resurrected by J.P. Houry and Chantier Naval de Cordouan simply as the K380. The design is still based on Pro Kennex's first yacht, the original Kennex 380. Intended for offshore as well as coastal cruising, the K380 is both seaworthy and fast, ideal for long-term family cruising. Sailing performance is excellent and easy to control, even when short-handed. Below decks, the airy interior, generous headroom, capacious storage space and abundant room make this an easy boat to live aboard for extended cruising. The galley up arrangement allows the hulls to be used exclusively for staterooms and storage. A charter version is also available with a slightly reduced sail plan and a more appropriate interior layout, including an additional stateroom forward.

SPECIFICATIONS

Displacement	12,000 lbs, 5443 kg	
Standard Auxiliary	2 x 18 hp inboard	
Overall Length	38'0"	11.59 m
Waterline Length	38'0"	11.59 m
Bridgedeck Length	22'0"	6.71 m
Wing Deck Clearance		
Beam (max.)	20'0"	6.00 m
Draft (max.)	3'8"	1.12 m
Mast Hgt. Off Deck		
Mast Hgt. Off Water	55'0"	16.78 m

SAIL AREA

Mainsail	592 sf	56 sm
Genoa	376 sf	35 sm
Total Area	968 sf	90 sm
Spinnaker	946 sf	88 sm

CAPACITY

Berths	3 doubles	
Staterooms	3	
Heads	2	
Fuel	53 gal	200 ltr
Fresh Water	185 gal	700 ltr
Payload		

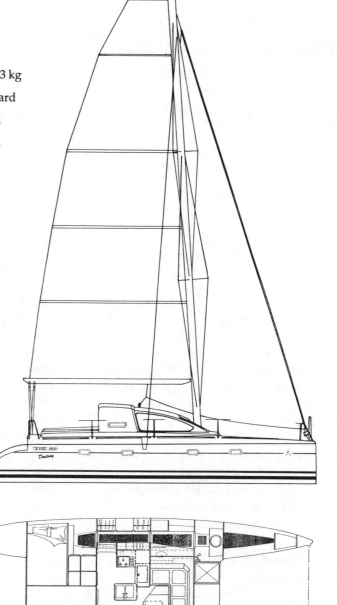

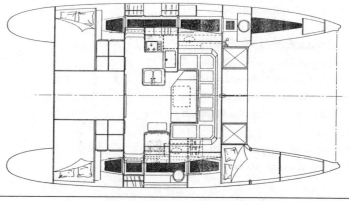

KENNEX 445

GENERAL INFORMATION

Classification   Production catamaran,
                     Cruiser

Approx. Cost   Call for current price

Designers   Van Peteghem,
                     Lauriot-Prevost

Builder   Naval de Cordouan
                     1 quai Verical de Port Bloc,
                     33123 Le Verdon-Sur-Mer
                     France
                     Tel: (33) 5 56 09 69 06
                     Fax: (33) 5 56 09 69 06
                     email:

Year Introduced

Number of boats built

N. American Dealers   Buy factory direct

Other Cruising Multihulls By Builder
   Kennex 380
New for 1998: Kennex 395 and Kennex 555

KEY FEATURES

Hull & Sail Plan
- Integral keels, inboard rudders, reverse transoms with steps, near-plumb bows
- Fractional sloop rig, fully roached main, roller-furling jib

Deck Layout
- Trampoline forward with central walkway rigid foredeck just aft with lockers
- Large cockpit with table, sunning platforms aft of cockpit port and starboard

Standard Accommodations
- Galley up to starboard, large settee and table forward, navigation area to port
- Starboard hull has large staterooms fore & aft, dual-compartment head midships
- Port hull has large staterooms fore & aft, dual-compartment head midships

Mechanical
- Wheel steering, dual helms aft in cockpit
- Twin inboards, access from aft cabins

DESCRIPTION

Formerly the Kennex 445 *Legendary* , this boat is now being built by J.P. Houry and Chantier Naval de Corouan, and being marketed simply as the K445. It is a larger, more luxurious version of their K380. Notable improvements to an already solid cruising concept include the addition of a solid mooring platform on the foredeck for ease of anchoring; an additional stateroom forward; larger staterooms, with the forward double cabins featuring additional forepeak single berths; an expanded galley layout on the bridgedeck; two heads with private compartments for both marine toilets and showers; and a large folding table in the truly expansive (172 sf) cockpit. The K445 has an outstanding amount of living space and level of comfort for a boat its size.

SPECIFICATIONS

Displacement	16,000 lbs, 7258 kg	
Standard Auxiliary	2 x 28 hp inboard	
Overall Length	44'5"	13.55 m
Waterline Length		
Bridgedeck Length	29'0"	8.85 m
Wing Deck Clearance		
Beam (max.)	25'0"	7.62 m
Draft (max.)	4'0"	1.22 m
Mast Hgt. Off Deck		
Mast Hgt. Off Water	60'0"	18.30 m

SAIL AREA

Mainsail	730 sf	68 sm
Genoa	500 sf	47 sm
Total Area	1230 sf	114 sm
Spinnaker	1120 sf	104 sm

CAPACITY

Berths	2 sgls, 4 dbls	
Staterooms	4	
Heads	2	
Fuel	53 gal	400 ltr
Fresh Water	211 gal	800 ltr
Payload		

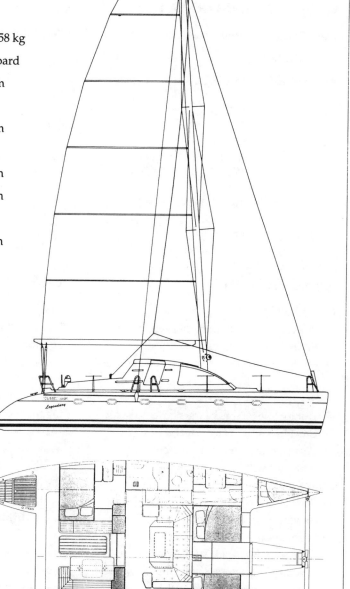

PIANA 30

GENERAL INFORMATION

Classification   Semi-custom catamaran, Cruiser

Approx. Cost   FF 475,000

Designer   B. Desray

Builder   Naval Force 3
Rue Sénac de Meilhan
17042 La Rochelle Cédex 1
France
Tel: (33) 5 46 45 04 15
Fax: (33) 5 46 45 43 76
email:

Year Introduced   1991

Number of boats built   7   (as of Sep 97)

N. American Dealers   Buy factory direct

Other Cruising Multihulls By Builder
   Piana 37, Tropic 12m & 15m catamarans;
Drop 26 & Challenge 30 folding trimarans;
Challenge 37 trimaran (foldable or not),
custom multihulls

KEY FEATURES

Hull & Sail Plan
- Wood-epoxy hulls, integral keels, inboard rudders, reverse transoms with steps
- Fractional sloop rig, fully roached main, roller-furling jib

Deck Layout
- Trampoline forward, large lockers just aft
- Good foot space at side decks
- Cockpit offers ample seating port and starboard with large sundeck aft

Standard Accommodations
- Bridgedeck has large settee and table that converts to double berth
- Starboard hull has stateroom aft, smaller cabin forward, head/storage midships
- Port hull has stateroom or galley aft, galley or nav area midships, small cabin forward

Mechanical
- Tiller steering connected to aft rudder bar
- Twin outboards off transom

DESCRIPTION

Designed by B. Desray and sistership to the Piana 37, the Piana 30 is a fine example of an affordable family boat. This modest-size cruising catamaran has an abundance of exterior lounging areas and a surprising amount of interior accommodations, including the potential for two aft double berths and two forward single permanent berths, as well as a saloon seating area that converts to another double berth. The galley can be aft in the port hull as shown, or midships in the port hull. She has sparkling performance, yet is easy to handle by one person. The Piana 30 is available in three different closed bridgedeck versions, the "budget", "standard", and "comfort", as well as an open bridgedeck configuration with separate hull access hatches. This boat is a good choice for those wanting to cruise comfortably on a small budget.

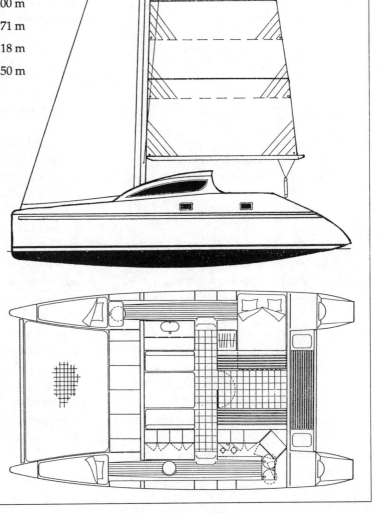

SPECIFICATIONS

Displacement	4,400 lbs, 2,000 kg	
Standard Auxiliary	2 x 8 hp outboard	
Overall Length	29'6"	9.00 m
Waterline Length	29'0"	8.84 m
Bridgedeck Length	18'0"	5.46 m
Wing Deck Clearance	1'10"	0.55
Beam (max.)	16'4"	5.00 m
Draft (max.)	2'4"	0.71 m
Mast Hgt. Off Deck	40'0"	12.18 m
Mast Hgt. Off Water	44'4"	13.50 m

SAIL AREA

Mainsail	300 sf	28 sm
Genoa	215 sf	20 sm
Total Area	515 sf	48 sm
Spinnaker	753 sf	70 sm

CAPACITY

Berths	2 sgls, 2-3 dbls	
Staterooms	2	
Heads	1	
Fuel	13 gal	50 ltr
Fresh Water	53 gal	200 ltr
Payload	1,540 lbs, 700 kg	

PIANA 37

GENERAL INFORMATION

Classification   Semi-custom catamaran,
                      Cruiser

Approx. Cost   FF 830,000

Designer   Naval Force 3 Design

Builder: Naval Force 3
                Rue Sénac de Meilhan
                17042 La Rochelle Cédex 1
                France
                Tel: (33) 5 46 45 04 15
                Fax: (33) 5 46 45 43 76
                email:

Year Introduced   1994

Number of boats built

N. American Dealers   Buy factory direct

Other Cruising Multihulls By Builder
   Piana 30, Tropic 12m & 15m catamarans;
Drop 26 & Challenge 30 folding trimarans;
Challenge 37 trimaran (foldable or not),
custom multihulls

KEY FEATURES

Hull & Sail Plan
- Wood-epoxy hulls, integral keels, inboard rudders, reverse transoms with steps
- Fractional sloop rig, fully roached main, roller-furling jib

Deck Layout
- Trampoline forward, large lockers just aft
- Wide side decks, good foot space
- Large cockpit offers ample seating and storage lockers, sundeck aft

Standard Accommodations
- Bridgedeck has galley and nav area aft and dual circular seating areas forward
- Starboard hull has stateroom aft, smaller stateroom forward, head-storage midships
- Port hull has stateroom aft, smaller stateroom forward, large head midships

Mechanical
- Wheel steering, forward to port
- Twin inboards, access from aft deck

DESCRIPTION

The largest boat in the Piana line, the Piana 37 incorporates the nice features of her highly successful 30 foot sistership in a much larger, more comfortable package for long-distance cruising. Her graceful lines, sturdy construction, and well-conceived interior design should guarantee the success of this boat, too. The interior layout in the hulls includes two large double staterooms aft with hanging lockers and seat, two head compartments midships with two sinks in the starboard compartment, and two single cabins up forward. The bridgedeck cabin has a fully equipped galley and navigation area aft and two separate settee areas up forward, a truly great layout for living aboard. Above decks there are abundant spaces for sunbathing, including a large aft deck behind the cockpit.

SPECIFICATIONS

Displacement	9,900 lbs,	4500 kg
Standard Auxiliary	2 x 18 hp inboard	
Overall Length	36'1"	11.00 m
Waterline Length	35'0"	10.67 m
Bridgedeck Length	24'0"	7.33 m
Wing Deck Clearance	2'2"	0.65
Beam (max.)	19'8"	6.00 m
Draft (max.)	3'0"	0.92 m
Mast Hgt. Off Deck	45'0"	13.70 m
Mast Hgt. Off Water	51'4"	15.65 m

SAIL AREA

Mainsail	430 sf	40 sm
Genoa	204 sf	19 sm
Total Area	634 sf	59 sm
Spinnaker	860 sf	80 sm

CAPACITY

Berths	3 sgls, 2 dbls
Staterooms	4
Heads	2
Fuel	24 gal 90 ltr
Fresh Water	106 gal 400 ltr
Payload	4,400 lbs, 2000 kg

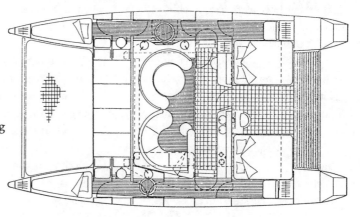

NEWPORT 5400

GENERAL INFORMATION

Classification	Semi-custom catamaran, Cruiser/racer
Approx. Cost	US $575,000
Designer	John Marples, Newport 5400 design team
Builder	Shaw Boats
Agent	Newport Multihulls 2560 Hwy 20, Newport, OR 97365 USA Tel: (541) 265-5501 Fax: (541) 265-6755 email: Rich5501@netbridge.net

Year Introduced	1996
Number of boats built	2 (as of Sep 97)
N. American Dealers	Scott Rush 2222 N. Pacific Seattle, WA 98103

Other Cruising Multihulls By Builder

A variety of Newport 5400 versions, and a number of custom multihull projects that include designs from John Marples, Ian Farrier, Chris White, Robert Perry, and Morrelli & Melvin

KEY FEATURES

Hull & Sail Plan
- Full round hulls, daggerboards, near plumb bows, wide reverse transoms
- Fractional sloop rig, fully battened main, roller-furling headsail, asym. spinnaker

Deck Layout
- Trampoline forward, wide deck just aft, wide side decks, sleek cabin lines, aft decks
- Cockpit has port seating with table, unique raised pilothouse helm station

Standard Accommodations
- Bridgedeck has galley aft to port, huge lounge area & nav station/library forward
- Starboard hull has large aft stateroom, central head, large stateroom forward
- Port hull has large aft stateroom, central head, large stateroom/head forward

Mechanical
- Wheel, helms in cockpit and in saloon area
- Twin inboards, access from aft cabins

DESCRIPTION

The Newport 5400 Series blends tried and true multihull technology with updated construction methods and materials. The pedigree of these boats is a charter trade work horse with good sailing performance. From this solid heritage the Newport design team has developed a modem cruising version that suits the needs of experienced cruisers. Sailing speeds over the 20 knot mark and motoring speeds of 8 to 16 knots are commmon. The generous interior lends itself to a number of custom configurations with full headroom throughout. Features include two aft queen staterooms, galley up with large salon/settee, aft sundeck, and exterior as well as an interior helm stations. The sail plan and deck arrangement are modernized for those owners who appreciate the balance of ease of handling and sailing at a good rate of speed.

SPECIFICATIONS

Displacement	22,000 lbs, 9988 kg	
Standard Auxiliary	2 x 79 hp inboard	
Overall Length	54'0"	16.47 m
Waterline Length	51'0"	15.56 m
Bridgedeck Length	24'0"	7.32 m
Wing Deck Clearance	3'0"	0.92 m
Beam (max.)	30'0"	9.15 m
Draft (min.)	3'2"	0.98 m
Mast Hgt. Off Deck	67'0"	20.44 m
Mast Hgt. Off Water	76'0"	23.18 m

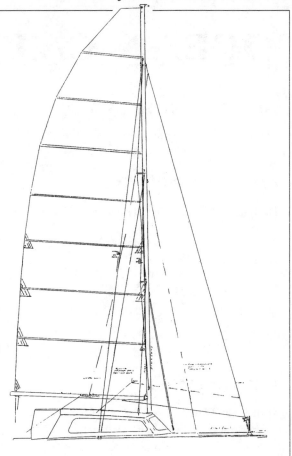

SAIL AREA

Mainsail	1117 sf	104 sm
Jib	740 sf	69 sm
Total Area	1857 sf	173 sm
Spinnaker	2700 sf	251 sm

CAPACITY

Berths	3-4
Staterooms	3-4
Heads	2
Fuel	150 gal 151 ltr
Fresh Water	200 gal 757 ltr
Payload	8,000 lbs, 3632 kg

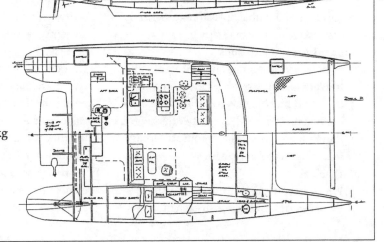

OCEAN CAT 48

GENERAL INFORMATION

Classification   Semi-custom catamaran, Cruiser

Approx. Cost   US $140,000 kit form

Designer   Ocean Catamarans

Builder   Ocean Catamarans
509-107th St.
Marathon, FL 33050 USA
Tel: (305) 289-7679
Fax: (305) 289-7680
email:

Year Introduced   1997

Number of boats built   3   (as of Sep 97)

N. American Dealers   Buy factory direct

Other Cruising Multihulls By Builder
Ocean Cat 42 and 60 in design stages

KEY FEATURES

Hull & Sail Plan
- Integral keels, inboard rudders, reverse transoms with boarding steps
- Fractional sloop rig, fully-battened main, roller-furling genoa

Deck Layout
- Semi-circular trampoline forward with walkway, lockers just aft, sleek cabintop
- Large cockpit with ample storage lockers, easy access to transom steps

Standard Accommodations
- Bridgedeck has lounge and nav areas forward, galley & entertainment area aft
- Starboard hull has stateroom aft, double berth midships, head/single berth forward
- Port hull has owners stateroom aft, storage midships, head/storage foward

Mechanical
- Wheel steering, helm forward in cockpit
- Twin inboards, aft access in each hull

DESCRIPTION

The Ocean Cat 48, similar in design to the popular Manta 40, was conceived for the knowledgeable sailor looking for a design which has truly exceptional sailing qualities, low maintenance, and comfortable accommodations for long-term occupancy. Built with Airlight or Core-Cell foam, vinylester and isopthalic resins, this unique boat is offered in a basic form assembled as an empty shell with steering and counter-balanced rudders, ready to be delivered to your destination. You can design and customize the interior to meet your cruising needs; the final result is limited only by the customer's imagination and budget. Interior moldings and various rig options (standard rig shown in specs) are available. The price of the basic package is less than half of finished, comparably sized cruising catamarans currently on the market.

SPECIFICATIONS

Displacement	13,000 lbs, 5900 kg	
Standard Auxiliary	2 x 18-30 hp inboard	
Overall Length	48'8"	14.84 m
Waterline Length	48'0"	14.64 m
Bridgedeck Length	25'0"	7.63 m
Wing Deck Clearance	3'0"	0.92 m
Beam (max.)	24'4"	7.42 m
Draft (max.)	3'0"	0.92 m
Mast Hgt. Off Deck	53'0"	16.17 m
Mast Hgt. Off Water	62'0"	18.91 m

SAIL AREA

Mainsail	599 sf	49 sm
Genoa	388 sf	21 sm
Total Area	987 sf	70 sm
Spinnaker	1382 sf	95 sm

CAPACITY

Berths	3-6 doubles	
Staterooms	3-6	
Heads	2	
Fuel	60 gal	227 ltr
Fresh Water	100 gal	379 ltr
Payload	5,000 lbs, 2270 kg	

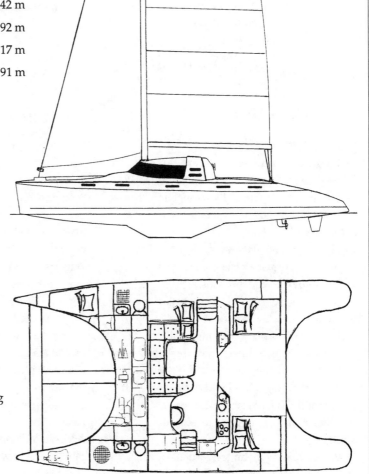

LIGHTWAVE 10.5

GENERAL INFORMATION

Classification   Semi-custom catamaran,
Cruiser/racer

Approx. Cost   Call for current price of
complete boat or kit

Designer   Tony Grainger

Builder   Overell & Stanton
PO Box 960
Nerang 4210, Qld
Australia
Tel: (61) 7 5533 7134
Fax: (61) 7 5533 7703
email:

Year Introduced   1997

Number of boats built   2 (as of Sep 97)

N. American Dealers
California Multihulls
Tel: (619) 222-9694 Fax: (619) 222-9693

Other Cruising Multihulls By Builder
None at present

KEY FEATURES

Hull & Sail Plan
- Integral keels, inboard rudders, reverse transoms, DeltaPod under bow bridgedeck
- Fractional sloop rig, fully-battened main, roller-furling genoa, spinnaker on prowler

Deck Layout
- Small trampoline forward, large rigid deck with lockers just aft, sleek cabin lines
- Large covered cockpit seats eight, with walkways from cockpit to aft steps

Standard Accommodations
- Bridgedeck has large lounge/seating area forward, entertainment/nav area aft
- Starboard hull has comfortable stateroom forward, storage/head midships, shower aft
- Port hull has large stateroom forward, galley midships, large stateroom aft

Mechanical
- Wheel steering, helm forward in cockpit
- Twin inboards, aft access in each hull

DESCRIPTION

First design priority for the Lightwave 10.5 was to provide pure sailing enjoyment, along with an interior suitable for pleasant cruising. A compromise has been struck between a yacht appropriate for family sailing and extended cruising, and one with strong enough performance for racing enthusiasts. With her chosen sailplan, most of the area is in the mainsail, an efficient, easy rig to handle. The resulting smaller headsails and fully battened mainsail in lazy jacks can be handled by two people. The Lightwave is available with either centerboards for shallow draft and high performance, or fixed keels for the simplicity and protection of the hulls and steering gear, plus additional buoyancy reserve, giving more load carrying capacity. Accommodations feature three double-berth cabins, a head with separate shower, galley, and comfortable saloon seating.

SPECIFICATIONS

Displacement	9,503 lbs, 4300 kg	
Standard Auxiliary	2 x 20 hp inboard	
Overall Length	34'5"	10.50 m
Waterline Length	33'9"	10.30 m
Bridgedeck Length	24'7"	7.50 m
Wing Deck Clearance	2'6"	0.75 m
Beam (max.)	21'10"	6.67 m
Draft (max.)	3'3"	1.00 m
Mast Hgt. Off Deck	47'0"	14.30 m
Mast Hgt. Off Water	53'0"	16.25 m

SAIL AREA

Mainsail	527 sf	49 sm
Genoa	226 sf	21 sm
Total Area	753 sf	70 sm
Spinnaker	1014 sf	95 sm

CAPACITY

Berths	1-2 sgls, 3 dbls
Staterooms	3
Heads	1
Fuel	48 gal 180 ltr
Fresh Water	111 gal 420 ltr
Payload	2,652 lbs, 1200 kg

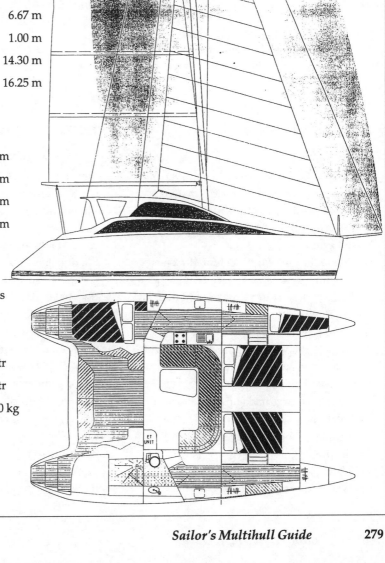

PDQ 32 MkII

GENERAL INFORMATION

Classification Production catamaran, Cruiser

Approx. Cost US $126,500

Designer Alan Slater

Builder PDQ Yachts Inc.
1710 Charles St., Whitby,
ON Canada L1N 1C2
Tel: (905) 430-2582
Fax: (905) 430-8306
email: pdqcats-idirect.com

Year Introduced 1994

Number of boats built 28 (as of Sep 97)

N. American Dealers
Contact PDQ for dealer list

Other Cruising Multihulls By Builder
PDQ 36 MkIII

KEY FEATURES

Hull & Sail Plan
- Integral keels, inboard rudders, reverse transoms with molded boarding steps
- Masthead sloop rig, fully roached main, roller-furling, self-tacking jib

Deck Layout
- Trampoline forward; rigid foredeck just aft with comfortable seating/sunning area
- Large cockpit with hardtop & soft dodger
- Cockpit lockers and storage areas

Standard Accommodations
- Large U-shaped dining area forward with table that converts to a double berth
- Starboard hull has large stateroom aft, nav area and lockers midships, head forward
- Port hull has large stateroom aft, galley midships and refrig./freezer forward

Mechanical
- Wheel steering, helm forward in cockpit
- Twin outboards, inboards available

DESCRIPTION

The PDQ 32 MkII is an affordable family cruising catamaran that includes two double-berth staterooms, panoramic windows in the saloon and standing headroom throughout. Two innovative design features are the comfortable sun lounge on the foredeck and the rigid hardtop over the forward part of the cockpit for all-weather protection. Construction materials such as premium glass fabrics, carbon fiber, Core-Cell foam and modified epoxy resin are all selected for strength and safety on this modest-size blue water yacht. The PDQ 32 MkII is capable of carrying 5-7 people, while retaining good performance under sail. She offers an excellent feeling of space, good load-carrying capacity and a livable layout that includes a large owner's cabin and standing headroom throughout. The standard cruising rig includes a fully battened mainsail and self-tending jib.

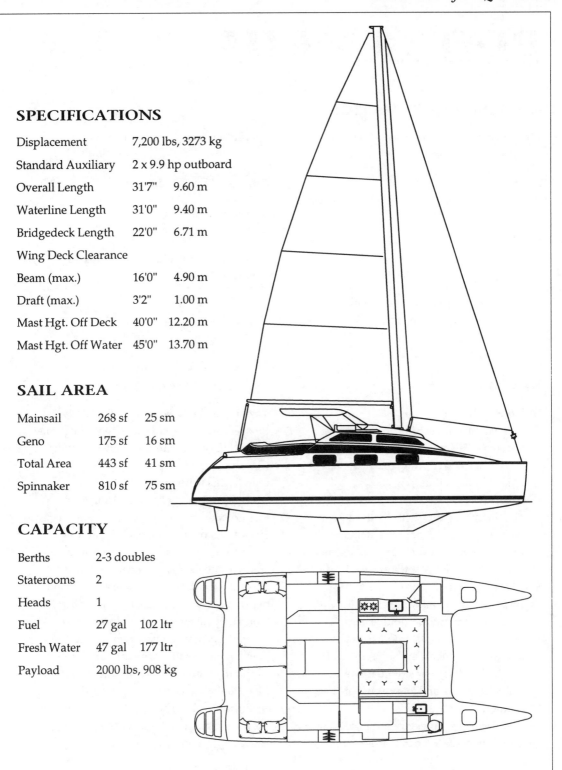

SPECIFICATIONS

Displacement	7,200 lbs, 3273 kg	
Standard Auxiliary	2 x 9.9 hp outboard	
Overall Length	31'7"	9.60 m
Waterline Length	31'0"	9.40 m
Bridgedeck Length	22'0"	6.71 m
Wing Deck Clearance		
Beam (max.)	16'0"	4.90 m
Draft (max.)	3'2"	1.00 m
Mast Hgt. Off Deck	40'0"	12.20 m
Mast Hgt. Off Water	45'0"	13.70 m

SAIL AREA

Mainsail	268 sf	25 sm
Geno	175 sf	16 sm
Total Area	443 sf	41 sm
Spinnaker	810 sf	75 sm

CAPACITY

Berths	2-3 doubles	
Staterooms	2	
Heads	1	
Fuel	27 gal	102 ltr
Fresh Water	47 gal	177 ltr
Payload	2000 lbs, 908 kg	

PDQ 36 MkIII

GENERAL INFORMATION

Classification   Production catamaran,
                       Cruiser/racer

Approx. Cost   US $240,000

Designer   Alan Slater

Builder   PDQ Yachts Inc.
                       1710 Charles St., Whitby,
                       ON Canada L1N 1C2
                       Tel: (905) 430-2582
                       Fax: (905) 430-8306
                       email: pdqcats-idirect.com

Year Introduced   1989
                           (as the PDQ 34)

Number of boats built 63   (as of Sep 97)

N. American Dealers
Contact PDQ for dealer list

Other Cruising Multihulls By Builder
  PDQ 32 MkII

KEY FEATURES

Hull & Sail Plan
- Integral keels, inboard rudders, reverse transoms with molded boarding steps
- Masthead sloop rig, fully roached main, roller-furling, self-tacking jib

Deck Layout
- Trampoline forward with rigid walkway
- Foredeck just aft blends into cabin top
- Large cockpit with U-shaped seating and ample lockers and storage areas

Standard Accommodations
- Large u-shaped dining area forward with table that converts to a double berth
- Starboard hull has stateroom forward, nav area with pilot berth midships, head aft
- Port hull has large stateroom forward, galley midships, and all-purpose area aft

Mechanical
- Wheel steering, helm forward in cockpit
- Twin outboards; twin inboards optional

DESCRIPTION

The PDQ 36 MkIII is a true cruiser designed for speed, comfort and ease of handling. She comes in two configurations, the sporty Classic and the voyaging LRC (long range cruiser) that features twin inboards, increased tankage, and a long list of cruising gear. Construction materials such as premium glass fabrics, carbon fiber, Core-Cell foam and modified epoxy resin are all selected for strength and safety. Intended for bluewater as well as coastal cruising, she is stable and dependable, with a spacious interior that has panoramic saloon cabin windows, a well-equipped galley, full headroom, large opening ports, and luxury interior finish. Accommodations include 2 large staterooms forward with queen-size berths, and saloon seating for eight. The aft cabin layout is up to the owner; possibilities include workshop, stateroom, laundry, and sitting area.

SPECIFICATIONS

Displacement	8,000 lbs, 3629 kg	
Standard Auxiliary	2 x 9.9 hp outboard	
Overall Length	36'5"	11.10 m
Waterline Length	34'4"	10.50 m
Bridgedeck Length	24'5"	7.45 m
Wing Deck Clearance		
Beam (max.)	18'3"	5.60 m
Draft (max.)	2'10"	0.90 m
Mast Hgt. Off Deck	42'0"	12.81 m
Mast Hgt. Off Water	47'0"	14.30 m

SAIL AREA

Mainsail	275 sf	26 sm
Geno	325 sf	30 sm
Total Area	600 sf	56 sm
Spinnaker	950 sf	88 sm

CAPACITY

Berths	1 sgle, 2-3 dbls	
Staterooms	2	
Heads	1	
Fuel	55 gal	208 ltr
Fresh Water	85 gal	321 ltr
Payload	2000 lbs, 908 kg	

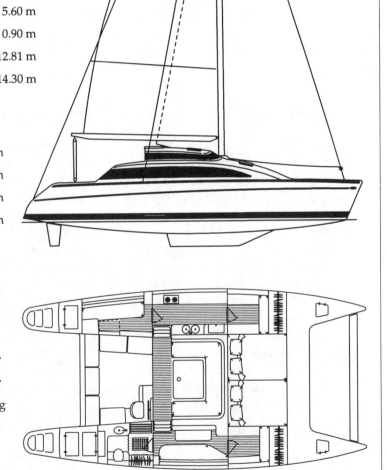

SHUTTLECAT 52

GENERAL INFORMATION

Classification Semi-custom catamaran, Luxury cruiser

Approx. Cost Call for price quote

Designer John Shuttleworth

Builder Pedigree Cats
1835 Ocean Avenue
Raymond, WA 98577 USA
Tel: (360) 942-2810
Fax: (360) 942-2936
email: PedigreCat@AOL.com

Year Introduced 1997

Number of boats built 1 (as of Sep 97)

N. American Dealers Buy factory direct

Other Cruising Multihulls By Builder
Thirty different models of semi-custom stock design catamarans between 50 and 130 feet.

KEY FEATURES

Hull & Sail Plan
- Airex foam core with carbon fiber, daggerboards, inboard rudders, reverse transoms with molded steps
- Fractional sailplan on an AeroRig™

Deck Layout
- Trampoline forward w/ central support, lockers just aft, steps to mast base
- large cockpit with partial or full hardtop, ample seating, lockers and storage areas

Standard Accommodations
- Bridgedeck has two lounge areas, nav area, full galley to starboard aft
- Starboard hull has stateroom aft, storage midships, stateroom with private forward
- Port hull has staterooms with private heads fore and aft, work area midships

Mechanical
- Wheel steering, raised helm in cockpit
- Twin inboards, access from aft deck

DESCRIPTION

The Shuttlecat 52 from Pedigree Cats is a luxury craft with high-performance characteristics, built on a custom basis for discriminating clients using a popular John Shuttleworth stock design as the basis for the project. The exterior of the Shuttlecat 52 is sleek and modern, with an efficient AeroRig™ sailplan. The interior is dramatically spacious, taking full advantage of the boat's 33'6" beam. After the structural needs of an individual design are met, owners are encouraged to participate in the selection of all machinery and electronics, as well as the interior layout and decor. All Pedigree boats are built from composite foam core, E-glass, Kevlar and carbon fiber reinforcement, vinylester and epoxy resins, epoxy barrier coating below the waterlines, and Dupont Imron polyurethane exteriors. This is an exceptionally strong, luxurious catamaran.

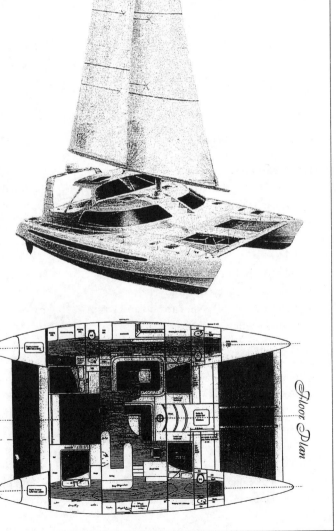

SPECIFICATIONS

Displacement	16,500 lbs, 7500 kg	
Standard Auxiliary	2 x 47 hp inboard	
Overall Length	52'2"	15.89 m
Waterline Length	50'0"	15.25 m
Bridgedeck Length	32'0"	9.71 m
Wing Deck Clearance	3'0"	0.92 m
Beam (max.)	33'6"	10.21 m
Draft (boards up)	2'10"	0.89 m
Draft (boards down)	6'0"	1.83 m
Mast Hgt. Off Deck	70'0"	21.25 m

SAIL AREA

Mainsail		
Jib		
Total Area	1184 sf	110 sm
Spinnaker		

CAPACITY

Berths	4 doubles
Staterooms	4
Heads	3-4
Fuel	200 gal 757 ltr
Fresh Water	500 gal 1892 ltr
Payload	8,800 lbs, 4000 kg

Floor Plan

GEMINI 105M

GENERAL INFORMATION

Classification Production catamaran, Cruiser

Approx. Cost US $105,000

Designer Tony Smith

Builder Performance Cruising
7364 Edgewood Rd.
Annapolis, MD 21403 USA
Tel: (410) 626-2720
Fax: (410) 626-2726
email: gem105M@aol.com

Year Introduced 1995 (as 105M)

Number of boats built 84 (as of Sep 97)
  (hundreds of boats built as Gemini 3000, 3200, and 3400)

N. American Dealers
  Contact Performance Cruising for their dealer list

Other Cruising Multihulls By Builder
  Gemini 32 and 34 past-production cruisers.

KEY FEATURES

Hull & Sail Plan
- Centerboard, inboard rudders, reverse transoms with molded boarding steps
- Masthead sloop rig, partially-battened main, working jib, opt'l roller-furling genoa

Deck Layout
- Full rigid foredeck with lockers aft
- Sleek cabin top blends into hardtop aft
- Protected cockpit with hardtop and wrap-around seating, ample storage lockers

Standard Accommodations
- Nav area aft, U-shaped settee with table midships, large master berth forward
- Starboard hull has stateroom aft, galley midships, master stateroom access forward
- Port hull has stateroom aft, storage midships, and large head forward

Mechanical
- Wheel steering, helm forward in cockpit
- Single inboard with Sonic drive optional

DESCRIPTION

Following in the wake of the immensely popular Gemini 3000, 3200 and 3400, the new 105M continues the tradition of offering an affordable, family-type cruiser. With the exception of a few familiar Gemini features like dual centerboards, tilting rudders and two-level cabintop, the entire boat had been redesigned. The new planing hull, longer waterline length, narrow bows, repositioned centerboards and keels, and wide flat transom combine good load-carrying capacity with improved performance and stability. The interior now feels light and spacious with a living-room style saloon, three double-berth cabins (including wider aft berths and a forward master cabin), well-equipped galley, and comfortable head. One of the best selling catamarans of all time, the Gemini continues to be a good choice for comfortable cruising.

SPECIFICATIONS

Displacement	8,000 lbs, 3630 kg	
Standard Auxiliary	1 x 27 hp inboard	
Overall Length	33'6"	10.21 m
Waterline Length	31'9"	9.68 m
Bridgedeck Length	29'6"	9.00 m
Wingdeck Clearance	1'6"–3'3" (varies)	
Beam (max.)	14'0"	4.27 m
Draft (boards up)	1'6"	0.45 m
Draft (boards down)	5'0"	1.53 m
Mast Hgt. Off Water	45'0"	13.73 m

SAIL AREA

Mainsail	270 sf	25 sm
Geno	350 sf	34 sm
Total Area	620 sf	59 sm
Spinnaker	850 sf	79 sm

CAPACITY

Berths	3 doubles	
Staterooms	3	
Heads	1	
Fuel	36 gal	136 ltr
Fresh Water	60 gal	227 ltr
Payload	3,000 lbs, 1362 kg	

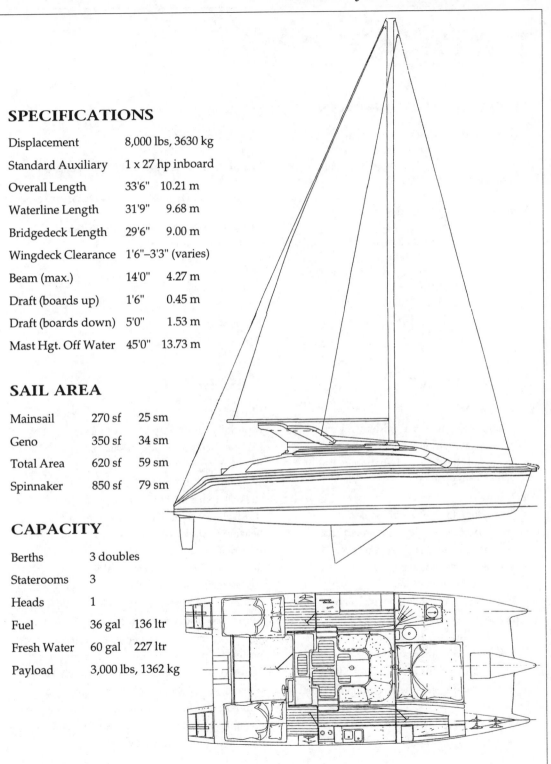

PROCAT 43

GENERAL INFORMATION

Classification	Semi-custom catamaran, Day charter cruiser
Approx. Cost	US $259,000
Designer	ProCat design team
Builder	ProCat Marine Internation'l 770a Mullet Rd. Cape Canaveral, FL 32920 USA Tel: (407) 799-0997 Fax: (407) 799-1077 email:

Year Introduced 1996

Number of boats built 2 (as of Sep 97)

N. American Dealers Buy factory direct

Other Cruising Multihulls By Builder
  Cruiser version of ProCat 43

KEY FEATURES

Hull & Sail Plan
- Integral keels, inboard rudders, reverse transoms with molded boarding steps
- Fractional sloop rig, fully-battened main, roller-furling genoa

Deck Layout
- Trampoline foredeck with walkway
- Open bridgedeck with windshield and hardtop to protect large seating area
- Aft area has seating behind helm

Standard Accommodations
- Bridgedeck is open with forward and aft passenger seating areas
- Starboard hull has berths aft, storage and head midships, stateroom/storage forward
- Port hull has berths aft, storage and head midships, stateroom/storage forward

Mechanical
- Wheel steering, helm aft in cockpit
- Twin inboards, access from aft deck

DESCRIPTION

The ProCat 43 is a new catamaran designed especially for the day charter market. Emphasis has been put on ease of maintenance and use, plus efficient sailing with a minimum crew. The hull, with fixed fin keel, reinforced bottom and four-foot draft, allows sailing in shallow waters and beaching. Standard cruising accommodations include four separate double-berth cabins, head with shower, spacious saloon and bridgedeck galley. Layout can also be tailored to suit the day charter business, with two optional staterooms for crew. The ProCat 43 is a proven ocean cruising catamaran, perfect for private ownership or charter fleet operations, with USCG approval for 42 day passengers. Seventeen of these boats, by a different builder and under another name, are currently in operation. A liveaboard cruising version of this design is available.

SPECIFICATIONS

Displacement	18,000 lbs, 8172 kg	
Standard Auxiliary	2 x 18 hp inboard	
Overall Length	42'8"	13.01 m
Waterline Length	40'5"	12.34 m
Bridgedeck Length	24'10"	7.59 m
Wingdeck Clearance	2'6"	0.76 m
Beam (max.)	23'10"	7.29 m
Draft (max.)	3'8"	1.12 m
Mast Hgt. Off Deck	57'0"	17.39 m
Mast Hgt. Off Water	63'0"	19.22 m

SAIL AREA

Mainsail	656 sf	61 sm
Genoa	240 sf	22 sm
Total Area	896 sf	83 sm
Spinnaker		

CAPACITY

Berths	up to 8
Passengers	42
Heads	1-2
Fuel	78 gal 295 ltr
Fresh Water	200 gal 757 ltr
Payload	8,800 lbs, 3995 kg

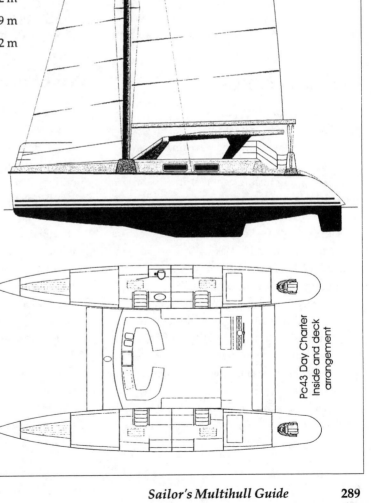

Pc43 Day Charter
Inside and deck
arrangement

PROUT 34

GENERAL INFORMATION

Classification	Production catamaran, Cruiser
Approx. Cost	$170,000
Designer	Prout
Builder	Prout Catamarans Kings Close, Charfleets, Canvey Island, Essex SS8 0QZ, England Tel: 44 (0) 1 268 511500 Fax: 44 (0) 1 268 510094 email: Sales@Prout-Catamarans.com

Year Introduced
 (as the Event 34)

Number of boats built

N. American Agent
 Prout Catamarans USA
 326 First Street, Suite 33
 Annapolis, MD 21403
 Tel: (410) 280-8500 Fax: (410) 280-6095

Other Cruising Multihulls By Builder
 Prout 26 (semi-custom basis), Prout 37,
Prout 38, Prout 39, Prout 45, Prout 50

KEY FEATURES

Hull & Sail Plan
- Integral keels, inboard rudders, reverse transoms with molded boarding steps
- Mast-aft cutter rig w/small mainsail, large roller furling genoa, staysail

Deck Layout
- Full rigid foredeck with lockers aft
- Large U-shaped cockpit with ample lockers
- Sundeck aft of the cockpit

Standard Accommodations
- Bridgedeck saloon cabin has U-shaped seating with large dining table forward
- Starboard hull has comfortable staterooms fore and aft with long galley midships
- Port hull has stateroom aft, storage and nav area midships, and large head forward

Mechanical
- Wheel steering, helm forward to starboard
- Single engine midships aft of cockpit or twin engines, one each hull

DESCRIPTION

Formerly the Event 34, the Prout 34 is one of the newer generation of cruising cats from Prout incorporating high volume hulls and wider beam in a luxury, high-performance cruiser. The high aspect ratio rig, full length nacelle, planing wedges and high prismatic hull design all enable the Prout 34 to perform exceptionally under a variety of conditions while still maintaining the ease of handling associated with Prout boats. Sail controls all lead to the cockpit, allowing easy handling by one person. She has a light and airy interior available in both the Family and Open plan, with abundant room and impressive load-carrying capacity. The Excel option features the new fully molded luxurious interior with twin inboard diesels. Suitable for liveaboard and extended cruising, the Prout 34 is a good choice for superior sailing performance with comfort.

SPECIFICATIONS

Displacement	8,800 lbs, 4000 kg	
Standard Auxiliary	1 x 20 hp inboard	
Overall Length	34'0"	10.36 m
Waterline Length	30'3"	9.20 m
Bridgedeck Length	28'10"	8.80 m
Wing Deck Clearance	varies	
Beam (max.)	15'7"	4.75 m
Draft (max.)	2'8"	0.81 m
Mast Hgt. Off Deck	38'0"	11.50 m
Mast Hgt. Off Water		

SAIL AREA

Mainsail	185 sf	17 sm
Genoa	380 sf	35 sm
Staysail	96 sf	9 sm
Total Area	660 sf	61 sm
Spinnaker	800 sf	75 sm

CAPACITY

Berths	3-4 doubles	
Staterooms	3	
Heads	1	
Fuel	15 gal	70 ltr
Fresh Water	70 gal	318 ltr
Payload	3,000 lbs, 1361 kg	

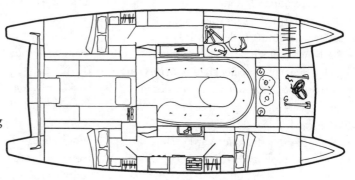

PROUT 37

GENERAL INFORMATION

Classification   Production catamaran, Cruiser

Approx. Cost   US $210,000

Designer   Prout

Builder   Prout Catamarans
Kings Close, Charfleets,
Canvey Island, Essex
SS8 0QZ, England
Tel: 44 (0) 1 268 511500
Fax: 44 (0) 1 268 510094
email: Sales@Prout-Catamarans.com

Year Introduced
(as the Snowgoose 37)

Number of boats built

N. American Agent
Prout Catamarans USA
326 First Street, Suite 33
Annapolis, MD 21403
Tel: (410) 280-8500 Fax: (410) 280-6095

Other Cruising Multihulls By Builder
Prout 26 (semi-custom basis), Prout 34,
Prout 38, Prout 39, Prout 45, Prout 50

KEY FEATURES

Hull & Sail Plan
- Integral keels, inboard rudders, plumb transoms, central nacelle underbody
- Mast-aft cutter rig w/small mainsail, large roller-furling genoa, staysail

Deck Layout
- Full rigid foredeck with lockers just aft
- Cockpit seating port and starboard
- Sundeck aft the cockpit

Standard Accommodations
- Bridgedeck saloon cabin has long U-shaped settee with dining table forward
- Starboard hull has large stateroom aft, galley midships, smaller stateroom forward
- Port hull has large stateroom aft, storage and nav area midships, large head forward

Mechanical
- Wheel steering, helm forward to starboard
- Single engine midships aft of cockpit or twin engines, one each hull

DESCRIPTION

For many years a popular cruiser worldwide, the Prout 37 (formerly the Snowgoose 37) combines ocean sailing capabilities and a legendary safety record with comfort. She boasts a proven design employing traditional Prout innovations and modern construction techniques. The result is a fast, responsive craft under sail, with spacious accommodations, excellent load-carrying capacity for her size, and ease of handling. As with other Prout boats, sail handling can be done exclusively from the cockpit. A good family boat, the Prout 37 now features a new Italian luxuriously-styled interior, available in both the Family and Open plan layouts. Other changes include optional twin engines, a new cutter rig, and a lighter-weight structure that improves her load-carrying capacity. The 37 remains Prout Catamaran's best choice for family cruising in a medium-priced boat.

SPECIFICATIONS

Displacement	11,500 lbs, 5216 kg	
Standard Auxiliary	1 x 30 hp inboard	
Overall Length	37'0"	11.30 m
Waterline Length	33'11"	10.30 m
Bridgedeck Length	32'4"	9.86 m
Wing Deck Clearance	varies	
Beam (max.)	16'3"	4.95 m
Draft (max.)	2'8"	0.81 m
Mast Hgt. Off Deck	40'0"	12.20 m
Mast Hgt. Off Water		

SAIL AREA

Mainsail	200 sf	19 sm
Genoa	416 sf	39 sm
Staysail	84 sf	8 sm
Total Area	700 sf	66 sm
Spinnaker	1500 sf	140 sm

CAPACITY

Berths	1 sgle, 2-3 dbls	
Staterooms	3	
Heads	1	
Fuel	15 gal	70 ltr
Fresh Water	90 gal	410 ltr
Payload		

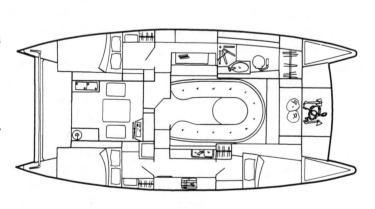

PROUT 38

GENERAL INFORMATION

Classification   Production catamaran, Cruiser

Approx. Cost   US $253,000

Designer   Prout

Builder   Prout Catamarans
Kings Close, Charfleets,
Canvey Island, Essex
SS8 0QZ, England
Tel: 44 (0) 1 268 511500
Fax: 44 (0) 1 268 510094
email: Sales@Prout-Catamarans.com

Year Introduced   1998

Number of boats built   1 (as of Sep 97)

N. American Agent
Prout Catamarans USA
326 First Street, Suite 33
Annapolis, MD 21403
Tel: (410) 280-8500 Fax: (410) 280-6095

Other Cruising Multihulls By Builder
Prout 26 (semi-custom basis), Prout 37, Prout 38, Prout 39, Prout 45, Prout 50

KEY FEATURES

Hull & Sail Plan
- Integral keels, inboard rudders, reverse transoms, mini-nacelle underbody
- Mast-aft sloop rig w/small mainsail, large roller-furling genoa

Deck Layout
- Curved rigid foredeck with lockers just aft
- U-shaped cockpit seating on level with transom access, storage lockers
- Boarding steps molded into transoms

Standard Accommodations
- Bridgedeck saloon cabin has U-shaped settee with dining table, nav station
- Starboard hull has large stateroom aft, galley midships, smaller stateroom forward
- Port hull has large stateroom aft, storage midships, large head forward

Mechanical
- Wheel steering, helm forward to starboard
- Twin inboards, access from aft cabins

DESCRIPTION

The Prout 38 is a portent of things to come from the "second generation" of Prout catamarans. This stylish cruising catamaran is designed along the same lines as the Prout 45. The central nacelle has been replaced with a mini-nacelle and an arched bridgedeck with substantial clearance from the waterline. The deck and cabin lines are sleeker and the foredeck has a curved design that creates a center peak for attaching anchor and forestay. Central to the boat's concept is a new high-volume hull (with reduced weight in the bows and transoms) that provides increased load carrying, smoother, more comfortable sea-keeping, and a dramatic improvement in performance. The main saloon cabin has a spacious lounge area and nav station. Hull accommodations include two aft staterooms, a long galley, forward stateroom, and a large head with shower compartment.

SPECIFICATIONS

Displacement	14,300 lbs, 6500 kg	
Standard Auxiliary	2 x 10 hp inboard	
Overall Length	38'0"	11.58 m
Waterline Length	34'6"	10.52 m
Bridgedeck Length	31'0"	9.50 m
Wing Deck Clearance		
Beam (max.)	17'5"	5.30 m
Draft (max.)	3'3"	1.00 m
Mast Hgt. Off Deck	40'0"	12.20 m
Mast Hgt. Off Water	53'0"	16.31 m

SAIL AREA

Mainsail	262 sf	24 sm
Genoa	446 sf	42 sm
Total Area	708 sf	66 sm
Spinnaker	1020 sf	95 sm

CAPACITY

Berths	3 doubles
Staterooms	3
Heads	1
Fuel	variable
Fresh Water	variable
Payload	

PROUT 39

GENERAL INFORMATION

Classification   Production catamaran,
Cruiser

Approx. Cost   US $325,000 (Family)

Designer   Prout

Builder   Prout Catamarans
Kings Close, Charfleets,
Canvey Island, Essex
SS8 0QZ, England
Tel: 44 (0) 1 268 511500
Fax: 44 (0) 1 268 510094
email: Sales@Prout-Catamarans.com

Year Introduced
(as the Escale 39)

Number of boats built

N. American Agent
Prout Catamarans USA
326 First Street, Suite 33
Annapolis, MD 21403
Tel: (410) 280-8500 Fax: (410) 280-6095

Other Cruising Multihulls By Builder
Prout 26 (semi-custom basis), Prout 34,
Prout 37, Prout 38, Prout 45, Prout 50

KEY FEATURES

Hull & Sail Plan
- Integral keels, inboard rudders, reverse transoms, central nacelle
- Mast-aft cutter rig, small fully battened main, large roller-furling genoa, staysail

Deck Layout
- Full rigid foredeck w/ self-draining lockers
- Wrap-around cockpit seating; lockers
- Sundeck aft with twin swim platforms

Standard Accommodations
- Bridgedeck saloon cabin has oval dining area forward, settees; cocktail unit aft
- Starboard hull has comfortable staterooms fore and aft, long galley midships
- Port hull has stateroom aft, storage and nav area midships, and large head forward

Mechanical
- Wheel steering, helm forward to starboard
- Single engine midships aft of cockpit or twin engines, one each hull

DESCRIPTION

Formerly the Escale 39, the Prout 39 combines state-of-the-art construction techniques with excellent performance. Various options are offered, from sport model to family cruiser, resulting in a boat with more than the usual amount of versatility. The roller-furling cutter rig with all sail controls leading to the cockpit provides easy handling. Belowdecks, four different layouts are offered, all designed to reflect a subtle Italian style: a charter version of four double cabins with private heads; an open layout with two double cabins and enormous living area; a stateroom option with a king-sized cabin suite; and the family version with four double berths, master head, and choice of up to two more bath or dressing rooms. No matter which you choose, you'll get a superior level of comfort in a cruiser with all the usual Prout seakeeping and safety characteristics.

SPECIFICATIONS

Displacement	14,392 lbs, 6534 kg	
Standard Auxiliary	1 x 40 hp inboard	
Overall Length	39'0"	11.90 m
Waterline Length	35'0"	10.66 m
Bridgedeck Length	33'6"	10.21 m
Wing Deck Clearance		
Beam (max.)	18'4"	5.60 m
Draft (max.)	3'2"	0.95 m
Mast Hgt. Off Deck	45'0"	13.70 m
Mast Hgt. Off Water	53'0"	16.15 m

SAIL AREA

Mainsail	243 sf	23 sm
Genoa	475 sf	44 sm
Staysail	125 sf	12 sm
Total Area	843 sf	78 sm
Spinnaker		

CAPACITY

Berths	3-4 doubles	
Staterooms	3-4	
Heads	1, 2, or 3	
Fuel	26 gal	120 ltr
Fresh Water	143 gal	650 ltr
Payload		

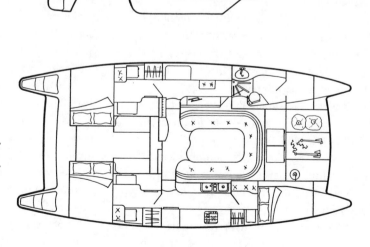

PROUT 45

GENERAL INFORMATION

Classification   Production catamaran, Cruiser

Approx. Cost   US $459,000 (Family)

Designer   Prout

Builder   Prout Catamarans
Kings Close, Charfleets,
Canvey Island, Essex
SS8 0QZ, England
Tel: 44 (0) 1 268 511500
Fax: 44 (0) 1 268 510094
email: Sales@Prout-Catamarans.com

Year Introduced   1996

Number of boats built

N. American Agent
Prout Catamarans USA
326 First Street, Suite 33
Annapolis, MD 21403
Tel: (410) 280-8500 Fax: (410) 280-6095

Other Cruising Multihulls By Builder
Prout 26 (semi-custom basis), Prout 34,
Prout 37, Prout 38, Prout 39, Prout 50

KEY FEATURES

Hull & Sail Plan
- Integral keels, inboard rudders, reverse transoms with molded boarding steps
- Mast-aft cutter rig w/small mainsail, large genoa with roller furling, staysail

Deck Layout
- Partial rigid foredeck with 2 trampolines, central walkway with anchor mount
- Large cockpit with table aft, lockers
- Sundeck at the stern behind the cockpit

Standard Accommodations
- Bridgedeck saloon cabin has semi-circular dining table, settee and nav area to port
- Starboard hull has stateroom with head aft, long galley midships, stateroom forward
- Port hull has large stateroom aft, storage midships, and large head forward

Mechanical
- Wheel steering, helm forward to starboard
- Dual engines; access from deck and cabins

DESCRIPTION

The Prout 45, the newest ocean-going catamaran from Prout, looks and performs quite differently from most of her sisterships. New design features include hydrodynamic winglets on the integral keels to reduce pitching and greatly improve windward performance. Skeg-mounted, counter-balanced rudders improve responsiveness and lighten helm loads, while diagonal torsion control bulkheads virtually eliminate twist between the two hulls in short, steep seas. The aft-stepped mast, unique in a boat of this size, ensures simple operation of the powerful sail area. Four interior layouts are available: the Open Plan, Family, Charter and Master Suite. Both the Family and Open Plan feature an inside helm station with a 300 degree view and full-size navigation table. The boat comes with an extensive liveaboard cruising inventory.

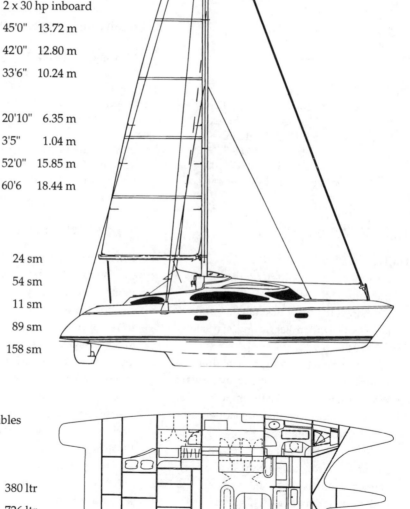

SPECIFICATIONS

Displacement	21,450 lbs, 9750 kg	
Standard Auxiliary	2 x 30 hp inboard	
Overall Length	45'0"	13.72 m
Waterline Length	42'0"	12.80 m
Bridgedeck Length	33'6"	10.24 m
Wing Deck Clearance		
Beam (max.)	20'10"	6.35 m
Draft (max.)	3'5"	1.04 m
Mast Hgt. Off Deck	52'0"	15.85 m
Mast Hgt. Off Water	60'6	18.44 m

SAIL AREA

Mainsail	360 sf	24 sm
Genoa	582 sf	54 sm
Staysail	115 sf	11 sm
Total Area	1057 sf	89 sm
Spinnaker	1700 sf	158 sm

CAPACITY

Berths	3-4 doubles	
Staterooms	3-4	
Heads	2-4	
Fuel	85 gal	380 ltr
Fresh Water	160 gal	726 ltr
Payload		

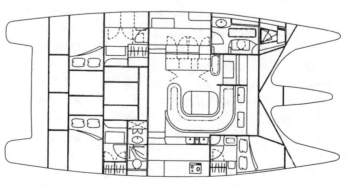

PROUT 50

GENERAL INFORMATION

Classification   Production catamaran,
Luxury Cruiser

Approx. Cost   US $647,000

Designer   Prout

Builder: Prout Catamarans
Kings Close, Charfleets,
Canvey Island, Essex
SS8 0QZ, England
Tel: 44 (0) 1 268 511500
Fax: 44 (0) 1 268 510094
email: Sales@Prout-Catamarans.com

Year Introduced
(as the Quasar 50)

Number of boats built

N. American Dealers
Prout Catamarans USA
326 First Street, Suite 33
Annapolis, MD 21403
Tel: (410) 280-8500 Fax: (410) 280-6095

Other Cruising Multihulls By Builder
Prout 26 (semi-custom basis), Prout 34,
Prout 37, Prout 38, Prout 39, Prout 45

KEY FEATURES

Hull & Sail Plan
- Integral keels, inboard rudders, reverse transoms with molded boarding steps
- Mast-aft cutter rig with small mainsail, large genoa with roller furling, staysail

Deck Layout
- Aft part of foredeck is rigid, with dual trampolines and central walkway forward
- Wrap-around cockpit with ample lockers
- Large sundeck, built-in swim ladders aft

Standard Accommodations
- Galley up to starboard aft, nav with helm station forward, dual seating area to port
- Starboard hull has large stateroom aft, head midships, stateroom with head forward
- Port hull same as starboard, with opt'l frig./freezer compartment midships

Mechanical
- Wheel steering, helm forward to starboard
- Dual engines with access from hull flooring

DESCRIPTION

Formerly the Quasar 50, the Prout 50 is a luxury craft of high quality. She offers a veritable ocean-going home, ideal for extended family cruising or the charter trade. In 1996, Prout introduced a new lightweight bulkhead system, new double diamond rig, and changes to the cockpit and aft deck layout. The spacious accommodations include four double staterooms, a 12 ft x 14 ft main saloon, large galley, inside helm position, and masses of locker space. All finish and upholstery can be chosen to suit each individual owner. Despite her large size and the fact that her mast is stepped further forward than most other Prout designs, the 50 handles with the ease, safety and pronounced sailing performance of all Prout craft. An open bridgedeck day charter version of the Prout 50 is also available, with crew cabin and large guest head compartments.

SPECIFICATIONS

Displacement	20,000 lbs, 9090 kg	
Standard Auxiliary	2 x 30 hp inboard	
Overall Length	49'0"	14.90 m
Waterline Length	45'0"	13.70 m
Bridgedeck Length	36'9"	11.21 m
Wing Deck Clearance		
Beam (max.)	23'6"	7.16 m
Draft (max.)	3'4"	1.02 m
Mast Hgt. Off Deck	55'0"	16.76 m
Mast Hgt. Off Water		

SAIL AREA

Mainsail	492 sf	45 sm
Genoa	486 sf	45 sm
Staysail	200 sf	21 sm
Total Area	1178 sf	111 sm
Spinnaker	2200 sf	205 sm

CAPACITY

Berths	2 sgls opt'l, 4 dbls	
Staterooms	4	
Heads	2-4	
Fuel	100 gal	454 ltr
Fresh Water	200 gal	910 ltr
Payload		

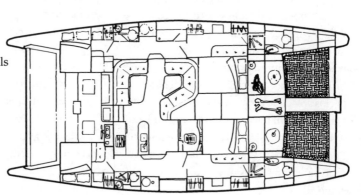

SEAWIND 1000

GENERAL INFORMATION

Classification   Production catamaran,
Cruiser

Approx. Cost   US $155,000

Designer   Seawind Catamarans

Builder   Seawind Catamarans
PO Box 5, Rozelle
NSW 2039 Australia
Tel: (61) 2 9810 1844
Fax: (61) 2 9810 9040
email:

Year Introduced

Number of boats built

N. American Dealer
Havre de Grace Yacht Sales
Maryland: Tel: (410) 939-2161
Florida: Tel: (941) 795-5591
Contact Seawind for other dealers

Other Cruising Multihulls By Builder
Custom multihulls

KEY FEATURES

Hull & Sail Plan
- Integral keels, inboard rudders, reverse transoms with molded boarding steps
- Fractional sloop rig, fully roached main, roller-furling, self-tacking jib

Deck Layout
- Trampoline forward with walkway, lockers just aft, open bridgedeck with soft cover
- Cockpit has soft enclosure over metal frame, generous seating and dining table

Standard Accommodations
- Bridgedeck accommodations under soft enclosure; table converts to a double berth
- Starboard hull has staterooms fore and aft with galley and storage lockers midships
- Port hull has large head aft, double berth midships, and stateroom forward

Mechanical
- Wheel steering, dual helms aft in cockpit
- Twin outboards, inboards optional

DESCRIPTION

The Seawind 1000 is designed and built as a comfortable family crusier or charter yacht. Sail handling is easy, with all controls leading to the central cockpit and modest-size sails and rig. Molded seating on the foredeck and a well protected, bimini-covered cockpit make this a comfortable yacht to sail. The interior is simple yet elegantly appointed. Four private cabins, a spacious saloon and well-equipped galley are available in the charter version, while the private owner layout features a port hull master suite with midships double berth and private head and shower aft. Awarded the 1994 Cruising Sailboat of the Year award by the Australian Boating Industry Association, the Seawind 1000 is designed to appeal to a wide range of sailors, from offshore passagemakers with an eye for safety and speed, to comfort seeking families with children.

SPECIFICATIONS

Displacement	8,800 lbs, 4000 kg	
Standard Auxiliary	2 x 9.9 hp outboard	
Overall Length	33'0"	10.00 m
Waterline Length		
Bridgedeck Length	20'3"	6.18 m
Wingdeck Clearance	2'8"	0.80 m
Beam (max.)	19'5"	5.90 m
Draft (max.)	2'11"	0.90 m
Mast Hgt. Off Deck		
Mast Hgt. Off Water		

SAIL AREA

Mainsail	480 sf	45 sm
Jib	200 sf	18 sm
Total Area	680 sf	63 sm
Spinnaker	654 sf	60 sm

CAPACITY

Berths	4-5 doubles
Staterooms	3-4
Heads	1
Fuel	32 gal 120 ltr
Fresh Water	120 gal 450 ltr
Payload	2,210 lbs, 1000 kg

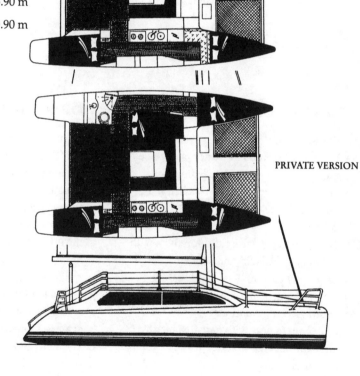

CHARTER VERSION

PRIVATE VERSION

ST. FRANCIS 44 MkII

GENERAL INFORMATION

Classification Production catamaran, Cruiser

Approx. Cost US $265,500

Designer Angelo Lavranos

Builder St. Francis Marine
P.O. Box 16, St.
Francis Bay 6312, S. Africa
Tel: (27) 423-940654
Fax: (27) 423-940553
email: stfrancispgp@intekom.co.za

Year Introduced 1991
(as the St. Francis 43)

Number of boats built 27 (as of Sep 97)

N. American Dealers Buy factory direct

Other Cruising Multihulls By Builder
None at present

KEY FEATURES

Hull & Sail Plan
- Integral keels, inboard rudders, reverse transoms with molded boarding steps
- Fractional sloop rig, fully roached main, roller-furling, self-tacking jib

Deck Layout
- Trampoline forward, ridid foredeck with lockers just aft, wide side decks
- Large cockpit with U-shaped seating
- Swim platform aft of the cockpit

Standard Accommodations
- Galley up to port with nav area nearby, large dining area to starboard
- Starboard hull has comfortable staterooms fore and aft with central common head
- Port hull has the master stateroom with berth aft and large head forward

Mechanical
- Wheel steering, helm forward in cockpit
- Twin inboards, access from aft cabins

DESCRIPTION

Formerly the St. Francis 43, the St. Francis 44 is a finely appointed, high-performance cruising catamaran, one ideally suited for the charter trade or private ownership. Boat construction has been meticulously undertaken, with numerous elegant touches to both the interior and topsides. Easy to sail, the St. Francic 44 has a fully battened mainsail and roller-furling genoa, plus optional reacher, spinnaker (in various weights), working jib, trysail and storm jib. The layout features a spacious saloon upholstered in leather, teak and holly floors, beechwood furniture, four double cabins with private heads (two with sit-type baths), extensive navigation table inventory, and deluxe galley with all the modern appliances. The overall impression is one of elegance and comfort. She is a boat well-suited to charter operations or liveaboard cruising.

SPECIFICATIONS

Displacement	15,435 lbs, 7000 kg	
Standard Auxiliary	2 x 27 hp inboard	
Overall Length	44'2"	13.45 m
Waterline Length	39'7"	12.10 m
Bridgedeck Length	27'8"	8.50 m
Wing Deck Clearance	2'0"	0.60 m
Beam (max.)	23'7"	7.20 m
Draft (max.)	3'0"	0.95 m
Mast Hgt. Off Deck	56'5"	17.20 m
Mast Hgt. Off Water	61'4"	18.71 m

SAIL AREA

Mainsail	676 sf	62 sm
Genoa	394 sf	36 sm
Total Area	1070 sf	99 sm
Spinnaker	968 sf	90 sm

CAPACITY

Berths	1 sgle, 4 dbls
Staterooms	4
Heads	4
Fuel	100 gal 379 ltr
Fresh Water	160 gal 600 ltr
Payload	5,512 lbs, 2500 kg

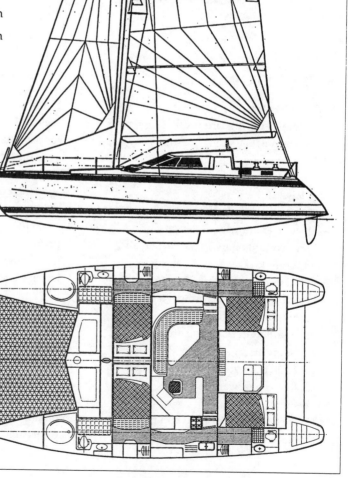

AQUILON 800

GENERAL INFORMATION

Classification   Production catamaran,
                      Trailerable sport cruiser

Approx. Cost   FF 355,000

Designer   Paul Stanek

Builder   Stanek Marine
               6 Ave. Julien
               06100 Nice, France
               Tel: (33) 4 92 08 04 22
               Fax: (33) 4 92 08 04 23
               email:

Year Introduced   1995

Number of boats built

N. American Agent   Buy factory direct

Other Cruising Multihulls By Builder
   None at present

KEY FEATURES

Hull & Sail Plan
- Integral keels, inboard rudders, reverse transoms with molded boarding steps
- Fractional sloop rig, fully roached main, self-tacking jib, spinnaker on prowler

Deck Layout
- Trampoline forward, large lockers just aft
- Open rigid bridgedeck design
- Large cockpit offers ample seating and aft sundeck

Standard Accommodations
- Open bridgedeck has dodger and optional hardtop for cockpit protection
- Starboard hull has dining area aft, galley midships, storage forward
- Port hull has stateroom aft, head midships, single berth forward

Mechanical
- Tiller steering, helm aft in cockpit
- Single outboard in cockpit well

DESCRIPTION

The Aquilon 800 is a reasonably priced trailerable catamaran, ideal for a cruising couple. She can be assembled/disassembled by two adults in about three hours and towed easily behind a regular family car. An optional mast-raising system and special trailer equipped with a cockpit lifting system to aid the assembly process are also available. Performance is fast on this light craft with fully-battened mainsail and cutter rig. The interior is amazingly light and airy with a large galley and saloon dining area to starboard. The port hull has a double berth aft, head/shower amidships, and single berth forward. Full standing headroom is found throughout both hulls. With no bridgedeck cabin, the cockpit comes with a table and teak-trimmed benches, plus an optional bimini top with windows for all-weather protection.

SPECIFICATIONS

Displacement	1,875 lbs, 850 kg	
Standard Auxiliary	1 x 9.9 hp outboard	
Overall Length	26'3"	7.99 m
Waterline Length	25'0"	7.65 m
Bridgedeck Length	13'6"	4.13 m
Wing Deck Clearance		
Beam (max.)	14'9"	4.50 m
Draft (max.)	2'0"	0.60 m
Mast Hgt. Off Deck	36'1	11.00 m
Mast Hgt. Off WL		

SAIL AREA

Mainsail	237 sf	22 sm
Genoa	134 sf	15 sm
Total Area	371 sf	37 sm
Spinnaker	409 sf	38 sm

CAPACITY

Berths	1 sgls, 1-2 dbls	
Staterooms	1	
Heads	1	
Fuel	variable	
Fresh Water	52 gal	200 ltr
Payload		

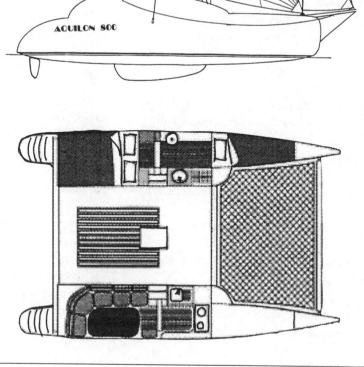

AQUILON 800

HIRONDELLE 23

GENERAL INFORMATION

Classification   Production catamaran,
Coastal cruiser

Approx. Cost   £30,000

Designer   Chris Hammond

Builder   Prout Catamarans for:
Swallow Yachts
Old Cross House, Stogursey
Sommerset TA5 1TE
England
Tel: (44) 1278 733089
Fax: (44) 1278 733089
email:

Year Introduced

Number of boats built

N. American Dealers   Buy factory direct

Other Cruising Multihulls By Sales Agent
None at present

KEY FEATURES

Hull & Sail Plan
- U-shaped hulls with integral keels, inboard rudders, reverse transoms
- Fractional sloop rig, fully roached main, roller-furling jib, AeroRig™ optional

Deck Layout
- Full rigid foredeck with large lockers, narrow side decks, cozy cockpit with seating port and starboard
- Engine in central cockpit well

Standard Accommodations
- Dual access hatches to saloon, settee/table converts to double berth
- Starboard hull has single berth aft, galley midships, storage forward
- Port hull has single berth aft, storage midships, head forward

Mechanical
- Tiller steering, cross bar aft in cockpit
- Single outboard in cockpit well

DESCRIPTION

The Hirondelle is a great little family coastal cruiser. Small yet speedy and surprisingly comfortable despite her size, this new version of a tried and true design remains one of the most affordable cruising options, with performance that will delight any sailing enthusiast. The wide aft cockpit, small rig and stable design make her an ideal choice for a small family or a couple just learning to sail. The cleverly designed, uncluttered interior layout includes two aft single berths, a dinette that converts to a double berth, roomy galley, navigation area, separate head, and commodious storage space. The latest version of the Hirondelle 23 is offered with an AeroRig™ for complete ease of sail handling, although those who wish to handle sails may still order the boat with a conventional sailplan. This boat is well-suited for the self-sufficient, budget-minded sailor.

SPECIFICATIONS

Displacement	2,500 lbs, 1132 kg	
Standard Auxiliary	1 x 9.9 hp outboard	
Overall Length	23'0"	7.02 m
Waterline Length		
Bridgedeck Length	20'9"	6.34 m
Wing Deck Clearance		
Beam (max.)	12'6"	3.81 m
Draft (max.)	2'6"	0.76 m
Mast Hgt. Off Deck	31'4"	9.55 m
Mast Hgt. Off Water	36'9"	11.22 m

SAIL AREA

Mainsail	135 sf	13 sm
Jib	115 sf	11 sm
Total Area	250 sf	24 sm
Spinnaker	220 sf	20 sm

CAPACITY

Berths	2 sgls, 1 dble	
Staterooms	none	
Heads	1	
Fuel	6 gal	22 ltr
Fresh Water	26 gal	100 ltr
Payload		

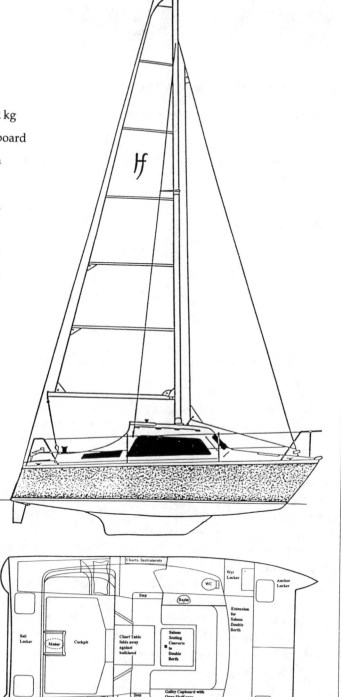

C-CAT 3214

GENERAL INFORMATION

Classification   Production catamaran, Cruiser

Approx. Cost   US $105,000

Designer   Bill Symons

Builder/Agent   Symons Choice
8401 9th St. N
St. Petersburg, FL 33702
USA
Tel: (813) 576-3993
Fax: (813) 576-3993
email:

Year Introduced   1991

Number of boats built   87*   (as of Sep 97)
(*boats of the same concept built under various names)

N. American Dealers   Buy factory direct

Other Cruising Multihulls By Builder/Agent
None at present

KEY FEATURES

Hull & Sail Plan
- Integral keels, inboard rudders, reverse transoms with molded boarding steps
- Cat rig, fully roached and battened main, no jib

Deck Layout
- Fully rigid foredeck, large lockers on deck,
- Low cabin roof for good visibility
- Large cockpit offers ample seating and storage lockers

Standard Accommodations
- Bridgedeck has long dinette settee/table that converts to an over-size berth
- Starboard hull has stateroom aft, storage midships, and large head/shower forward
- Port hull has stateroom aft, storage midships, and galley forward

Mechanical
- Wheel steering, forward in cockpit
- Single outboard hung off transom

DESCRIPTION

The C-CAT 3214, developed by long-time multihull enthusiast Bill Symons, is an improved and expanded version of Symons' C-CAT 3014. It is a true family cruising boat, incorporating a unique catboat sail plan that's remarkably trouble-free. She's a safe, comfortable, modest-size, easily handled boat for those outside the luxury market. She is a good choice for liveaboards. Storage and load-carrying capacity are excellent for her size, and accommodations are ample for up to six people with the two large aft staterooms and a comfortable saloon dinette that converts to an oversize double berth. It should be noted that emphasis with this design has been placed on safety, comfort and sea-kindliness. Performance is pleasing and easy to come by with the self-tending, single-sail rig, though she has no pretensions of being a high-performance cat.

SPECIFICATIONS

Displacement	6,700 lbs, 3042 kg	
Standard Auxiliary	1 x 25 hp outboard	
Overall Length	31'8"	9.66 m
Waterline Length	31'0"	9.46 m
Bridgedeck Length	29'6"	9.00 m
Wing Deck Clearance	variable (nacelle)	
Beam (max.)	14'9"	4.50 m
Draft (max.)	2'6"	0.76 m
Mast Hgt. Off Deck	41'6"	12.61 m
Mast Hgt. Off Water	47'6"	14.48 m

SAIL AREA

Mainsail	430 sf	40 sm
Total Area	430 sf	40 sm
Spinnaker	950 sf	88 sm

CAPACITY

Berths	2-3 doubles
Staterooms	2
Heads	1
Fuel	30 gal
Fresh Water	60 gal 197 ltr
Payload	6,000 lbs, 2724 kg

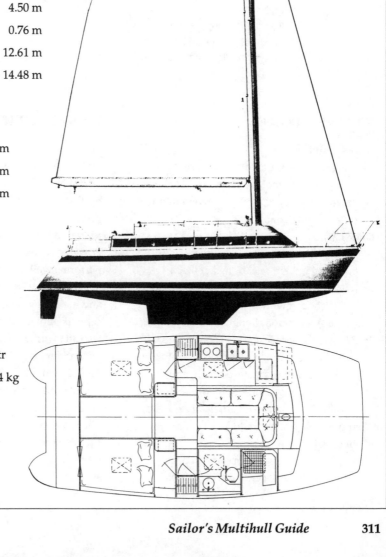

TASMAN ELITE 4000

GENERAL INFORMATION

Classification Production catamaran,
Luxury motorsailer cruiser

Approx. Cost AUS $326,000

Designer Roger Hill

Builder Tasman Yachts Australia
PO Box 256, Robina
QLD 4226, Australia
Tel: (61) 7 5593 8922
Fax: (61) 7 5593 8922
email: tyachts@ozemail.com.au

Year Introduced 1994

Number of boats built

N. American Dealers Buy factory direct

Other Cruising Multihulls By Builder
Tasman Elite 5000 motorsailer

KEY FEATURES

Hull & Sail Plan
- Integral keels, inboard rudders, reverse transoms with molded boarding steps
- Fractional sloop rig, fully battened main, roller-furling genoa

Deck Layout
- Trampoline forward with catwalk and boarding ladder, anchor locker just aft
- Raised coach roof with overhang aft
- Large cockpit with ample seating

Standard Accommodations
- Bridgedeck has lockers aft, seating area with table forward, dual hull access steps to port
- Starboard hull has stateroom aft, galley midships, double stateroom forward
- Port hull has stateroom aft, head midships, and double stateroom forward

Mechanical
- Wheel steering, helm forward to port
- Twin inboards, access from aft cabins

DESCRIPTION

The Tasman Elite 4000 is a comfortable motorsailer catamaran designed by Roger Hill of New Zealand and built and marketed by Tasman Yachts of Australia. She is a good combination of style, comfort and performance, with a strong focus on safety. Powered by twin 40hp diesel saildrives, she performs well under sail or power. Thanks to her shallow draft this boat can be beached, and the drop-down ladder from the foredeck catwalk allows easy shore access. There are also aft swim platforms with integrated steps and ladders for ease of swimming or diving. The Tasman Elite 4000 has full headroom throughout and a luxurious finish using high-grade lumber, quality fabrics and furnishings. There are four double staterooms (two with private head compartments), spacious saloon cabin, and fully equipped galley. (Note: the sideview shown is of the new Elite 5000)

SPECIFICATIONS

Displacement	13,200 lbs, 6000 kg	
Standard Auxiliary	2 x 40 hp inboard	
Overall Length	40'0"	12.20 m
Waterline Length	39'0"	11.90 m
Bridgedeck Length	28'4"	8.64 m
Wing Deck Clearance	2'3"	0.69 m
Beam (max.)	20'0"	6.02 m
Draft (max.)	3'0"	0.90 m
Mast Hgt. Off Deck	53'9	16.40 m
Mast Hgt. Off Water	63'7"	19.40 m

SAIL AREA

Mainsail	505 sf	47 sm
Genoa	398 sf	37 sm
Total Area	903 sf	84 sm
Spinnaker	936 sf	87 sm

CAPACITY

Berths	4 doubles	
Staterooms	4	
Heads	3	
Fuel	95 gal	360 ltr
Fresh Water	264 gal	197 ltr
Payload		

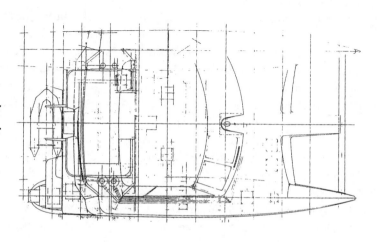

TOMCAT 6.2

GENERAL INFORMATION

Classification   Production catamaran,
Coastal sport cruiser

Approx. Cost   Call for current price

Designer   Ted & Tom Strain

Builder   TomCat Boats, Strain Assoc.
RR 1, Caledon East
Ontario, Canada L0N 1E0
Tel: (905) 584-1236
Fax: (905) 584-1236 (plus *)
email: emstrain@flexnet.com

Year Introduced   1996

Number of boats built   5   (as of Sep 97)

N. American Dealers   Buy factory direct

Other Cruising Multihulls By Builder
None at present

KEY FEATURES

Hull & Sail Plan
- Rockered hulls, centerboards, inboard rudders, reverse transoms
- Fractional sloop rig, fully battened main, optional roller-furling jib

Deck Layout
- Open foredeck area between hulls, central cockpit on bridgedeck with windshield to protect helmsman
- Cockpit extends to transom, which has twin storage boxes and outboard engine

Standard Accommodations
- Bridgedeck area is essentially open, with two seats facing forward and a windshield for spray protection
- A boom tent is available to provide overnight accommodations.

Mechanical
- Wheel steering, helm forward in cockpit
- Single outboard, access from transom

DESCRIPTION

The TomCat 6.2 is a versatile, trailerable day sailing or sport cruising catamaran. The rotating mast, fully battened mainsail with vang for sail shape control, and six-part ratchet mainsheet give good performance on all points of sail, with speeds of 10-12 knots or more common in a breeze. Lazy jacks and roller furling jib make sail handling safe and easy from the cockpit. With centerboards and rockered hulls, she tacks surely and can be easily beached. Motoring is as easy as handling a runabout, with wheel steering pinned to the rudders and a protected helm position with a windshield and soft top. The sport cruising option includes a mahogany dining table, provision for one double and one single berth, pull-out head with privacy curtain and a camper top with windows, screens, and zip-out panels providing full sitting headroom throughout the bridgedeck.

SPECIFICATIONS

Displacement	1,000 lbs, 454 kg	
Standard Auxiliary	1 x 5-25 hp outboard	
Overall Length	20'3"	6.20 m
Waterline Length	20'0"	6.10 m
Bridgedeck Length	11'0"	3.30 m
Wing Deck Clearance	1'0"	0.30 m
Beam (max.)	11'2"	3.40 m
Draft (boards up)	0'9"	0.20 m
Draft (boards down)	3'6"	1.10 m
Mast Hgt. Off Water	31'0"	9.50 m

SAIL AREA

Mainsail	155 sf	14 sm
Jib	45 sf	5 sm
Total Area	200 sf	19 sm
Spinnaker		

CAPACITY

Berths	1 sgle, 1 dble
Staterooms	none
Heads	1 pull out
Fuel	portable
Fresh Water	portable
Payload	1200 lbs, 545 kg

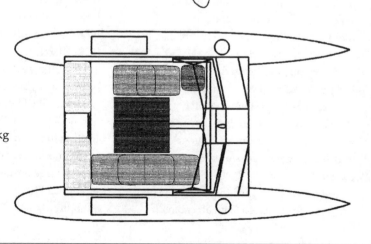

LAGOON 35ccc

GENERAL INFORMATION

Classification Production catamaran, Cruiser

Approx. Cost Call for current price

Designers Morrelli & Melvin

Builder TPI
Agent Lagoon America
105 Eastern Ave., Suite 202
Annapolis, MD 21403
Tel: (410) 280-9400
Fax: (410) 280-9401
email: lagoonam@aol.com

Year Introduced 1996

Number of boats built 11 (as of Sep 97)

N. American Dealers
Contact Lagoon America for dealer list

Other Cruising Multihulls By Builder
Custom boats

KEY FEATURES

Hull & Sail Plan
- Integral low asect ratio keels
- Near-plumb bows, long reverse transoms
- Fractional sloop rig
- Fully roached main, roller-furling jib

Deck Layout
- Large trampoline area forward, wide rigid deck just aft with self-draining lockers
- Wrap-around seating in cockpit
- Molded boarding steps

Standard Accommodations
- Galley up on port bridgedeck, with L-shaped seating area to starboard
- Starboard hull has stateroom aft, storage midships, large head forward
- Port hull has stateroom aft, storage midships, large single stateroom forward

Mechanical
- Wheel steering forward to port in cockpit
- Twin inboards, access from aft cabins

DESCRIPTION

The new Lagoon 35ccc (for coastal cruising catamaran) is the smallest of the renowned Lagoon line of yachts. She draws from a long lineage of impressive multihull designs and continues with the collaboration of Lagoon, one of the world's leading producers of quality catamarans, and TPI, a U.S. builder of sophisticated production sailboats. Construction is unique—she is the first multihull in the world with a hull constructed utilizing the SCRIMP® infusion method of lamination. The resulting balsa cored composite offers one of the highest strength-to-weight ratios possible. She features a large cockpit, mast and boom internal halyards, and all lines leading to the cockpit. Her comfortable accommodations include two queen-size aft cabins, large head forward, and saloon with galley, dinette, 6'3" headroom and panoramic visibility.

SPECIFICATIONS

Displacement	9,500 lbs, 4313 kg	
Standard Auxiliary	2 x 9 hp inboard	
Overall Length	34'6"	10.50 m
Waterline Length	33'3"	10.10 m
Bridgedeck Length	23'3"	7.10 m
Wing Deck Clearance	1'8"	0.51 m
Beam (max.)	15'9"	4.80 m
Draft (max.)	3'3"	1.00 m
Mast Hgt. Off Deck	42'3"	12.94 m
Mast Hgt. Off Water	49'3"	15.02 m

SAIL AREA

Mainsail	422 sf	39 sm
Genoa	198 sf	18 sm
Total Area	620 sf	57 sm
Spinnaker	500 sf	47 sm

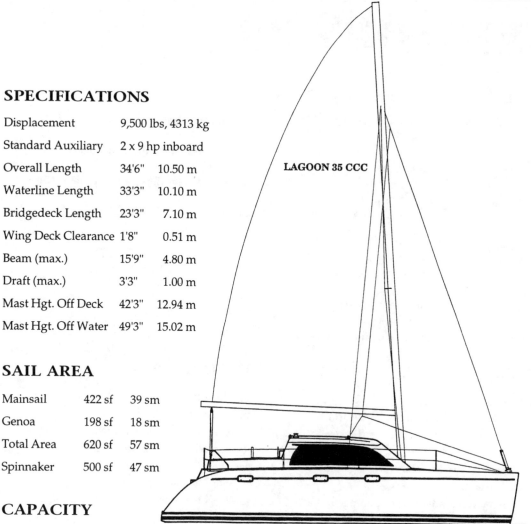

LAGOON 35 CCC

CAPACITY

Berths	1 sgle, 2 dbls	
Staterooms	3	
Heads	1	
Fuel	40 gal	151 ltr
Fresh Water	68 gal	257 ltr
Payload	2,627 lbs, 1195 kg	

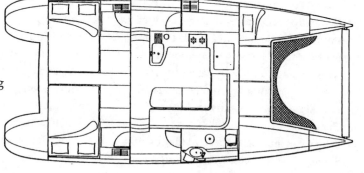

VICTORY 35

GENERAL INFORMATION

Classification   Production catamaran, Cruiser

Approx. Cost   US $192,900

Designer   B. Hepburn
Tradewinds Yacht Design

Builder   Endeavour
Agent   Victory Catamarans
74 20th St. Brooklyn, NY
11232 USA
Tel: (718) 965-8600
Fax: (718) 965-9729
email: ppr@interport.net

Year Introduced   1994

Number of boats built   13   (as of Sep 97)

N. American Dealers   Buy factory direct

Other Cruising Multihulls By Agent
None at present

KEY FEATURES

Hull & Sail Plan
- Integral keels, inboard rudders, reverse transoms with molded boarding steps
- Masthead sloop rig, fully battened main with lazy jacks; roller-furling genoa

Deck Layout
- Fully ridid foredeck with storage lockers wide side decks, good foot space
- large cockpit with wrap-around seating and side sundecks

Standard Accommodations
- Galley up to port aft with large nav area to starboard aft, lounge area/table forward
- Starboard hull has large stateroom aft, work/storage midships, head forward
- Port hull has large staterooms fore & aft, with storage, sink/vanity midships

Mechanical
- Wheel steering, helm forward in cockpit
- Single inboard, access from cockpit

DESCRIPTION

The Victory 35 is an innovative catamaran designed for liveaboard or short term cruising. Design features include shoal-draft keels, moderate beam for canal cruising or easy berthing at marinas, and an easily driven underbody that adds to her performance under sail or power. Skeg-hung rudders provide directional stability. Unique hull design and fine waterline entry allow the boat to tack easily, with downwind speeds in excess of 10 knots commonplace. Very livable for a boat this size, her accommodations include three double-berth cabins, a large head compartment forward in the starboard hull, and a comfortable bridgedeck layout with saloon seating and dining area, a full navigation center and a well-appointed galley. This boat is a good choice for extended family cruising.

SPECIFICATIONS

Displacement	9,000 lbs, 4082 kg	
Standard Auxiliary	1 x 27 hp inboard	
Overall Length	35'0"	10.68 m
Waterline Length	34'10"	10.63 m
Bridgedeck Length	32'10"	10.02 m
Wing Deck Clearance	2'0"	0.61 m
Beam (max.)	16'0"	4.88 m
Draft (max.)	2'10"	0.87 m
Mast Hgt. Off Deck	39'0"	11.90 m
Mast Hgt. Off Water	48'0"	14.64 m

SAIL AREA

Mainsail	320 sf	30 sm
Genoa	300 sf	28 sm
Total Area	620 sf	58 sm
Spinnaker	1100 sf	102 sm

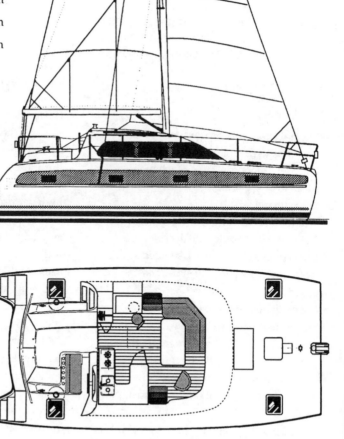

CAPACITY

Berths	3 doubles
Staterooms	3
Heads	1 & $^1/_2$
Fuel	36 gal 136 ltr
Fresh Water	85 gal 322 ltr
Payload	4,000 lbs, 1814 kg

NORSEMAN 430

GENERAL INFORMATION

Classification   Production catamaran,
                     Cruiser/charter cruiser

Approx. Cost   US $272,000

Designer   Alexander Simonis

Builder   Voyage Yachts, S. Africa
Agent   Voyage Charters BVI
              PO Box 1788
              Cruz Bay, St. John
              USVI 00831
              Tel: (809) 494-0740
              Fax: (809) 494-0741
              email: VOYAGE@caribsurf.com

Year Introduced   1993
                           (as the Norseman 400)

Number of boats built   35   (as of Sep 97)

N. American Dealers
   Contact Voyage Yachts for dealer list

Other Cruising Multihulls By Builder
   Mayotte 500

KEY FEATURES

Hull & Sail Plan
- Integral keels, inboard rudders, reverse transoms with molded boarding steps
- Fractional sloop rig, fully roached main, roller-furling genoa

Deck Layout
- Trampoline forward, ridid foredeck with lockers just aft, wide side decks
- Comfortable cockpit w/ U-shaped seating, table, ample lockers and storage areas

Standard Accommodations
- Galley up to port with large lounge/dining area to starboard, well-placed nav area aft
- Starboard hull–large staterooms/private heads fore & aft, heads are midships
- Port hull has large staterooms/private heads fore & aft, head/storage midships

Mechanical
- Wheel steering, helm forward in cockpit
- Twin inboards, access from aft cabins

DESCRIPTION

Designed by Alexander Simonis, built by Voyage Yachts of South Africa, and marketed by Voyage Charters, the Norseman 430 is a durable, fast bluewater cruising catamaran. Formerly the Norseman 400, she combines high performance, style, and comfort, and is well-suited to private ownership and the crewed or bareboat charter trade. Her interior is spacious and elegant. The main saloon cabin has two hull access steps for each hull, allowing four private double staterooms complete with head compartments (the two forward staterooms also have additional single berths). The bridgedeck features a galley, semi-circular settee with table, and navigation center with swing-out seat. At the stern is a wide sun or bathing deck. Numerous touches of luxury have been incorporated into this yacht, making her a very livable boat for world cruising.

SPECIFICATIONS

Displacement	16,020 lbs, 7250 kg	
Standard Auxiliary	2 x 27 hp inboard	
Overall Length	42'11"	13.07 m
Waterline Length	39'7"	12.10 m
Bridgedeck Length	27'0"	8.24 m
Wing Deck Clearance	2'2"	0.65 m
Beam (max.)	25'0"	7.60 m
Draft (max.)	3'7"	1.10 m
Mast Hgt. Off Deck	56'9"	17.30 m
Mast Hgt. Off Water	62'0"	18.90 m

SAIL AREA

Mainsail	646 sf	60 sm
Genoa	484 sf	45 sm
Total Area	1130 sf	105 sm
Spinnaker	1184 sf	110 sm

CAPACITY

Berths	0-2 sgls, 4 dbls
Staterooms	4
Heads	2, 3, or 4
Fuel	106 gal 400 ltr
Fresh Water	106 gal 400 ltr
Payload	8,730 lbs, 3950 kg

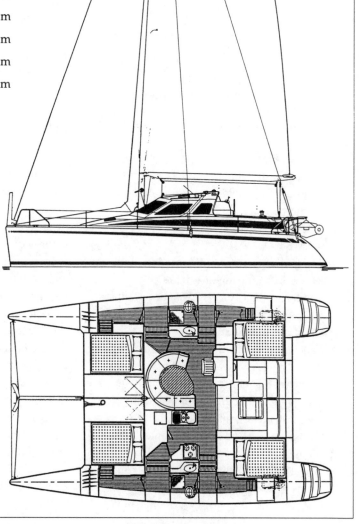

MAYOTTE 500

GENERAL INFORMATION

Classification	Production catamaran, Cruiser/charter cruiser	**Year Introduced**	1994 (as the Mayotte 470)

Classification Production catamaran, Cruiser/charter cruiser

Approx. Cost US $457,000

Designer Alexander Simonis

Builder Voyage Yachts, S. Africa
Agent Voyage Charters Intn'l
PO Box 1788
Cruz Bay, St. John
USVI 00831
Tel: (809) 494-0740
Fax: (809) 494-0741
email: VOYAGE@caribsurf.com

Year Introduced   1994
(as the Mayotte 470)

Number of boats built   18 (as of Sep 97)

N. American Dealers
Contact Voyage Yachts for dealer list

Other Cruising Multihulls By Builder
Norseman 430

KEY FEATURES

Hull & Sail Plan
- Integral keels, inboard rudders, reverse transoms with molded boarding steps
- Fractional sloop rig, fully roached main, roller-furling genoa

Deck Layout
- Trampoline forward, ridid foredeck with lockers just aft, wide side decks
- Comfortable cockpit w/ U-shaped seating, table, ample lockers and storage areas

Standard Accommodations
- Galley up to port with large lounge/dining area to starboard, well-placed nav area aft
- Starboard hull–large staterooms/private heads fore & aft, berth/storage midships
- Port hull has large staterooms/private heads fore & aft, head/storage midships

Mechanical
- Wheel steering, helm forward in cockpit
- Twin inboards, access from aft cabins

DESCRIPTION

The Mayotte 500 is a comfortable, seaworthy catamaran designed for both private ownership and the charter trade. Sail handling has been kept simple with roller-furling genoa, mainsail, and all lines leading to the cockpit. Twin transom boarding ladders lead to a convenient swim platform and the large cockpit area with seating for ten. The standard charter layout includes four queen-berth cabins with private head/shower compartments. A spacious galley is located on the bridgedeck alongside the large dining/seating area and bar counter with stools. For crewed charter, three single berths have been incorporated into the bow and starboard amidships, along with a separate head. Standing headroom is 7 feet throughout the saloon and cabins. Ventilation is excellent, with numerous opening ports and hatches.

SPECIFICATIONS

Displacement	19,575 lbs, 8863 kg
Standard Auxiliary	2 x 38 hp inboard
Overall Length	49'10" 15.20 m
Waterline Length	47'6" 14.50 m
Bridgedeck Length	30'0" 9.15 m
Wing Deck Clearance	2'7" 0.80 m
Beam (max.)	27'3" 8.30 m
Draft (max.)	3'11" 1.20 m
Mast Hgt. Off Deck	61'6" 18.75 m
Mast Hgt. Off Water	68'3" 20.80 m

SAIL AREA

Mainsail	775 sf	72 sm
Genoa	516 sf	48 sm
Total Area	1291 sf	120 sm
Spinnaker	1345 sf	125 sm

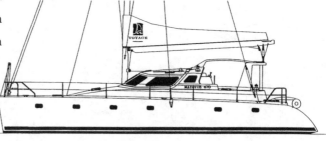

MAYOTTE

CAPACITY

Berths	3 sgls, 4 dbls
Staterooms	4
Heads	5
Fuel	132 gal 500 ltr
Fresh Water	264 gal 1000 ltr
Payload	10,387 lbs, 4700 kg

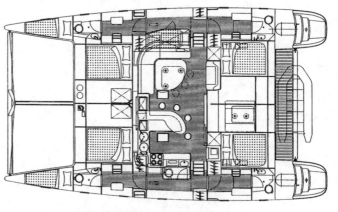

MAYOTTE   • CHARTER LAYOUT

Production &
Semi-Custom
Trimarans

F-25C/G

GENERAL INFORMATION

Classification   Production trimaran,
Trailerable sport cruiser kit

Approx. Cost   US $29,300 major parts C
US $60,000 complete boat C
US $19,900 major parts G
US $40,000 complete boat G

Designer   Ian Farrier

Builder   Colorado Composites
PO Box 3283
Evergreen, CO 80437 USA
Tel: (303) 674-2580
Fax: (303) 674-2758

Year Introduced   1994

Number of boats built   47 (as of Sep 97)

N. American Dealers   Buy factory direct

Other Cruising Multihulls By Builder
CFR-20

KEY FEATURES

Hull & Sail Plan
- U-shaped main hull with high-buoyancy amas, daggerboard, sugar-scoop transom
- Fractional sloop rig, fully battened main, 100% jib, roller-furling screecher

Deck Layout
- Full rigid foredeck with trampoline netting between the main hull and amas.
- Cockpit has seats port and starboard, cabin hatch with dodger, storage in amas

Standard Accommodations
- Main hull aft–standing headroom under sliding hatch, quarterberths
- Main hull midships–settees that convert to single berths, folding dining table
- Main hull forward–double V-berth with minimal headroom

Mechanical
- Tiller steering, outboard rudder
- Transom-hung outboard

DESCRIPTION

The F-25C/G is actually two kit versions of the same folding, trailable F-25 sport trimaran design from Ian Farrier. The F-25C, constructed of lightweight carbon fiber, has quite a reputation for speed on the race course and for comfort on weekend cruises. The F-25G is an all-glass model constructed from the same tooling. It is about a third less expensive and therefore more attractive for those who simply want to cruise and don't mind the extra weight. The F-25C/G is offered in kit form by the builder, either as individual hulls, decks, beams, and folding hardware, or as a structurally complete boat with all folding hardware installed. With the exception of the 4' x 7'3" V-berth, which is a structural part of the boat, the interior layout is entirely up to the builder. There is room for two quarter berths, a galley, a chart table, and a dining area.

SPECIFICATIONS

Displacement	C: 1,480 lbs, G: 2,095 lbs	
Standard Auxiliary	1 x 9.9 hp outboard	
Overall Length	26'10"	8.20 m
Waterline Length	24'4"	7.42 m
Beam (max.)	19'0"	5.80 m
Beam (folded)	8'6"	2.90 m
Draft (board up)	4'4"	1.32 m
Draft (board down)	0'8"	0.20 m
Mast Hgt. Off Deck	36'6"	11.13 m
Mast Hgt. Off Water	41'0"	12.51 m

SAIL AREA

Mainsail	291 sf	27 sm
Jib	149 sf	14 sm
Total Area	440 sf	41 sm
Screecher	321 sf	30 sm
Spinnaker	695 sf	65 sm

CAPACITY

Berths	2 sgls, 1 dble
Staterooms	none
Heads	1 (portable)
Fuel	variable
Fresh Water	variable
Payload	

Galley (position is optional)

Double berth

Single quarter berth and settee

CONTOUR 30 MkII

GENERAL INFORMATION

Classification   Production trimaran,
                       Trailerable sport cruiser

Approx. Cost   US $90,000

Designer   Cole Beadon

Builder: Contour Yachts, PC Mould
                       25 Shamrock Rd.
                       Erin, ON NOB 1TO Canada
                       Tel: (519) 833-9490
                       Fax: (519) 833-7246
                       email:

Year Introduced

Number of boats built

N. American Dealers   Buy factory direct

Other Cruising Multihulls By Builder
   Contour 34 SC, Contour 40 custom

KEY FEATURES

Hull & Sail Plan
- Main hull with "swing wing" amas for easy docking and trailerability; daggerboard
- Fractional sloop rig, rotating mast, fully battened loose-footed main, self-tacking jib

Deck Layout
- Full rigid foredeck with trampoline netting between the main hull and amas.
- Cockpit has seats port & starboard, sliding cabin hatch, storage in amas

Standard Accommodations
- Main hull aft–standing headroom in main hull, galley aft
- Main hull midships–settees that convert to single berths, folding dining table
- Main hull forward–enclosed head, double V-berth stateroom

Mechanical
- Tiller steering, outboard rudder
- Transom-hung outboard

DESCRIPTION

The Contour 30 MkII combines trimaran performance with true cruising accommodations. Standing headroom throughout the main cabin, two full-length settees, a complete galley, a fully enclosed head, and private forward cabin with a 6'5" V-berth allow you to cruise in style. The interior is bright and airy with good ventilation. This boat owes her outstanding performance to her powerful rig, well-balanced hull design and large amas. She regularly cruises at 10 to 15 knots, and her self-tacking jib makes single-handed sailing a breeze. The folding amas mean the Contour 30 MkII can fit in a regular slip. The amas demount for easy trailering. This boat is a good option for those who like to cruise fast or who want to put in some time on the racing circuit.

SPECIFICATIONS

Displacement	3,000 lbs, 1361 kg	
Standard Auxiliary	1 x 9.9 hp outboard	
Overall Length	30'0"	9.15 m
Waterline Length	28'6"	8.69 m
Beam (max.)	23'10"	7.27 m
Beam (folded)	11'0"	3.36 m
Draft (board up)	1'4"	0.41 m
Draft (board down)	5'9"	1.75 m
Mast Hgt. Off Water	46'6"	14.18 m

SAIL AREA

Mainsail	360 sf	34 sm
Jib	150 sf	14 sm
Total Area	510 sf	48 sm
Genoa	230 sf	21 sm
Spinnaker	950 sf	88 sm

CAPACITY

Berths	0-2 sgls, 1-2 dbls	
Staterooms	1	
Heads	1	
Fuel	15 gal	68 ltr
Fresh Water	20 gal	91 ltr
Payload	2,000 lbs, 907 kg	

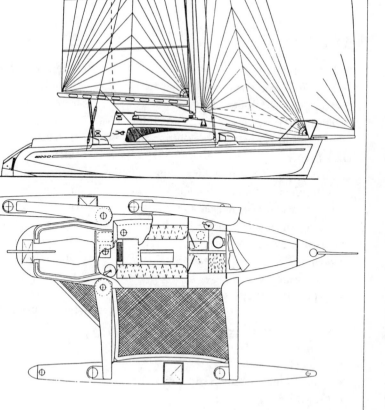

CONTOUR 34 SC

GENERAL INFORMATION

Classification   Production trimaran, Trailerable sport cruiser

Approx. Cost   US $139,000

Designer   Cole Beadon

Builder: Contour Yachts, PC Mould
25 Shamrock Rd.
Erin, ON NOB 1TO Canada
Tel: (519) 833-9490
Fax: (519) 833-7246
email:

Year Introduced   1996

Number of boats built

N. American Dealers   Buy factory direct

Other Cruising Multihulls By Builder
Contour 30 MkII, Contour 40 custom

KEY FEATURES

Hull & Sail Plan
- Main hull with swing-wing amas for easy docking and trailerability; daggerboard
- Fractional sloop rig, rotating mast, fully battened loose-footed main, self-tacking jib

Deck Layout
- Full rigid foredeck with trampoline netting between the main hull and amas.
- Large cockpit seats with storage under, sliding cabin hatch, storage/berths in amas

Standard Accommodations
- Main hull aft–standing headroom in main cabin, galley aft
- Main hull midships–settees that convert to single berths, folding dining table
- Main hull forward–enclosed private head, double V-berth stateroom

Mechanical
- Tiller steering, outboard rudder
- Transom-hung outboard

DESCRIPTION

Sistership to the popular Contour 30 MkII, the Contour 34 SC is the largest trailerable trimaran in production. This boat is designed for serious offshore cruising with a high level of structural integrity. The amas on this boat extend inboard, creating the rigidity of a fixed beam. The accommodations are bright and spacious—the layout is designed for extended cruising by two couples or a family. Large amas provide great form stability, while the powerful rig makes this boat extremely fast with a smooth, flat ride. All systems on deck are set up for single-handed sailing. This boat is a good choice for those who want to get to their cruising destination quickly and in style.

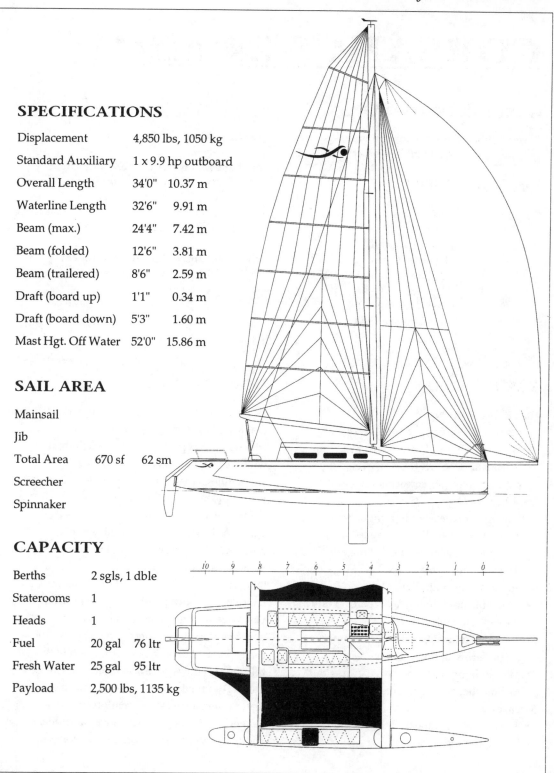

SPECIFICATIONS

Displacement	4,850 lbs, 1050 kg	
Standard Auxiliary	1 x 9.9 hp outboard	
Overall Length	34'0"	10.37 m
Waterline Length	32'6"	9.91 m
Beam (max.)	24'4"	7.42 m
Beam (folded)	12'6"	3.81 m
Beam (trailered)	8'6"	2.59 m
Draft (board up)	1'1"	0.34 m
Draft (board down)	5'3"	1.60 m
Mast Hgt. Off Water	52'0"	15.86 m

SAIL AREA

Mainsail		
Jib		
Total Area	670 sf	62 sm
Screecher		
Spinnaker		

CAPACITY

Berths	2 sgls, 1 dble	
Staterooms	1	
Heads	1	
Fuel	20 gal	76 ltr
Fresh Water	25 gal	95 ltr
Payload	2,500 lbs, 1135 kg	

CORSAIR F-24 MkII

GENERAL INFORMATION

Classification   Production trimaran, Trailerable sport cruiser

Approx. Cost   US $36,500

Designer   Ian Farrier

Builder   Corsair Marine
150 Reed Court
Chula Vista, CA 91911 USA
Tel: (619) 585-3005
Fax: (619) 585-3092
email: corsair33@aol.com

Year Introduced   1994

Number of boats built   102 (as of Sep 97)
*156 F-24s were previously built

N. American Dealers
Contact Corsair Marine for dealer list

Other Cruising Multihulls By Builder
F-28, F-28R, F-31 trailerable sport trimarans
Corsair 3600 cruising catamaran

KEY FEATURES

Hull & Sail Plan
- Main hull with folding amas for docking and trailerability, daggerboard main hull
- Fractional sloop rig, rotating mast, fully battened main, jib, screacher on bowsprit

Deck Layout
- Full rigid foredeck with trampoline netting between the main hull and amas.
- Cockpit has molded seats, sliding cabin hatch; storage in the amas

Standard Accommodations
- Main hull aft–standing headroom aft under pop-up companion hatch
- Main hull midships–settees that convert to single berths, optional galley
- Main hull forward–double V-berth with minimal headroom, marine toilet under

Mechanical
- Tiller steering, outboard kick-up rudder
- Transom-hung outboard

DESCRIPTION

The F-24 MkII is a one-design cruiser-racer that the whole family can enjoy. This trimaran is compact, easily trailerable, and with the addition of optional cruising ammenities a highly mobile pocket cruiser. But it's the boat's high performance—20+ knots speed capability—that really sets it apart. A flexible, easy-to-handle sail plan gives the F-24 excellent all-round perfor-mance in a wide range of conditions. Its fully battened square-top mainsail places more sail area aloft to take best advantage of light air, yet in heavy wind gusts the sail twists to depower the sail for safety. The working jib can be hanked on or roller-furled, and with the optional bowsprit a screacher or asym-metrical spinnaker can be flown. Additional features include a carbon-reinforced daggerboard, transom-hung kick-up rudder, and the famous Farrier Folding System™.

SPECIFICATIONS

Displacement	1,800 lbs, 816 kg	
Standard Auxiliary	1 x 5 hp outboard	
Overall Length	24'2"	7.30 m
Waterline Length	23'7"	7.20 m
Beam (max.)	17'11"	5.50 m
Beam (folded)	8'2"	2.50 m
Draft (board up)	1'0"	0.30 m
Draft (board down)	4'8"	1.40 m
Mast Hgt. Off Deck	31'10"	9.71 m
Mast Hgt. Off Water	36'8"	11.18 m

SAIL AREA

Mainsail	251 sf	23 sm
Jib	118 sf	11 sm
Total Area	369 sf	34 sm
Screacher	328 sf	30 sm
Spinnaker	496 sf	46 sm

CAPACITY

Berths	2 sgls, 1 dble
Staterooms	none
Heads	1 (portable)
Fuel	3 gal (portable)
Fresh Water	optional tank
Payload	

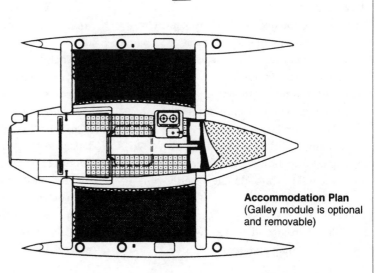

Accommodation Plan
(Galley module is optional
and removable)

CORSAIR F-28

GENERAL INFORMATION

Classification   Production trimaran, Trailerable sport cruiser

Approx. Cost   US $61,900

Designer   Ian Farrier

Builder   Corsair Marine
150 Reed Court
Chula Vista, CA 91911 USA
Tel: (619) 585-3005
Fax: (619) 585-3092
email: corsair33@aol.com

Year Introduced   1997

Number of boats built   28 (as of Sep 97)
  *453 F-27s were previously built

N. American Dealers
  Contact Corsair Marine for dealer list

Other Cruising Multihulls By Builder
  F-24 MkII, F-28R, F-31 trailerable sport trimarans, Corsair 3600 cruising catamaran

KEY FEATURES

Hull & Sail Plan
- Main hull with folding amas for docking and trailerability, daggerboard main hull
- Fractional sloop rig, rotating mast, fully battened main, jib, screacher on bowsprit

Deck Layout
- Full rigid foredeck with trampoline netting between the main hull and amas.
- Cockpit has long molded seats, sliding cabin hatch, storage in the amas

Standard Accommodations
- Main hull aft–single berth under cockpit, galley module to port
- Main hull midships–settees that convert to single berths, folding table, marine toilet
- Main hull forward–double V-berth with low headroom

Mechanical
- Tiller steering, outboard kick-up rudder
- Transom-hung outboard

DESCRIPTION

The new Corsair F-28 is a total redesign of one of the world's most popular trimaran sport cruisers, the F-27. After 10 years on the market and over 450 boats sold, the F-27 has been replaced by a slightly longer boat with more beam, yet less weight. Designed to be a roomy, fun cruiser that's easy for everyone, the F-28 is still fast enough under sail to tow a water skier! The Farrier Folding System™ used on all Corsair tris is well proven, easy to use and structurally sound. Rigging and launching can be done single-handed in about 30 minutes, half that for two persons. Balanced design eliminates the need for an oversize rig. The F-28 has a single spreader rotating mast with the latest flush square top fully battened main and blade jib for an efficient sail combination. The mast is actually shorter than before but overall speed potential is greater.

SPECIFICATIONS

Displacement	2,690 lbs, 1224 kg	
Standard Auxiliary	1 x 8 hp outboard	
Overall Length	28'5"	8.66 m
Waterline Length	26'3"	8.00 m
Beam (max.)	19'9"	6.10 m
Beam (folded)	8'2"	2.50 m
Draft (board up)	1'2"	0.36 m
Draft (board down)	4'11"	1.50 m
Mast Hgt. Off Deck	36'10"	11.22 m

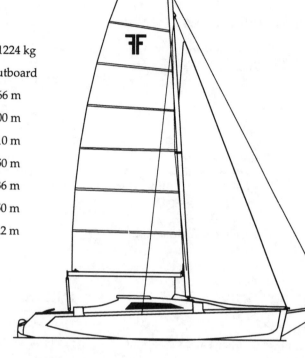

SAIL AREA

Mainsail	300 sf	28 sm
Jib	175 sf	16 sm
Total Area	475 sf	44 sm
Screacher	358 sf	33 sm
Spinnaker	780 sf	73 sm

CAPACITY

Berths	3 sgls, 1 dble
Staterooms	none
Heads	1 (portable)
Fuel	6 gal (portable)
Fresh Water	18 gal 68 ltr
Payload	

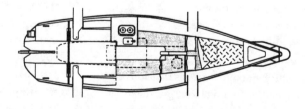

F-28 INTERIOR

CORSAIR F-31

GENERAL INFORMATION

Classification   Production trimaran,
                      Trailerable sport cruiser

Approx. Cost   US $100,000

Designer   Ian Farrier

Builder   Corsair Marine
                      150 Reed Court
                      Chula Vista, CA 91911 USA
                      Tel: (619) 585-3005
                      Fax: (619) 585-3092
                      email: corsair33@aol.com

Year Introduced   1991

Number of boats built   91   (as of Sep 97)

N. American Dealers
  Contact Corsair Marine for dealer list

Other Cruising Multihulls By Builder
  F-24 MkII, F-28, F-28R, F-31R tris
  Corsair 3600 cruising cat

KEY FEATURES

Hull & Sail Plan
- Main hull with folding amas for docking and trailerability, daggerboard main hull
- Fractional sloop rig, rotating mast, fully battened main, jib, screacher on bowsprit

Deck Layout
- Full rigid foredeck with trampoline netting between the main hull and amas.
- Cockpit has long molded seats, sliding cabin hatch, storage in the amas

Standard Accommodations
- Main hull aft–single berth under cockpit, galley module to port
- Main hull midships–settees that convert to single berths, folding table, marine toilet
- Main hull forward–double V-berth with low headroom

Mechanical
- Tiller steering, outboard kick-up rudder
- Transom-hung outboard

DESCRIPTION

The Corsair F-31 is a true long-range performance cruiser and racer that is also trailerable. Designed along the same lines as the F-27, this boat has more spacious cruising accommodations. The F-31 was originally built by Ostac Yachts in Australia. All tooling was sent to Corsair in 1994, where production continues with this popular trimaran. The Corsair F-31 has all the high-performance characteristics of her sisterships, with an efficient fractional sailplan, fully battened mainsail with roller-furling boom, and bowsprit for flying an asymmetrical spinnaker. There are two interior layouts, the aft cockpit model and the aft cabin model. The aft cockpit layout allows for a large open cockpit, while the double-berth aft cabin provides privacy or a great place for children to play while under sail. Both layouts feature a galley, head, and double V-berth forward.

SPECIFICATIONS

Displacement	3,850 lbs, 1746 kg	
Standard Auxiliary	1 x 9.9 hp outboard	
Overall Length	30'10"	9.40 m
Waterline Length	30'0"	9.15 m
Beam (max.)	22'5"	6.84 m
Beam (folded)	8'2"	2.50 m
Draft (board up)	1'4"	0.41 m
Draft (board down)	5'6"	1.68 m
Mast Hgt. Off Deck	40'0"	12.20 m
Mast Hgt. Off Water	44'11"	13.70 m

SAIL AREA

Mainsail	389 sf	36 sm
Jib	210 sf	20 sm
Total Area	599 sf	56 sm
Genoa	278 sf	26 sm
Spinnaker	1004 sf	93 sm

CAPACITY

Berths	1 sgle, 2 dbls	
Staterooms	1-2 (aft cabin model	
Heads	1	
Fuel	6 gal	23 ltr
Fresh Water	18 gal	68 ltr
Payload		

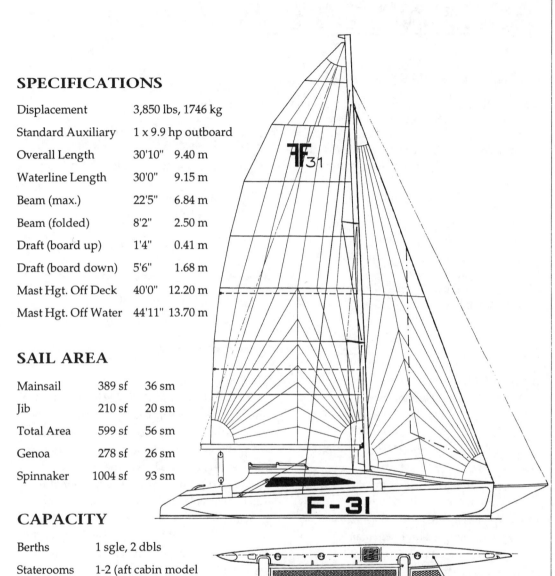

ESSENTIAL 8

GENERAL INFORMATION

Classification   Production trimaran, Trailerable sport cruiser

Approx. Cost   AUS $87,000 complete boat (also available in kit form)

Designer   Tony Grainger

Builder   Essential Boats
12 Bradford Rd.
Gladstone, QNLD 4680
Australia
Tel: (61) 07 979 3313
Fax: (61) 07 979 3313
email:

Year Introduced   1996

Number of boats built   (as of Sep 97)

N. American Dealers   Buy factory direct

Other Cruising Multihulls By Builder
None at present

KEY FEATURES

Hull & Sail Plan
- Main hull with high-buoyancy folding amas, daggerboard, kick-up rudder
- Fractional sloop rig, rotating mast, fully battened main, jib, screacher on bowsprit

Deck Layout
- Full rigid foredeck with trampoline netting between the main hull and amas.
- Cockpit has molded seats, pop-up hatch allows standing headroom in main cabin

Standard Accommodations
- Main hull aft–standing headroom at galley under pop-up main hatch
- Main hull midships–settees that convert to single berths, quarter berth, folding table
- Main hull forward–small double V-berth with minimal headroom, marine toilet

Mechanical
- Tiller steering, kick-up rudder
- Transom-hung outboard

DESCRIPTION

The Essential Eight is a trailerable, high-performance trimaran available in kit form at any stage, or as a complete boat. Design features include a modern folding mechanism for quick assembly/disassembly, wide beam for overall stability, kick-up rudders, and fractional rig. Interior layout is functional yet still comfortable. A pop-top in the main cabin provides standing headroom when raised. There is a double V-berth in the forepeak and three single berths in the main saloon, plus head, folding table, dining area, and small galley. Stowage space is sufficient for short cruises, although the cockpit area offers more than enough room for sailing equipment. Layout can easily be adjusted to suit the needs of each individual owner, such as the number of berths and galley layout. This exciting boat is affordable, fast, and sufficiently comfortable for cruising.

SPECIFICATIONS

Displacement	2,600 lbs, 1182 kg	
Standard Auxiliary	1 x 5 hp outboard	
Overall Length	26'0"	8.00 m
Waterline Length	24'6"	7.52 m
Beam (max.)	22'3"	6.80 m
Beam (folded)	8'2"	2.50 m
Draft (board up)	1'2"	0.39 m
Draft (board down)		
Mast Hgt. Off Deck	36'1"	11.00 m

SAIL AREA

Mainsail	313 sf	29 sm
Genoa	215 sf	20 sm
Total Area	528 sf	49 sm
Reacher	310 sf	29 sm

CAPACITY

Berths	3 sgls, 1 dble
Staterooms	none
Heads	1 (portable)
Fuel	3 gal 11 ltr
Fresh Water	
Payload	

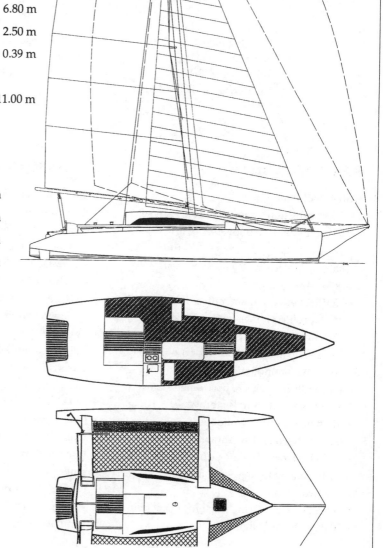

GOLD COAST 56C Tri

GENERAL INFORMATION

Classification   Semi-custom trimaran,
                     Cruiser/racer

Cost   US $325,000

Designer   Joe Colpit, Gold Coast

Builder   Gold Coast Yachts
                     P.O. Box 1980, Kingshill,
                     St. Croix, USVI 00851
                     Tel: (809) 778-1004
                     Fax: (809) 778-2859
                     email:

Year introduced   1996

Number of boats sold   1   (as of Sep 97)

N. American dealers   Buy factory direct

Other Cruising Multihulls By Builder
   Gold Coast 44C, 53C cats (cruisers)
   Gold Coast 46, 53, 62, & 70 (day charters)
   Gold Coast 55 (worlds fastest motor-sailer)

KEY FEATURES

Hull & Sail Plan
- Composite hulls, daggerboards, reverse transoms, built-in buoyancy
- Fractional sloop rig, wing mast, fully battened main, furling jib, bowsprit

Deck Layout
- Netting between main hull and amas, sleek cabin profile, storage lockers forward
- Cockpit aft with ample seating and storage lockers, open deck area aft for dinghy, etc.

Standard Accommodations
- Main hull aft–galley to port, dinette converts to double berth, ample storage
- Main hull midships–pilot berth to port, large head compartment with shower
- Main hull forward–large double stateroom with hanging lockers, seat, storage

Mechanical
- Wheel steering, helm midships in cockpit
- 50 hp outboard engine

DESCRIPTION

The Gold Coast 56 cruising/racing trimaran is the culmination of a dream for multihull ocean racing veteran Joe Colpitt. Working closely with the Gold Coast design team he integrated his concepts into a functional structure using 3D computer design and engineering. As a cruiser/racer, this boat was designed to dominate in all of the local races, be capable of crossing any ocean and yet be a full time home as well. With her working sail she is capable of reaching at 150% of wind speed and climbing upwind at 80% of wind speed on any given day. Interior layout sleeps five comfortably and can easily carry twelve people for the charter trade. There is standing headroom throughout, a functional galley, head, panoramic settee seating that converts to a double berth, and ample stowage as well as multiple watertight compartments in both amas.

SPECIFICATIONS

Displacement	14,000 lbs, 6356 kg	
Standard Auxiliary	1 x 50 hp outboard	
Overall Length	56'0"	17.07 m
Waterline Length	53'0"	16.15 m
Beam (max.)	32'0"	9.75 m
Draft (boards up)	2'2"	0.66 m
Draft (boards down)	10'0"	3.05 m
Mast Hgt. Off Water	78'0"	23.80 m

SAIL AREA

Wing Mast	135 sf	13 sm
Mainsail	1050 sf	98 sm
Jib	410 sf	38 sm
Total Area	1595 sf	149 sm
Spinnaker	710 sf	66 sm

CAPACITY

Berths	1 sgle, 2 dbls
Staterooms	2
Heads	1
Fuel	variable
Fresh Water	80 gal 303 ltr
Payload	6,000 lbs, 2724 kg

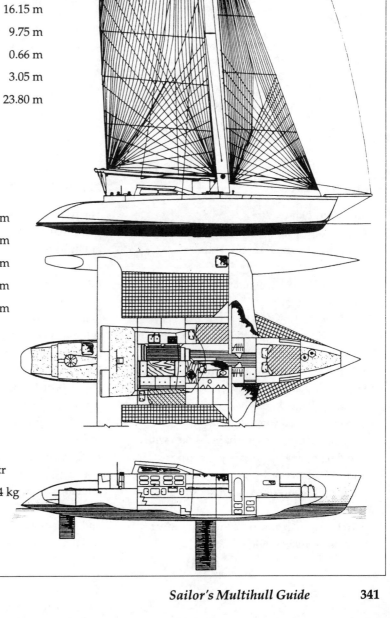

ANTRIM 30+

GENERAL INFORMATION

Classification   Production trimaran,
                      Trailerable sport cruiser

Approx. Cost   Call for current price

Designer   Jim Antrim, Antrim Assoc.

Builder   Moore Sailboats
Agent   Helms Yachts Sales
                      2415 Mariner Square Dr.
                      Alameda, CA 94501 USA
                      Tel: (510) 865-2511
                      Fax: (510) 865-0215
                      email: helmz@aol.com

Year Introduced

Number of boats built

N. American Dealers   Helms Yacht Sales

Other Cruising Multihulls By Builder
  Pacific Class 34 trimaran

KEY FEATURES

Hull & Sail Plan
- composite foam construction, main hull with folding amas for trailerability, asymmetric daggerboards in amas
- Fractional sloop rig, rotating mast, fully battened main, roller-furling jib, bowsprit

Deck Layout
- Full rigid foredeck with trampoline netting between the main hull and amas.
- Sheltered cockpit, aft deck swim platform

Standard Accommodations
- Main hull aft–double berth with low headroom, accessed from main cabin
- Main hull midships–L-shaped settee with folding dining table, galley to starboard
- Main hull forward–double V-berth with minimal headroom, storage lockers

Mechanical
- Tiller steering, inboard swing-up rudder
- Transom-hung outboard

DESCRIPTION

The Antrim 30+ is one of the popular high-performance trimaran designs from the office of Jim Antrim Associates. A fast cruiser that is equally at home on any race course, this tri folds to a mere 10'0" beam for convenient docking, hauling out, or trailering. Easy handling and performance sailing are combined with safety because of the high-buoyancy and dynamic lift of the ama design. Her features include symmetric daggerboards, located in the amas to prevent main hull interior space from being compromised, a high-aspect rig and touches such as the unique whipstaff tiller. The Antrim 30+ has good interior accommodations for a 30 foot trimaran. There is a wide double berth aft that extends under the cockpit, a comfortable double berth up forward, a wet locker and changing bench aft for foul weather gear, and a workable galley and table arrangement.

SPECIFICATIONS

Displacement	3,600 lbs, 1633 kg	
Standard Auxiliary	1 x 8-9 hp outboard	
Overall Length	30'10"	9.42 m
Waterline Length	30'8"	9.35 m
Beam (max.)	24'5"	7.45 m
Beam (folded)	10'0"	3.05 m
Draft (boards up)	4'2"	1.28 m
Draft (boards down)	5'0"	1.52 m
Mast Hgt. Off Water	48'0"	14.63 m

SAIL AREA

Mainsail	468 sf	44 sm
Jib	159 sf	15 sm
Total Area	627 sf	59 sm
Spinnaker	570 sf	53 sm

CAPACITY

Berths	2 doubles
Staterooms	none
Heads	1 (portable)
Fuel	variable
Fresh Water	variable
Payload	

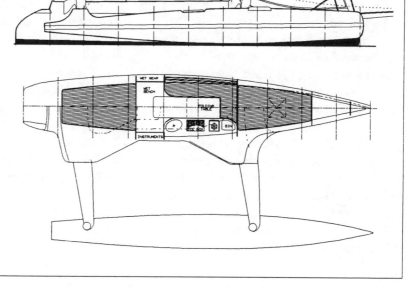

PACIFIC CLASS 34

GENERAL INFORMATION

Classification   Production trimaran,
Trailerable sport cruiser

Approx. Cost   US $135,000

Designer   Jim Antrim, Antrim Assoc.

Builder   Moore Sailboats
Agent   Helms Yachts Sales
2415 Mariner Square Dr.
Alameda, CA 94501 USA
Tel: (510) 865-2511
Fax: (510) 865-0215
email: helmz@aol.com

Year Introduced

Number of boats built

N. American Dealers   Helms Yacht Sales

Other Cruising Multihulls By Builder
Antrim 30+ trimaran

KEY FEATURES

Hull & Sail Plan
- composite foam construction, main hull with folding amas for trailerability, asymmetric daggerboards in amas
- Fractional sloop rig, rotating mast, fully battened main, roller-furling jib, bowsprit

Deck Layout
- Full rigid foredeck with trampoline netting between the main hull and amas.
- Sheltered cockpit, aft deck swim platform

Standard Accommodations
- Main hull aft–double berth with low head-room, accessed from main cabin
- Main hull midships–Settee to port with folding dining table, galley to starboard
- Main hull forward–double V-berth with minimal headroom, private marine toilet

Mechanical
- Tiller steering, inboard swing-up rudder
- Transom-hung outboard

DESCRIPTION

The Pacific Class 34 is an extended version of the Antrim 30+. She perform equally well as an agressive racer or high-performance cruiser. As with the 30+, this tri folds to a mere 10'0" beam for convenient docking, hauling out, or trailering. Easy handling and performance sailing are combined with safety because of the high buoyancy and dynamic lift of the ama design. Her features include symmetric daggerboards, located in the amas to prevent main hull interior space from being compromised, a high-aspect rig and touches such as the unique whipstaff tiller. The Pacific Class 34 interior layout includes a large double berth aft that extends under the cockpit, wet locker and nav area beside the companionway, and a comfortable double berth up forward with private head compartment.

SPECIFICATIONS

Displacement	3,700 lbs, 1678 kg	
Standard Auxiliary	1 x 8-9 hp outboard	
Overall Length	33'9"	10.29 m
Waterline Length	32'9"	9.98 m
Beam (max.)	24'5"	7.45 m
Beam (folded)	10'0"	3.05 m
Draft (board up)	4'2"	1.28 m
Draft (board down)	5'0"	1.52 m
Mast Hgt. Off Water	48'0"	14.63 m

SAIL AREA

Mainsail	426 sf	40 sm
Jib	174 sf	16 sm
Total Area	600 sf	56 sm
Spinnaker	853 sf	79 sm

CAPACITY

Berths	2 doubles
Staterooms	none
Heads	1
Fuel	variable
Fresh Water	variable
Payload	

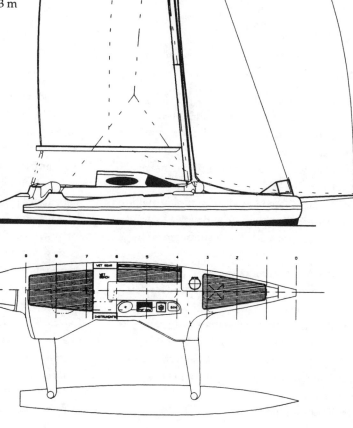

ELAN 26

GENERAL INFORMATION

Classification   Semi-custom trimaran,
Trailerable sport cruiser

Approx. Cost $65,000 US

Designer   Multi-Winds Design

Builder   Multi-Winds International
655 Maid Marion Hill
Sherwood Forest, MD
21405 USA
Tel: (410) 849-3316
Fax:
email:

Year Introduced   1994

Number of boats built   3   (as of Sep 97)

N. American Dealers   Buy factory direct

Other Cruising Multihulls By Builder
Elan 7.7 tri, Elan Extreme 36 cat

KEY FEATURES

Hull & Sail Plan
- U-shaped main hull with high-buoyancy amas, reverse transom with swim platform
- Fractional sloop rig, fully battened main, roller-furling jib, asymmetric spinnaker

Deck Layout
- Full rigid foredeck with trampoline netting between the main hull and amas
- Cockpit has seats port & starboard; storage in amas

Standard Accommodations
- Main hull aft–Mini-galley aft under sliding main hatch
- Main hull midships–settees that convert to single berths, folding dining table
- Main hull forward–double V-berth with minimal headroom, marine toilet under

Mechanical
- Tiller steering, outboard rudder
- Transom-hung outboard

DESCRIPTION

Based on the former Firefly design, the Elan 26 is a high-performance trailerable sport cruiser that gives an exhilarating ride under sail. The fractional rig with rotating mast offers an easy-to-handle sailplan with all controls leading to the cockpit. Asymmetrical daggerboards in the amas, canted inward for extra lift, ensure good windward performance. The Elan 26 doesn't have a folding mechanism like the Elan 7.7, but the amas demount for easy trailering. Down below the accommodations are Spartan yet functional for short-term cruising for up to four persons. There's a mini-galley consisting of a small sink and stove. The main cabin has twin settees that convert to single berths, and a folding dining table. Up forward is a V-berth with minimal headroom, with a portable marine toilet stored below the berth cushion.

SPECIFICATIONS

Displacement	1,300 lbs, 590 kg	
Standard Auxiliary	1 x 8 hp outboard	
Overall Length	26'0"	7.93 m
Waterline Length	25'5"	7.76 m
Beam (max.)	20'0"	6.10 m
Draft (board up)	1'1"	0.34 m
Draft (board down)	3'5"	1.05 m
Mast Hgt. Off Deck		
Mast Hgt Off Water		

SAIL AREA

Mainsail	245 sf	23 sm
Jib	150 sf	14 sm
Total Area	395 sf	37 sm
Spinnaker		

CAPACITY

Berths	2 sgls, 1 dble	
Staterooms	none	
Heads	1 (portable)	
Fuel	6 gal	23 ltr
Fresh Water	16 gal	60 ltr
Payload		

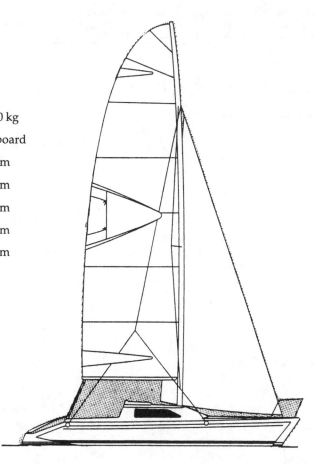

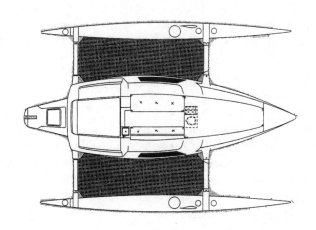

CHALLENGE 30

GENERAL INFORMATION

Classification   Semi-custom trimaran, Trailerable sport cruiser

Approx. Cost   FF 500,000

Designer   P. Gaudry

Builder   Naval Force 3
Rue Sénac de Meilhan
17042 La Rochelle Cédex 1
France
Tel: (33) 5 46 45 04 15
Fax: (33) 5 46 45 43 76
email:

Year Introduced   1995

Number of boats built   9   (as of Sep 97)

N. American Dealers   Buy factory direct

Other Cruising Multihulls By Builder
Piana 30 & 37, Tropic 12m & 15m catamarans; Drop 26 & Challenge 37 trimaran (foldable or not), custom multihulls

KEY FEATURES

Hull & Sail Plan
- High-performance main hull, high-buoyancy amas, reverse transom
- Fractional sloop rig, rotating mast, fully battened main, roller-furling jib

Deck Layout
- Full rigid foredeck with trampoline netting between the main hull and amas.
- Cockpit has seats port and starboard, boarding ladder at the stern

Standard Accommodations
- Main hull aft–double berth in low headroom area under cockpit
- Main hull midships–small galley and berth to starboard, settee/folding table to port
- Main hull forward–large head with a shower and storage lockers

Mechanical
- Tiller steering aft in cockpit
- Transom-hung outboard engine

DESCRIPTION

The Challenge 30 is a foldable trimaran built in France using the West Epoxy System method of construction. This wood-epoxy system was chosen to allow the boat to be light (and therefore easily trailerable), fast and comfortable under sail. Performance is excellent, with a fully-battened, full-roach mainsail and jib. Belowdecks, the Challenge 30 is cozy yet livable, with a large double berth aft, main cabin seating with folding table, small galley beside the companionway, and forward hanging locker and head. Perhaps most appropriate as a weekend (or longer) cruiser, the Challenge 30 is destined to appeal to those who like the excitement of a high-performance trimaran.

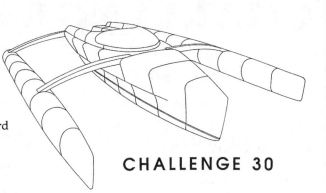

SPECIFICATIONS

Displacement	3,094 lbs, 1400 kg	
Standard Auxiliary	1 x 9.9 hp outboard	
Overall Length	29'6"	9.00 m
Waterline Length	26'3"	8.00 m
Beam (max.)	21'0"	6.40 m
Beam (folded)	7'10"	2.40 m
Draft (board up)	1'4"	0.40 m
Draft (board down)	5'10"	1.80 m
Mast Hgt. Off Water	45'3"	13.80 m

CHALLENGE 30

SAIL AREA

Mainsail	366 sf	34 sm
Genoa	215 sf	20 sm
Total Area	581 sf	54 sm
Spinnaker	807 sf	75 sm

CAPACITY

Berths	1 sgle, 1-2 dbls
Staterooms	none
Heads	1
Fuel	varies
Fresh Water	varies
Payload	1,326 lbs, 600 kg

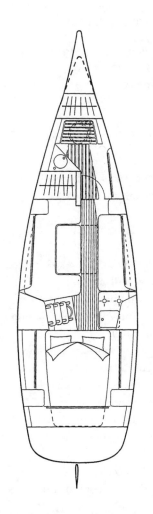

CHALLENGE 37

GENERAL INFORMATION

Classification   Semi-custom trimaran, Performance cruiser

Approx. Cost   FF 1,000,000

Designer   Marc Lombard

Builder   Naval Force 3
Rue Sénac de Meilhan
17042 La Rochelle Cédex 1
France
Tel: (33) 5 46 45 04 15
Fax: (33) 5 46 45 43 76
email:

Year Introduced   1997

Number of boats built   1 (as of Sep 97)

N. American Dealers   Buy factory direct

Other Cruising Multihulls By Builder
Piana 30 & 37, Tropic 40 & 50 catamarans;
Drop 26 & Challenge 30 folding trimaran,
custom multihulls

KEY FEATURES

Hull & Sail Plan
- High-performance main hull, high-buoyancy amas, reverse transom
- Fractional sloop rig, rotating mast, fully battened main, roller-furling jib

Deck Layout
- Full rigid foredeck with trampoline netting between the main hull and amas.
- Aft crossbeam forms back of cockpit area, sugar-scoop transom with outboard option

Standard Accommodations
- Main hull aft–large double cabin in low headroom area under cockpit
- Main hull midships–galley, head & lockers aft, settees/berths with table
- Main hull forward–large double cabin with storage lockers

Mechanical
- Tiller steering aft in cockpit
- Transom-hung outboard or inboard

DESCRIPTION

Like her smaller sistership, the Challenge 37 offers high performance in a cruising trimaran. Built on a semi-custom basis of plywood-epoxy construction, she can be designed according to each owner's specifications. Both a foldable and non-foldable version are available. The foldable version allows for trailering and the West Epoxy System allows the boat to remain light yet durable. With her fully-battened mainsail, fractional rig, and roller-furling genoa, performance is excellent and the boat exciting to sail. Speeds of up to 20 knots are possible in a variety of conditions. Interior layout is comfortable, with a large aft double-berth cabin, main cabin seating that converts to two single berths, forward single-berth cabin, head, and large galley area.

SPECIFICATIONS

Displacement	5,525 lbs, 2500 kg	
Standard Auxiliary	1 x 18 hp inboard	
Overall Length	36'3"	10.99 m
Waterline Length	34'9"	10.60 m
Beam (max.)	26'7"	8.10 m
Beam (folded)	11'2"	3.40 m
Draft (board up)	2'0"	0.60 m
Draft (board down)	6'6"	2.00 m
Mast Hgt. Off Deck	56'3"	17.15 m

SAIL AREA

Mainsail	527 sf	49 sm
Genoa	323 sf	30 sm
Total Area	850 sf	79 sm
Drifter	753 sf	70 sm

CAPACITY

Berths	1 sgls, 2-3 dbls
Staterooms	2
Heads	1
Fuel	varies
Fresh Water	varies
Payload	3,315 lbs, 1500 kg

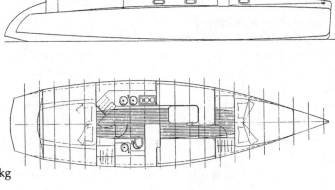

DRAGONFLY 800

GENERAL INFORMATION

Classification   Production trimaran, Trailerable sport cruiser

Approx. Cost   US $50,000

Designer   Børge Quorning

Builder   Quorning Boats
Skærbæk, DK-7000
Fredericia, Denmark
Tel: (45) 75 56 26 26
Fax: (45) 75 51 31 31
email:

Year Introduced   1981
  (as the Dragonfly 25)

Number of boats built   268 (as of Sep 97)

N. American Agent
Dragonfly Sailboats, 103 Center St.,
Garwood, NJ 07027 USA
Tel: (908) 232-7890 Fax: (908) 233-0620
email: Dragonfly@microsysinc.com

Other Cruising Multihulls By Builder
Dragonfly 920, Dragonfly 1000

KEY FEATURES

Hull & Sail Plan
- U-shaped main hull with high-buoyancy amas, pivoting centerboard
- Fractional sloop rig, rotating mast, fully battened main, roller-furling jib

Deck Layout
- Full rigid foredeck with trampoline netting between the main hull and amas.
- Cockpit has teak seats and cabin hatch that converts to a table; storage in amas

Standard Accommodations
- Main hull aft–standing headroom at galley under sliding main hatch
- Main hull midships–settees that convert to single berths, folding dining table
- Main hull forward–double V-berth with minimal headroom, marine toilet under

Mechanical
- Tiller steering, outboard lifting rudder
- Transom-hung outboard

DESCRIPTION

The Dragonfly 800 sailboat is a high-performance, trailerable coastal cruiser, comparable to the F-27. Its "Swing Wing" system allows both amas to fold back easily and in close to the hull for convenient docking. When trailering, you simply remove one ama to reduce the total width to the required nine feet in the U.S.A. Sailing is fast, exciting and competitive on the racing circuit, with her fractional sailplan, rotating mast, and the fact that all controls are easily handled from the cockpit. Accommodations belowdecks are compact, ideal for a couple or small family. There is a small galley aft with standing headroom under a sliding hatch, comfortable seating around a folding table, and double V-berth up forward. While the Dragonfly 800 does claim offshore capabilities, it is probably best suited to spirited, short-term coastal cruising.

SPECIFICATIONS

Displacement	2,315 lbs, 1050 kg	
Standard Auxiliary	1 x 6 hp outboard	
Overall Length	26'2"	8.00 m
Waterline Length	24'11"	7.60 m
Beam (max.)	19'7"	5.94 m
Beam (folded)	9'6"	2.90 m
Draft (board up)	1'1"	0.34 m
Draft (board down)	4'7"	1.39 m
Mast Hgt. Off Deck	39'4"	12.00 m

SAIL AREA

Mainsail	226 sf	21 sm
Genoa	151 sf	14 sm
Total Area	377 sf	35 sm
Spinnaker	538 sf	50 sm

CAPACITY

Berths	2 sgls, 1 dble	
Staterooms	none	
Heads	1 (portable)	
Fuel	6 gal	23 ltr
Fresh Water	16 gal	60 ltr
Payload	882 lbs, 400 kg	

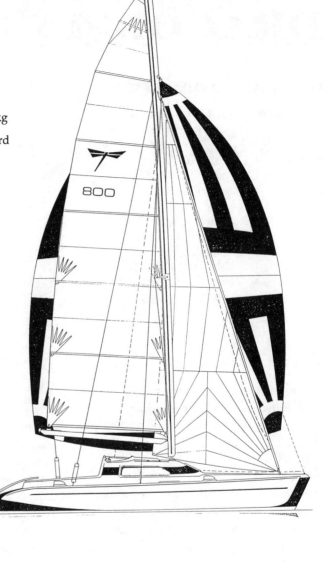

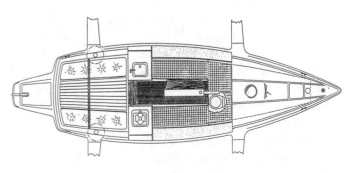

DRAGONFLY 920

GENERAL INFORMATION

Classification   Production trimaran,
                     Trailerable sport cruiser

Approx. Cost   US $150,000

Designer   Børge Quorning

Builder   Quorning Boats
                     Skærbæk, DK-7000
                     Fredericia, Denmark
                     Tel: (45) 75 56 26 26
                     Fax: (45) 75 51 31 31
                     email:

Year Introduced   1996

Number of boats built   23   (as of Sep 97)

N. American Agent
   Dragonfly Sailboats, 103 Center St.,
   Garwood, NJ 07027 USA
   Tel: (908) 232-7890 Fax: (908) 233-0620
   email: Dragonfly@microsysinc.com

Other Cruising Multihulls By Builder
   Dragonfly 800, Dragonfly 1000

KEY FEATURES

Hull & Sail Plan
- U-shaped main hull with high-buoyancy amas, pivoting centerboard and rudder
- Fractional sloop rig, rotating mast, fully battened main, roller-furling jib

Deck Layout
- Full rigid foredeck with trampoline netting between the main hull and amas.
- Cockpit has teak seats and cabin hatch that converts to a table; storage in amas

Standard Accommodations
- Main hull aft–galley and storage lockers forward of companionway
- Main hull midships–folding table with settees that convert to single berths
- Main hull forward–small private head and lockers, large V-berth forward

Mechanical
- Tiller steering, lifting inboard rudder
- Outboard engine mounted at stern

DESCRIPTION

Designed to fill the gap between the Dragonfly 800 and 1000, the new 920 continues the Dragonfly tradition of a high-performance, trailerable cruiser-racer. Big enough for a family, even on an extended cruise, she is also ideal for singlehanding. With her "Swing Wing" system she can be reduced to a mere 2.5m beam for trailering or winter storage. Fast, easy to sail, and competitive on the racing circuit, she has a fully-battened mainsail and roller-furling genoa, large cockpit, high-buoyancy floats, all controls leading to the cockpit, kick-up centerboard, and watertight compartments which make her virtually unsinkable. The teak interior gives a feeling of coziness and quality to both cabins. The layout includes one forward double berth, two fold-out berths in the saloon, folding table, functional galley, private head and stowage areas.

SPECIFICATIONS

Displacement	3,960 lbs, 1800 kg	
Standard Auxiliary	1 x 9.9 hp outboard	
Overall Length	30'2"	9.20 m
Waterline Length	28'8"	8.75 m
Beam (max.)	22'2"	6.75 m
Beam (folded)	10'2"	3.10 m
Draft (board up)	1'5"	0.45 m
Draft (board down)	4'11"	1.50 m
Mast Hgt. Off Deck	42'8"	13.00 m

SAIL AREA

Mainsail	355 sf	33 sm
Genoa	237 sf	22 sm
Total Area	592 sf	55 sm
Spinnaker	807 sf	75 sm

CAPACITY

Berths	2 sgls, 1 dble
Staterooms	1
Heads	1
Fuel	6 gal	23 ltr
Fresh Water	16 gal	60 ltr
Payload	1,760 lbs, 800 kg

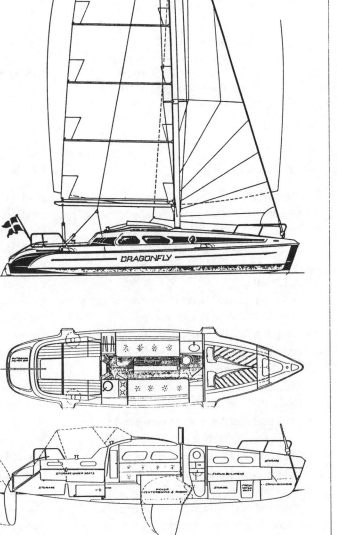

DRAGONFLY 1000

GENERAL INFORMATION

Classification Production trimaran, Trailerable sport cruiser

Approx. Cost US $150,000

Designer Børge Quorning

Builder Quorning Boats
Skærbæk, DK-7000
Fredericia, Denmark
Tel: (45) 75 56 26 26
Fax: (45) 75 51 31 31
email:

Year Introduced 1991

Number of boats built 31 (as of Sep 97)

N. American Agent
Dragonfly Sailboats, 103 Center St.,
Garwood, NJ 07027 USA
Tel: (908) 232-7890 Fax: (908) 233-0620
email: Dragonfly@microsysinc.com

Other Cruising Multihulls By Builder
Dragonfly 800, Dragonfly 920

KEY FEATURES

Hull & Sail Plan
- U-shaped main hull with high-buoyancy amas, pivoting centerboard and rudder
- Fractional sloop rig, rotating mast, fully battened main, roller-furling jib

Deck Layout
- Full rigid foredeck with trampoline netting between the main hull and amas.
- Cockpit has teak seats and cabin hatch that converts to a table; storage in amas

Standard Accommodations
- Main hull aft–galley and storage lockers forward of companionway
- Main hull midships–settee converts to single, folding table forms double berth
- Main hull forward–small private head and lockers, large V-berth forward

Mechanical
- Tiller steering, lifting inboard rudder
- Inboard engine under cockpit

DESCRIPTION

Built on the same design principles as her smaller sistership, the Dragonfly 800, the Dragonfly 1000 is a popular high-performance sport cruiser that is capable of long-distance voyages. The craftsmanship of this boat is superb, and she offers many luxury touches not usually found in a boat of this size. Aided by the easy-to-operate "Swing Wing" folding system, the boat's width can be reduced to thirteen feet when docking or being hauled. Interior accommodations are much more spacious than the 800 model, with elegant saloon seating, a fully-equipped galley, separate head compartment and private forward cabin. Sail handling is kept simple with all controls leading to the cockpit. Sailing is exciting and competitive, with speeds of up to 25 knots possible. This boat is a good choice for fast cruising or racing.

SPECIFICATIONS

Displacement	5,100 lbs, 2300 kg	
Standard Auxiliary	1 x 18 hp inboard	
Overall Length	33'0"	10.00 m
Waterline Length	30'3"	9.20 m
Beam (max.)	25'0"	7.60 m
Beam (folded)	12'8"	3.85 m
Draft (board up)	1'7"	0.50 m
Draft (board down)	5'2"	1.60 m
Mast Hgt. Off Deck	49'3"	15.00 m

SAIL AREA

Mainsail	388 sf	36 sm
Genoa	259 sf	24 sm
Total Area	647 sf	60 sm
Spinnaker	1023 sf	95 sm

CAPACITY

Berths	1 sgle, 2 dbls	
Staterooms	1	
Heads	1	
Fuel	13 gal	50 ltr
Fresh Water	27 gal	102 ltr
Payload	2,200 lbs, 1000 kg	

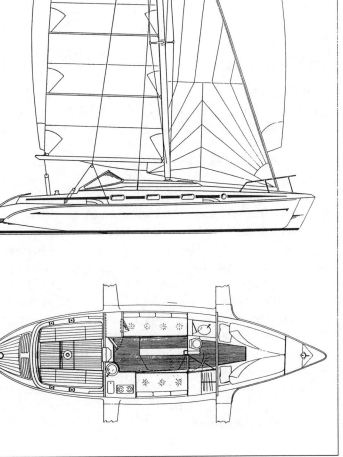

T-GULL 25

GENERAL INFORMATION

Classification   Production trimaran, Trailerable sport cruiser

Approx. Cost   US $26,250 + sails, trailer

Designer   Dick Newick

Builder   Tremolino Boat Co.
411 East 6th Street
Chaska, MN 55318
Tel: (612) 448-6855
Fax:
email:

Year Introduced   1996

Number of boats built   3 (as of Sep 97)
(15 as T-Gull 23)

N. American Dealers   Buy factory direct

Other Cruising Multihulls By Builder
    Tremolino 23, Argonauta 27

KEY FEATURES

Hull & Sail Plan
- Main hull with folding symmetrical amas for efficient sailing, buoyancy
- Fractional sloop rig, rotating mast, fully battened main, self-tacking jib

Deck Layout
- Full rigid main deck with trampoline netting between the main hull and amas.
- Split cabin arrangement fore & aft, cozy center cockpit

Standard Accommodations
- Main hull aft–double berth, rear hatch gives sitting headroom for harbor cooking
- Main hull midships–cockpit with 5'7" long seats that serve as small camping berths
- Main hull forward–storage area under low-profile cabintop

Mechanical
- Tiller steering, vertical tiller or jackstaff
- Transom-hung outboard

DESCRIPTION

The T-Gull 25 provides you with sparkling daysailing performance and Spartan yet comfortable camper accommodations for longer cruising excursions. The pop-top rear hatch gives sitting headroom for harbor cooking, as well as a cozy interior and full-size double berth. A rotating mast and the latest cuts of sails maximize windward performance. The boat normally comes with a self-tending Camber-Spar™ jib which always sets properly on or off the wind. The foredeck widens out ahead of the mast to accommodate the pivoting forward cross-arm, making the boat dry at high speeds. The generous cockpit seats can be used as berths by the younger members of the family. This boat is designed for easy trailering, with a very simple sequence for folding the amas and raising or lowering the mast. The T-Gull 25 is exciting to sail yet simple to handle.

SPECIFICATIONS

Displacement	1,950 lbs, 885 kg	
Standard Auxiliary	1 x 5 hp outboard	
Overall Length	25'0"	7.63 m
Waterline Length	24'2"	7.38 m
Beam (max.)	19'0"	5.80 m
Beam (folded)	8'4"	2.54 m
Draft (board up)	1'5"	0.44 m
Draft (board down)	4'6"	1.37 m
Mast Hgt. Off Deck	29'8"	9.05 m
Mast Hgt. Off Water	33'4"	10.17 m

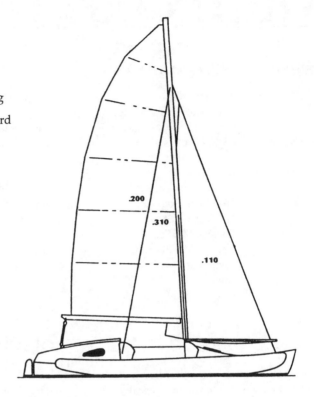

SAIL AREA

Mainsail	200 sf	19 sm
Jib	110 sf	10 sm
Total Area	310 sf	29 sm
Spinnaker		

CAPACITY

Berths	2 sgls, 1 dble
Staterooms	none
Heads	1 (portable)
Fuel	portable
Fresh Water	portable
Payload	600 lbs, 275 kg

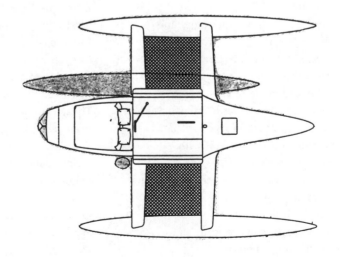

ARGONAUTA 27

GENERAL INFORMATION

Classification   Production trimaran, Trailerable sport cruiser

Approx. Cost   US $34,000 + sails, trailer

Designer   Dick Newick

Builder   Tremolino Boat Co.
411 East 6th Street
Chaska, MN 55318
Tel: (612) 448-6855
Fax:
email:

Year Introduced   1995

Number of boats built   3 (as of Sep 97)
(3 as the Argonauta 26)

N. American Dealers   Buy factory direct

Other Cruising Multihulls By Builder
Tremolino 23, T-Gull 25

KEY FEATURES

Hull & Sail Plan
- Main hull with folding symmetrical amas for efficient sailing, buoyancy
- Fractional sloop rig, rotating mast, fully battened main, self tacking jib

Deck Layout
- Full rigid main deck with trampoline netting between the main hull and amas.
- Split cabin arrangement fore & aft, cozy center cockpit

Standard Accommodations
- Main hull aft–double berth with seat under, small galley to port, storage locker
- Main hull midships–cockpit with comfortable seating for four adults
- Main hull forward–single berth, storage and space for a portable head

Mechanical
- Wheel steering, aft in cockpit
- Transom-hung outboard

DESCRIPTION

The Argonauta trimaran, designed by Dick Newick and built by the Tremolino Boat Co., has been lengthened from the previous 26 foot version to give a sharper water entry and reduced spray at high speeds. Along the bow the foredeck has been raised for improved headroom and space forward. Access to the forward compartment is from the cockpit, just below the windshield. The advantages gained from the lengthened hull also have improved the overall aesthetics of the boat. The new hulls are 22 foot long, symmetrical in shape. All Argonautas come with a permanently installed A-frame for raising and lowering the mast, an easy one-person job. Folding and deploying the outriggers is also easy for one person. This boat is truly exciting yet simple to sail, with wheel steering and all controls and auxiliary power in easy reach of the skipper.

SPECIFICATIONS

Displacement	2,850 lbs, 1295 kg	
Standard Auxiliary	1 x 5 hp outboard	
Overall Length	27'4"	8.34 m
Waterline Length	26'0"	7.93 m
Beam (max.)	20'0"	6.10 m
Beam (folded)	8'4"	2.54 m
Draft (board up)	1'3"	0.38 m
Draft (board down)	4'6"	1.37 m
Mast Hgt. Off Deck	34'0"	10.37 m
Mast Hgt. Off Water	36'0"	10.98 m

SAIL AREA

Mainsail	272 sf	25 sm
Jib	88 sf	8 sm
Total Area	360 sf	33 sm
Spinnaker		

CAPACITY

Berths	1 sgle, 1 dble
Staterooms	none
Heads	1 (portable)
Fuel	portable
Fresh Water	portable
Payload	800 lbs, 363 kg

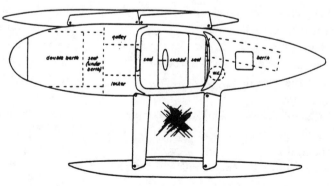

ZEFYR 43

GENERAL INFORMATION

Classification	Production trimaran, Wingsail cruiser	**Year Introduced**	1996
Approx. Cost	£290,000	**Number of boats built**	6 (as of Sep 97)
Designer	John Walker, WWS team	**N. American Dealers**	Buy factory direct

Builder   Walker Wingsail Systems
Devonport Royal Dockyard
Plymouth, Devon PL1 4SG
UK
Tel: (44) 1752 605 426
Fax: (44) 1752 605 428
email: info@walkerwing.co.uk

Other Cruising Multihulls By Builder
Custom wingsail trimarans

KEY FEATURES

Hull & Sail Plan

- Epoxy/unidirectional glass/balsa composite hulls, skeg-hung rudder
- Walker Wingsail computer-controlled raked monoplane 1/33

Deck Layout

- Rigid main deck with locker forward, rigid decks between the main hull and amas
- Wide side decks with storage in the outer hulls, protected aft cockpit

Standard Accommodations

- Main hull aft–storage locker to port, double stateroom with lockers to starboard
- Main hull midships–galley to port, head to starboard
- Main hull forward–helm and nav station, dinette, private stateroom with head

Mechanical

- Wheel steering, helm in cabin and cockpit
- Inboard diesel, access from main cabin

DESCRIPTION

An enlarged and updated version of the original Zefyr 40, the 43 uses the same type of innovative monoplane wingsail, which exceeds double the drive of similar size cloth sails. The carbon fiber wingsail is mounted on a free bearing and operates in similar fashion to a weathervane. The wingsail automatically responds to every wind shift to keep the wing section perfectly trimmed. Hurricane tested, the manufacturer claims these boats are unbroachable. Belowdecks she has two separate staterooms, each with its own head and shower compartment, and another couple can sleep in the saloon cabin where the settee and table convert to a double berth. The functional galley, located aft beside the companionway, has ample counter and storage space. The inside pilot position is forward and to port; separate outside helm and controls are provided.

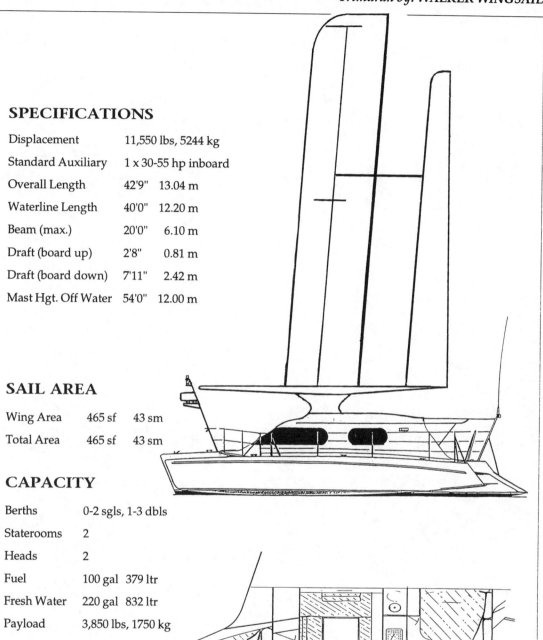

SPECIFICATIONS

Displacement	11,550 lbs, 5244 kg	
Standard Auxiliary	1 x 30-55 hp inboard	
Overall Length	42'9"	13.04 m
Waterline Length	40'0"	12.20 m
Beam (max.)	20'0"	6.10 m
Draft (board up)	2'8"	0.81 m
Draft (board down)	7'11"	2.42 m
Mast Hgt. Off Water	54'0"	12.00 m

SAIL AREA

Wing Area	465 sf	43 sm
Total Area	465 sf	43 sm

CAPACITY

Berths	0-2 sgls, 1-3 dbls
Staterooms	2
Heads	2
Fuel	100 gal 379 ltr
Fresh Water	220 gal 832 ltr
Payload	3,850 lbs, 1750 kg

Stock Catamaran Designs

ANTRIM 37

GENERAL INFORMATION

Classification	Stock boat design, Cruiser/racer	**Year Introduced**	
		Number of boats built	
Approx. Cost	Call for current price		
Designer	Jim Antrim, Antrim Assoc.	**N. American Stockists**	Buy plans direct

Designs Available From
Antrim Associates
4018 Archery Way
El Sobrante, CA 94803 USA
Tel: (510) 223-9680
Fax: (510) 262-0303
email: antrimna@hotcoco.infi.net

Other Cruising Multihulls By Designer
Antrim 52 and other stock design catamarans and trimarans; Antrim 30+ and Pacific Class 34 semi-custom complete boats from Helms Yacht Sales (see pages 342-345)

KEY FEATURES

Hull & Sail Plan
- Unique bow "knuckles" for optimal trim/ buoyancy, daggerboards, reverse transoms
- Fractional sloop rig, rotating wing mast, fully battened main, self-tacking jib

Deck Layout
- Trampoline forward, deck storage to port, sleek cabintop, U-shaped cockpit seating
- Raised cockpit for good visibility
- Dinghy storage under cockpit

Standard Accommodations
- The bridgedeck has two seating areas, port and starboard, each with a table
- The starboard hull has a stateroom aft, galley midships, wet locker/berths forward
- The port hull has stateroom aft, workshop/ lockers midships, head forward

Mechanical
- Wheel steering, helm forward in cockpit
- Inboard in port hull with hydraulic drives

DESCRIPTION

As Jim Antrim will be the first to tell you, this is a design for the serious cruiser or liveaboard owner. Modern "plush" interior features such as carpeting, fabric hull liners, and multitudes of mirrors, heads and staterooms have been discarded in favor of a simple yet attractive low-maintenance finish. There is an enormous amount of interior storage room for sails and recreational gear. The easily handled three-sail rig has rotating wing mast and main, self-tending jib and asymmetric spinnaker. The raised cockpit provides good visibility ahead when seated or standing. Under the cockpit there's room to hang an eight foot dinghy in a protected compartment. The saloon cabin has two separate seating areas with tables, and steps leading to the two hulls placed diagonally across from each other. This boat should be a good choice for long-distance cruising.

SPECIFICATIONS

Displacement	11,000 lbs,	4990 kg
Standard Auxiliary	1 x 18-27 hp inboard	
Overall Length	37'5"	11.41 m
Waterline Length	35'0"	10.68 m
Bridgedeck Length	21'0"	6.41 m
Wing Deck Clearance		
Beam (max.)	21'8"	6.61 m
Draft (min.)	3'6"	1.07 m
Draft (max.)	5'6"	1.68 m
Mast Hgt. Off Water	52'0"	15.86 m

SAIL AREA

Mainsail/mast	551 sf	51 sm
Jib	209 sf	19 sm
Total Area	760 sf	70 sm
Spinnaker	670 sf	62 sm

CAPACITY

Berths	1 sgle, 2-3 dbls
Staterooms	2-3
Heads	1
Fuel	125 gal 473 ltr
Fresh Water	125 gal 473 ltr
Payload	3,500 lbs, 1587 kg

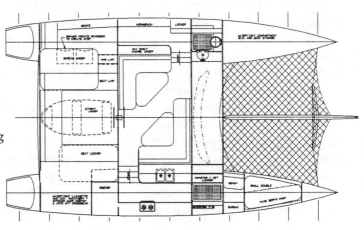

ANTRIM 52

GENERAL INFORMATION

Classification   Stock boat design,
                      Cruiser/charter cruiser

Cost of plans   Call for current price

Designer   Jim Antrim, Antrim Assoc.

Designs   Antrim Associates
Available   4018 Archery Way
From   El Sobrante, CA 94803 USA
                      Tel: (510) 223-9680
                      Fax: (510) 262-0303
                      email: antrimna@hotcoco.infi.net

Year Introduced

Number of boats built

N. American Stockists   Buy plans direct

Other Cruising Multihulls By Designer
  Antrim 37 and other stock design
catamarans and trimarans; Antrim 30+ and
Pacific Class 34 semi-custom complete boats
from Helms Yacht Sales (see pages 342-345)

KEY FEATURES

Hull & Sail Plan
- Unique bow "knuckles" for optimal trim/
  buoyancy, daggerboards, reverse transoms
- Fractional sloop rig, rotating wing mast,
  fully battened main, self-tacking jib

Deck Layout
- Trampoline foredeck with center walkway,
  twin cockpit areas with seating port and
  starboard, outdoor "patio" acts as vestibule
  for main cabin, transom access to the hulls

Standard Accommodations
- The bridgedeck has spacious saloon cabin
  w/ dual seating areas, nav area with helm
- The starboard hull has storage/engine room
  aft, head midships, stateroom forward
- The port hull has master stateroom aft,
  galley midships, stateroom/head forward

Mechanical
- Dual helms in cockpit plus inside helm
- Engine to starboard with hydraulic drives

DESCRIPTION

The Antrim 52 cruising catamaran is a true
luxury craft, ideal for serious liveaboards or
the crewed charter trade. Large and state-of-
the-art, she features a number of innovative
touches guaranteed to please the luxury-
minded client. Twin raised cockpits to port
and starboard with an outdoor "patio" area
between, a walkway around the entire deck
perimeter, walk-through transom access to
the hulls, elegant staterooms with queen-size
berths, and separate dining and lounge areas
are all conducive to sailing in ultimate
comfort. Sail handling is easy, with three
separate helm stations (one in each cockpit
and one inside), a self-tending jib, and
hydraulic mainsheet with an automatic
overload release. This boat offers passengers
and crew members a wide choice of environ-
ments for living and entertaining, from light
and airy to warm and cozy.

SPECIFICATIONS

Displacement	19,000 lbs, 8618 kg	
Standard Auxiliary	1 x 27-37 hp inboard	
Overall Length	52'0"	15.85 m
Waterline Length	47'0"	14.33 m
Bridgedeck Length	30'0"	9.14 m
Wing Deck Clearance		
Beam (max.)	32'0"	9.75 m
Draft (min.)	3'11"	1.20 m
Draft (max.)	8'4"	2.54 m
Mast Hgt. Off Water	74'0"	22.56 m

SAIL AREA

Mainsail/mast	935 sf	87 sm
Jib	302 sf	28 sm
Total Area	1237 sf	115 sm
Spinnaker	870 sf	81 sm

CAPACITY

Berths	3 sgls, 3 dbls
Staterooms	3-4
Heads	4
Fuel	250 gal 946 ltr
Fresh Water	300 gal 946 ltr
Payload	9,000 lbs, 4082 kg

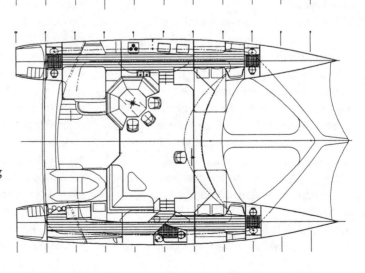

CATSEYE BAY 10.8

GENERAL INFORMATION

Classification   Stock catamaran design, Cruiser

Approx. Cost   AUS $3,500 plans
AUS $280,000 sail-away

Designer   Peter Brady

Designs or Complete Boat   Peter Brady & Associates
33 Curtin Ave. West
Brisbane 4007, Australia
Tel: (61) 7 3868 3773
Fax: (61) 7 3868 3774
email:

Year Introduced   1995

Number of boats built

N. American stockists
Purchase plans from Peter Brady & Assoc.

Other Cruising Multihulls By Builder
   Other cruising catamarans, Saracen 13.2 and other motorsailer cats, and a wide range of power cats

KEY FEATURES

Hull & Sail Plan
- Strip-planked composite hulls, fixed keels, reverse tramsoms with boarding steps
- Fractional sloop rig, fully battened main, roller-furling genoa

Deck Layout
- Small trampoline forward with central walkway, lockers just aft, wide side decks
- Large cockpit with hardtop over supported by aft arch

Standard Accommodations
- The bridgedeck has a large lounge area with table to port, full-size galley to starboard
- The starboard hull has staterooms fore & aft, with galley fridge/freezer midships
- The port hull has large head aft, nav station midships, and stateroom forward

Mechanical
- Wheel steering, raised helm in cockpit
- Dual inboards, access from hulls

DESCRIPTION

The Catseye Bay is the latest cruising catamaran design from Peter Brady and Associates. Originally conceived as a production yacht, the versatility of the design attracted so much interest from amateur builders that it was released as a stock plan. On deck a light targa top over the large cockpit is utilized to provide sun protection for the crew, with a cut-out and dual-height seat giving the helmsman both an unrestricted all round vision for sailing and a sheltered position for motoring. All sailing controls lead back to a work station to port of the central helm position. Other design features include a spreaderless fractional rig and either mini-keels or daggerboards. By using a far wider bridgedeck and cabin arrangements than usual, the Catseye Bay gives the impression of a much larger boat when you step inside.

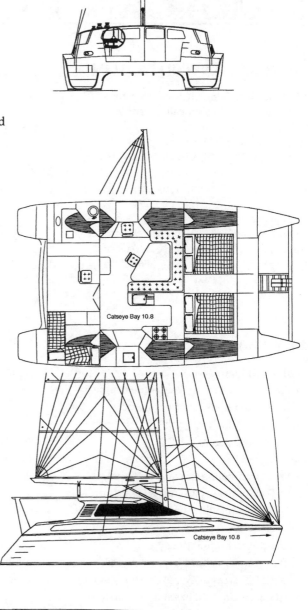

SPECIFICATIONS

Displacement	9,253 lbs, 4206 kg	
Standard Auxiliary	2 x 10-30 hp inboard	
Overall Length	35'5"	10.80 m
Waterline Length	33'2"	10.10 m
Bridgedeck Length	27'3"	8.32 m
Wing Deck Clearance	2'2"	0.65 m
Beam (max.)	20'4"	6.20 m
Draft (max.)	3'1"	0.93 m
Mast Hgt. Off Deck	45'10"	14.00 m
Mast Hgt. Off Water	55'9"	17.00 m

SAIL AREA

Mainsail	409 sf	38 sm
Genoa	301 sf	28 sm
Total Area	710 sf	66 sm
Spinnaker		

CAPACITY

Berths	2 sgls, 2 dbls	
Staterooms	3	
Heads	1	
Fuel	61 gal	230 ltr
Fresh Water	92 gal	350 ltr
Payload	2,200 lbs, 1000 kg	

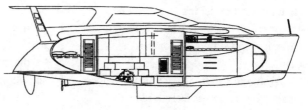

SARACEN 13.2

GENERAL INFORMATION

Classification Stock catamaran design, Motorsailer/cruiser

Approx. Cost AUS $5,500 plans
AUS $480,000 sail-away

Designer Peter Brady

Designs or Complete Boat Peter Brady & Associates
33 Curtin Ave. West
Brisbane 4007, Australia
Tel: (61) 7 3868 3773
Fax: (61) 7 3868 3774
email:

Year Introduced 1995

Number of boats built (as of Sep 97)

N. American stockists Buy plans direct

Other Cruising Multihulls By Builder
Other motorsailer cats, Catseye Bay 10.8 and other cruising catamarans, and a wide range of power cats

KEY FEATURES

Hull & Sail Plan
- Strip-planked cedar, Balsa-core composite hulls, fixed keels, reverse tramsoms
- Fractional sloop rig, fully battened main, roller-furling genoa

Deck Layout
- Small trampoline forward with central walkway, lockers just aft, wide side decks
- Large cockpit with hardtop over supported by aft arch

Standard Accommodations
- The bridgedeck has a large lounge area with table, full-size galley, nav/steering station
- The starboard hull has staterooms fore & aft, with head midships
- The port hull has large head aft, storage midships, and stateroom forward

Mechanical
- Wheel steering, helm in cockpit and saloon
- Dual inboards, access from hulls

DESCRIPTION

Saracen is the latest in the line of motorsailers designed and built by Peter Brady & Associates. At 13.2 meters long, Saracen is large enough to be comfortably lived aboard, yet small enough to be easily handled by a couple. She is designed more as a coastal cruiser with emphasis put on performance rather than range and carrying capacity. She has a simple fractional rig, fully-battened main in lazy jacks, and self furling jib. The extensive use of balsa cores and composites, combined with a minimal yet comfortable interior, has provided large weight savings. Customized accommodations are possible; one option features a port side master suite with extra dressing/storage area and a huge head. The starboard hull has two single berths in the forward cabin, a walk-through shower and head area, and two more single berths aft. The galley is on the bridgedeck.

SPECIFICATIONS

Displacement	20,900 lbs, 9500 kg	
Standard Auxiliary	2 x 50-75 hp inboard	
Overall Length	43'4"	13.20 m
Waterline Length	39'1"	11.90 m
Bridgedeck Length	35'10"	10.92 m
Wing Deck Clearance	2'5"	0.75 m
Beam (max.)	23'0"	7.00 m
Draft (max.)	3'4"	1.02 m
Mast Hgt. Off Deck	53'2"	16.20 m
Mast Hgt. Off Water	62'0"	18.90 m

SAIL AREA

Mainsail	538 sf	50 sm
Genoa	549 sf	51 sm
Total Area	1087 sf	101 sm
Spinnaker		

CAPACITY

Berths	4 sgls, 1 dbls
Staterooms	3
Heads	2
Fuel	145 gal 550 ltr
Fresh Water	145 gal 550 ltr
Payload	4,400 lbs, 2000 kg

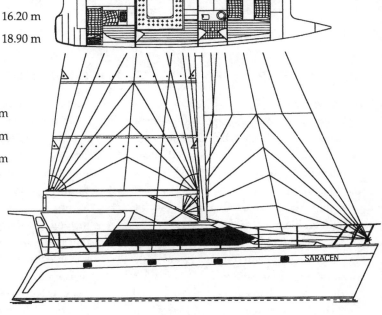

CROWTHER 40 MkII

GENERAL INFORMATION

Classification Stock catamaran design,
Cruiser

Cost of plans Call for current price

Designer Lock Crowther

Designs Crowther Associates
PO Box 204, Newport
NSW 2106, Australia
Tel: (61) 2 9970 8300
Fax: (61) 2 9970 8023
email: brettac@crowther.com.au

Year introduced

Number of boats built

N. American Stockists
California Multihulls
Tel: (619) 222-9694 Fax: (619) 222-9693

Other Cruising Multihulls By Designer
A wide range of performance sailing and
power multihulls

KEY FEATURES

Hull & Sail Plan
- Unique bulb bows, daggerboards, reverse transoms with integral boarding steps
- Fractional cutter rig, fully battened main, roller-furling headsails

Deck Layout
- Trampoline forward with central walkway, rigid foredeck just aft with lockers
- Aft cockpit with U-shaped seats, ample lockers, raised helm station forward

Standard Accommodations
- The bridgedeck has galley aft to port, wide U-shaped settee with dining table forward
- Starboard hull–large stateroom or storage cabin aft, head midships, stateroom forward
- Port hull–stateroom aft, storage midships, large stateroom and private head forward

Mechanical
- Wheel steering, helm forward in cockpit
- Dual inboards, access from aft cabins

DESCRIPTION

Similar to all other Crowther performance cruising catamarans, the popular MkII version of the 40 foot design is an extremely capable craft with a good turn of speed. Intended for extended world cruising, she has a high payload as well as dependable stability for open ocean conditions. Design features include a modern fractional cutter sail plan that's easy to handle, the Crowther bulb bows and integral boarding steps and swim platforms in the transoms. Based on the popular No. 85 design, she is an excellent liveaboard, long-distance cruising yacht, with four private double-berth cabins, a comfortable bridgedeck galley, a large U-shaped lounge seating area with dining table, and two or three private head compartments. The helm station forward in the cockpit is protected by a cabintop overhang, and an aft deck provides a boarding/sunbathing area.

SPECIFICATIONS

Displacement	12,000 lbs, 5444 kg	
Standard Auxiliary	2 x 18-27 hp inboard	
Overall Length	40'0"	12.20 m
Waterline Length	37'0"	11.27 m
Bridgedeck Length	20'2"	6.14 m
Wing Deck Clearance		
Beam (max.)	20'10"	6.35 m
Draft (min.)	5'0"	1.50 m
Draft (max.)	2'3"	0.69 m
Mast Hgt. Off Water	63'3"	19.29 m

SAIL AREA

Mainsail	618 sf	57 sm
Jib	350 sf	33 sm
Total Area	968 sf	90 sm
Spinnaker	1400 sf	130 sm

CAPACITY

Berths	4 doubles
Staterooms	4
Heads	2-3
Fuel	80 gal 360 ltr
Fresh Water	120 gal 540 ltr
Payload	4,400 lbs, 2000 kg

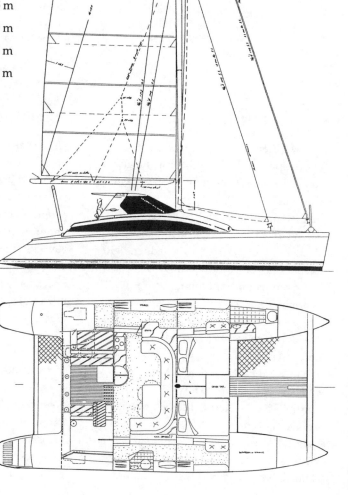

GOLD COAST 53

GENERAL INFORMATION

Classification   Stock catamaran design, Charter cruiser

Approx. Cost   US $345,000 complete boat

Designer   R. Hatfield, Gold Coast

Designs or Complete Boat   Gold Coast Yachts
P.O. Box 1980, Kingshill,
St. Croix, USVI 00851
Tel: (809) 778-1004
Fax: (809) 778-2859
email:

Year Introduced   1988

Number of boats built   17   (as of Sep 97)

N. American Stockists   Buy plans direct

Other Cruising Multihulls By Builder
Gold Coast cruisers include the 44C & 53C cats (see pages 200-203) and 56C tri (see pages 340-341), Gold Coast 42, 46, 62, & 70 day charter cats, and Gold Coast 55 (worlds fastest motor-sailer)

KEY FEATURES

Hull & Sail Plan
- wood/epoxy hull, daggerboards, sugar scoop transoms, watertight compartments
- Fractional sloop rig, wing mast, fully roached main, roller-furling genoa

Deck Layout
- Trampoline forward w/ swim ladder, rigid foredeck just aft, wide decks
- Mid helm station with comfortable seat
- Enormous open cockpit with seating areas

Standard Accommodations
- The aft bridgedeck has two seating areas, port and starboard, each with a table
- The forward bridgedeck area has seating under a protective hard top
- The hulls have watertight compartments, storage, and crew quarters

Mechanical
- Wheel steering, raised helm aft midships
- Dual outboards, access off stern transom

DESCRIPTION

The 49 passenger GC 53 represents a standard for excellence in layout, styling, performance, durability and cost. With sixteen sister ships carrying a total of a quarter of a million people annually, the GC 53 series reflects the unique needs of the charter industry today. Her most unusual feature is her wingmast which has proven itself through daily charter operations, offshore deliveries and many hurricanes. Four U-shaped cushioned seating areas, each with a varnished coffee table, surround a central bar. The bar has split levels with large working counter, deep ice boxes, sink and storage, and protection under a roof with full windshield and standing headroom. The captain is located aft in a commanding position allowing unobstructed focus on all sail operations. The large foredeck has ample sunbathing space and a pivoting stairway to the water.

SPECIFICATIONS

Displacement	19,500 lbs, 8845 kg	
Standard Auxiliary	2 x 45 hp outboards	
Overall Length	53'0"	16.15 m
Waterline Length	51'0"	15.56 m
Bridgedeck Length	20'0"	6.10 m
Wing Deck Clearance	3'0"	0.92 m
Beam (max.)	28'6"	8.69 m
Draft (min.)	3'0"	0.92 m
Draft (max.)	8'0"	2.44 m
Mast Hgt. Off Water	70'6"	21.50 m

SAIL AREA

Wing Mast	120 sf	11 sm
Mainsail	727 sf	68 sm
Genoa	440 sf	41 sm
Total Area	1287 sf	120 sm
Spinnaker	1016 sf	95 sm

CAPACITY

Berths	variable	
Passengers	49	
Heads	2	
Fuel	10 gal	38 ltr
Fresh Water	140 gal	530 ltr
Payload	10,000 lbs, 4536 kg	

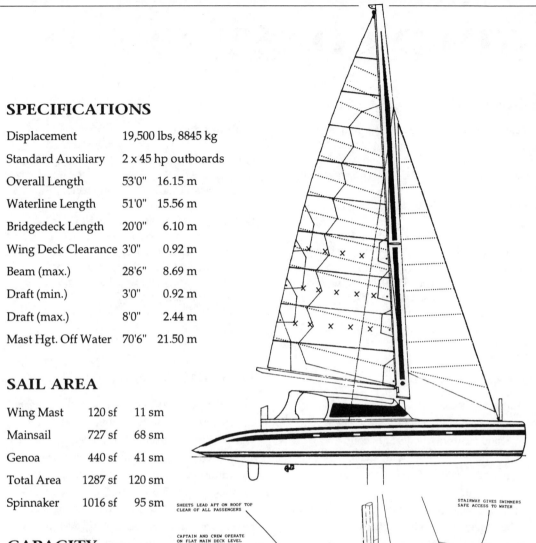

SHEETS LEAD AFT ON ROOF TOP CLEAR OF ALL PASSENGERS

STAIRWAY GIVES SWIMMERS SAFE ACCESS TO WATER

CAPTAIN AND CREW OPERATE ON FLAT MAIN DECK LEVEL

SECONDARY CONTROLS FOLLOW PERIMETER OF VESSEL TO CAPTAIN

MULTIPLE WATER-TIGHT BULKHEADS

VARIABLE DEPTH DAGGERBOARDS WITH CRASHBOX GIVE 8' DRAFT

49 PASSENGERS CAN BE SAFELY SEATED IN 20'x20' WELL DECK AREA

GOLD COAST 70

GENERAL INFORMATION

Classification Stock catamaran design, Day charter cruiser

Approx. Cost US $450,000 (finished boat)

Designer R. Hatfield, Gold Coast

Designs or Complete Boat
Gold Coast Yachts
P.O. Box 1980, Kingshill,
St. Croix, USVI 00851
Tel: (809) 778-1004
Fax: (809) 778-2859
email:

Year Introduced 1996

Number of boats built 1 (as of Sep 97)

N. American Dealers Buy factory direct

Other Cruising Multihulls By Builder
Gold Coast cruisers include the 44C & 53C cats (see pages 200-203) and 56C tri (see pages 340-341), Gold Coast 42, 46, 53 & 62 day charter cats, and Gold Coast 55 (worlds fastest motor-sailer)

KEY FEATURES

Hull & Sail Plan
- composite hull, daggerboards, sugar scoop transoms, watertight compartments
- Fractional sloop rig, wing mast, fully roached main, roller-furling genoa

Deck Layout
- Trampoline foredeck, self-draining lockers just aft in large solid deck area
- Raised helm station, numerous seating areas in the open cockpit or under hardtop

Standard Accommodations
- The bridgedeck has 1200 sf of passenger deck space, 30% is protected by hardtop
- The starboard hull has crew quarters foreward, huge food storage midships
- The port hull same as starboard but with 3 heads instead of food storage

Mechanical
- Wheel steering, raised helm aft midships
- Dual inboards, access from aft deck, hulls

DESCRIPTION

The Gold Coast 70 deisgn is one of the largest commercial day charter sailing vessels in the world. She was designed to carry and service 105 passenger with a variety of amenities including ergonmetric seating, three swim ladders, three heads and complete food and beverage service. On several occasions she has shown a full complement of guests an exhilarating 18 knots of speeds. Her towering wingspar sports over 2,000 sqare feet of sail. Accommodations include living space for two crew, five hundred cubic feet of storage space for food and beverages located adjacent to the service bar, and large engine compartments. The 1,2000 square feet of deck is devoted soley to the comfort and safety of the passengers, with nearly 30% protected by the windshield and roof.

SPECIFICATIONS

Displacement	32,000 lbs, 14,515 kg	
Standard Auxiliary	2 x 50 hp inboards	
Overall Length	70'0"	21.30 m
Waterline Length	66'0"	20.10 m
Bridgedeck Length	43'0"	13.13 m
Wing Deck Clearance	3'3"	1.00 m
Beam (max.)	30'0"	9.14 m
Draft (boards up)	3'4"	1.02 m
Draft (boards down)	10'0"	3.05 m
Mast Hgt. Off Water	88'0"	26.80 m

SAIL AREA

Wing Mast	185 sf	17 sm
Mainsail	1338 sf	124 sm
Jib	510 sf	47 sm
Total Area	2033 sf	188 sm
Spinnaker		

CAPACITY

Berths	2 doubles
Passengers	105
Heads	3
Fuel	variable
Fresh Water	165 gal 624 ltr
Payload	20,000 lbs, 9080 kg

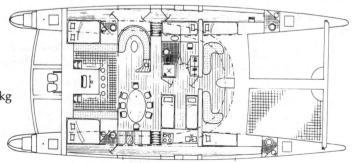

GRAINGER 430

GENERAL INFORMATION

Classification   Stock catamaran design,
Cruiser

Cost of plans   Call for current price

Designer   Grainger Designs

Designs   Grainger Designs
PO Box 212, Kingscliff
NSW 2487 Australia
Tel: (61) 66 74 1090
Fax: (61) 66 74 4129
email:

Year Introduced

Number of boats built

N. American Dealers   Buy plans direct

Other Cruising Multihulls By Designer
   A wide range of sailing and power cruising
catamarans, including the Grainger 480

KEY FEATURES

Hull & Sail Plan
- cedar or foam and glass composite hulls,
  fixed keels or daggerboards
- Fractional sloop rig, fully battened main,
  furling headsail, spinnaker on bowsprit

Deck Layout
- Trampoline forward with central walkway,
  rigid deck just aft with lockers
- Large open cockpit with ample seating, yet
  sufficiently sheltered for ocean cruising

Standard Accommodations
- The bridgedeck has a large lounge area
  forward with L-shaped settee and table
- The starboard hull has fore & aft staterooms,
  a long galley midships and a head forward

- The port hull has fore & aft staterooms, with
  a large head midships

Mechanical
- Wheel steering, helm forward in cockpit
- Dual inboards, access from aft deck

DESCRIPTION

The Grainger 430 was developed from the
earlier Grainger 37 (also Azure 37) and G1250
concepts. Produced specifically to optimize
some of the features of those two earlier
designs, she also incorporates some new
developments in hull shape and keel design.
The basic philosophy was to use the same
accommodation platform with longer hulls to
provide a more seakindly boat without
adding significantly to the cost or overall
weight. Moderate beam has been retained for
the 430 so she can make use of marina berths
and travel lift facilities. New design features
include wider side decks, increased
headroom forward, a longer cockpit with a
revised layout, and greater flexibility with the
interior accommodations. A raised helm
station provides comfortable steering with
good vision over the cabin top. Options
include daggerboards or fixed keels.

SPECIFICATIONS

Displacement	15,560 lbs, 7073 kg	
Standard Auxiliary	2 x 27 hp inboard	
Overall Length	43'0"	13.00 m
Waterline Length	38'6"	11.73 m
Bridgedeck Length		
Wing Deck Clearance	2'8"	0.85 m
Beam (max.)	21'11"	6.70 m
Draft (hull)	1'10"	0.55 m
Draft (fixed keels)	3'7"	1.10 m
Mast Hgt. Off Water		

SAIL AREA

Mainsail	722 sf	67 sm
Genoa	487 sf	45 sm
Total Area	1209 sf	112 sm
Spinnaker		

CAPACITY

Berths	4 doubles
Staterooms	4
Heads	2
Fuel	variable
Fresh Water	variable
Payload	

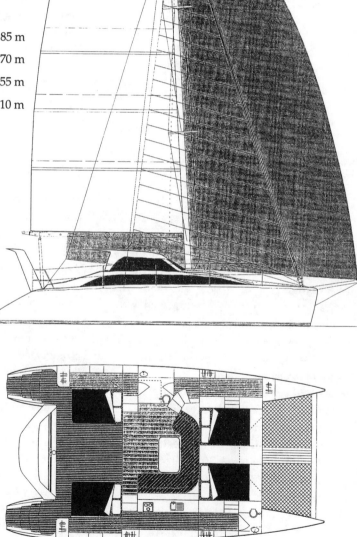

GRAINGER 480

GENERAL INFORMATION

Classification   Stock catamaran design, Cruiser

Cost of plans   Call for current price

Designer   Grainger Designs

Designs   Grainger Designs
PO Box 212, Kingscliff
NSW 2487 Australia
Tel: (61) 66 74 1090
Fax: (61) 66 74 4129
email:

Year Introduced

Number of boats built

N. American Dealers   Buy plans direct

Other Cruising Multihulls By Designer
A wide range of sailing and power cruising catamarans, including the Grainger 430

KEY FEATURES

Hull & Sail Plan
- cedar or foam and glass composite hulls, fixed keels or daggerboards
- Fractional sloop rig, fully battened main, furling headsail, spinnaker on bowsprit

Deck Layout
- Trampoline forward with central walkway, rigid deck just aft with lockers
- Large open cockpit with ample seating, yet sufficiently sheltered for ocean cruising

Standard Accommodations
- The bridgedeck has a large lounge area forward with L-shaped settee and table
- The starboard hull has fore & aft staterooms, a long galley midships, and a head forward
- The port hull has fore & aft staterooms, with a large head midships

Mechanical
- Wheel steering, helm forward in cockpit
- Dual inboards, access from aft deck

DESCRIPTION

This design owes its heritage to a number of previous Grainger designs in this size range, including the Ocean 460 and the more recent Grainger 460. The newer 480 offers two design versions, the first being performance oriented and featuring a streamlined coach-house. The other has a longer coach-house which allows a second set of steps to access the hull from the main saloon, a popular arrangement for charter work and long term liveaboard purposes. Although layout can be customized, a standard option includes two aft double berth cabins and two forward doubles, one with en suite head. A second head with shower is located to port, with the galley to starboard. The comfortable, spacious saloon supplies table seating and navigation station. The Grainger 480 can be built in foam glass or cedar strip composite and be fitted with keels or daggerboards.

SPECIFICATIONS

Displacement	17,928 lbs, 8149 kg	
Standard Auxiliary	2 x 35-51 hp inboard	
Overall Length	47'10"	14.60 m
Waterline Length	44'3"	13.53 m
Bridgedeck Length	30'0"	9.15 m
Wing Deck Clearance	3'0"	0.90 m
Beam (max.)	25'0"	7.62 m
Draft (hull)	2'0"	0.62 m
Draft (fixed keels)	3'7"	1.10 m
Mast Hgt. Off Water		

SAIL AREA

Mainsail	789 sf	73 sm
Genoa	535 sf	50 sm
Total Area	1324 sf	123 sm
Spinnaker		

CAPACITY

Berths	4 doubles
Staterooms	4
Heads	2
Fuel	variable
Fresh Water	variable
Payload	

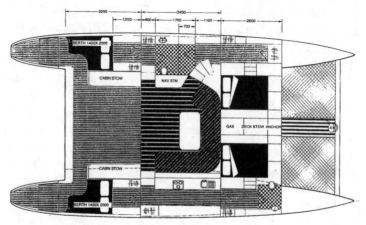

HARRIS 38 Cat

GENERAL INFORMATION

Classification Stock catamaran design, Cruiser

Cost of plans Call for current price
Complete boat $170,000 owner-built

Designer Robert Harris

Designs Robert B. Harris Design
#408-611 Alexander St.
Vancouver, BC V6A 1E1
Canada
Tel: (61) 7 3868 3773
Fax: (61) 7 3868 3774
email:

Year Introduced 1996

Number of boats built 1 (as of Sep 97)

N. American stockists Buy plans direct

Other Cruising Multihulls By Designer
A wide range of cruising multihulls

KEY FEATURES

Hull & Sail Plan
- Strip-planked composite hulls, round bilge, fixed keels, reverse tramsoms with steps
- Fractional sloop rig, fully battened main, roller-furling genoa

Deck Layout
- Small trampoline forward with central walkway, deckhouse with panoramic view
- Large cockpit with circular seating and partial hardtop to protect helm

Standard Accommodations
- The bridgedeck has long table with settees, galley, and access to hulls in deckhouse
- The starboard hull has staterooms fore & aft, with lockers, head, shower midships
- The port hull has staterooms fore & aft, with lockers, head, shower midships

Mechanical
- Wheel steering, raised helm in cockpit
- Dual outboards off stern, access aft deck

DESCRIPTION

The Harris 38 catamaran, Robert Harris stock design No. 667, is a comfortable motorsailer/cruiser designed for the owner-builder. Construction is of strip plank western red cedar, with a hull design that incorporates a round bilge and mini-keels. The easily managed sail plan includes a fractional sloop rig with fully-battened main, slab reefing, and roller furling jib. Wheel steering is located in the deckhouse with sighting through a wind screen, plus an emergency tiller mounted at the aft end of the hulls. Layout can be customized, but a standard plan features four double-berth cabins, (two forward, two aft), twin heads with shower, and spacious galley and table seating in the deckhouse forward of the helm station. Auxiliary power is provided by two 20 hp outboards retracting in wells with flush closure plates at the hull ends.

SPECIFICATIONS

Displacement	8,000 lbs, 3636 kg	
Standard Auxiliary	2 x 20 hp outboard	
Overall Length	38'0"	11.59 m
Waterline Length	35'5"	10.81 m
Bridgedeck Length	29'0"	8.85 m
Wing Deck Clearance	2'4"	0.71 m
Beam (max.)	20'6"	6.27 m
Draft (max.)	2'9"	0.84 m
Mast Hgt. Off Deck	50'0"	15.25 m
Mast Hgt. Off Water	60'0"	18.30 m

SAIL AREA

Mainsail	545 sf	51 sm
Genoa	277 sf	26 sm
Total Area	822 sf	77 sm
Spinnaker		

CAPACITY

Berths	4 doubles
Staterooms	4
Heads	2
Fuel	60 gal 227 ltr
Fresh Water	120 gal 454 ltr
Payload	3,000 lbs, 1362 kg

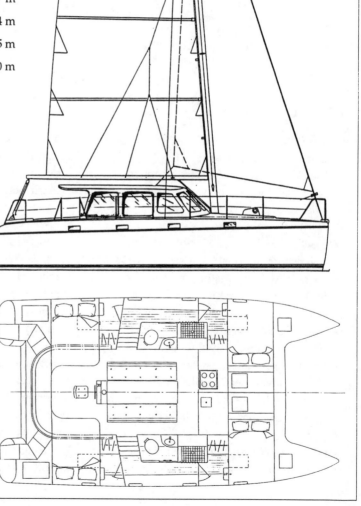

HARRIS 55 Cat

GENERAL INFORMATION

Classification   Stock catamaran design,
Charter cruiser/cruiser

Cost of plans   Call for current price
Complete boat   US $350,000 owner-built

Designer   Robert Harris

Designs   Robert B. Harris Design
#408-611 Alexander St.
Vancouver, BC V6A 1E1
Canada
Tel: (61) 7 3868 3773
Fax: (61) 7 3868 3774
email:

Year Introduced   1997

Number of boats built

N. American stockists   Buy plans direct

Other Cruising Multihulls By Designer
A wide range of cruising multihulls

KEY FEATURES

Hull & Sail Plan
- Composite GRP hulls, round bilge, fixed keels, reverse tramsoms with steps
- Fractional sloop rig, fully battened main, roller-furling genoa

Deck Layout
- Small trampoline forward with central walkway, lockers just aft, wide side decks
- Large cockpit with seating and open areas, full hardtop protects cockpit and helm

Standard Accommodations
- The bridgedeck has dual lounges with tables, nav station, bar/entertainment area
- The starboard hull has staterooms fore & aft with private heads, galley midships
- The port hull has staterooms fore & aft with private heads, head & crew berths midships

Mechanical
- Wheel steering, dual raised helm in cockpit
- Dual inboards, access from aft deck

DESCRIPTION

the Harris 55 is a larger version of the 38, designed for the owner builder and intended as a comfortable motorsailer/cruiser. Construction is of composite GRP, with a hull design that incorporates a round bilge and mini-keels. The easily handled sail plan features a fractional sloop rig, fully-battened main, slab reefing, roller-furling jib, and retracting bow sprit for larger headsails. Standard accommodations include four private double-berth cabins with en suite head and shower compartments. A fifth head services the saloon area, with navigation station and dual table seating located on the bridgedeck. The central starboard hull section serves as a large galley. This layout is ideal for the charter trade, with room for 6-8 guests plus two crew. Wheel steering is located forward and center in the large cockpit, with an emergency tiller aft.

SPECIFICATIONS

Displacement	30,000 lbs, 13,620 kg	
Standard Auxiliary	2 x 42 hp inboard	
Overall Length	55'0"	16.78 m
Waterline Length	51'8"	15.76 m
Bridgedeck Length	40'0"	12.20 m
Wing Deck Clearance	3'1"	0.96 m
Beam (max.)	28'0"	8.54 m
Draft (max.)	3'8"	1.12 m
Mast Hgt. Off Deck	76'0"	23.18 m
Mast Hgt. Off Water	83'6"	25.47 m

SAIL AREA

Mainsail	1181 sf	110 sm
Genoa	569 sf	53 sm
Total Area	1650 sf	163 sm
Spinnaker		

CAPACITY

Berths	4-5 doubles
Staterooms	4
Heads	4 + 1 day head
Fuel	300 gal 1135 ltr
Fresh Water	200 gal 757 ltr
Payload	10,000 lbs, 1362 kg

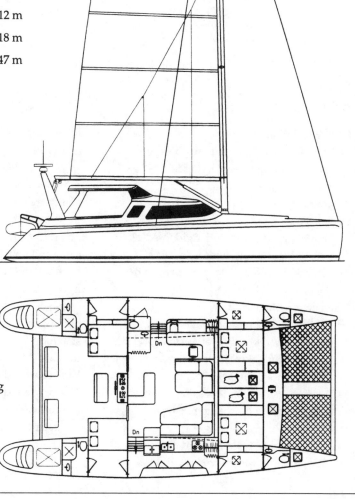

TRI-STAR 38 Cat

GENERAL INFORMATION

Classification   Stock catamaran design, Cruiser

Cost of plans   Call for current price

Designer   Ed Horstman

Designs   Tri-Star Tris/Cats
PO Box 286
Venice, CA 90294 USA
Tel: (310) 396-6154
Fax:
email:

Year introduced

Number of boats built

N. American stockists
Tri-Star Tris/Cats

Other Cruising Multihulls By Designer
A wide range of cruising trimaran and catamaran designs, including the Tri-Star 38-39 trimaran

KEY FEATURES

Hull & Sail Plan
- Long hulls with near-plumb bows and reverse transoms, daggerboards
- Masthead sloop rig, standard main, Overlapping roller-furling genoa

Deck Layout
- Trampoline area forward, rigid foredeck with lockers just aft, wide side decks
- Aft cockpit with seating to port, raised helm station forward to port

Standard Accommodations
- The bridgedeck has wet lockers, storage aft and U-shaped lounge area & table forward
- Starboard hull–double staterooms fore & aft with storage, galley midships
- Port hull–same as starboard hull, only with chart and navigation area midships

Mechanical
- Wheel steering, helm forward in cockpit
- Dual inboards, access from aft deck

DESCRIPTION

Ed Horstman's Tri-Star 38 Cat, one of the newest of his cruising catamaran designs, is spacious and fast, an enjoyable catamaran to sail. Her accommodations and load carrying ability are more typical of larger yachts than those in the 38 foot range. Because of the raised cabin roof, the large bridgedeck saloon cabin and both hull accommodation areas have over 6'4" of headroom throughout. The interior layout can be arranged to suit the owner, with either two cabins with queen-size berths forward, or a single full-width owner's stateroom forward. The starboard hull has the galley midships, while the port hull has a large chart and navigation area midships. The large cockpit, designed for easy sailing or comfortable lounging, can be protected with a boom tent in harbor or a dodger at sea.

SPECIFICATIONS

Displacement	8,800 lbs, 2851 kg	
Standard Auxiliary	2 x 27 hp inboard	
Overall Length	38'7"	11.80 m
Waterline Length	37'7"	11.45 m
Bridgedeck Length	26'3"	8.00 m
Wing Deck Clearance		
Beam (max.)	20'6"	6.25 m
Draft (boards up)	2'4"	0.71 m
Draft (boards down)	5'6"	1.68 m
Mast Hgt. Off Water	52'0"	15.86 m

SAIL AREA

Mainsail		
Jib		
Total Area	837 sf	78 sm
Spinnaker		

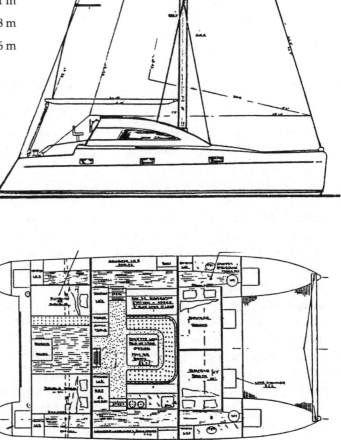

CAPACITY

Berths	3-4 doubles	
Staterooms	3-4	
Heads	2	
Fuel	35 gal	132 ltr
Fresh Water	60 gal	227 ltr
Payload	4,100 lbs, 1860 kg	

HUGHES 45 Cat

GENERAL INFORMATION

Classification   Stock catamaran design
Cruiser/racer

Cost of plans   US $2,700

Designer   Kurt Hughes

Designs   K. Hughes Sailing Designs
612-1/2 West McGraw St.
Seattle, WA 98119 USA
Tel: (206) 284-6436
Fax: (206) 283-4106
email: khughes@isomedia.com

Year introduced   1993

Number of boats built

N. American Stockists   Buy plans direct

Other Cruising Multihulls By Designer
   Over 75 other multihull designs from 12 to
79 feet

KEY FEATURES

Hull & Sail Plan
- Easily-driven hulls w/ full round sections, daggerboards, reverse transoms
- Fractional sloop rig, fully battened main, furling headsails, asymmetric spinnaker

Deck Layout
- Trampoline forward with central walkway, rigid foredeck just aft, wide side decks
- Aft cockpit with seating to port, raised helm station forward to starboard

Standard Accommodations
- The bridgedeck has galley aft, interior helm area, dual lounge areas with tables to port
- Starboard hull–double staterooms fore & aft with storage, head compartments midships outboard with storage inboard
- Port hull–same as starboard hull

Mechanical
- Dual helms, in cockpit and in main cabin
- Dual inboards, access from aft deck

DESCRIPTION

The Hughes 45 Cat is a versatile performance cruiser capable of long-distance voyaging, racing or charter work. The hull construction is cylinder-molded, vacuum-bagged plywood or triaxial roving on pvc foam using epoxy resin. The hulls have full round sections for minimum wetted surface, wide transoms for power reaching, and a relatively low drag at high speed. Extra attention is given to impact resistance, and the high bridgedeck clearance from waterline of 3 feet allows the boat to keep moving in big water. Specs for the tradewind rig are given; a performance rig is available. There are dual seating areas in the main cabin and four separate staterooms, each with a large double berth, closet, dresser, and other storage. There is an interior helm station and adjacent nav area with large flat counter space. The cockpit helm is protected by the cabin yet offers good visibility.

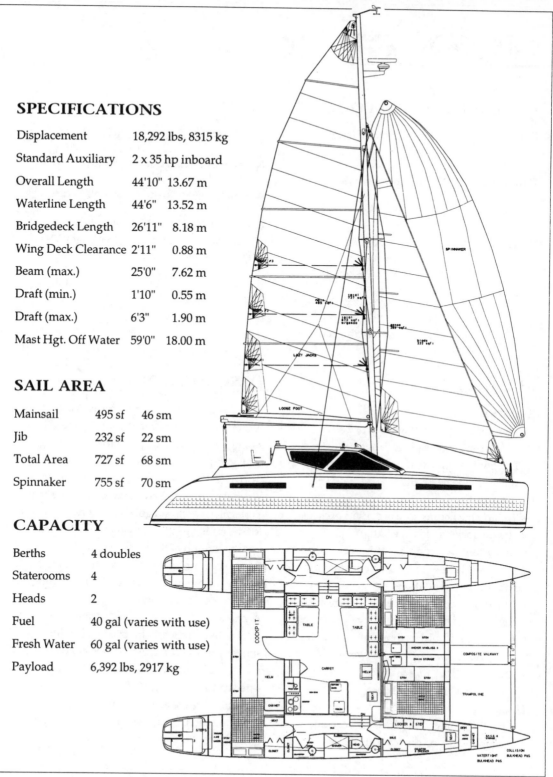

SPECIFICATIONS

Displacement	18,292 lbs,	8315 kg
Standard Auxiliary	2 x 35 hp inboard	
Overall Length	44'10"	13.67 m
Waterline Length	44'6"	13.52 m
Bridgedeck Length	26'11"	8.18 m
Wing Deck Clearance	2'11"	0.88 m
Beam (max.)	25'0"	7.62 m
Draft (min.)	1'10"	0.55 m
Draft (max.)	6'3"	1.90 m
Mast Hgt. Off Water	59'0"	18.00 m

SAIL AREA

Mainsail	495 sf	46 sm
Jib	232 sf	22 sm
Total Area	727 sf	68 sm
Spinnaker	755 sf	70 sm

CAPACITY

Berths	4 doubles
Staterooms	4
Heads	2
Fuel	40 gal (varies with use)
Fresh Water	60 gal (varies with use)
Payload	6,392 lbs, 2917 kg

NOSE BE 36

GENERAL INFORMATION

Classification   Stock catamaran design, Cruiser

Cost of plans   Call for current price

Designer   Angelo Lavranos

Designs   Lavranos & Associates
33 Jellicoe Road,
Murry's Bay, Auckland
New Zealand
Tel: (64) 9 478 1942
Fax: (64) 9 478 1943
email: lavranos@ihug.co.nz

Year Introduced

Number of boats built   8   (as of Sep 97)

N. American stockists   Buy plans direct

Other Cruising Multihulls By Designer
   Admiral 48, St. Francis 44 (see pages 304-305), and other cruising multihulls

KEY FEATURES

Hull & Sail Plan
- Hull construction using foam or Balsa panels over a male plug, fixed keels
- Fractional sloop rig, fully battened main, roller-furling headsails

Deck Layout
- Trampoline netting forward, rigid deck just aft with lockers, sleek cabintop
- Aft cockpit with ample seating, yet sufficiently sheltered for ocean cruising

Standard Accommodations
- The bridgedeck has a circular lounge area nav station, and full-size galley
- The starboard hull has fore & aft staterooms, with a head compartment between
- The port hull has fore & aft staterooms, with a head compartment between

Mechanical
- Wheel steering, helm forward in cockpit
- Dual inboards, access from aft cabins

DESCRIPTION

The Nose Be 36 is a comfortable cruising catamaran designed for offshore or coastal sailing. Care has been taken to produce hulls with good reserve buoyancy in the bows. Bridgedeck clearance is excellent, reducing wave slap, particularly in the ends of the boat. Waterplane area and good clearances make for the cruising load-carrying capability of a light monohull of the same length. She features a runnerless fractional rig with fully battened main in lazyjacks and roller-furling genoa for easy sail handling.

Accommodations include four double-berth cabins (two in each hull), two heads with shower, and a bridgedeck galley and dining area. Additional "home comforts" can be fitted to suit the budget. Power is provided by twin saildrive engines, with the propellers mounted directly in front of the rudders for good maneuverability.

SPECIFICATIONS

Displacement	9,240 lbs, 4200 kg	
Standard Auxiliary	2 x 10 hp inboard	
Overall Length	36'1"	11.00 m
Waterline Length	32'10"	10.00 m
Bridgedeck Length	23'4"	7.10 m
Wing Deck Clearance	2'1"	0.65 m
Beam (max.)	23'0"	7.00 m
Draft (max.)	2'8"	0.80 m
Mast Hgt. Off Deck	49'3"	15.00 m
Mast Hgt. Off Water	56'1"	17.10 m

SAIL AREA

Mainsail	495 sf	46 sm
Genoa	301 sf	28 sm
Total Area	796 sf	74 sm
Spinnaker	624 sf	58 sm

CAPACITY

Berths	4 doubles	
Staterooms	4	
Heads	2	
Fuel	66 gal	250 ltr
Fresh Water	66 gal	250 ltr
Payload	3,520 lbs, 1600 kg	

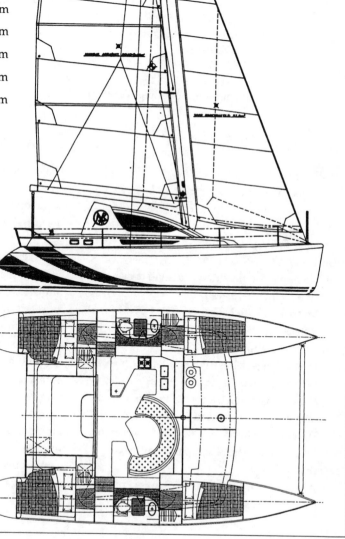

ADMIRAL 48

GENERAL INFORMATION

Classification   Stock catamaran design, Cruiser

Cost of plans   Call for current price

Designer   Angelo Lavranos

Designs   Lavranos & Associates
33 Jellicoe Road,
Murry's Bay, Auckland
New Zealand
Tel: (64) 9 478 1942
Fax: (64) 9 478 1943
email: lavranos@ihug.co.nz

Year Introduced   1994

Number of boats built   4   (as of Sep 97)

N. American stockists   Buy plans direct

Other Cruising Multihulls By Designer
Nose Be 36, St. Francis 44 (see pages 304-305), and other cruising multihulls

KEY FEATURES

Hull & Sail Plan
- Hull construction using foam or Balsa panels over a male plug, fixed keels
- Fractional sloop rig, fully battened main, roller-furling headsails

Deck Layout
- Trampoline netting forward, rigid deck just aft with lockers, sleek cabintop
- Aft cockpit with U-shaped seating, yet sufficiently sheltered for ocean cruising

Standard Accommodations
- The bridgedeck has a circular lounge area, nav station, work area, and full-size galley
- The starboard hull has fore & aft staterooms, each with a private head compartment
- The port hull has fore & aft staterooms, each with a private head compartment

Mechanical
- Wheel steering, helm forward in cockpit
- Dual inboards, access from aft cabins

DESCRIPTION

The Admiral 48 is currently the largest production catamaran in South Africa. Built of vacuum-bagged sandwich construction, she is designed for high performance as well as comfort and good load-carrying capacity. The fractional sloop rig features a fully battened mainsail, roller-furling jib, and runnerless rig with swept back cap shrouds for safety and easy of use. Overall beam is large to provide the necessary stability for a modern performance cat. Other safety features include a topsides flare, good buoyancy reserves, and watertight collision bulkheads. Although she has been designed with a four cabin layout, a six cabin arrangement specifically for charter work may be fitted. Standard layout incorporates four cabins in the hulls with en suite heads, plus the galley, dining/seating area and navigation station all on the bridgedeck.

SPECIFICATIONS

Displacement	23,100 lbs, 10,500 kg
Standard Auxiliary	2 x 27 hp inboard
Overall Length	46'10" 14.30 m
Waterline Length	45'3" 13.80 m
Bridgedeck Length	31'2" 9.50 m
Wing Deck Clearance	2'7" 0.80 m
Beam (max.)	27'10" 8.50 m
Draft (max.)	4'3" 1.30 m
Mast Hgt. Off Deck	61'0" 18.60 m
Mast Hgt. Off Water	68'5" 20.85 m

SAIL AREA

Mainsail	861 sf	80 sm
Genoa	484 sf	45 sm
Total Area	1345 sf	135 sm
Spinnaker	925 sf	86 sm

CAPACITY

Berths	4 doubles
Staterooms	4
Heads	4
Fuel	158 gal 600 ltr
Fresh Water	212 gal 800 ltr
Payload	8,360 lbs, 3800 kg

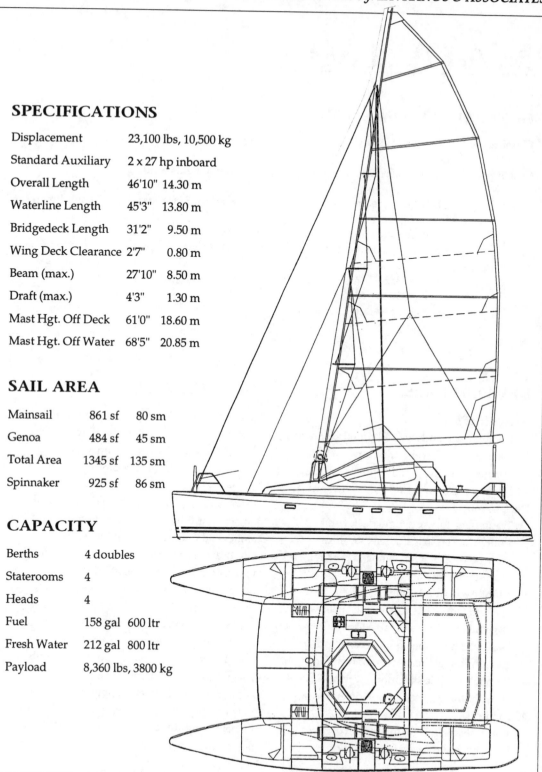

MAÏA 160

GENERAL INFORMATION

Classification   Cruiser/racer

Cost of plans   Call for current price

Designer   Erik LeRouge Yacht Design

Designs   Erik LeRouge International
Maison Conan, Le Rohello
56250 Sulniac France
Tel: (33) 2 97 43 16 05
Fax: (33) 2 97 43 13 47
email: elerouge@club-internet.fr

Year introduced   1997

Number of boats built

N. American Stockists   Buy plans direct

Other Cruising Multihulls By Designer
A wide range of high-performance cruising and racing multihulls, including the Maïa 80, a fast open-bridgedeck, trailerable catamaran

KEY FEATURES

Hull & Sail Plan
- Easily-driven hulls w/ full round sections, daggerboards, reverse transoms
- Fractional sloop rig, fully battened main, rotating wing mast, furling jib, bowsprit

Deck Layout
- Trampoline forward, rigid deck with storage lockers just aft, sleek topsides
- Wide aft cockpit with seating to port, raised helm station forward

Standard Accommodations
- The bridgedeck has galley and nav area aft, large saloon settee and table forward
- Starboard hull–double staterooms fore & aft with storage, head with shower midship
- Port hull–double staterooms fore & aft with storage, head with shower midship

Mechanical
- Wheel steering, helm forward in cockpit
- Dual inboards, access from aft deck

DESCRIPTION

The Maïa 160 is designed to provide cruising comfort on a boat capable of sailing in excess of wind speed. Her wide beam, good buoyancy, short bridgedeck located high above the water, and minimum windage make her a dependable sea boat. Deep daggerboards ensure excellent pointing ability and reduced drag off the wind, while elliptical spade rudders provide good control with minimum drag. She is fitted with a carbon fiber rotating mast and Spectra sails for an efficient rig in all conditions, but she's kept light for safety and ease of handling. Accommodations feature four comfortable double-berth cabins, panoramic saloon with galley and chart table, and two heads with showers. A twin diesel version provides 10+ knots of speed under power, plus easy harbor maneuvering. Other options are available for ocean voyaging or the charter trade.

SPECIFICATIONS

Displacement	18,700 lbs, 8500 kg	
Standard Auxiliary	2 x 50 hp inboard	
Overall Length	52'6"	15.99 m
Waterline Length	52'6"	15.99 m
Bridgedeck Length	24'7"	7.50 m
Wing Deck Clearance	3'6"	1.05 m
Beam (max.)	29'2"	8.90 m
Draft (boards up)	1'10"	0.56 m
Draft (boards down)	9'2"	2.78 m
Mast Hgt. Off Water	69'0"	21.50 m

SAIL AREA

Wing Mast	130 sf	12 sm
Mainsail	1120 sf	102 sm
Jib	640 sf	58 sm
Total Area	1890 sf	172 sm
Spinnaker	1960 sf	178 sm

CAPACITY

Berths	4 doubles
Staterooms	4
Heads	2
Fuel	106 gal 400 ltr
Fresh Water	106 gal 600 ltr
Payload	6,400 lbs, 2900 kg

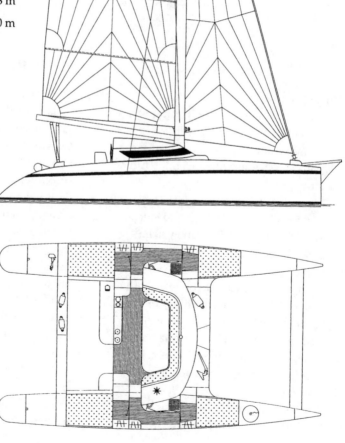

CONSTANT CAMBER C440

GENERAL INFORMATION

Classification   Stock catamaran design,
Cruiser

Cost of plans   US $2,000
($50,000 material estimate)

Designer   John Marples

Designs   John R. Marples
Multihull Designs
PO Box 1437, St. Augustine,
FL 32085 USA
Tel: (904) 824-2688
Fax: (904) 824-2688
email:

Year introduced   1989

Number of boats built   5 (as of Sep 97)

N. American Stockists   Buy plans direct

Other Cruising Multihulls By Designer
A wide range of cruising catamaran and trimaran designs, including the Constant Camber™, Searunner (in partnership with Jim Brown), and the Seaclipper series

KEY FEATURES

Hull & Sail Plan
- Wood-epoxy U-shaped hulls, aft skegs, daggerboards, built-in buoyancy
- Masthead cutter rig, standard mainsail, genoa and staysail with opt'l roller furling

Deck Layout
- Trampoline forward with central walkway, rigid foredeck just aft, sleek bridgedeck
- Aft cockpit with ample seating, helm station midships, trampoline netting aft

Standard Accommodations
- The open bridgedeck has berth extensions from midships and forward sections
- Starboard hull–galley aft with dinette seating, single berth, forward stateroom
- Port hull–work station and nav area aft, double berth midships, head, storage

Mechanical
- Wheel steering or tiller midships in cockpit
- Dual inboards, access from hulls

DESCRIPTION

Another innovative Marples design, the C440 cat is a fast, dependable cruising craft that is safe and strong yet easy to build. Construction utilizes the patented Constant Camber™ technique, which can be used successfully by most home builders. The deck and interior layout is unusual—all accommodations are accessed separately through the hulls, yet several of the berths in the midships portion of the boat extend partially onto the flush bridgedeck area. This allows the cabin roof profile to remain sleek and uncluttered, while providing comfortable accommodations and a large cockpit seating area. There is a comfortable galley in the aft section of the starboard hull, and a work station or additional storage or berth area aft in the port hull. The Constant Camber C440 is a good boat for group day sailing or extended family cruises.

SPECIFICATIONS

Displacement	10,800 lbs, 4900 kg	
Standard Auxiliary	2 x 15-20 hp inboard	
Overall Length	40'0"	12.20 m
Waterline Length	37'0"	11.20 m
Bridgedeck Length	19'2"	5.85 m
Wing Deck Clearance	3'0"	0.92 m
Beam (max.)	16'0"	4.88 m
Draft (boards up)	1'8"	0.46 m
Draft (boards down)	5'3"	1.60 m
Mast Hgt. Off Water	50'0"	15.20 m

SAIL AREA

Mainsail	390 sf	36 sm
Genoa	512 sf	48 sm
Staysail	160 sf	15 sm
Total Area	1062 sf	73 sm
Spinnaker	1300 sf	121 sm

CAPACITY

Berths	1 sgle, 3-4 dbls	
Staterooms	3	
Heads	2	
Fuel	30 gal	114 ltr
Fresh Water	50 gal	190 ltr
Payload	2,800 lbs, 1270 kg	

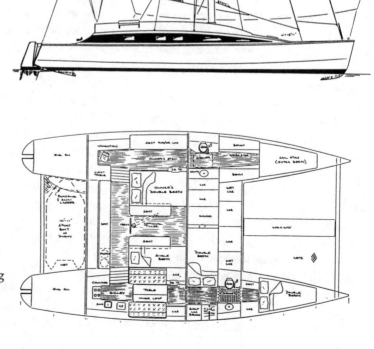

WILDERNESS 930

GENERAL INFORMATION

Classification   Stock catamaran design, Cruiser/racer

Cost of plans   AUS $2,500

Designer   Jeff Schionning

Designs   Jeff Schionning Designs
20 David Muir St.
Slade Point, Mackay
Qld 4740, Australia
Tel: (61) 79 55 45 77
Fax: (61) 79 55 40 59
email:

Year Introduced

Number of boats built   (as of Sep 97)

N. American Dealers
Purchase plans from Jeff Schionning Designs

Other Cruising Multihulls By Designer
A wide range of cruising catamarans, including the Wilderness series and the Cosmos series

KEY FEATURES

Hull & Sail Plan
- hard-chine hulls with chamfer panels on the hull/wing-deck joint, daggerboards
- Fractional sloop rig, fully battened main, furling headsail, spinnaker on bowsprit

Deck Layout
- Trampoline forward with central walkway, rigid deck just aft with lockers & buoyancy
- Large open cockpit with semi-circular seating, arch at stern, swim platforms

Standard Accommodations
- The bridgedeck has a settee aft and large U-shaped lounge area with table forward
- The starboard hull has double stateroom aft, single berth forward, galley midships
- The port hull has double stateroom aft, large head forward, and nav area midships

Mechanical
- Tiller steering, inboard kick-up rudders
- Single outboard mounted in cockpit well

DESCRIPTION

The Wilderness 930, designed for shorter cruises or "lightweight" liveaboard, is a high-performance cruising catamaran from Australian designer Jeff Schionning. Incorporating a hard-chine hull configuration that is surprisingly graceful and relatively easy to construct, the design calls for the use of DuraKore panels for their superior strength and light weight. Layout features two aft double-berth cabins, galley, workbench/navigation area (or additional double berth option), head with shower, functional galley, spare forward single berth in the forepeak, and large saloon seating area with wrap around windows. There are two access doors from the cockpit into the main cabin to ensure a smooth traffic flow in the bridgedeck area. The Wilderness 930 is pleasing to look at and easy to handle, with all lines leading to the cockpit and the use of tiller steering.

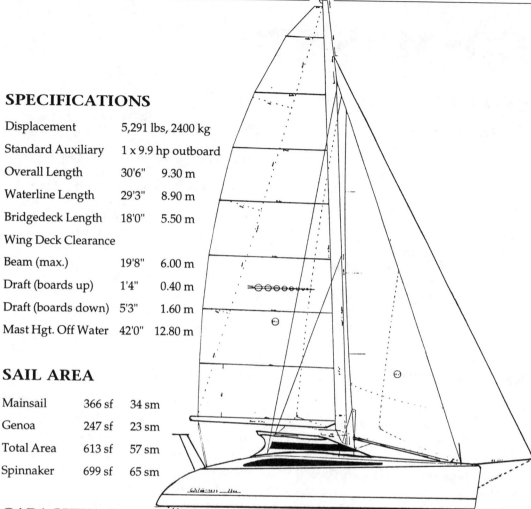

SPECIFICATIONS

Displacement	5,291 lbs, 2400 kg	
Standard Auxiliary	1 x 9.9 hp outboard	
Overall Length	30'6"	9.30 m
Waterline Length	29'3"	8.90 m
Bridgedeck Length	18'0"	5.50 m
Wing Deck Clearance		
Beam (max.)	19'8"	6.00 m
Draft (boards up)	1'4"	0.40 m
Draft (boards down)	5'3"	1.60 m
Mast Hgt. Off Water	42'0"	12.80 m

SAIL AREA

Mainsail	366 sf	34 sm
Genoa	247 sf	23 sm
Total Area	613 sf	57 sm
Spinnaker	699 sf	65 sm

CAPACITY

Berths	1-2 sgls, 2 dbls
Staterooms	2-3
Heads	1
Fuel	6 gal (portable)
Fresh Water	53 gal 200 ltr
Payload	2,200 lbs, 1000 kg

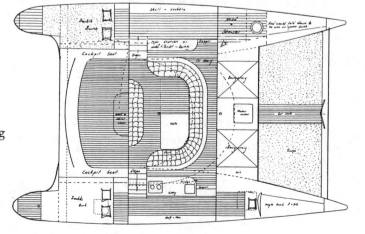

COSMOS 930

GENERAL INFORMATION

Classification Stock catamaran design, Cruiser/racer

Cost of plans AUS $2,500

Designer Jeff Schionning

Designs Jeff Schionning Designs
20 David Muir St.
Slade Point, Mackay
Qld 4740, Australia
Tel: (61) 79 55 45 77
Fax: (61) 79 55 40 59
email:

Year Introduced

Number of boats built (as of Sep 97)

N. American Dealers Buy plans direct

Other Cruising Multihulls By Designer
A wide range of cruising catamarans, including the Wilderness series and the Cosmos series

KEY FEATURES

Hull & Sail Plan
- High-performance hulls, daggerboards, reverse transoms
- Fractional sloop rig, fully battened main, furling headsail, spinnaker on bowsprit

Deck Layout
- Trampoline forward with central walkway, rigid deck just aft with lockers & buoyancy
- Large open cockpit with semi-circular seating, arch at stern, swim platforms

Standard Accommodations
- The bridgedeck has a settee aft and large U-shaped lounge area with table forward
- The starboard hull has double stateroom aft, single berth forward, galley midships
- The port hull has double stateroom aft, large head midships, single berth forward

Mechanical
- Wheel steering, inboard kick-up rudders
- Single outboard mounted in cockpit well

DESCRIPTION

The Cosmos 930 is a cruising catamaran built using strip-planked construction methods, which produces a strong, light composite multihull without requiring high skill levels or complex, expensive tools. The 930, known as the Convertible, offers three choices: one with a full bridgedeck cabin, one with open bridgedeck and soft bimini for cockpit shade, and a third with open bridgedeck and hard cabin top, on legs over the cockpit, with zip in sides, ideal for the tropics. All three options offer a galley, head, two aft double berths and two forward singles, with the bridgedeck cabin version adding an interior saloon seating area. Performance is a high priority, with low profile hulls and daggerboards. A single winch station in the cockpit handles all halyards and single-line reefing, allowing easy sail handling. The Comos 930 joins the wide range of other Cosmos cats.

SPECIFICATIONS

Displacement	5,720 lbs, 2600 kg	
Standard Auxiliary	1 x 9.9 hp outboard	
Overall Length	30'6"	9.30 m
Waterline Length	29'3"	8.90 m
Bridgedeck Length	18'0"	5.50 m
Wing Deck Clearance	2'0"	0.60
Beam (max.)	19'8"	6.00 m
Draft (boards up)	1'5"	0.45 m
Draft (boards down)	5'3"	1.60 m
Mast Hgt. Off Water	39'4"	12.00 m

SAIL AREA

Mainsail	355 sf	33 sm
Genoa	204 sf	19 sm
Total Area	659 sf	52 sm
Spinnaker	1043 sf	97 sm

CAPACITY

Berths	2 sgls, 2 dbls
Staterooms	4
Heads	1
Fuel	6 gal (portable)
Fresh Water	53 gal 200 ltr
Payload	2,200 lbs, 1000 kg

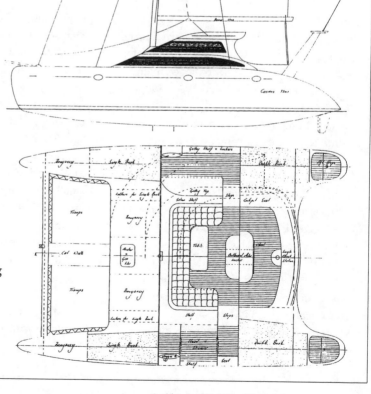

GROUND EFFECT 9m

GENERAL INFORMATION

Classification Stock catamaran design, Cruiser/racer

Cost of plans Call for current price

Designer Simpson Design

Designs Simpson Design
PO Box 2, Hemmant,
Qld 4174 Australia
Tel: (61) 7 3396 5135
Fax: (61) 7 3893 1624
email: simdes@ozemail.com.au

Year Introduced

Number of boats built

N. American Dealers   Buy plans direct

Other Cruising Multihulls By Designer
  A wide range of cruising and cruising/racing multihulls, including the Slipstream 15m

KEY FEATURES

Hull & Sail Plan
- strip-planked composite hulls with knuckle, daggerboards (opt'l keels), reverse transoms
- Fractional sloop rig, fully battened main, self-tending headsail

Deck Layout
- Large trampoline forward, semi-open bridgedeck design, cambered cabintop
- Large open cockpit with ample seating, good access to tiller steering

Standard Accommodations
- The bridgedeck is a semi-open design with bridgedeck berths accessed from the hulls
- The starboard hull has head aft, storage and berth acccess midships, and berth forward
- The port hull has galley aft, dinette and berth access midships, and berth forward

Mechanical
- Tiller steering, transom-hung rudders
- Single outboard mounted in cockpit pod

DESCRIPTION

In just under 30 feet (9 meters), Roger Simpson's Ground Effect 9m offers just about the most boat for the least effort and cost in a semi-bridgedeck catamaran. By not offering a full bridgedeck cabin, this design can be built far from the water and dismantled for trucking and final assembly near the launch site. The builder has a choice of keels or daggerboards, kick-up or skeg-hung rudders. The "knuckle" in the hull section allows for a small waterline imprint, yet ample accommodations above waterline. Those accommodations include three double berths and one single berth, a combination galley and dinette area in the port hull, a head compartment in the starboard hull, and ample storage areas. The full plans are prepared with the amateur builder in mind and come complete with a copy of the book *Simpson On Boatbuilding*.

SPECIFICATIONS

Displacement	5,553 lbs, 2524 kg	
Standard Auxiliary	1 x 9.9 hp outboard	
Overall Length	29'8"	9.05 m
Waterline Length	28'4"	8.64 m
Bridgedeck Length	13'11"	4.24 m
Wing Deck Clearance		
Beam (max.)	19'8"	6.00 m
Draft (boards up)	1'8"	0.50 m
Draft (boards down)		
Mast Hgt. Off Water	47'6"	13.00 m

SAIL AREA

Mainsail	395 sf	37 sm
Jib	164 sf	15 sm
Total Area	559 sf	52 sm
Spinnaker		

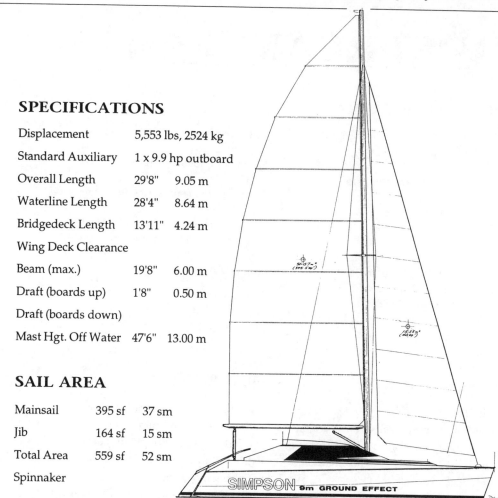

CAPACITY

Berths	1 sgle, 3 dbls
Staterooms	none
Heads	1
Fuel	6 gal (portable)
Fresh Water	50 gal 227 ltr
Payload	4,400 lb, 2000 kg

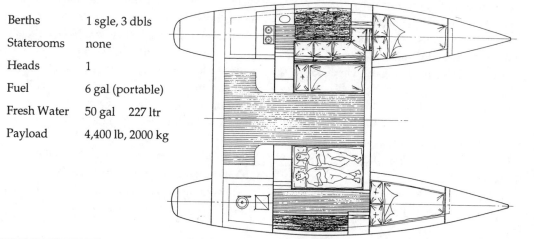

SLIPSTREAM 15m

GENERAL INFORMATION

Classification   Stock catamaran design,
Cruiser/racer

Cost of plans   Call for current price

Designer   Simpson Design

Designs   Simpson Design
PO Box 2, Hemmant,
Qld 4174 Australia
Tel: (61) 7 3396 5135
Fax: (61) 7 3893 1624
email: simdes@ozemail.com.au

Year Introduced

Number of boats built

N. American Dealers   Buy plans direct

Other Cruising Multihulls By Designer
A wide range of cruising and cruising/
racing multihulls, including the
Ground Effect 9m

KEY FEATURES

Hull & Sail Plan
- strip-planked composite hulls with knuckle, daggerboards (opt'l keels), reverse transoms
- Fractional sloop rig, fully battened main, self-tending headsail

Deck Layout
- Trampoline netting forward, rigid deck just aft with lockers, cambered cabintop
- Large cockpit with U-shaped seating, aft swim platforms, helm forward

Standard Accommodations
- The bridgedeck has lounge and table to port, full-size galley to starboard
- The starboard hull has double staterooms fore & aft, large head midships
- The port hull has double staterooms fore & aft, large head midships

Mechanical
- Wheel steering, inboard skeg-hung rudders
- Dual inboards or outboard in cockpit pod

DESCRIPTION

This catamaran is designed as a fast cruising yacht for the home builder, with all the comforts of home brought into the design. Although the standard plans call for a Simpson Strip-Wing Mast, a more conservative rig is available. By using the "knuckle" hull section, the interior space is vastly increased beyond what one would normally expect in a boat this size. The off-set head compartments allow complete walk-through hulls, while the galley on the bridgedeck keeps everyone together and involved during social occasions. Sleeping accommodations include large double staterooms up forward, with the berths transverse on the bridgedeck, and slightly smaller double staterooms aft in the hulls. The Slipstream 15m is a big catamaran that is relatively simple to build, a practical boat for those who enjoy fast cruising in style.

SPECIFICATIONS

Displacement	18,920 lbs, 8600 kg	
Standard Auxiliary	inboards or outboard	
Overall Length	49'10"	15.19 m
Waterline Length	47'7"	14.51 m
Bridgedeck Length	27'2"	8.29 m
Wing Deck Clearance		
Beam (max.)	27'6"	8.40 m
Draft (boards up)	2'0"	0.60 m
Draft (boards down)		
Mast Hgt. Off WL	65'8"	20.00 m

SAIL AREA

Mainsail	980 sf	91 sm
Jib	435 sf	41 sm
Total Area	1415 sf	132 sm
Spinnaker		

CAPACITY

Berths	4 doubles	
Staterooms	4	
Heads	2	
Fuel	60 gal	273 ltr
Fresh Water	100 gal	379 ltr
Payload	7,700 lb, 3500 kg	

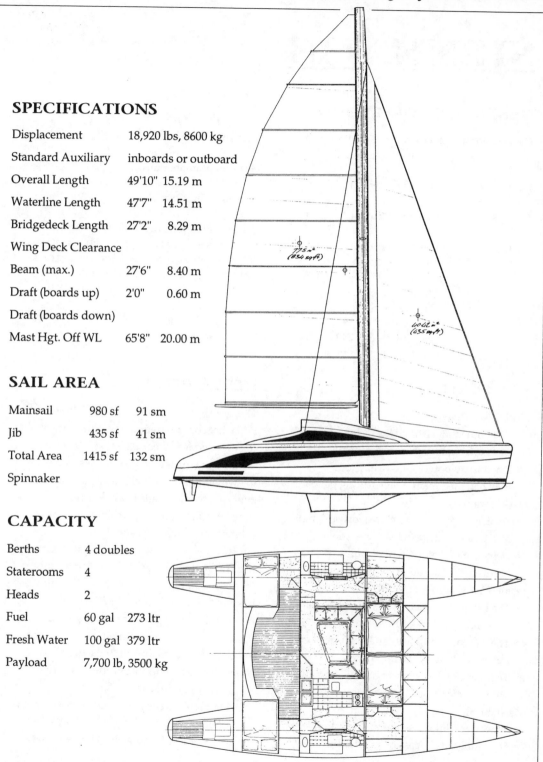

SIENNA 38

GENERAL INFORMATION

Classification   Stock catamaran design, Cruiser

Cost of plans   Call for current price

Designer   Malcolm Tennant

Designs   Malcolm Tennant
Multihull Design
PO Box 21-857, Henderson,
Auckland 1008
New Zealand
Tel: (64) 9 838 6593
Fax: (64) 9 836 6749
email: brianh@netbyte.co.nz

Year Introduced   1997

Number of boats built   2   (as of Sep 97)

N. American Stockists   Buy plans direct

Other Cruising Multihulls By Designer
   Indigo 43, Turissimo 9m & 10m, Great Barrier Express, Northern 11m cruising cats, and many other sail and power multihulls

KEY FEATURES

Hull & Sail Plan
- Full bodied hulls, fixed keels, reverse transoms, watertight compartments
- Fractional sloop rig, aft-swept spreaders, fully battened main, roller-furling genoa

Deck Layout
- Small trampoline netting area forward, rigid foredeck just aft with lockers, wide decks
- Helm station on raised platforms to provide headroom in aft cabins, wide seating area

Standard Accommodations
- The bridgedeck has a wide lounge seating area and table forward
- The starboard hull has staterooms fore and aft, with a long galley midships
- The port hull has staterooms fore and aft with private head compartment midships

Mechanical
- Wheel steering, raised helm in cockpit
- Dual inboards, access from aft deck

DESCRIPTION

This cruising catamaran features full-bodied hulls that ensure adequate performance when fully loaded for extended voyaging. Her "underwing girder" eases the transition from the wing to the hulls, with no right angle joints in the bulkheads to allow stress concentrations. The rig is a simple, non-rotating, aft-swept spreader type with upper spreaders and shrouds that allow the carrying of light weather extras without using runners. Standard sail plan shows slab reefing lines leading to the cabin top winches, while a boom roller furling set up is a suggested option. The helm is mounted on a plinth for good visibility, also providing extra head-room over the aft double berths. Saildrives are the auxiliary of choice. She has the interior of an "English style" cruising cat, with four doubles, two singles, a comfortable lounge area, head, and well equipped galley.

SPECIFICATIONS

Displacement	11,607 lbs, 5276 kg
Standard Auxiliary	2 x 18 hp inboard
Overall Length	38'2" 11.63 m
Waterline Length	36'7" 11.17 m
Bridgedeck Length	23'3" 7.10 m
Wing Deck Clearance	2'4" 0.71 m
Beam (max.)	20'7" 6.30 m
Draft (min.)	3'3" 1.00 m
Mast Hgt. Off Deck	48'6" 14.80 m
Mast Hgt. Off Water	57'0" 17.40 m

SAIL AREA

Mainsail	512 sf	47 sm
Genoa	282 sf	26 sm
Total Area	794 sf	73 sm
Spinnaker		

CAPACITY

Berths	2 sgls, 4 dbls	
Staterooms	4	
Heads	1	
Fuel	53 gal	200 ltr
Fresh Water	105 gal	400 ltr
Payload	4264 lbs, 1938 kg	

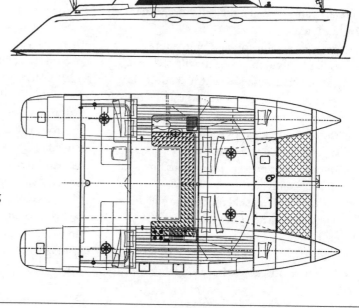

INDIGO 43

GENERAL INFORMATION

Classification   Stock catamaran design, Charter cruiser

Cost of plans   Call for current price

Designer   Malcolm Tennant

Designs   Malcolm Tennant
Multihull Design
PO Box 21-857, Henderson,
Auckland 1008
New Zealand
Tel: (64) 9 838 6593
Fax: (64) 9 836 6749
email: brianh@netbyte.co.nz

Year Introduced   1996

Number of boats built   2 (as of Sep 97)

N. American Stockists   Buy plans direct

Other Cruising Multihulls By Designer
Sienna 38, Turissimo 9m & 10m, Great Barrier Express, Northern 11m cruising cats, and many other sail and power multihulls

KEY FEATURES

Hull & Sail Plan
- Full bodied hulls, fixed keels, reverse transoms, watertight compartments
- Fractional sloop rig, aft-swept spreaders, fully battened main, roller-furling genoa

Deck Layout
- Small trampoline forward with central walkway, rigid foredeck aft with lockers
- Helm station on raised central platform in cockpit, expansive aft deck & seating area

Standard Accommodations
- The bridgedeck has two lounge areas and large U-shaped galley forward
- The starboard hull has staterooms fore and aft, with a private head midships
- The port hull has staterooms fore and aft with a private head midships

Mechanical
- Wheel steering, raised helm in cockpit
- Dual inboards, access from aft deck

DESCRIPTION

The Indigo 43 was designed primarily for charter work, hence the centrally located heads in the hulls and the galley in the wing. Twin cockpit doors either side of the helm facilitate the movement of the larger numbers of people usually found on a charter vessel. There are walk-through transoms, and the inboard side of the hulls aft are cut away to create a larger than usual boarding platform that allows the dinghy to come in along side to transfer passengers. The cockpit has generous seating and features a barbecue and removable game fishing chair. The boat is helmed from a raised platform which has the electric main sheet winch ready to hand. Charter layout includes four double-berth cabins (two aft, two forward), two forward singles for crew quarters, and two heads. Seating in the saloon is spacious and the galley well equipped.

SPECIFICATIONS

Displacement	15,642 lbs, 7110 kg	
Standard Auxiliary	2 x 38 hp inboard	
Overall Length	43'4"	13.20 m
Waterline Length	40'7"	12.38 m
Bridgedeck Length	25'3"	7.70 m
Wing Deck Clearance	2'5"	0.75 m
Beam (max.)	25'1"	7.65 m
Draft (max.)	4'1"	1.25 m
Mast Hgt. Off Deck	55'8"	17.00 m
Mast Hgt. Off Water	64'8"	19.70 m

SAIL AREA

Mainsail	676 sf	62 sm
Genoa	343 sf	32 sm
Total Area	1012 sf	94 sm
Spinnaker		

CAPACITY

Berths	4 sgls, 4 dbls	
Staterooms	4	
Heads	2	
Fuel	53 gal	200 ltr
Fresh Water	132 gal	500 ltr
Payload	4950 lbs, 2250 kg	

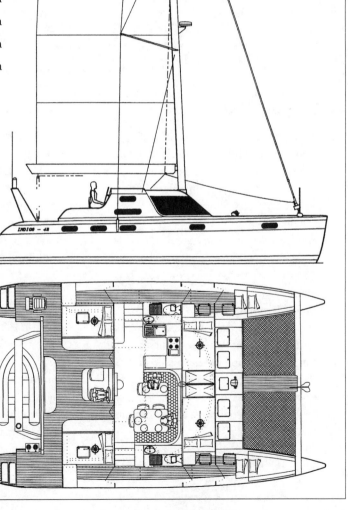

TIKI 30

GENERAL INFORMATION

Classification	Stock design catamaran, Cruiser
Cost of plans	£505
Designer	James Wharram, H. Boon
Designs	James Wharram Designs Greenbank Rd., Devoran, Truro, Cornwall TR3 6PJ UK Tel: (44) 1872 864792 Fax: (44) 1872 864792 email:

Year Introduced

Number of boats built

N. American Stockists
T. Milano
PO Box 35177, Sarasota, FL 34242

Other Cruising Multihulls By Designer
A wide range of cruising catamarans including the complete Tiki series, the Pahi series, and other classic Wharram designs

KEY FEATURES

Hull & Sail Plan
- canoe-shaped hulls with integral fixed keels, outboard rudders on skegs
- Gaff-headed sloop rig, boomless soft-wing mainsail, roller-furling genoa

Deck Layout
- Trampoline netting forward, rigid bridgedeck floor, trampoline seats
- Cockpit has netting seats port & starboard, access to hulls from deck hatches

Standard Accommodations
- The bridgedeck is an open design with a removeable shelter and access to the hulls
- The starboard hull has nav station aft, berth midships, berth or storage forward
- The port hull has small galley aft, double berth midships, berth or storage forward

Mechanical
- Tiller steering, transom-hung rudders
- Single outboard mounted in cockpit pod

DESCRIPTION

The Tiki 30 is the largest of the "Trailerable Coastal Trek" catamarans from Wharram Designs. Like the smaller Tiki 26 and 28, accommodations are modest yet serviceable, perfectly comfortable for coastal cruising. There's a simple galley that has a sliding seat for ease of cooking, a double berth midships and single berth or storage forward in each hull, and a pop-up flexible shelter over the bridgedeck that adds a convertible double berth and table seating. Production versions of the Tiki 30 have been produced in Zimbabwe and Germany, although none are being marketed at present. The Tiki 30 continues the Wharram tradition of simplicity and self-sufficiency. Eminently seaworthy, she features the familiar gaff-headed soft wingsail main, canoe-shaped hulls, and trampoline foredeck.

SPECIFICATIONS

Displacement	2,205 lbs, 1000 kg	
Standard Auxiliary	1 x 9.9 hp outboard	
Overall Length	30'0"	9.15 m
Waterline Length	25'5"	7.74 m
Bridgedeck Length	13'0"	3.96 m
Wing Deck Clearance		
Beam (max.)	16'4"	4.98 m
Draft (max.)	2'1"	0.64 m
Mast Hgt Off Deck	30'10"	9.40 m
Mast Hgt. Off Water	34'0"	10.40 m

SAIL AREA

Mainsail	234 sf	22 sm
Genoa	151 sf	15 sm
Total Area	385 sf	37 sm
Spinnaker	500 sf	45 sm

CAPACITY

Berths	1-2 sgls, 2-3 dbls
Staterooms	none
Heads	1 (portable)
Fuel	6 gal (portable)
Fresh Water	12 gal (portable)
Payload	2,205 lb, 1000 kg

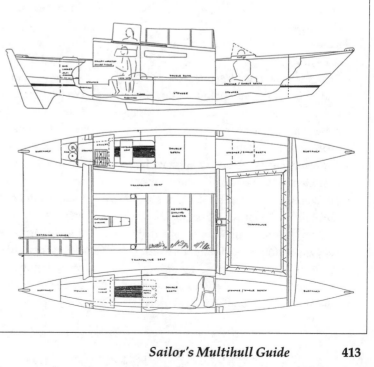

TIKI 38

GENERAL INFORMATION

Classification   Stock catamaran design, Cruiser

Cost of plans   £920

Designer   James Wharram, H. Boon

Designs   James Wharram Designs
Greenbank Rd., Devoran,
Truro, Cornwall TR3 6PJ
UK
Tel: (44) 1872 864792
Fax: (44) 1872 864792
email:

Year Introduced   1996

Number of boats built

N. American Stockists
T. Milano
PO Box 35177, Sarasota, FL 34242

Other Cruising Multihulls By Designer
A wide range of cruising catamarans including the complete Tiki series, the Pahi series, and other classic Wharram designs

KEY FEATURES

Hull & Sail Plan
- canoe-shaped hulls with integral fixed keels, outboard rudders on skegs
- Gaff-headed schooner rig, boomless soft-wing mainsails, roller-furling genoa

Deck Layout
- Trampoline netting forward, wooden bridgedeck floor, trampoline netting aft
- Cockpit with watch bunk and seats, engine boxes, hull access deck hatches

Standard Accommodations
- The bridgedeck is an open design with a protected helm and access to the hulls
- The starboard hull has head aft, berth midships, and cabin or workshop forward
- The port hull has galley aft, dinette that converts to double, and cabin forward

Mechanical
- Wheel steering, helm forward in cockpit
- Dual outboards mounted in cockpit pods

DESCRIPTION

The Tiki 38 design evolved from the vast experience James Wharram and his partner Hanneke Boon have accumulated over the past 12 years of selling the Tiki series of catamaran designs (over 1800 Tiki plans were sold for boats 26 to 36 feet). With their emphasis on function and simplicity, Wharram cats have been described as the Landrover or Jeep of multihulls. Now the Tiki 38 and her sistership the Tiki 46 bring an extra level of comfort to these fast, seaworthy, relatively inexpensive craft. The two soft wingsails set in schooner rig are easily handled and point 45 degrees off the true wind. Accommodations include two wide double berths midships, two single private cabins forward, and a watch berth in the cockpit with a protective steering pod. The Tiki 38 can comfortably cruise at 7 to 8 knots, with top speeds of 15 knots.

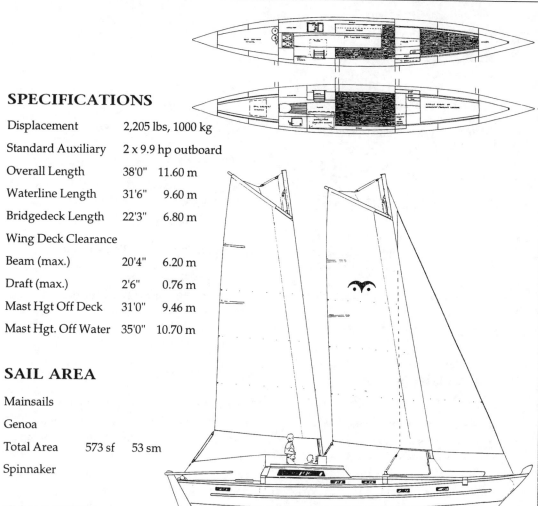

SPECIFICATIONS

Displacement	2,205 lbs, 1000 kg	
Standard Auxiliary	2 x 9.9 hp outboard	
Overall Length	38'0"	11.60 m
Waterline Length	31'6"	9.60 m
Bridgedeck Length	22'3"	6.80 m
Wing Deck Clearance		
Beam (max.)	20'4"	6.20 m
Draft (max.)	2'6"	0.76 m
Mast Hgt Off Deck	31'0"	9.46 m
Mast Hgt. Off Water	35'0"	10.70 m

SAIL AREA

Mainsails		
Genoa		
Total Area	573 sf	53 sm
Spinnaker		

CAPACITY

Berths	1-2 sgls, 2-3 dbls	
Staterooms	1-2	
Heads	1	
Fuel	6 gal (portable)	
Fresh Water	75 gal	340 ltr
Payload	3,500 lb, 1600 kg	

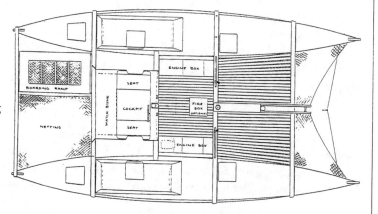

TIKI 46

GENERAL INFORMATION

Classification	Stock design catamaran, Cruiser
Cost of plans	£1,950
Designer	James Wharram, H. Boon
Designs	James Wharram Designs Greenbank Rd., Devoran, Truro, Cornwall TR3 6PJ UK Tel: (44) 1872 864792 Fax: (44) 1872 864792 email:

Year Introduced   **1997**

Number of boats built

N. American Stockists
  T. Milano
  PO Box 35177, Sarasota, FL 34242

Other Cruising Multihulls By Designer
  A wide range of cruising catamarans including the complete Tiki series, the Pahi series, and other classic Wharram designs

KEY FEATURES

Hull & Sail Plan
- canoe-shaped hulls with integral fixed keels, outboard rudders on skegs
- Gaff-headed schooner rig, boomless soft-wing mainsails, roller-furling genoa

Deck Layout
- Trampoline netting forward, rigid bridgedeck floor, net for dinghy storage aft
- Large open bridgedeck with engine boxes midships, ample cockpit seating under pod

Standard Accommodations
- The bridgedeck is an open design with a cockpit shelter and access to the hulls
- The starboard hull has a double cabin aft, galley & dinette midships, head forward
- The port hull has double cabins fore & aft, head with shower midships, storage

Mechanical
- Wheel steering, protected helm in cockpit
- Dual outboards mounted in cockpit pods

DESCRIPTION

The largest in the Tiki design series from James Wharram Designs, the Tiki 46 offers the extra comforts sailors look for in ocean-going cruisers. All the usual Wharram design features are present: the classic gaff-headed schooner rig with soft wingsails, trampoline netting fore and aft, wide open bridgedeck, and separately accessed canoe-shaped hulls. And Wharram's design criteria remain the same: freedom from capsize, structural strength, ease of building, and traditional styling. But this design features proper steering protection, a full-size galley with standing headroom and adjacent relaxation platform or dinette area, three full staterooms with double berths and storage, optional double berths near the galley and in the cockpit, and two separate head compartments with showers. This layout may prove to be Wharram's most popular Tiki design.

SPECIFICATIONS

Displacement	10,000 lbs, 4500 kg	
Standard Auxiliary	2 x 9.9 hp outboard	
Overall Length	46'0"	14.00 m
Waterline Length	38'1"	11.60 m
Bridgedeck Length	29'0"	8.84 m
Wing Deck Clearance		
Beam (max.)	24'0"	7.30 m
Draft (max.)	3'0"	0.90 m
Mast Hgt Off Deck	38'0"	11.60 m
Mast Hgt. Off Water	42'9"	13.09 m

SAIL AREA

Mainsails		
Genoa		
Total Area	880 sf	82 sm
Spinnaker		

CAPACITY

Berths	3-5 doubles
Staterooms	3
Heads	2
Fuel	variable
Fresh Water	variable
Payload	3000-4000 kg

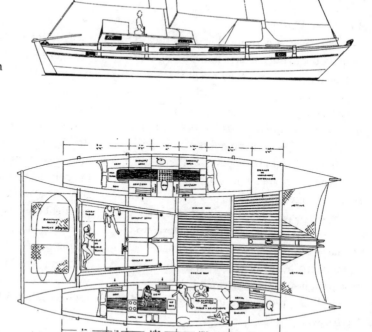

VOYAGER 45

GENERAL INFORMATION

Classification   Stock catamaran design, Cruiser/racer

Approx. Cost   US $425,000 (estimate)

Designer   Chris White

Designs   Chris White Designs
5 Smith's Way
S. Dartmouth, MA 02748
USA
Tel: (508) 636-6111
Fax: (508) 636-6110
email: cwdesign@ma.ultranet.com

Year introduced   1995

Number of boats built   3 (as of Sep 97)

N. American Stockists   Buy plans direct

Other Cruising Multihulls By Designer
   Atlantic 42 (see pages 242-243),
Hammerhead 54 Tri (see pages 444-445),
Hammerhead 34 Tri (available late 1997),
other cruising designs

KEY FEATURES

Hull & Sail Plan
- integral keels plus retracting daggerboard in starboard hull, reverse transoms w/steps
- Fractional sloop rig, fully roached main, roller-furling genoa

Deck Layout
- Trampoline forward, rigid foredeck just aft, wide decks, good hand holds
- Aft cockpit with U-shaped seats, ample lockers, helm station forward to port

Standard Accommodations
- The bridgedeck has nav area and wet locker/storage aft, seating/table forward
- Starboard hull–stateroom aft, storage midships, head/single stateroom forward
- Port hull–stateroom aft, long galley midships, head/single stateroom forward

Mechanical
- Wheel steering, helm forward in cockpit
- Dual inboards, access from aft deck

DESCRIPTION

From the design board of well respected yacht designer Chris White comes the Voyager 45, a high-performance, elegant cruising catamaran. This sleek yet powerful cat has a slim, efficient hull shape that is essential for high speed and maneuverability. Constructed of epoxy-composite with cedar strip hulls, foam-cored decks, and carbon-fiber cross beams, the Voyager 45 is lighter than other fiberglass cruising cats of equal size. Windward work and tacking ability are excellent through the use of fixed keels and a retracting daggerboard in the starboard hull. The accommodations are well conceived, with four separate staterooms, plenty of locker and work space, and good visibility from the saloon cabin windows. The large cockpit has a table to starboard. She is a livable ocean cruiser that doesn't sacrifice performance.

SPECIFICATIONS

Displacement	15,500 lbs, 7037 kg	
Standard Auxiliary	2 x 27 hp inboard	
Overall Length	44'8"	13.62 m
Waterline Length	43'0"	13.12 m
Bridgedeck Length	24'5"	7.50 m
Wing Deck Clearance	2'0"	0.61 m
Beam (max.)	23'4"	7.12 m
Draft (min.)	3'0"	0.92 m
Draft (board down)	7'9"	2.36 m
Mast Hgt. Off Water	63'0"	19.22 m

SAIL AREA

Mainsail	630 sf	59 sm
Genoa	340 sf	32 sm
Total Area	970 sf	91 sm
Spinnaker	1250 sf	116 sm

CAPACITY

Berths	2-3 sgls, 2 dbls	
Staterooms	4	
Heads	2	
Fuel	45 gal	170 ltr
Fresh Water	50 gal	189 ltr
Payload		

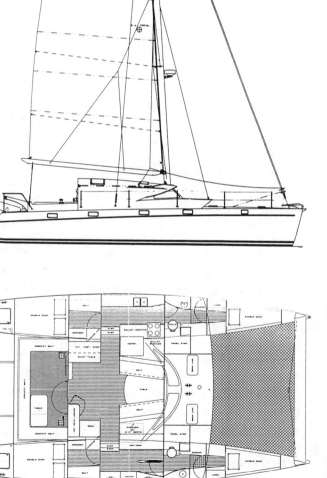

FLICKA 30

GENERAL INFORMATION

Classification   Stock catamaran design, Cruiser

Cost of plans   Call for current price

Designer   Richard & Lilian Woods

Designs   Woods Designs
6 Elm Park, Southdown,
Milbrook, Torpoint,
Cornwall, PL10 1HD UK
Tel: (44) 752 823301
Fax:
email:

Year introduced

Number of boats built

N. American Stockists
Purchase plans from Woods Designs

Other Cruising Multihulls By Designer
Savannah 26; Woods 30 series: Symphony, Sagitta, Scorpio; Flica series; Woods 35 series: Mira, Scylla, Banshee; Nimbus 40; others

KEY FEATURES

Hull & Sail Plan
- U-shaped or hard-chine hulls, fixed keels, reverse transoms
- Fractional sloop rig, standard main, roller-furling genoa

Deck Layout
- Small trampoline netting forward, rigid deck just aft with lockers
- Aft cockpit with seating to port & starboard, storage under, large locker to starboard

Standard Accommodations
- The bridgedeck has a wet locker aft and comfortable lounge with table forward
- Starboard hull–head aft, nav area midships, double cabin with vanity and sink forward
- Port hull–double berth aft, galley midships, double cabin with vanity and sink forward

Mechanical
- Tiller steering, inboard skeg-hung rudders
- Dual inboards, access from aft cabins

DESCRIPTION

Purely a cruising boat, the Flica 30 is fast, weatherly and seaworthy. A moderate beam, fractional rig, low aspect ratio keels and easily handled sails make her stable and manageable for a single-handed novice or family with small children. Designed for the homebuilder, she can be made using either hard chine plywood or flat panel GRP hulls. Accommodations include three separate double cabins with full standing headroom in the hulls, a large galley and head, and light, airy saloon cabin with adequate seating and all-round vision. Wing deck clearance is reputed to be marginal on this otherwise well-designed craft. Modifications could be discussed with the designer to improve this condition. Modest in size, this is one of the more affordable options for a family bluewater cruiser.

SPECIFICATIONS

Displacement	5,952 lbs, 2700 kg	
Standard Auxiliary	2 x 9.9 hp inboard	
Overall Length	29'10"	9.10 m
Waterline Length	26'11"	8.20 m
Bridgedeck Length	22'4"	6.81 m
Wing Deck Clearance		
Beam (max.)	16'4"	4.98 m
Draft (min.)	2'11"	0.90 m
Mast Hgt Off Deck		
Mast Hgt. Off Water	41'0"	12.51 m

SAIL AREA

Mainsail	199 sf	19 sm
Genoa	215 sf	20 sm
Total Area	414 sf	39 sm
Spinnaker	646 sf	60 sm

CAPACITY

Berths	3 doubles
Staterooms	2
Heads	1
Fuel	variable
Fresh Water	variable
Payload	1,764 lbs, 800 kg

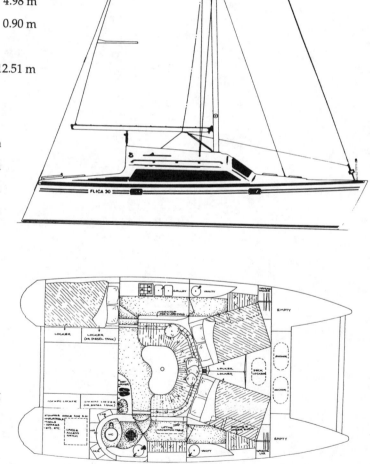

Stock
Trimaran
Designs

FARRIER F-36

GENERAL INFORMATION

Classification   Stock trimaran design, Cruiser/racer

Approx. Cost   Call for current price

Designer   Ian Farrier

Designs   Farrier Marine
PO Box 40675
Bellevue, WA 98015-4675
USA
Tel: (206) 957-1903
Fax: (206) 957-1915
www.farriermarine.com

Year introduced

Number of boat built

N. American Stockists   Buy plans direct

Other Cruising Multihulls By Designer
The F-25 and the Corsair Marine series of sport triamarans including the F-24, the former F-27 and current F-28, and the F-31

KEY FEATURES

Hull & Sail Plan
- Main hull with demountable or folding amas, daggerboard, built-in buoyancy
- Fractional sloop rig, fully battened main, roller-furling jib, spinnaker on bowsprit

Deck Layout
- Sleek main hull design, trampolines between main hull and amas
- Protected center cockpit with U-shaped seats, ample lockers, helm midships

Standard Accommodations
- Main hull aft—double stateroom (2 sgle or 1 double), passageway from main cabin
- Main hull midships—full galley, wet locker, nav area, dinette/double berth, settee
- Main hull forward–storage, private head with shower, double V-berth

Mechanical
- Wheel steering, helm midships in cockpit
- Single inboard, access from main cabin

DESCRIPTION

The F-36 was designed to provide a large, offshore cruiser that still has the capability of being demounted and trailered. The fractional rig is efficient and easy to sail, with all halyards and controls in the cockpit. A self-tacking jib is optional with the centerboard version and the boom can be roller-furling. This conservative rig, coupled with the F-36's excellent righting moment, makes her a safe cruising boat. Standard layout has room for six to eight adults with standing headroom throughout. A galley, chart table, wet locker and dinette seating for five that converts to a double berth are all located in the saloon cabin, while forward is a private head with shower and double berth cabin. Optional layouts include an aft cabin, a pilothouse providing an all weather passage between the two cabins, and an aft cockpit version for more space in the main cabin.

SPECIFICATIONS

Displacement	6,500 lbs, 2950 kg	
Standard Auxiliary	1 x 20-30 hp inboard	
Overall Length	36'10"	11.20 m
Waterline Length	35'8"	10.88 m
Beam (max.)	26'1"	7.95 m
Beam (trailered)	10'0"	3.05 m
Draft (board up)	1'8"	0.50 m
Draft (board down)	6'9"	2.07 m
Mast Hgt. Off Deck	49'0"	14.94 m

SAIL AREA

Mainsail	552 sf	51 sm
Jib	286 sf	27 sm
Total Area	838 sf	78 sm
Spinnaker		

CAPACITY

Berths	2-4 sgls, 2-3 dbls
Staterooms	2
Heads	1
Fuel	variable
Fresh Water	variable
Payload	

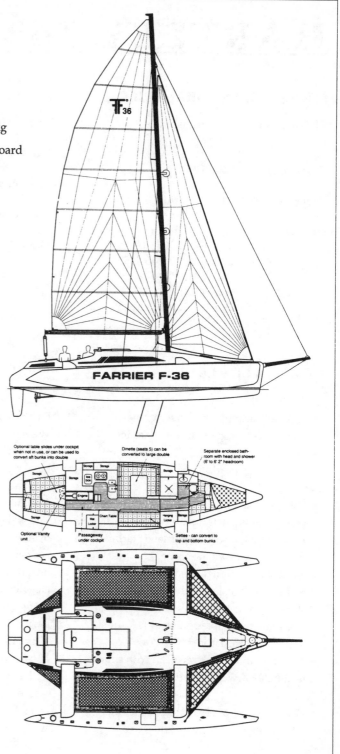

HARTLEY 363

GENERAL INFORMATION

Classification   Stock trimaran design,
Cruiser

Cost of plans   US $890

Designer   Allan J. Hartley

Designs   Hartley Trimaran Designs
3354 Helton Hartley Pl.
Lenoir, NC 28645 USA
Tel: (704) 758-7426
Fax: (704) 754-7255
email: AJHARTLEY@twave.net

Year Design Introduced

Number of plans sold

N. American Stockists   Buy plans direct

Other Cruising Multihulls By Designer
   Other cruising trimaran designs include 30,
34, and 38 foot models

KEY FEATURES

Hull & Sail Plan
- Hulls are strip planking over frames, pivoting centerboard, kick-up rudder
- Masthead sloop rig, fully battened main, roller-furling headsail

Deck Layout
- Full rigid deck midships between the main hull and amas, netting fore and aft
- Aft cockpit has seating port and starboard, storage lockers and lazarette

Standard Accommodations
- Main hull aft–galley with double sink and stove to port, refrig., instrument console
- Main hull midships–double berths and lockers outboard, dinette between
- Main hull forward–large head with shower leading to forward V-berth

Mechanical
- Tiller steering, outboard kick-up rudder
- Inboard engine under cockpit

DESCRIPTION

The 363 is a new design from Allan Hartley. His trimarans are true cruisers, with good average cruising speeds but no pretense of high performance on the race course. The 363 has a rigid deck midships between the main hull and amas, creating added interior accommodations and exterior storage space. The wide decks have no obstructions to trip over when maneuvering above. The kick-up rudder and centerboard design makes the boat beachable for exploring ashore or cleaning the bottom. Water, fuel and load carrying capacity have been thoughtfully designed for long-distance cruising. Ventilation is provided by standard deck hatches combined with underwing vents, both of which can be fully closed in cold weather. Headroom throughout the main cabin is 6'4". The cockpit seats are long and wide enough to serve as extra berths.

SPECIFICATIONS

Displacement	7,044 lbs, 3198 kg	
Standard Auxiliary	1 x 18-27 hp inboard	
Overall Length	36'0"	10.98 m
Waterline Length	33'6"	10.22 m
Beam (max.)	21'0"	6.41 m
Draft (board up)	2'0"	0.61 m
Draft (board down)	8'4"	2.54 m
Mast Hgt. Off Deck	43'9"	13.34 m
Mast Hgt. Off Water	49'9"	15.17 m

SAIL AREA

Mainsail	310 sf	29 sm
Jib	250 sf	23 sm
Total Area	560 sf	52 sm
Spinnaker		

CAPACITY

Berths	0-1 sgle, 2-3 dbls
Staterooms	1
Heads	1
Fuel	50 gal 189 ltr
Fresh Water	80 gal 303 ltr
Payload	2,950 lbs, 1340 kg

HARTLEY 381

GENERAL INFORMATION

Classification   Stock trimaran design, Cruiser

Cost of plans   US $970

Designer   Allan J. Hartley

Designs   Hartley Trimaran Designs
3354 Helton Hartley Pl.
Lenoir, NC 28645 USA
Tel: (704) 758-7426
Fax: (704) 754-7255
email: AJHARTLEY@twave.net

Year Design Introduced

Number of plans sold

N. American Stockists   Buy plans direct

Other Cruising Multihulls By Designer
Other cruising trimaran designs include 30, 34, and 36 foot models

KEY FEATURES

Hull & Sail Plan
- Hulls are strip planking over frames, pivoting centerboard, kick-up rudder
- Masthead sloop rig, fully battened main, roller-furling headsail

Deck Layout
- Full rigid deck midships between the main hull and amas, netting fore and aft
- Aft cockpit has seating port and starboard, storage lockers and lazarette

Standard Accommodations
- Main hull aft–galley with double sink and stove to port, refrig., instrument console
- Main hull midships–double berths and lockers outboard, dinette between
- Main hull forward–large head with shower leading to forward V-berth

Mechanical
- Tiller steering, outboard kick-up rudder
- Inboard engine under cockpit

DESCRIPTION

The 381 is the sistership to the 363 design from Allan Hartley. As with all Hartley designs, this boat has good average cruising speeds that should satisfy the cruiser's quest for fast passages. The 381 also has a rigid deck midships between the main hull and amas and trampoline netting fore and aft. There is an extra 18 inches of beam over the 363 design, making the outboard double berths in the main cabin more comfortable. The wide decks have no obstructions to trip over when maneuvering above. The kick-up rudder and centerboard design makes the boat beachable for exploring ashore or cleaning the bottom. The ample water, fuel and load carrying capacity illustrates the boat's intention for long-distance cruising. Headroom throughout the main cabin is 6'4". The cockpit seats are long and wide enough to serve as extra berths.

SPECIFICATIONS

Displacement	7,655 lbs, 3475 kg	
Standard Auxiliary	1 x 27 hp inboard	
Overall Length	38'0"	11.59 m
Waterline Length	35'6"	10.83 m
Beam (max.)	22'6"	6.86 m
Draft (board up)	2'0"	0.61 m
Draft (board down)	8'6"	2.59 m
Mast Hgt. Off Deck	44'0"	13.42 m
Mast Hgt. Off WL	50'0"	15.25 m

SAIL AREA

Mainsail	330 sf	31 sm
Jib	280 sf	26 sm
Total Area	600 sf	57 sm
Spinnaker		

CAPACITY

Berths	3 doubles	
Staterooms	1	
Heads	1	
Fuel	50 gal	189 ltr
Fresh Water	100 gal	378 ltr
Payload	3,330 lbs, 1512 kg	

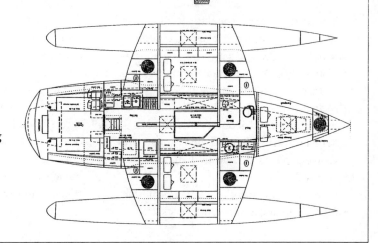

TRI-STAR 38-39 Tri

GENERAL INFORMATION

Classification   Stock trimaran designs, Cruiser

Cost of plans   Call for current price

Designer   Ed Horstman

Designs   Tri-Star Tris/Cats
PO Box 286
Venice, CA 90294 USA
Tel: (310) 396-6154
Fax:
email:

Year Design Introduced

Number of boats built

N. American Stockists   Buy plans direct

Other Cruising Multihulls By Designer
   A complete line of Tri-Star cruising and cruising/racing trimarans and catamarans

KEY FEATURES

Hull & Sail Plan
• Round section main hull with flared bow and reverse transom, daggerboards in amas
• Fractional sloop or yawl rig, self-tending club-footed jib, roller furling genoa

Deck Layout
• Full rigid main deck and side decks between the main hull and amas
• Sheltered center cockpit with hardtop over, private aft cabin accessible from cockpit

Standard Accommodations
• Main hull aft–aft stateroom with double berth, desk, seat, hanging locker
• Main hull midships–galley aft, storage, two sitting areas, double berths outboard
• Main hull forward–head compartment with shower, lockers, double berth in forepeak

Mechanical
• Wheel steering in cockpit, inboard rudder
• Inboard engine located under cockpit

DESCRIPTION

The Horstman Tri-Star 38-39 is a versatile design that can be built as either a 38 foot standard yacht or a 39 foot custom version similar to the Casanovas' boat that was the first trimaran to round Cape Horn (the extra one foot added to the length gives a larger aft cabin). She can be aptly described as a boat with good performance and spacious accommodations at an affordable price. The rounded hull shape and flared bows give ample reserve buoyancy, while the high bow height and flush decks make her a safe, comfortable ocean cruiser. Unlike many trimaran designs, this boat allows for accommodations in the wing deck areas. This design has been proven in serious offshore cruising situations. She's a good choice for owner-builders who want a seaworthy craft that is reasonably easy to construct.

SPECIFICATIONS

Displacement	9,000 lbs, 4082 kg	
Standard Auxiliary	1 x 18-30 hp inboard	
Overall Length	38'6"	11.73 m
Waterline Length	34'4"	10.47 m
Beam (max.)	22'4"	6.81 m
Draft (board up)	2'3"	0.69 m
Draft (board down)	4'0"	1.22 m
Mast Hgt. Off Deck		
Mast Hgt. Off Water		

SAIL AREA

Mainsail		
Jib		
Total Area	841 sf	78 sm
Spinnaker		

CAPACITY

Berths	3-4 doubles	
Staterooms	3	
Heads	1	
Fuel	35 gal	132 ltr
Fresh Water	60 gal	227 ltr
Payload	4,200 lbs, 1905 kg	

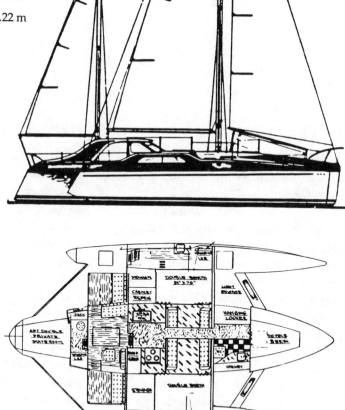

HUGHES 37C Tri

GENERAL INFORMATION

Classification   Stock trimaran design, Cruiser/racer

Cost of plans   US $2,000

Designer   Kurt Hughes

Designs   K. Hughes Sailing Designs
612-1/2 West McGraw St.
Seattle, WA 98119 USA
Tel: (206) 284-6436
Fax: (206) 283-4106
email: khughes@isomedia.com

Year Design Introduced   1995

Number of plans sold   (as of Sep 97)

N. American Stockists   Buy plans direct

Other Cruising Multihulls By Designer
Over 75 other multihull designs from 12 to 79 feet

KEY FEATURES

Hull & Sail Plan
- Round section flared main hull, large amas, wide beam, daggerboard
- Fractional sloop rig, fully battened main, furling headsails, spinnaker on bowsprit

Deck Layout
- Full rigid main deck with netting between the main hull and amas
- Center cockpit is protected but with good visibility, U-shaped seating with lockers

Standard Accommodations
- Main hull aft–double berth with storage compartments and lockers
- Main hull midships–full galley aft, dinette to port, double berth to starboard
- Main hull forward–comfortable double V-berth, head compartment, nav station

Mechanical
- Tiller steering, outboard rudder
- Transom-hung outboard

DESCRIPTION

The 37C trimaran from the office of Kurt Hughes Sailing Designs is a high-performance cruising boat with great accommodations for long-distance cruising. Construction of the hulls and connectives is of unidirectional or triaxial roving on pvc foam using epoxy resin. The main hull has a skinny waterline but flares up above waterline to give inside room where it is needed. It is intended to be easily driven but still carry the weight. The amas are very big (200%+) and the wide beam gives maximum righting moment. The interior has $2\text{-}1/2$ staterooms, each with a double berth, cabinets and other storage. There is a private head with shower, a galley with stove, double sink and refrigeration, and a main saloon with dining area and lounge seating for five. An outboard engine is preferred, but space is available for an inboard under the cockpit.

SPECIFICATIONS

Displacement	6,810 lbs, 3089 kg	
Standard Auxiliary	outboard or inboard	
Overall Length	37'9"	11.54 m
Waterline Length	37'4"	11.38 m
Beam (max.)	31'9"	9.68 m
Draft (board up)	1'8"	0.51 m
Draft (board down)	8'4"	2.54 m
Mast Hgt. Off Deck	49'3"	15.02 m
Mast Hgt. Off Water	54'8"	16.63 m

SAIL AREA

Mainsail	568 sf	56 sm
Jib	197 sf	18 sm
Total Area	765 sf	74 sm
Spinnaker	875 sf	81 sm

CAPACITY

Berths	3 doubles
Staterooms	$2\text{-}1/2$
Heads	1
Fuel	20 gal (variable)
Fresh Water	35 gal (variable)
Payload	2,835 lbs, 1286 kg

SEARUNNER 34

GENERAL INFORMATION

Classification   Stock trimaran design,
Cruiser

Cost of plans   US $600
($40,000 material estimate)

Designer   Jim Brown, John Marples

Designs   John R. Marples
Multihull Designs
PO Box 1437, St. Augustine,
FL 32085 USA
Tel: (904) 824-2688
Fax: (904) 824-2688
email:

Year Design Introduced   1975

Number of plans sold   115   (as of Sep 97)

N. American Stockists   Buy plans direct

Other Cruising Multihulls By Designer
   A wide range of cruising catamaran and
trimaran designs, including the Constant
Camber™, the Searunner (in partnership with
Jim Brown), and the Seaclipper series

KEY FEATURES

Hull & Sail Plan
- wood/wood-epoxy hulls, fine entry bows,
  fin keel centerboard, built-in buoyancy
- Masthead cutter rig (sloop rig opt'l),
  standard mainsail, roller furling headsails

Deck Layout
- Full rigid main deck and side decks
  between the main hull and amas
- Sheltered center cockpit with cabin areas
  forward & aft, storage in amas and cockpit

Standard Accommodations
- Main hull aft–aft cabin has dinette with
  seats, galley and storage areas forward
- Main hull midships–center cockpit with
  access hatches to fore and aft cabins
- Main hull forward–comfortable double
  berth and single berth, head compartment

Mechanical
- Wheel steering, outboard skeg-hung rudder
- Inboard engine located under cockpit

DESCRIPTION

The Searunner 34 trimaran, co-designed by
Jim Brown and John Marples, is a relatively
new addition to perhaps the most popular
series of home-built cruising multihulls of all
time. Fast, seaworthy, spacious, and
manageable, she is still popular with those
wanting an affordable, dependable cruising
trimaran. Every inch a family cruiser, the
Searunner 34 features a cutter rig, well-
protected center cockpit, aft saloon cabin with
dinette, galley and roll-up single berth,
comfortable forward berths that extend
toward the amas, easy sail handling, and
enough storage capacity to meet the needs of
any extended cruise. The centerboard, fine
entry bow & amas give good windward
performance on this safe, speedy yacht. Jim
Brown and John Marples offer other
Searunner tris and their new line of
Searunner cats for family cruising or charter.

SPECIFICATIONS

Displacement	8,000 lbs, 3629 kg	
Standard Auxiliary	1 x 25 hp inboard	
Overall Length	34'4"	10.46 m
Waterline Length	30'3"	9.22 m
Beam (max.)	20'11"	6.39 m
Draft (board up)	2'10"	0.85 m
Draft (board down)	6'5"	1.97 m
Mast Hgt. Off Deck	44'6"	13.60 m
Mast Hgt. Off Water	46'9"	14.20 m

SAIL AREA

Mainsail	215 sf	20 sm
Jib	329 sf	31 sm
Total Area	537 sf	51 sm
Spinnaker	1100 sf	102 sm

CAPACITY

Berths	2 sgls, 1 dble	
Staterooms	1	
Heads	1	
Fuel	40 gal	152 ltr
Fresh Water	40 gal	152 ltr
Payload	2,000 lbs, 907 kg	

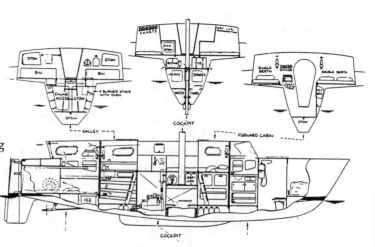

CONSTANT CAMBER T35

GENERAL INFORMATION

Classification   Stock trimaran design,
                      Cruiser

Cost of plans   US $900
                      ($40,000 material estimate)

Designer   John Marples

Designs   John R. Marples
                      Multihull Designs
                      PO Box 1437, St. Augustine,
                      FL 32085 USA
                      Tel: (904) 824-2688
                      Fax: (904) 824-2688
                      email:

Year Design Introduced   1983

Number of plans sold   17   (as of Sep 97)

N. American Stockists   Buy plans direct

Other Cruising Multihulls By Designer
   A wide range of cruising catamaran and
trimaran designs, including the Constant
Camber™, the Searunner (in partnership with
Jim Brown), and the Seaclipper series

KEY FEATURES

Hull & Sail Plan
- wood-epoxy hulls, retracting centerboard,
  built-in buoyancy
- Fractional sloop rig, standard mainsail with
  reef points, inner stay, opt'l furling jib

Deck Layout
- Combination of rigid deck and trampoline
  netting between the main hull and amas
- Sheltered center cockpit with cabin areas
  forward & aft, storage in amas and cockpit

Standard Accommodations
- Main hull aft–aft cabin has dinette with
  seats, galley and storage areas forward
- Main hull midships–center cockpit with
  access hatches to fore and aft cabins
- Main hull forward–comfortable double
  berth and single berth, head compartment

Mechanical
- Wheel steering, outboard skeg-hung rudder
- Inboard engine located under cockpit

DESCRIPTION

A true bluewater cruiser, the Constant
Camber T35 was designed to satisfy the needs
of the self-sufficient sailor. Combining
simplicity and efficiency with speed and
comfort, she represents an ocean-going family
cruiser, one that John Marples calls his perfect
boat. As her name implies, construction
utilizes the patented Constant Camber™
system, a revolutionary labor-saving
technique that even home-builders find easy
to use. The result is a strong boat that sails
well while carrying a full cruising load.
Accommodations are ideal for a couple or
small family. They include an aft cabin with
dinette, galley, and convertible berth, a center
cockpit with access to the fore & aft cabins,
comfortable berths midships, and head and
storage compartments forward. Aft cockpit
and new "Swing-Wing" versions are also
available.

SPECIFICATIONS

Displacement	7,200 lbs, 3266 kg	
Standard Auxiliary	1 x 8-12 hp inboard	
Overall Length	35'0"	10.67 m
Waterline Length	32'9"	9.98 m
Beam (max.)	22'0"	6.71 m
Draft (board up)	2'5"	0.75 m
Draft (board down)	5'8"	1.73 m
Mast Hgt. Off Deck	40'0"	12.19 m
Mast Hgt. Off Water	45'6"	13.87 m

SAIL AREA

Mainsail	240 sf	22 sm
Jib	390 sf	36 sm
Total Area	630 sf	58 sm
Spinnaker	950 sf	88 sm

CAPACITY

Berths	2 sgls, 1 dble
Staterooms	1
Heads	1
Fuel	20 gal 76 ltr
Fresh Water	50 gal 189 ltr
Payload	2,000 lbs, 907 kg

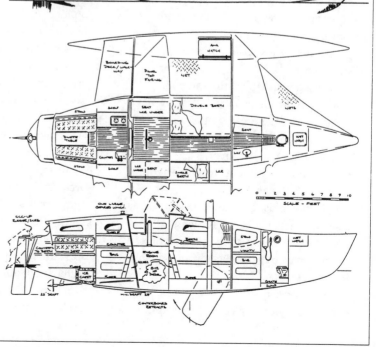

SEACLIPPER 41

GENERAL INFORMATION

Classification   Cruiser

Cost of plans   US $1,000
($40,000 material estimate)

Designer   John Marples

Designs   John R. Marples
Multihull Designs
PO Box 1437, St. Augustine,
FL 32085 USA
Tel: (904) 824-2688
Fax: (904) 824-2688
email:

Year Design Introduced   1982

Number of plans sold   9 (as of Sep 97)

N. American Stockists   Buy plans direct

Other Cruising Multihulls By Designer
A wide range of cruising catamaran and
trimaran designs, including the Constant
Camber™, the Searunner (in partnership with
Jim Brown), and the Seaclipper series

KEY FEATURES

Hull & Sail Plan
- wood-epoxy hulls, single-chine main hull,
  V-shaped amas, kick-up centerboard
- Fractional cutter rig, standard mainsail,
  roller furling headsails optional

Deck Layout
- Full rigid main deck with trampoline
  netting between the main hull and amas
- Sheltered center cockpit with cabin areas
  forward & aft, storage in amas and cockpit

Standard Accommodations
- Main hull aft–aft cabin has single berth,
  seat, and storage areas
- Main hull midships–center cockpit, galley
  and navigation area just forward
- Main hull forward–folding table with seats
  that convert to berths, head, double cabin

Mechanical
- Wheel steering, outboard skeg-hung rudder
- Inboard engine located under cockpit

DESCRIPTION

The Seaclipper 41 is an economy cruising
trimaran intended primarily for the homebuilder. Both design and construction
techniques have been kept as simple as
possible, with V-section amas, a single-chine
main hull, flush deck, and wood or wood/
epoxy construction. Sea-kindly and fast, she
performs well to windward, aided by the
efficient kick-up centerboard design.
Accommodations are functional yet
comfortable, with a private single-berth aft
cabin and a large main cabin and forepeak
area capable of sleeping four in two
convertible single berths and one double V-
berth. This design also features a large chart
and navigation area opposite the galley just
forward of the cockpit. Optional wing berths
outboard of the main hull are available. The
Seaclipper 41 continues the Brown/Marples
tradition of affordable, easy-to-build cruisers.

SPECIFICATIONS

Displacement	12,500 lbs, 5670 kg	
Standard Auxiliary	1 x 25 hp inboard	
Overall Length	41'9"	12.70 m
Waterline Length	39'3"	11.96 m
Beam (max.)	27'2"	8.30 m
Draft (board up)	3'3"	1.00 m
Draft (board down)	5'11"	1.81 m
Mast Hgt. Off Deck	50'0"	15.25 m
Mast Hgt. Off Water	56'6"	17.22 m

SAIL AREA

Mainsail	400 sf	37 sm
Jib	550 sf	51 sm
Total Area	950 sf	88 sm
Spinnaker	1260 sf	117 sm

CAPACITY

Berths	3 sgls, 1 dble	
Staterooms	2	
Heads	1	
Fuel	40 gal	152 ltr
Fresh Water	50 gal	190 ltr
Payload	3,500 lbs, 1588 kg	

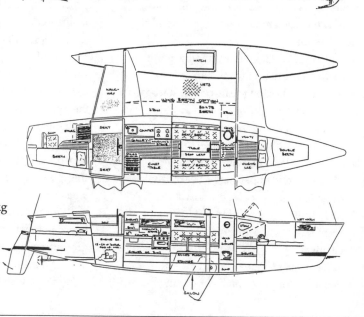

ECHO 36

GENERAL INFORMATION

Classification   Cruiser/racer

Cost of Plans   US $2,400

Designer   Dick Newick

Designs   Dick Newick
5 Sheppards Way
Kittery Point, ME 03905
USA
Tel: (207) 439-3768
Fax: (207) 439-8591
email: dnewick@gwi.net

Year Design Introduced

Number of Boats Built

N. American Stockists   Buy plans direct

Other Cruising Multihulls By Designer
  A wide range of fast cruising trimaran designs and a 44 foot charter catamaran design

KEY FEATURES

Hull & Sail Plan
- Strip-planked hulls (Core-Cell, Durakore, or cedar) with glass, Kevlar or carbon fiber
- Fractional sloop rig, rotating wing mast, fully battened main, furling jib, bowsprit

Deck Layout
- Rigid main deck with trampoline netting between the main hull and amas
- Aft cockpit has long seats port & starboard, storage lockers, aft sloping deck

Standard Accommodations
- Main hull aft–seat and galley to starboard, folding table, single berths outboard
- Main hull midships–daggerboard trunk by galley, large lockers outboard
- Main hull forward–V-berth with low headroom and storage areas

Mechanical
- Tiller steering, inboard rudder
- Outboard engine behind connecting beam

DESCRIPTION

Echo is a 36 foot high-performance cruising trimaran from well-respected multihull designer Dick Newick. His racing and cruising trimarans are fast and uniquely sculptured. Echo is the younger sister to Newick's 1970 Tricia design. She is a cruiser capable of high speeds, yet she can easily be single-handed since all sail controls lead to the cockpit. As with most Newick designs, the interior layout is Spartan yet comfortable, with the cruising emphasis on fast, safe passages. The accommodations can be expanded by using the long cockpit seats or trampoline netting as extra berths in fair weather. Other features include a 19 inch draft for beaching, a "crash box" abaft the board in the trunk to prevent serious grounding damage, and kick-up rudders. Echo is a good choice for owner-builders who enjoy fast cruising with simple luxuries.

SPECIFICATIONS

Displacement	5,600 lbs, 2542 kg
Standard Auxiliary	1 x 10 hp outboard
Overall Length	36'6" 11.13 m
Waterline Length	35'10" 10.95 m
Beam (max.)	30'0" 9.15 m
Draft (board up)	1'9" 0.53 m
Draft (board down)	7'9" 2.36 m
Mast Hgt. Off Deck	
Mast Hgt. Off Water	48'8" 14.84 m

SAIL AREA

Wing Mast		
Mainsail		
Jib		
Total Area	660 sf	61 sm
Spinnaker		

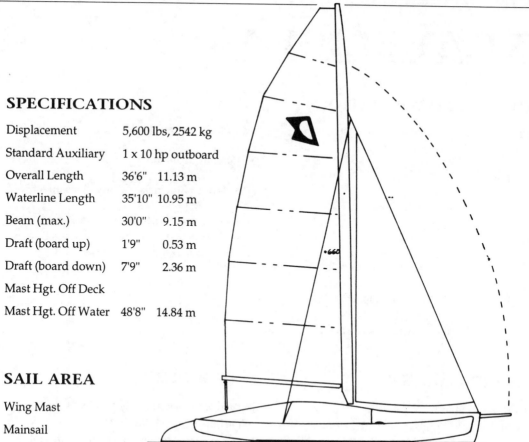

CAPACITY

Berths	2 sgls, 1 dble
Staterooms	none
Heads	1 (portable)
Fuel	variable
Fresh Water	variable
Payload	

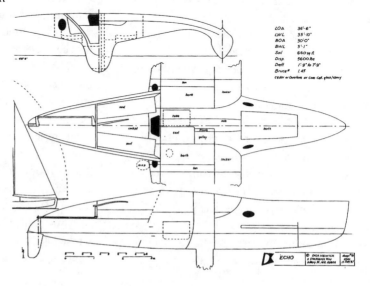

LOA	36'-6"
LWL	35'-10"
BOA	30'0"
BWL	3'-1"
Sail	660 sq ft.
Disp.	5600 lbs
Draft	1'9" to 7'9"
Bruce #	1.45

Cedar or Duraleare or Cons.-Cell. glass/epoxy

ECHO   © DICK NEWICK

TRAVELER 48

GENERAL INFORMATION

Classification   Stock trimaran design, Cruiser/racer

Cost of Plans   US $6,000

Designer   Dick Newick

Designs   Dick Newick
5 Sheppards Way
Kittery Point, ME 03905
USA
Tel: (207) 439-3768
Fax: (207) 439-8591
email: dnewick@gwi.net

Year Design Introduced

Number of Boats Built

N. American Stockists   Buy plans direct

Other Cruising Multihulls By Designer
A wide range of fast cruising trimaran designs and a 44 foot charter catamaran design

KEY FEATURES

Hull & Sail Plan
- Strip-planked hulls (Core-Cell, Durakore, or cedar) with glass, Kevlar or carbon fiber
- Fractional sloop rig, rotating wing mast, fully battened main, furling jib, bowsprit

Deck Layout
- Wide connecting beams, trampoline netting between the main hull and amas
- Aft cockpit has long seats port & starboard, storage lockers, short aft deck

Standard Accommodations
- Main hull aft–small head, lockers, settees with folding table, single berths outboard
- Main hull midships–ice box, galley, trunk for daggerboard, nav & instrument area
- Main hull forward–head with shower, seat and lockers, large double berth

Mechanical
- Tiller steering, inboard kick-up rudder
- Inboard engine under cockpit

DESCRIPTION

Named after General Robert E. Lee's big white horse, Traveler is a strong, seaworthy, high-performance trimaran from the design board of well-respected multihull designer Dick Newick. Emphasis is on speed, sea-kindliness, and simplicity. Dick feels things such as easy motion, low stress sailing and short passages are regarded as the true luxuries of cruising. Averaging speeds of 12-16 knots, she still maintains a high strength-to-weight ratio which allows her to carry a normal cruising load. Traveler is for a couple to sail anyplace in the world quickly, comfortably, and with a minimum of effort. There is room for two guests, the essentials, and perhaps a few of the modern "luxuries". The boat is designed to fly a spinnaker on a short bowsprit. Construction can be strip-planked (Core-Cell, Durakore, or cedar) with glass, Kevlar or carbon-fiber skins and epoxy.

SPECIFICATIONS

Displacement	11,650 lbs,	5284 kg
Standard Auxiliary	1 x 27-40 hp inboard	
Overall Length	47'11"	14.62 m
Waterline Length	47'7"	14.50 m
Beam (max.)	34'2"	10.39 m
Draft (board up)	2'0"	0.61 m
Draft (board down)	8'6"	2.59 m
Mast Hgt. Off Deck	59'6"	18.12 m
Mast Hgt. Off Water	64'0"	19.50 m

SAIL AREA

Wing Mast	85 sf	8 sm
Mainsail	700 sf	65 sm
Jib	395 sf	37 sm
Total Area	1180 sf	110 sm
Spinnaker		

CAPACITY

Berths	2 sgls, 1 dble	
Staterooms	1	
Heads	1-2	
Fuel	40 gal	152 ltr
Fresh Water	40 gal	152 ltr
Payload	2,000 lbs, 908 kg	

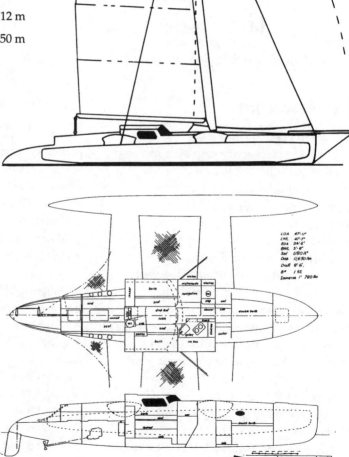

TRAVELER

HAMMERHEAD 54

GENERAL INFORMATION

Classification   Stock trimaran design, Cruiser/racer

Approx. Cost   US $500-$700,000

Designer   Chris White

Designs   Chris White Designs
5 Smith's Way
S. Dartmouth, MA 02748
USA
Tel: (508) 636-6111
Fax: (508) 636-6110
email: cwdesign@ma.ultranet.com

Year introduced   1995

Number of Boats Built   2 (as of Sep 97)

N. American Stockists   Buy plans direct

Other Cruising Multihulls By Designer
   Atlantic 42 cat (see page 242-243), Voyager 45 cat (see pages 418-419), Hammerhead 34 tri (late 1997), other cruising designs

KEY FEATURES

Hull & Sail Plan
- Epoxy-composite, cedar strip hulls, pivoting centerboard, built-in buoyancy
- Masthead cutter rig, fully roached main, roller-furling jib & staysail

Deck Layout
- Sleek main hull design, trampolines between main hull and amas
- Protected center cockpit with U-shaped seats, ample lockers, helm midships

Standard Accommodations
- Main hull aft—double stateroom (2 single or 1 large double), storage, private head
- Main hull midships—center cockpit, galley/nav area aft, seat/table & berth forward
- Main hull forward–2 single berths with storage, head with shower forward

Mechanical
- Wheel steering, helm midships in cockpit
- Single inboards, access from cockpit

DESCRIPTION

The Hammerhead 54 is an extremely high performance cruising trimaran with comfortable accommodations. Construction is epoxy composite, with cedar strip hulls, foam-cored decks, and carbon-fiber crossbeams. Sailing performance is excellent, with the Hammerhead capable of doing 20 knots under mainsail and jib alone. At high speed the helm is easy and balanced, with no feeling of loosing control or broaching. Stronger winds can produce speeds of 24 to 25 knots without surfing. With her centerboard-down draft of 9 ft, she also shows an excellent ability to drive to windward. A large main cabin contains the galley, full navigation station, seating with table, and settee/berth. Forward is a double cabin (or two singles) with en suite head and shower. The large aft cabin, located behind the cockpit, supplies a huge double berth complete with head and shower.

SPECIFICATIONS

Displacement	16,500 lbs, 7491 kg	
Standard Auxiliary	2 x 27 hp inboard	
Overall Length	54'0"	16.47 m
Waterline Length	52'0"	15.86 m
Beam (max.)	34'4"	10.47 m
Draft (board up)	2'6"	0.76 m
Draft (board down)	9'0"	2.75 m
Mast Hgt. Off Deck		
Mast Hgt. Off Water	63'6"	19.37 m

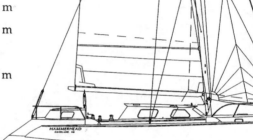

SAIL AREA

Mainsail	858 sf	80 sm
Jib	492 sf	46 sm
Staysail	252 sf	23 sm
Total Area	1602 sf	149 sm
Spinnaker	1400 sf	130 sm

CAPACITY

Berths	2-3 sgls, 1-2 dbls	
Staterooms	2	
Heads	2	
Fuel	70 gal	265 ltr
Fresh Water	80 gal	303 ltr
Payload		

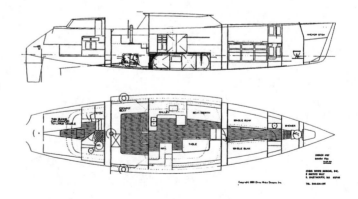

Reference
Section

Glossary Of Terms

Aft: Stern, back, rear, after the rear section.

Ama: The outer floats (hulls) of a trimaran.

Anchor: (verb) To hold something in position. (noun) A device to hold a vessel in position in an anchorage; also at anchor, anchored.

Apparent Wind: The direction from which the wind appears to blow. On a moving boat, it is never the same as the true wind. The apparent wind is either more or less than the true wind, depending upon which direction you are going.

Aka: The cross beams connecting the floats to the main hull of a trimaran. Aka & Ama are derived from Polynesian. Many designers and writers prefer them to the more mundane crossarm or crossbeam, and outer float. Time will tell if they became the standard generic notation.

Aspect Ratio: The height vs. the width of a boat component. Commonly used to describe the keels on a catamaran or the rig type on a cat or tri.

Back: To force a sail against the wind when maneuvering. A jib is "backed" when you want to force the bow to fall off the wind (see backwind), *sails are aback* (archaic) to allow or cause the boat to move backward with the bows pointed into the wind.

Backwind: To impair the effectiveness of a mainsail by sheeting in the jib so far as to deflect a stream of air against the lee side of the mainsail, thus destroying its partial vacuum. Also see *back*.

Backstay: A supporting wire cable for a mast, leading to the deck aft of the mast, as opposed to the headstay which supports the mast from forward. Many catamarans have twin backstays leading from the masthead to the aftermost corners of the boat, while others have no backstays at all, relying upon shrouds and the mainsheet for mast support.

Bahamian Moor: Two anchors laid out in roughly 180 degree opposition.

Ballast: Weight on a boat to give it stability, counterweight.

Barberhauler: A device of lines and blocks for changing the jib lead point, to haul it in or out.

Batten: (noun) A thin strip of wood or plastic inserted in a sail pocket to stiffen and hold the sail shape. A fully battened sail has battens extending across the full width of the sail. (verb) To securely close, as in "batten down" the hatches.

Beam: The width of a boat; this can refer to the maximum width or the folded width of a folding craft.

Beam Reach: The point of sailing with the wind directly abeam, or 90 degrees from the centerline.

Beat: (also beating) Close hauled, going to windward, generally denotes as close to the wind as that vessel is capable of achieving.

Bilge: The bottommost portion of the interior of the hull. That portion below the cabin sole.

Boom: A spar to which the foot of a fore-and-aft sail is attached.

Boom Vang: Most often a block-and-line device, but occasionally a hydraulic or rigid spar, attached between the underside of the boom and the hull or foot of the mast that prevents the boom from lifting and helps create proper sail shape. It also may be used as a "preventer", which prevents the boom from gibing accidentally.

Bow: The forward or front end of the boat.

Bow Wave: A continuing wave that forms on each side of the bow when a boat is in motion.

Bowsprit: A spar extending forward of the bow of a boat to take the tack of a sail, thus extending the base foretriangle of a sailboat.

Bridgedeck Length: The length of the rigid bridgedeck section of a catamaran.

Bridle: Cable wires running from each hull to the forestay, or lines to the anchor rode.

Broach: To swing or slew around toward the wind when running downwind, and thus come broadside to the sea. Major causes of broaching are the inability of a vessel to accelerate down a wave or to react quickly enough. Common broaching is almost unheard of in cruising multihulls.

Broad Reach: Any point of sailing between a beam reach and the wind quartering aft (from 90 to 165 degrees).

Broadside: The entire side of a boat, from stem to stern.

Catamaran: A twin-hulled vessel. According to *Webster's Unabridged Dictionary*: "A vessel noted for its safety."

Catboat/Cat-Rigged Boat: A sailboat with the mast stepped at the bow and only one large sail.

Center Of Effort: The theoretical pressure center of the combined area of all the sails being flown on a boat. This changes as you change sails.

Center Of Lateral Resistance: The theoretical center of the area of lateral resistance of a hull's underwater profile; the resistance to leeway; the center of the area that prevents the hull from slipping sideways.

Centerboard: A hinged board that passes through a slot in the hull to provide lateral resistance for a sailboat. It is enclosed in a trunk, may be raised in shallow water and adjusted during sailing.

Chainplate: The metal connectors bolted to the hull of a boat to which the wire rigging is attached.

Chock: A lead for docklines or anchor lines from the cleats to the points of attachment of the vessel.

Chord: A straight line intersecting a curve.

Cleat: A device used to belay or secure a line.

Clew: The corner of a sail at the juncture of the leech and the foot.

Close-Hauled: Sailing as close to the wind as possible; also see Beat.

Close Reach: A point of sailing between a beam reach and a beat.

Cockpit: The deck space that accommodates the helmsman and crew.

Come About: To tack.

Daggerboard: A non-pivoting board passed down through a slot or trunk in a sailboat to provide lateral resistance.

Dinghy: A small boat usually used to tend a larger boat.

Displacement: Technically, this equals the weight of the water displaced by a vessel as it sits afloat. *Displacement* usually refers to the boat's weight as it comes from the builder; *Designed Displacement* or *Displacement at Design Waterline* refers to the weight of the boat with its recommended cruising payload on board; *Maximum Displacement* refers to the weight of the boat with the designer's maximum recommended payload on board.

Displacement hull: A hull designed to pass through the water rather than skim over the surface.

Down: Away from the wind, opposite of Up (toward the wind).

Downhaul: (noun) A line for putting downward stress on a sail at the luff. (verb) The act of tightening the downhaul.

Downwind: Sailing with the wind up to 15 degrees either side of exactly downwind (165 through 195 degrees).

Draft: A boat's maximum depth of penetration into the water. Boats with centerboards or daggerboards have a *Minimum Draft* (depth with boards up) and *Maximum Draft* (the depth with boards completely down); also refers to the fullness of a sail, measured by the chord.

Eye: Eye of the wind, exactly into the wind direction; eye splice, a spliced loop in the end of a line.

Fathom: A unit of depth measuring six feet.

Following Sea: Seas coming up from behind.

Foot: The bottom edge of a sail.

Footing: Sailing to windward slightly less than close-hauled on the theory that the added speed more than offsets loss in pointing; the faster the catamaran or trimaran, the more this holds true.

Fore-And-Aft: Running, acting, or lying along the general length-wise line of a boat.

Foresail: The first working sail immediately forward of the main; the jib.

Forestay: A mast-supporting cable on which the jib luff is attached.

Forward: At, near, or belonging to the fore part of a boat; also more toward the bow than the stern.

Fouled: Tangled or caught, as in a fouled line or sheet.

Founder: To fill with water and sink.

Freeboard: The area on the sides of the hull from the water line to the gunwale.

Furl: To roll up a sail and secure it to a spar.

Gelcoat: The final resin gloss coating of a fiberglass hull (it typically contains the color pigment).

Genoa Jib: A large, overlapping jib with the foot parallel to the deck.

Ghoster: A sail capable of providing comparatively good speed in very light air.

Ghosting: Sailing in very light air.

Gooseneck: A metal two-way swivel device used for securing the boom to the mast.

Gudgeons: Socket fittings on the transom to accept rudder pintles.

Gunwale: The junction of the side of the boat and the deck.

Halyard: A line for hoisting or lowering a sail.

Hard Chine: An abrupt angle at the intersection of topside and bilges.

Haul: To pull with force; to remove a boat from the water; to sail closer to the wind.

Head: The top section of a sail.

Head: A marine toilet; also refers to the toilet compartment.

Head Board: A stiffening board inserted in the head of the sail.

Header: A wind shift that makes you steer down from your normal course to avoid luffing or losing speed.

Heading: Direction of travel of a boat; a course normally expressed in compass degrees.

Headsails: Any sails forward of the mainmast.

Head-To-Wind: The bow headed into the wind.

Heave To: To head into the wind; also, to keep a boat nearly stationary and headed into the wind, as when riding out a storm.

Heel: The lateral rotation of a sailboat under pressure of the wind (tipping, leaning).

Helm: (noun) The steering device of the vessel; the helm can be a wheel or tiller. (verb) To steer.

Helm Down: Turning to windward (archaic); refers to pushing the tiller down on a heeled vessel.

Hull: The basic external structure of a vessel.

Hull Speed: The maximum speed to which a displacement-type hull can be driven. It is limited by the length of the hull's water-line.

Irons/In Irons: The point at which a sailboat is dead in the water facing directly into the wind, sails flogging and making no way..

Jib: A triangular sail attached to the forestay and forward of the mainmast.

Jibe: Passing from one tack to another by swinging the stern of the boat through the eye of the wind.

Jury-Rig: Rig for temporary use.

Keel: The lower edge or backbone of a vessel extending along the center of the bottom from bow to stern. A lateral resistance device.

Knot: The speed of one nautical mile per hour.

Lateral Resistance: The ability of a hull, by means of the submerged surfaces, to resist being driven sideways by the pressure of wind on the sails.

Leach: The back edge of a sail; the edge usually supported with battens.

Lee: Shaded, protected, as "in the lee of..." Area shielded from the wind. The side of a boat away from the direction of the wind (opposite of *weather* side).

Lee Helm: A tendency to bear off the wind due to poor sail balance, caused by the center of effort being too far forward of the center of lateral resistance.

Lee Rail: The rail away from the wind.

Lee Shore: The shore towards which the wind is blowing; it is usually referred to in the context of danger.

Leeward: The side away from the wind, the opposite of windward.

Leeway: The amount a boat is pushed sideways by the wind, measured in degrees.

LOA: The overall length of a boat, including appendages such as davits, bowsprits, etc.

Luff: (noun) The leading edge of a sail; the fixed portion. (verb) To take the wind pressure off a sail by easing the sheet or by heading into the wind.

LWL: Waterline length of a boat.

Masthead: The top of a mast; often referred to as the *Truck*.

Multihull: A vessel with two or more hulls, typically refering to a catamaran, trimaran or proa.

Nautical Mile: A distance equal to one minute of arc of a great circle of the earth (usually given as 6,080 feet). When reading a chart, it's handy to remember that a nautical mile=one minute of latitude.

Pintle: An upright pivot pin forming a hinge on a rudder; a pintle (male) fits into a gudgeon (female).

Pitching/Hobby-Horsing: The quick, uncomfortable fore-and-aft motion exhibited by some multihulls; not as prevalent on newer models.

Pitchpole: To capsize a boat stern over bow.

Pointing: (noun *pointing ability)* A boat's level of efficiency sailing to windward. (verb) Sailing as close to the wind as the boat's design will allow.

Port: The left side of a boat when facing forward.

Port Tack: The point of sail with the wind coming over the port side.

Point of Sail: Denotes the sailing direction in relationship to the wind; beat, reach and run are three major points.

Pound: To strike the waves with a jarring force, as is characteristic of some hulls.

Proa: A two-hulled vessel that has one hull smaller than the other.

Rail: The top of the gunwales.

Rake: The inclination of a mast fore or aft, away from the perpendicular.

Reach: All points of sailing between a beat and a run. Close reach is between a beat and a beam reach; broad reach is between a beam reach and a run.

Reef: To shorten or reduce the area of sails.

Reef Points: Small grommets in the sail located in a row parallel to the foot, used for shortening sails.

Rhumb Line: A straight line between two points on a Mercator projection map or chart.

Rig: (noun) The type of sail plan and rigging. (verb) To step the mast and attach shrouds and stays while fitting out.

Rigging: Rope, wires, or cable used to support (standing rigging) or control (running rigging) masts, spars, or sails.

Righting Moment: A disposition of weight in relationship to buoyancy; the tendency to prevent a boat from capsizing or to return her to her normal attitude of flotation.

Roach: That portion of the sail leech that extends aft of an imaginary line from the head to the clew.

Rocker: A hull characteristic, low in the middle and sweeping upward at the ends, such as a rocker sheer or rocker chine.

Roller-Reefing/Roller-Furling Gear: A device for rolling a sail up on its attachment point (forestay or spar) like a window shade. These terms have become synonymous in popular speech, yet technically roller-reefing gear is used to make the sail smaller to match wind conditions, while roller-furling gear is only used as a sail storage device.

Round Up: To head into the wind.

Rub Rail: A sacrificial molding around the hull to prevent the hull from being damaged during docking or collision.

Running Rigging: All sheets, halyards, guys, runners, and other lines not permanently fixed that are used to control or support spars and sails.

Saloon/Saloon Cabin: The main cabin area on a sailboat. Also called commonly called "salon".

Scantlings: The engineering data for a vessel; the sizes and weights of the various components.

Sheer Line: The upward curve of the longitudinal lines of the hull as viewed from the side.

Shrouds: The stays for lateral mast support.

Skeg: An underwater appendage on the aft part of the hull to protect or secure the rudder.

Skin Friction: Surface resistance of a hull as it passes through water.

Spar: Any mast or boom that supports or extends the sail on a boat.

Spinnaker: A light, balloon-type headsail mostly used off the wind; can be symmetrical or asymmetrical in shape.

Stall: The slowing effect from sheeting the sails too tightly in relation to the wind direction, as in falling off without easing the sails.

Stanchion: A vertical lifeline support post.

Standing Rigging: The support rigging that is permanently fixed; as opposed to the running rigging.

Starboard: The right side of a boat when facing forward.

Starboard Tack: Sailing with the wind coming over the starboard side.

Stay: A wire rope used to support a mast or other spar; part of a boat's rigging.

Staysail: A sail with its luff attached to a stay.

Stem: A vessel's foremost timber or steel bar.

Step: (verb) To set and affix a mast in position.

Stern: The after end of a boat.

Sternway: Moving in reverse.

Tack: (noun) The corner of a sail at the juncture of luff and foot. (verb) To come about; to change the course of the boat by bringing the bows through the wind so that the wind is now on the opposite side.

Telltale: A short piece of wool, ribbon, plastic or feather attached to sails or shrouds for reading wind direction and monitoring sail trim.

Tiller: A steering handle linked to the rudder(s).

Topping Lift: A line by which the outer end of a boom is supported.

Topsides: The sides of a hull from the chine or the turn of the bilge to the sheer line.

Traveler: A horizontal track with a movable car for the purpose of controlling sail trim.

Trim: (verb) To haul in on a sheet, or to set the sails at their optimum position for efficiency; also to balance the hull in a proper attitude in the water.

Trimaran: A three-hulled vessel; the center hull is the main hull, the outer hulls are the amas.

Trunk: A shaft in which daggerboards and centerboards are lowered and lifted.

Turnbuckle: A mechanical device, consisting of end screws of opposite threads, connected to a center barrel that can be rotated for adjusting wire slack.

Wake: The temporary wave track left by a boat passing through the water.

Washboards: Occasionally called drop boards. The conventional closure for the main entry hatch of both monohulls and trimarans.

Waterline: The line of intersection of a hull with the water when the boat is in its normal attitude.

Waterplane: The footprint that the boat has in the water exactly at the waterline; the actual area at the water surface at that intersection.

Weather: (noun) Indicates the side of the boat toward the wind, also known as windward; "to weather" is to windward.

Weather Helm: When a boat has the tendency to head into the wind.

Weatherly: A term usually used to describe the condition or ability of a vessel to go to windward, as in "she is a very weatherly vessel."

Wetted Surface: The total area of the submerged portion of a hull and its appendages.

Whisker Pole: A spar used as a boom to hold the clew of a jib or spinnaker out, away from the boat.

Windward: The side from which the wind is blowing. The opposite of leeward.

Windward Ability: The ability of a vessel to sail into the wind.

Windward Leg: The portion of a sailed course that is towards the direction from which the wind is blowing.

Wing Mast: A rotating, foil-shaped mast with very large fore and aft axis that is considered part of the total mainsail area.

Yacht: Any pleasure boat.

Yaw: To go off course or swing from side to side; this term is usually associated with running before the wind in a sea.

Cruising Multihulls
By Length

Trimarans

Index

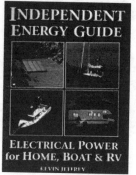
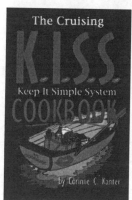

SAILOR'S MULTIHULL GUIDE
Second Edition

By Kevin Jeffrey & Charles E. Kanter

from Avalon House Publishing
in cooperation with

MULTIHULLS Magazine

Cover Photographs of Industry-Leading Multihulls:

FRONT COVER
upper left: Victory Catamarans, *Victory 35*
upper right: Island Packet Yachts, *Packet Cat 35*
lower left: PDQ Yachts, *PDQ 36 Mk III*
lower right: Contour Yachts, *Contour 34 SC*

BACK COVER
upper left: Voyage Yachts, *Mayotte 500*
upper right: KKG, *Macro Spaceshuttle*
lower left: Prout Catamarans, *Prout 45*
lower right: Lagoon/Jeanneau, *Lagoon 57*

INSIDE FRONT
upper left: Prout Catamarans, *Prout 37*
upper right: Performance Cruising, *Gemini 105M*
lower left: Fountaine Pajot, *Bahia 46*
lower right: Catana, *Catana 411*

INSIDE BACK
upper left: Manta Catamarans, *Manta 40*
upper right: Maine Cat, *Maine Cat 30*
lower left: Corsair Marine, *F-28*
lower right: Dufour Yachts, *Nautitech 395*

AVALON HOUSE
PUBLISHING
sustainable living • marine